FRAGILE POLITICS

MEHRAN KAMRAVA
Editor

Fragile Politics

Weak States in the Greater Middle East

GEORGETOWN UNIVERSITY

School *of* Foreign Service *in* Qatar
Center for International and Regional Studies

HURST & COMPANY, LONDON

First published in the United Kingdom in 2016 by
C. Hurst & Co. (Publishers) Ltd.,
41 Great Russell Street, London, WC1B 3PL
© Mehran Kamrava and the contributors, 2016
All rights reserved.
Printed in India

A Cataloguing-in-Publication data record for this book
is available from the British Library.

978-1-84904-482-0 *paperback*

This book is printed using paper from registered sustainable
and managed sources.

www.hurstpublishers.com

CONTENTS

ACKNOWLEDGEMENTS

This volume emerged as one of the research initiatives undertaken by the Center for International and Regional Studies of Georgetown University School of Foreign Service. A number of individuals were instrumental in helping shape the intellectual discussions that went into crafting this volume, chief among them Bridget Coggins, John Crist, Suzi Mirgani, Robert Rotberg, and Mahjoob Zweiri. The incomparable staff of CIRS was instrumental in ensuring the success of two working groups, one in Doha and another in Washington, DC, in which the contributors brainstormed ideas concerning weak states in the Middle East and critiqued each others' works. Without their hard work the task of editing the volume would have been much harder. Other colleagues at Georgetown University, Qatar were equally instrumental in shaping our ideas and providing helpful advice and insight into the topic. Grateful Acknowledgement goes also to the Qatar Foundation for its support of research and other scholarly endeavors.

1

WEAK STATES IN THE MIDDLE EAST

Mehran Kamrava

The outbreak and domino-like spread of uprisings in much of the Arab world beginning in 2011 has brought added urgency to the study of weak and failing states in the Middle East. Despite the region's history of wars and revolutions, the general scholarly consensus has often favored the prevalence of mammoth, strong states in the Middle East.[1] In fact, despite considerable regional variations in the political and institutional make-up of Middle Eastern countries, statism tends to be one of the most common denominators that an overwhelming majority of the region's countries share. Nevertheless, as this volume makes amply clear, not only are several states in the Middle East chronically "weak"—Lebanon, Yemen, and the Sudan—but most others have inherent structural and institutional features that compromise their capacity, devoid them of legitimacy, and make them prone to weakness.

This introductory chapter presents a broad survey of the study of weak states both as a scholarly exercise and in relation to the Middle East. The study of weak

[1] See, for example, Roger Owen, *State, Power and Politics in the Making of the Modern Middle East*, 3rd edn (London: Routledge, 2004); Nazih Ayubi, *Over-Stating the Arab State: Politics and Society in the Middle East* (London: I. B. Tauris, 1996); and Alan Richards and John Waterbury, *A Political Economy of the Middle East*, 3rd edn (Boulder, CO: Westview, 2013).

states, the chapter shows, is a contested terrain. Much of the controversy arises from the fact that the study of weak states is not merely an academic endeavor, but also goes to the heart of practical development policies.[2] Equally troubling is the frequent association of weak or collapsed states with terrorism and terrorist groups, as attested by the rise first of sea piracy and then the Al Shabaab group in Somalia, the March 23 Movement (M23) in the Democratic Republic of Congo, and al-Qaeda in the Arabian Peninsula (AQAP) in Yemen, to mention only a few examples. Not surprisingly, as Mark McGillivray's contribution to this volume shows, at times the concept of "failed states" and various indices for state failure have been used by policy experts to link international security with domestic stability and development promotion.[3]

The chapter begins with a discussion of some of the more salient controversies involving the weak and failed states discourse. These controversies bear on the very designation of states as weak, failing, or failed. The chapter then turns to the question of where weak states come from, examining the causes and characteristics of state weakness and failure. State weakness is rooted in diminished "capacity" and eroded or non-existent "legitimacy". At the broadest level, states feature two key ingredients. All have institutional frameworks within which their capacity is generated and through which it is exercised. They also have leaders who operate within these institutional frameworks and make choices along the way. Especially in non-democratic states, commonly found in the Middle East, leaders can at times craft or shape institutions to their own liking.[4] In understanding state weakness, in other words, both structure and agency are important.

In studying state weakness, our traditional conceptions of both notions of capacity and legitimacy need to be fine-tuned in order to take into account state leaders' ability to manipulate existing social cleavages for their own advantages and to further their tenure in office. This is particularly the case in the Middle East, as the chapters on Yemen and Sudan in this volume demonstrate, where despite significant state weakness leaders were able to remain in office through reliance on institutions that were just strong enough, and practices that were politically rewarding enough, to maintain them in power.

---

[2] Volker Boege, et al., "On Hybrid Political Orders and Emerging States: State Formation in the Context of 'Fragility'" (Berlin: Berghof Research Center for Constructive Conflict Management, October 2008), 4.

[3] Charles T. Call, "The Fallacy of the 'Failed State'", *Third World Quarterly*, Vol. 29, No. 8 (2008), 1494.

[4] Mehran Kamrava, "Preserving Non-Democracies: Leaders and State Institutions in the Middle East". *Middle Eastern Studies*, Vol. 46, No. 2 (March 2010), 231–50.

The Study of Weak States

There are essentially three, broad perspectives about failed states.[5] Some scholars view the concept of failed state as analytically useful, especially insofar as the study of international relations and security is concerned. A second group of scholars are open to the concept but do not see it as analytically useful because, they maintain, it is often hard to define. Fragile state terminology is often maligned because of its analytical imprecision.[6] Scholars in a third group are openly hostile to the concept, which they see as ethnocentric and motivated by hegemonic political agendas. They point to the fact that international and especially US interests in the study of weak and failed states peaked especially after the 9/11 attacks.[7] Because fragile states are seen as a threat to the United States and to international security, much of the state-building efforts around the world by the US and its allies have focused firstly and primarily on building up the security sector.[8]

Much of the controversy surrounding the discourse arises, in fact, because of its alleged concern with the protection of US and Western national and international security interests. In addition to a number of conceptual flaws in the "failed state" moniker, a number of scholars maintain, there are also ideological underpinnings to the concept that emphasize the use of power and advancing hegemony.[9] Realizing that weak states can threaten security, the more powerful states and international organizations have invested considerable sums of money in countering conflict and stabilizing societies.[10] The remedy needed to fix weak states is often assumed to be more order: "without security, nothing else is possible". Especially within the United Nations, there is an assumption that peace-building and state-building are connected. This entails placing emphasis on the strength and the coercive institutions of the state: the military, police, civil service, system of justice, and leadership.[11] The

[5] Edward Newman, "Failed State and International Order: Constructing a Post-Westphalian World", *Contemporary Security Policy*, Vol. 30, No. 3 (December 2009), 422–243.
[6] Claire Mcloughlin, *Topic Guide on Fragile States* (University of Birmingham: Governance and Social Development Resource Center, 2012), 9.
[7] Call, "The Fallacy of the 'Failed State'", 1493.
[8] Boege, et al., "On Hybrid Political Orders and Emerging States", 4.
[9] Charles T. Call, "Beyond the 'failed state': Toward conceptual alternatives", *European Journal of International Relations*, Vol. 20, No. 10 (2010), 19.
[10] Newman, "Failed State and International Order", 438.
[11] Call, "The Fallacy of the 'Failed State'", 1496–8.

relationship between peace-building and state-building is more complicated, with state-building potentially privileging one ethnic group over another, while peace deals may enable military leaders to divide the spoils of the state amongst themselves.[12]

Edward Newman's arguments in this respect are largely representative of the critiques of the weak state discourse. He argues that the idea of failed states is a political construct and a reflection of Western concerns over new security threats since 9/11. The securitization of failed states in political and academic discourse reflects this subjective, Western construction of international security threats and represents another constructivist process in international politics.[13] Newman concedes that no matter how problematic, the concept of failed states should not be abandoned. There is a distinction between the concept of failed state and the reality of failed states. It may therefore be academically useful to see how weak states and the threats they pose are constructed and perceived, and the meanings attached to them in policy and academic discourse.[14]

Others, Charles Call among them, have argued that the study of failed states is often informed by culturally specific assumptions about what a successful state should look like.[15] The failed state discourse is often value-driven, Call maintains, assuming that there is some "good" endpoint toward which states should be progressing.[16] Branwen Gruffyd Jones goes so far as to maintain that the prevailing discourse on weak and failed states "must be recognized as a contemporary successor to a much longer genealogy to a much longer imperial discourse about Africa and other non-European societies... The discourse of good governance and state failure reproduces a racialized imagination deeply entrenched in the structure of Western thought" and is "irredeemably rooted in an imperial imagination".[17]

Some scholars have also taken issue with the presumed relationship between weak and collapsed states and terrorism. The connection between state weakness and global threats is less clear than is commonly assumed. In

[12] Ibid., 1499.
[13] Newman, "Failed State and International Order", 437–9.
[14] Ibid., 433.
[15] Call, "The Fallacy of the 'Failed State'", 1494.
[16] Ibid., 1499.
[17] Branwen Gruffyd Jones, "'Good governance' and 'state failure': genealogies of imperial discourse", *Cambridge Review of International Affairs*, Vol. 26, No. 1 (2013), 49–50, 52.

fact, some cross-border threats are more likely to emerge from stronger states that possess critical gaps in capacity and will.[18] According to Stewart Patrick, weak and fragile states can provide useful assets to transnational terrorists, but they may be less important to the terrorists' operations than is widely believed. Patrick also questions the empirical evidence underpinning presumed multiple linkages between state weaknesses and international security threats.[19] The empirical link between state weakness and failure and terrorism is also questioned by Aidan Hehir. Hehir demonstrates that there is no strong evidence that most terrorist groups have a pronounced preference for associating with weak or failed states.[20]

Some criticism has also been raised against the "institutionalist" approach to state collapse, an approach that is largely adopted in this chapter. Broadly, institutionalist perspectives focus on the viability, functions, and capacity of the institutions of the state, while legitimacy approaches are more concerned with social and political cohesion and the legitimacy that central authorities can generate.[21] Institutionalist approaches run the danger of separating state-building from nation-building, and they attribute state weakness and collapse more to the collapse of institutions rather than lack of social and national cohesion.[22] These approaches often miss the political dimensions involved in a state's exercise of capacity, especially in relation to actors and currents in society. These social dynamics are often forged through conflict and have direct bearing on levels and exercise of state capacity. State capacity needs to be understood as a "socially constituted and dynamic phenomenon".[23]

Some of the controversy involving the study of weak and failed states has to do with the precise categories—or lack thereof—of states that deserve such designations, especially since donor agencies rely on typologies and degrees of

[18] Stewart Patrick, "Weak States and Global Threats: Assessing Evidence of 'Spillovers'", Center for Global Development, working paper No. 73, January 2006, 1.

[19] Ibid., 5.

[20] Aidan Hehir, "The Myth of the Failed State and the War on Terror: A Challenge to the Conventional Wisdom", *Journal of Intervention and Statebuilding*, Vol. 1, No. 3 (November 2007), 308.

[21] Nicolas Lemay-Hebert, "Statebuilding without Nation-Building? Legitimacy, State Failure and the Limits of the Institutionalist Approach", *Journal of Intervention and Statebuilding*, Vol. 3, No. 1 (March 2009), 22.

[22] Ibid., 40.

[23] Shahar Hameiri, "Failed states or a failed paradigm? State capacity and the limits of institutionalism", *Journal of International Relations and Development*, Vol. 10 (2007), 123.

state fragility to determine appropriate strategies for donor engagement.[24] The very definitions of "weak" and "collapsed" or "failed" states are contested.[25] In broad terms, the distinction between the two categories of "weak" and "failed" states is self-evident. Failed states occur in "a situation where governmental structures are overwhelmed by circumstances".[26] Robert Rotberg has offered what is a generally accepted definition of failed states:

> *Failed* states are tense, deeply conflicted, dangerous, and contested bitterly by warring factions. In most failed states, government troops battle armed revolts led by one or more rivals. Occasionally, the official authorities in a failed state face two or more insurgencies, varieties of civil unrest, different degrees of communal discontent, and a plethora of dissent directed at the state and at groups within the state.[27]

In these failed or collapsed states, "the state apparatus ceases to exist for a period of several months" and the services that are normally provided by the state are instead provided by sub-state or non-state actors.[28] Warning against the potential political uses of the concept of a failed state, Call maintains that the concept is useless unless it refers to wholly collapsed states in which there is no domestically or internationally recognizable authority.[29] This emphasis on the total collapse of state institutions and functions arises from the discrepancy between the de jure and de facto nature of many states.[30] Such states are marked by a collapse of central government authority and subsequent loss of territory or monopoly over the legitimate use of force. State collapse encompasses more than the failure of governmental institutions and also involves the complex dynamics having to do with the erosion of social and political cohesion.[31]

A weak state, according to the widely-used definition suggested by the Organisation for Economic Cooperation and Development (OECD), "has weak capacity to carry out basic functions of governing a population and its

---

[24] Mcloughlin, *Topic Guide on Fragile States*, 12.

[25] For an insightful analysis of the evolution of the concepts of weak and failed state, see Call, "Beyond the 'failed state'", 3.

[26] Gerald Helman and Steven Ratner, "Saving Failed States", *Foreign Policy*, Vol. 89 (1993), 5.

[27] Robert Rotberg, "The Failure and Collapse of Nation-States: Breakdown, Prevention, and Repair". In Robert Rotberg, ed., *When States Fail: Causes and Consequences* (Princeton, NJ: Princeton University Press, 2004), 5.

[28] Call, "The Fallacy of the 'Failed State'", 1501.

[29] Ibid., 1492.

[30] Newman, "Failed State and International Order", 423.

[31] Lemay-Hebert, "Statebuilding without Nation-Building?" 22.

territory", and lacks "the ability to develop mutually constructive and reinforcing relations with society".[32] The primary difference between a failed and a weak state is a matter of degree. In broad terms, state fragility can be defined as a state's inability to meet its citizens' basic needs and expectations. These states suffer from significant gaps in performance, legitimacy, security, and control over parts of their territory.[33] The state is a provider of public goods and service deliveries. Its core functions include the provision of security, legitimacy, and wealth and welfare. Gradations of state weakness and failure include measures of statehood against these core functions.[34] Fragile states can be conceptualized along a continuum of declining state performance, from weak states to failing and then failed states and finally collapsed states.[35] According to Rotberg, weak states in fact generally contain the "incubus of failure", as has been the case with Lebanon, Bolivia, Ecuador, and Guatemala, among others, or they may be "enduringly frail", as has been the case with Haiti.[36]

Paradoxically, the literature on weak states does not explicitly distinguish between "state" as an institutional construct in the Weberian sense and "state" as a sovereign territorial unit. This is an important distinction. Territorial entities designated as states often contain one or more nations, and it is in relation to these national or subnational groups—as well as in relation to other states—that states experience weakness or strength. From an institutionalist perspective, conceptualizing the state in purely political terms does not always provide a complete picture of the dynamics of state-building operations. States also have the ability to enforce a successful social contract that ensures a cohesion of the larger social entity they govern. There are even some "phantom states" that may have external resourcing but lack domestic social and political legitimacy.[37] Weak and failing states often possess legal but not empirical sovereignty.[38] In weak states informal institutions such as tribes,

---

[32] Louise Anten, Ivan Briscoe, and Marco Mezzera, "The Political Economy of State-Building in Situation of Fragility and Conflict: From Analysis to Strategy", Conflict Research Unit, Netherlands Institute of International Relations, January 2012, 12.

[33] Mcloughlin, *Topic Guide on Fragile States*, 9.

[34] Rolf Schwarz, "The political economy of state-formation in the Arab Middle East: Rentier states, economic reform, and democratization", *Review of International Political Economy*, Vol. 15, No. 4 (October 2008), 602.

[35] Boege, et al., "On Hybrid Political Orders and Emerging States", 3.

[36] Rotberg, "The Failure and Collapse of Nation-States", 18–19.

[37] Lemay-Hebert, "Statebuilding without Nation-Building?" 29, 37.

[38] Patrick, "Weak States and Global Threats", 7.

patron–client networks, or ethnically-based networks, rather than formal state institutions such as ministries, are the main channels of service delivery and allocation of public resources. Weak states feature low state capacity, and service delivery across social groups and territory is inconsistent.[39]

Causes and Characteristics of State Weakness

This leaves unanswered the question of where weak states come from, or, more accurately, what kinds of institutional and other factors cause state weakness. Weak states feature lack of institutional cohesion, bouts of political instability, violent competition over control of resources, fragmentation of society along multiple fault-lines, and citizens resort to alternative means of coping and surviving, including migration and crime.[40] The competition of political power-holders in the "political marketplace" is crucial to determining the path taken by a fragile state. Not surprisingly, such a state can give rise to a violent political marketplace, as Alex de Waal formulates in Chapter 8, one in which there is incessant armed confrontation, bargaining between the ruler and lower-level, local leaders, and where there are local militias. If there is no established balance of power, violence in the political marketplace has the potential to erupt into civil war.[41]

One of the most critical causes of state weakness is political fragmentation, as it "warps incentives, encouraging short-term opportunism at the expense of long-term investments that could advance development". Conflict between identity groups becomes a societal obsession and replaces other collective or individual endeavors that could enhance communal cohesion and harmony. Formal governing institutions and regulations become disconnected from the larger environment within which they operate, commanding at best superficial and perfunctory allegiance and compliance. "State laws go unheeded because no one acknowledges them as legitimate." Weak states invariably suffer from corrupt government, biased courts, and weak property rights.[42] Ghani and Lockhart refer to this as a "syndrome of dysfunctionality".[43] Not surprisingly,

---

[39] Call, "The Fallacy of the 'Failed State'", 1502.

[40] Louise Anten, Ivan Briscoe, and Marco Mezzera, "The Political Economy of State-Building in Situation of Fragility and Conflict", 21.

[41] Ibid., 23.

[42] Kaplan, *Fixing Fragile States*, 41.

[43] Ashraf Ghani and Clare Lockhart, *Fixing Failed States: A Framework for Rebuilding a Fractured World* (Oxford: Oxford University Press, 2008), 80.

in weak states allegiance to the state as a set of legitimate institutions with official power and compliance to its policies is in short supply.

Weak states invariably suffer from a disconnect between the state and social actors. In fact, in fragile states allegiances are more likely to be focused on a tribe, local notables, religious leaders, and other, more parochially focused entities instead of state institutions and political symbols and objects whose scope and purview is national in scale.[44] At times, as Charles Schimtz's contribution to this volume shows, the very process of state-building and political consolidation, which in Yemen for example occurred under the auspices of British rule, heavily favors one social group over others, setting into motion dynamics whose alienating consequences for large swathes of population have lasting results. Yemen's predicament may have changed today since the days of British rule, but strong local identities, often fed and nurtured by outside force, continue to dominate the country's political landscape, thus contributing to the state's chronic weakness. Whether fed endogenously or from the outside, strong local identities are one of the main contributors to state weakness. Not surprisingly, this weakness is not always inimical to the interests of actual or potential power centers. In Yemen's case, in fact, the state's weakness has entailed a number of functional benefits to many of the country's tribes, ruling coalitions, and to Saudi Arabia.

There are a range of other pathologies associated with state weakness. Perhaps the most glaring have to do with a state's diminished capacity and status in the international arena and its ability proactively to promote or even to defend its interests in dealing with regional and international forces and actors. These outside forces may be other states, multinational agencies and organizations, corporations, or, as a number of Middle Eastern states are learning the hard way, non-governmental actors such as al-Qaeda and the Islamic State in Iraq and the Levant (ISIL). But weak states often also have a host of domestic exigencies with which they need to contend. These internal difficulties may include forced migration; various forms of smuggling; the emergence of recalcitrant or aggressive governments; the emergence of war economies in which illegal networks and activities thrive; adverse impact on the environment; heightened health problems (such as the spread of cholera or the reappearance of polio); and the appearance of environments conducive to the establishment and operations of terrorist organizations.[45]

[44] Seth Kaplan, "Identity in Fragile States: Social cohesion and state building", *Development*, Vol. 52, No. 4 (2009), 469.
[45] Newman, "Failed State and International Order", 429–31.

At the broadest level, four clusters of factors combine to bring about state fragility: structural and economic factors, such as endemic poverty or chronic armed conflict; political and institutional factors, such as crisis of legitimacy and authority and the weakness of formal institutions; social factors, such as lack of social cohesion and sever identity fragmentation; and international factors, such as global economic shocks and loss of powerful patrons.[46] Weak states have "capacity gaps" in the security realm where they struggle to provide security against external and internal threats; in the political realm in the form of lack of legitimacy; in the economic realm insofar as trade, investments, and legal and regulatory environments are concerned; and thus are unable to meet the basic needs of their populations.[47] A state is failing when a government loses control over its territory; it lacks monopoly over legitimate use of force; its authority to make collective decisions is eroded; it is unable to provide reasonable public services; and it has diminished capacity to conduct formal relations with other states.[48]

The failure to perform functions of statehood, in other words, is central to state weakness or collapse. Charles Call conceives of state weakness as a series of core exigencies and gaps in capacity, security, and legitimacy. A "security gap" is when the state cannot "provide minimum levels of security in the face of organized armed groups". Not surprisingly, most of the states experiencing security gaps are those in the midst of armed conflict. A "legitimacy gap", which is the most difficult to conceptualize and operationalize, occurs when a "significant portion of political elite and society reject rules regulating the exercise of power and the accumulation and distribution of wealth".[49]

As evident, state weakness and/or collapse is driven by both institutional factors and by diminished legitimacy.[50] Insofar as institutional factors are concerned, the collapse or resilience of states is often directly tied to their capacity. State capacity owes much to institutional depth and breadth.[51] The "backbone of the state", political capacity is the ability to implement political decisions, especially in the face of actual or potential opposition from power-

[46] Mcloughlin, *Topic Guide on Fragile States*, 16.
[47] Patrick, "Weak States and Global Threats", 7–8.
[48] Zaryab Iqbal and Harvey Starr, "Bad Neighbors: Failed States and Their Consequences", *Conflict Management and Peace Science*, Vol. 25 (2008), 317.
[49] Call, "Beyond the 'failed state'", 5–6.
[50] Lemay-Hebert, "Statebuilding without Nation-Building?" 28.
[51] Linda Weiss, *The Myth of the Powerless State* (Ithaca, NY: Cornell University Press, 1998), 19.

ful social groups.[52] State weakness is a function of diminished state capacity. Among other things, diminished capacity opens the door to "political entrepreneurs" seeking to displace national allegiances with local ones.[53] State capacity refers to the capacity of the state to ensure the delivery of its core functions vis-à-vis providing security, rule of law, public finance management, and services.[54] A capacity gap exists where the institutions of the state are incapable of delivering minimal public goods and services to the population. "Minimal capacity", of course, differs from one society to another.

States only become operational in relation to other states and in relation to their own societies. According to Joel Migdal, a cohesive, strong state is perceived by its subjects as "a dominant, integrated, autonomous entity that controls, in a given territory, all rule making either directly through its own agencies or indirectly by sanctioning other authorized organizations—businesses, families, clubs, and the like—to make certain circumscribed rules".[55] Institutional capacity develops in an environment of social conflict and denotes the capacity of institutions to promote certain interests while marginalizing others.[56] Weak states, on the other hand, facilitate circumstances in which there are some groups that gain from the fluid circumstances and some that lose, and political collaboration and competition ensue over various material interests.[57] In such circumstances, "the state's 'outposts' are mediated by 'informal' indigenous societal institutions which follow their own logic and rules within the (incomplete) state structures".[58]

State capacity is often also directly impacted by a state's position within the international system and its relations with other states. More specifically, state fragility can often arise as a result of the dynamic interplay between internal and external factors. In addition to internal "malfunctions", a state's fragility

---

[52] Michael Bratton, "Peasant–State relations in postcolonial Africa: patterns of engagement and disengagement", in Joel S. Migdal, Atul Kohli, and Vivienne Shue, eds., *State Power and Social Forces: Domination and Transformation in the Third World* (Cambridge: Cambridge University Press, 1994), 235–6.

[53] Lemay-Hebert, "Statebuilding without Nation-Building?" 28.

[54] Call, "Beyond the 'failed state'", 4.

[55] Joel S. Migdal, *State in Society: Studying How States and Societies Transform and Constitute One Another* (Cambridge: Cambridge University Press, 2001), 16.

[56] Hameiri, "Failed states or a failed paradigm", 141.

[57] Anten, Briscoe, and Mezzera, "The Political Economy of State-Building in Situation of Fragility and Conflict", 11.

[58] Boege, et al., "On Hybrid Political Orders and Emerging States", 7.

or strength is often directly impacted by its place in the international system and the international political economy.[59] The fragile state's tenuous but nonetheless continued power and relevance to the life of society is further reinforced by a combination of international norms and forces that reinforce its de jure sovereignty and its de facto authority. More commonly, states use international as well as internal coalitions to enhance their capacity. Many, in fact, consolidate their domestic and international linkages as a way of increasing their power and capacity in both domestic and international arenas.[60]

Perhaps nowhere is this more apparent than the de facto break-up of Syria and Iraq as a result of the rise of the al-Qaeda offshoot calling itself the Islamic State of Iraq and the Levant. In their competition for regional influence in the chaos of the post-Arab Spring Middle East and to further their own international agendas, Turkey, Saudi Arabia, and Qatar lent what initially seemed like blanket support to groups fighting the Syrian state, among which the ISIL emerged as by far the most brutal and the most effective. Buoyed by parallel developments next door in Iraq and the Iraqi state's incapacity to extend its reach meaningfully beyond Baghdad and other key cities, ISIL also expanded its operations in northern Iraq. With continued though indirect and increasingly lessening support from outside backers, in June 2014 ISIL renamed itself the Islamic State and declared an independent, new country under the same name (*ad-Dawlah al-'Islāmiyyah*) in parts of northern Iraq and Syria. As of this writing, in late 2014, the fate of the new state and those of Iraq and Syria remains an open question. What is certain, however, is that neither the Iraqi and Syrian states nor the new entity are likely to have enough institutional capacity and military strength on their own to withstand the impact of outside influences.

The example of ISIL illustrates the importance of state capacity and its reach in areas not easily accessible to its agents and institutions. Particularly in developing countries, state capacity is often at its weakest in more remote, rural areas. Not surprisingly, as Daniel Esser's contribution here forcefully demonstrates, it is in the cities in which the full impact of the state's powers and capacities are most apparent, and where citizens come into the most sustained and meaningful contact with them. Cities are indeed, as Esser claims, important sites of state-building. But neglect of the countryside or of other non-central areas, as the cases of Iraq, Syria, Afghanistan, and Sudan demonstrate, can have perilous consequences for state weakness and failure.

[59] Mcloughlin, *Topic Guide on Fragile States*, 16.
[60] Weiss, *The Myth of the Powerless State*, 209.

The survival of weak states in the developing world is due to the support of an international political order that upholds existing boundaries and assists regimes against internal, at times even external, threats and challenges. This supportive international order has helped mask "the actual weakness and political incapacity of 'quasi-states'".[61] States seek to adapt to new and emerging challenges by forging domestic and international alliances. In fact, engaging with other states, as in globalization, can have the potential to enhance the powers of the state.[62] Globalization may also be an important contributor to state weakness, with neoliberal economic forces weakening state capacity and its provision of public goods.[63]

While regional and international dynamics can help maintain a weak state in power, they can also seriously undermine the strength and capacity of otherwise stable states. Declining superpower support, for example, is a critical factor in causing weakness, especially among more dependent states. Similarly, states neighboring failed states are likely to experience high levels of instability themselves.[64] Consequences of state failure may be destabilizing at the regional level as weak and failed states have a higher probability of getting involved in interstate conflict. Weak states cannot mitigate conflict diffusion and escalation from outside their borders. Moreover, as the cases of Iraq and Syria starkly demonstrate, state failure creates destabilizing conditions in a region, with possible incentives for violent behavior by other states. The failed state itself may present an attractive target for outside military intervention and interstate armed conflict.[65] In this respect, geographic contiguity plays a particularly important role in the spread of the effects of state collapse.[66]

Equally consequential to state weakness or strength is the legitimacy the state enjoys among its population. Although legitimacy's nebulous nature makes it difficult for the social sciences empirically to document its depth and extent among social actors, especially in non-democracies, it does nevertheless play a critical role in shaping the overall nature of state–society relations. As Seth Kaplan has argued, "state legitimacy lies at the base of any stable political order; it is an essential ingredient influencing any country's capacity to foster economic, political, or social progress and is a powerful predictor of economic

---

[61] Schwarz, "The political economy of state-formation in the Arab Middle East", 601.

[62] Weiss, *The Myth of the Powerless State*, 210–11.

[63] Newman, "Failed State and International Order", 424.

[64] Iqbal and Starr, "Bad Neighbors", 315.

[65] Ibid., 325.

[66] Ibid., 319.

growth and the quality of governance".[67] Fragile states are characterized by competing claims to power and logic of the formal state. They do not have a privileged position as the political framework that provides security, welfare, and representation, and are therefore forced to share authority, legitimacy, and capacity with others.[68]

States that are bereft of legitimacy are essentially non-democratic, there being a direct connection between state strength and democracy. The critical linkage between democracy and state strength, or lack thereof, lies in legitimacy. State legitimacy rooted in acceptable and responsive performance—the essence of democracy—fosters increased public confidence, "positive cycles of capacity development and institutionalisation, and a growth in legitimacy and constructive state-society relations".[69] Weak states may be able to perform security functions, but they cannot perform welfare and representation functions, thus suffering from eroded or diminished legitimacy. Failed states, on the other hand, can perform neither security nor welfare and representation functions, and have no legitimacy either.[70]

A number of scholars, Rotberg among them, see a lack of democracy as one of the most central elements of state weakness. Rotberg classifies state strength or weakness on the basis of a state's ability to deliver a series of "political goods", among which the provision of security, medical and healthcare services, arteries of commerce and transportation, and communication networks are key. Most notably, however, Rotberg points to a state's ability to provide its citizenry with the opportunities to participate freely in politics and the political process as one of the most important indicators of strength. Democracy equates with strength for Rotberg, and its absence denotes state weakness.[71]

Nevertheless, as the Middle East attests, the relationship between authoritarianism and state weakness is seldom direct. Authoritarian states may lack popular legitimacy but still be able to affect social and economic change and enjoy considerable capacities in institutional, security, economic, and diplomatic arenas. Although authoritarian regimes contain the seeds of their own demise, as their longevity and preponderance in the Middle East demonstrate, they often show remarkable staying power. Even if they may be "semi-stable",

---

[67] Kaplan, *Fixing Fragile States*, 37.

[68] Boege, et al., "On Hybrid Political Orders and Emerging States", 10.

[69] Derick W. Brinkerhoff, "State Fragility and Governance: Conflict Mitigation and Subnational Perspectives", *Development Policy Review*, Vol. 29, No. 2 (2011), 133.

[70] Schwarz, "The political economy of state-formation in the Arab Middle East", 603.

[71] Rotberg, "The Failure and Collapse of Nation-States", 4.

they are not necessarily weak since "state agencies are the main vehicle for the exercise of power and the delivery of services... [They] have generally refashioned the state along the lines they desire."[72] Even in instances of general state weakness, as this volume illustrates with specific reference to the cases of Pakistan, Yemen, and Sudan, the use of a "political budget", as de Waal puts it, to establish and maintain patronage and clientelist networks with strategically positioned social actors enables the state to continue holding on to power, and to maintain continued relevance in social and economic realms, despite significantly eroded capacities. As Barry Buzan reminds us, there are three critical elements to the state and its strength. They include its physical base (its sovereignty in a given territory); its institutional expression (the scope of its institutions); and the idea of the state (in terms of the implicit social contract on which it relies).[73] States may have weakened institutional capacities and eroded legitimacies, but the idea of the state and its ability to frame the context and continually influence norms and the environment will not easily dissipate.

Closely related to legitimacy is the equally nebulous notion of identity, which plays a key role in determining a state's strength and capacity. Identity is particularly critical in the creation of state legitimacy, since legitimate political orders are usually built around a cohesive group and use institutions that are reflective of that group's historical evolution.[74] As Robert Putnam has formulated, in most cohesive societies "virtuous circles" develop that feature "social equilibria with high levels of cooperation, trust, reciprocity, civic engagement, and collective well-being". At the opposite end, a combination of multiple identity groups on the one hand and absence of robust governing institutions on the other hand can result in a "vicious circle" in which "defection, distrust, shirking, exploitation, isolation, disorder, and stagnation intensify one another".[75] States work better when they are more deeply integrated with the societies they purport to represent. States that are structured around cohesive population groups are more effectively positioned to capitalize on the common identities and affinities found in society.[76]

---

[72] Call, "The Fallacy of the 'Failed State'", 1504.

[73] Barry Buzan, *People, States and Fear: An Agenda for International Security Studies in the Post-Cold War Era* (New York: Harvester Wheatsheaf, 1991), 64.

[74] Kaplan, "Identity in Fragile States", 468.

[75] Robert Putnam, *Making Democracy Work: Civic Traditions in Modern Italy* (Princeton, NJ: Princeton University Press, 1993), 177.

[76] Kaplan, "Identity in Fragile States", 470.

States that can take advantage of group synergies on a national level have considerable advantage over those that cannot.[77] Similarly, a cohesive society is central to both a state's robustness and enhanced capacity. Identity plays an important role in the construction of both formal and informal "productive" institutions of the state.[78] In weak states, in which formal institutions are fractured, the effects of diverse identities are magnified. Fluid, unstable environments in weak states encourage polities to split along the most salient cleavages. If they do not suffer from paralysis and debilitating fragility, states in fragmented societies are at best likely to remain "arenas of accommodation" instead of functioning as mechanisms for fostering major changes in people's social behavior.[79] Fragile states are unable to assert complete authority in their territories and are vulnerable to challenges from rival institutional systems. They feature "historically embedded disconnects between formal and informal institutions".[80] Where informal rules dominate governance, levels of institutionalization are generally low, and people have little trust in formal institutions, in turn undermining the possibility of reform through institutional design. When competing identity groups are tied to weak formal institutions, at the very least, they can cripple development.[81]

State weakness, in sum, is fundamentally a product of diminished capacity. It may be brought on endogenously, as a result of the nature of the state's relationship with the national groups and social actors over whom it seeks to rule; or exogenously, as a result of the nature of its interactions with other states. Among the more common catalysts of state weakness are wars and other forms of interstate conflict and tensions; international efforts to bring about "regime change" or changes in "regime behavior", such as trade sanctions and economic embargos; or cross-border attacks and attempts to foment ethnic unrest. As it happens, there has been no shortage of these endogenous and exogenous drivers of state weakness in the Middle East.

Weak States in the Middle East

The wave of mass-based rebellions that rocked the Arab world beginning in 2011 shook the very foundations of numerous Middle Eastern states, "weak"

---

[77] Ibid., 467.
[78] Ibid.
[79] Migdal, *State in Society*, 94.
[80] Anten, Briscoe, and Mezzera, "The Political Economy of State-Building in Situation of Fragility and Conflict", 31.
[81] Kaplan, "Identity in Fragile States", 467.

and "strong" alike. Seemingly invincible regimes like those of Ben Ali in Tunisia and Mubarak in Egypt fell like houses of cards, while the eternally revolutionary Qadhafi was dragged out of a sewer pipe at the bloody end of a civil war and shot dead while pleading for his life. Whatever edifice of a state he had erected in Libya over his forty-year rule—or, perhaps more aptly, *de*constructed—is now being dismantled and reassembled anew. The Syrian state, meanwhile, has so far proven more resilient, still standing as of this writing, despite a civil war raging since early 2011. But its very foundations have been shaken to their core. The Bahraini monarchy has been similarly jolted, the state's attempts at painting Shia protestors as Iran's fifth column having done little to stem the tide of popular anger or to strengthen its own hold on power.

In Yemen, the revolution succeeded, to a degree. The wily Ali Abdullah Saleh finally relented and gave up power after mass protests wouldn't subside until he left office, but the transition was only to that of his vice president, with little of the substance of politics, or even the many personalities manning state institutions, changing in any meaningful way. Yemen—along with Lebanon—has long been cited as the Middle East's prototypical weak state, and Saleh's departure has done little to change the fortunes of the state one way or another. The country's sovereignty continues to be violated with the same frequency by lethal US drones as it was during Saleh's last years in office. At the other end of the Arab world, in Sudan, Omar al-Bashir has so far had better luck keeping his hold on power using the same budgetary management of the political marketplace that Saleh resorted to in Yemen. But what Bashir could not do was to keep his country intact, by February 2011 having no alternative but to agree to the secession of South Sudan. But even in his now-truncated country, the Bashir state's hold over and reach into Sudanese society remains tenuous at best.

Along with Yemen and Sudan, Lebanon remains one of the Middle East's chronically weak states. Lebanon was born weak, with the institutional design of its state having sentenced it to a life of weakness. The unwritten National Pact of 1943 assigns state offices based on an archaic and artificial confessional distribution that from early on was more fiction that fact. The design of the state along confessional lines only perpetuated the hold of sub-national loyalties and identities, maintaining also the influence and powers of local notables (*zuama*), and impeding the development of state power and capacity. As if centrifugal forces were built into the state, the young country soon erupted into civil war, in 1958, and political stability remained elusive. By 1975, the additional burden of Palestinian presence in the country once again plunged

Lebanon into civil war, this time only to subside under the overpowering hand of the Syrian army's occupation in 1990.

Neither the Syrian presence nor the Tai'f Accord of 1994, meant to reconstitute and rejuvenate the state, brought the country stability or enhanced state power. The political elite continued to bicker; sectarian and confessional loyalties retained their strength within the country's fractured society; the army and the bureaucracy remained weak; Syria's heavy hand was matched by Israel's routine neglect of Lebanese sovereignty and occasional, destructive attacks; and non-state actors, especially the Hezbollah, operated at will and with impunity. By the time the impact of the Syrian civil war was felt in the northern parts of the country, the Lebanese state had already taken itself to the edge of the precipice and back several times. Today, the weakness continues.

Yemen, Sudan, and Lebanon join the countries of the Arab Spring—Tunisia, Egypt, Libya, Syria, and Bahrain—in exhibiting pronounced features and manifestations of state weakness. The extent to which the rest of the states of the Middle East can be classified as either "weak" or "strong", or something in between, is open to debate. Specific, national variations notwithstanding, state capacity in the Middle East is often greatly influenced by rentierism or war making, or both. Both of these developments bear directly on the capacity of the state, and both have been pervasive features of Middle Eastern politics for the last several decades.

War making, Charles Tilly has convincingly argued, directly contributed to the enhancement of state power in Europe as it helped to centralize the state, consolidated national boundaries, gave rise to political symbols at the employ of the state, and enhanced the state's penetrative and extractive reach within society.[82] In the Middle East, however, war making has had the opposite effect, significantly reducing the state's infrastructural power.[83] As is the case in the rest of the developing world, in the Middle East war making does not contribute to the development of state power and, in fact, may actually lead to a decline in state power.

Starting out from a position of relative weakness, disadvantage, and often dependence in the international arena, states in developing countries are likely to find it particularly taxing to marshal human and material resources for purposes of warfare. Throughout the Middle East, war making is likely to

---

[82] Charles Tilly, *Coercion, Capital and European States: AD 990–1992* (Oxford: Blackwell Publishers, 1992).

[83] Schwarz, "The political economy of state-formation in the Arab Middle East", 608.

result in a decline in state power due to three factors. They include the specific conditions of warfare prevailing in the region; the general financial challenges of war making; and the more specific fiscal crises that regimes face as a result of war making. Due to the pervasiveness of vast expanses of desert and large swathes of open, exposed territories, military conflicts in the Middle East—not the least of which have included the 1967 and 1973 Arab–Israeli wars and the 1980–88 Iran–Iraq war—have often entailed the destruction of massive quantities of military hardware and personnel, therefore exposing warring states to weakness and fragility. These conflicts have been costly not only in terms of human life but also insofar as the state's financial and overall economic health is concerned. In each of the three wars mentioned, as well as in Iraq's invasion of Kuwait in 1990 and the US invasion of Iraq in 2003, the damage to infrastructure in the countries affected reached into billions of dollars. Less obvious but still important has been the deepening dependence on Western weapons suppliers for purposes of war preparation.

In the case of Middle Eastern states involved in prolonged wars and international conflicts, the state does not gain power during sustained war making because the types of war making that exist in the region marginalize the value of domestic resources and instead increase the value of externally driven ones, including especially advanced weaponry, foreign currency, military assistance, and even skilled labor.[84] Ultimately, war making reduces the infrastructural power of the state, which is the power of the state to penetrate and centrally coordinate the activities of civil society through its own infrastructure.[85]

During the course of its eight-year war with Iran, for example, the Iraqi state's power over national economic resources declined precipitously as a direct result of the war, with the state's diminished capabilities bringing about important changes to the state–private sector relationship.[86] As evidence from Iran and Iraq in the 1980s and Egypt in the 1960s indicates, war making has also failed to provide impetus for growth in state power. In the lead-up to the 1967 war, in fact, war preparations placed great strains on the powers of the Egyptian state.[87]

The relationship between rentierism and state power is less clear. Benjamin Smith maintains that oil-rich states are particularly durable and have built-in

---

[84] Thierry Gangora, "War Making and State Power in the Contemporary Middle East", *International Journal of Middle East Studies*, Vol. 29 (1997), 331.

[85] Ibid., 324.

[86] Ibid., 326.

[87] Ibid., 330.

institutional immunity to slow-downs in the flow of oil revenues, thus ensuring their survival in tough economic times. Longevity, in fact, is their dominant distinguishing feature, regardless of whether or not they may be authoritarian or feature some hybrid of democratic and semi-democratic or non-democratic features.[88] Authoritarian leaders in oil-rich states invested their windfall revenues in building state institutions that could carry them through hard times, as in the 1980s, when their access to patronage rents decreased dramatically. He concludes that "oil wealth is robustly associated with increased regime durability".[89]

Rolf Schwarz, however, claims that rentierism has created fundamentally weak states in the Middle East. Arab states in particular, he argues, are "strong" in times of oil boom and weak in representative functions and, at times of fiscal crisis, in welfare functions as well.[90] Rentierism has permitted extensive militarization rather than resource extraction. This has significantly contributed to the weakness of the state internally. Extensive militarization has not fostered efficient bureaucracies, as large bureaucracies function as employers of last resort. The more a state relies on direct measures of taxation, the more the collection of taxes depends on an efficient bureaucracy and voluntary compliance. In the absence of voluntary compliance, which is mainly a function of lack of legitimacy, states have to rely on other indirect measures to accrue necessary revenues.[91]

Rentierism may erode the long-term efficacy of state institutions and their extractive capacity in relation to social actors, but it also facilitates the continued replenishing of a political budget at the disposal of state elites. Patronage and clientelism can be powerful substitutes for political legitimacy. The oft-predicted demise of the monarchical states of the Arabian Peninsula is nowhere near actually taking place, thanks largely to the benefits of rentierism accrued to state leaders.[92] And in times of crisis and economic slow-down, only states relying on indirect forms of rent or those with larger populations and comparatively lower rents suffer adverse political consequences. The others that are better endowed and have fewer mouths to feed—especially

---

[88] Benjamin Smith, "Oil Wealth and Regime Survival in the Developing World, 1960–1999", *American Journal of Political Science*, Vol. 48, No. 2 (April 2004), 242.
[89] Ibid., 232.
[90] Schwarz, "The political economy of state-formation in the Arab Middle East", 599.
[91] Ibid., 607.
[92] For the latest of such predictions, see Christopher Davidson, *After the Sheikhs: The Coming Collapse of Gulf Monarchies* (New York: Oxford University Press, 2013).

Saudi Arabia, Kuwait, Qatar, and the United Arab Emirates—tend to come out of crises relatively unscathed.[93]

Altogether, as the contributions to this volume make clear, we see in the Middle East a number of states in a condition of seemingly perpetual weakness—Sudan, Yemen, and Lebanon, plus Pakistan and Afghanistan, if the geographic designation of the region can be stretched slightly—and then the recurrence of episodes that push states toward weakness, most notable of which are wars, war making, and mass rebellions. State leaders, meanwhile, devise a variety of coping mechanisms and survival strategies, prolonging their own tenure in office and ensuring the operations of supportive institutions at sufficient, though not necessarily optimum, levels. Weakness persists, but failure and collapse are averted, at times just barely.

This Volume

Despite the growing importance of the topic, especially since 2011, so far the subject of weak states in the Middle East has not been studied in a systematic, in-depth manner through English-language sources. Scholars writing in Arabic have been equally inattentive to the broader topic of state weakness and failure in the region.[94] This omission has been mostly inadvertent rather than by design, a product, as Ayubi correctly asserts, of the largely mistaken impression that the expansive size and reach of the state in the Middle East entails a parallel growth in its size and efficacy.[95] This volume is designed to fill some of the scholarly gap left as a result.

Given the vast array of topics that could be studied under the broader umbrella of state weakness and failure, no single volume could possibly present a complete picture of the complex dynamics involved in a region as vast and diverse as the Middle East. Nevertheless, the contributors here have

[93] Mehran Kamrava, "The Political Economy of Rentierism in the Persian Gulf", in Mehran Kamrava, ed., *The Political Economy of the Persian Gulf* (New York: Oxford University Press, 2012), 54–62.

[94] Most scholars writing in Arabic examine state weakness within the context of challenges to state-building processes. See, for example, Khaled Mustafa Murab, *Moshkilat Bina' Aldawlah Alhadeetah fi Libnan was Al-Watan Al-Arabi* (Problems in Modern State-Building in Lebanon and Arab Countries) (Cairo: Dar Alnahze Alarabiyya, 2010); and Jihad Awda, *Fi Bina' Aldawlah Al-libraliyah Al-dasturiyah* (Building a Liberal, Republic State) (Cairo: n.p., 2013).

[95] Ayubi, *Over-Stating the Arab State*, 3.

sought to highlight some of the most pertinent, and in some cases the most understudied, examples of state weakness or state failure in the Middle East region. By design, the contributors approach the study of the topic from a variety of perspectives and angles, exploring various causes, facets, and consequences of state incapacity in relation to social groups, service delivery, and interactions with other states or with groups outside their borders (in Brand's case, their own citizens in the diaspora).

The contributions to the volume start with two treatments of Yemen, each from a different angle. Charles Schmitz presents a historical account of the evolution of the Yemeni state, drawing attention to its very genesis as a British creation meant to protect Britain's interests in Aden. Tribal chieftaincies were transformed into state institutions under the labels of "Paramouncy" or "Princely" rule. Whatever state-building ensued, whether under foreign auspices or a product of indigenous dynamics, it experienced severe strains during the Cold War, with centrifugal forces inspired by Nasserist pan-Arabism on the one side and Saudi conservatism on the other. The two Yemens that emerged had chronically weak institutions, and their unification into one in 1990 did little to enhance the reach and capacity of the new state. Schmitz shows that in the post-unification era and reaching well into and after the Arab Spring, foreign interference into Yemeni politics has not ceased. This level of persistent foreign machinations over time, Schmitz claims, is not adequately captured and accounted for by the literature on failed and weak states.

Complementing the historical analysis of Schmitz is Sarah Philips' focus on the security-oriented conceptions of the weakness of the Yemini state. Among other things, these conceptions, frequently perpetuated by Western publications such as the *Foreign Policy Failed State Index*, are all too often inspired by the perceived need to help "stabilize" the country in the face of terror attacks by al-Qaeda in the Arabian Peninsula (AQAP). Philips maintains that in Yemen's case what is commonly perceived as state weakness or failure is essentially a complex and multi-faceted process of state formation that is inherently fraught with unpredictability and conflict and violence. Within the context of today's globalized world, and more specifically given Yemen's strategic location, the violent travails of late state formation were assumed to be symptoms of state failure best remedied by development assistance the ultimate outcome of which was securing the state from its citizens. "Stabilization" has become a code word for regime stability through defeating the AQAP and ending its violence, in turn perpetuating a vicious cycle that has only eroded the state's functionality and its means of nexus with society.

Daniel Esser's chapter similarly critiques statist conceptualizations of governance that ignore sub-state dynamics as potential building blocks of improved human security and service delivery. Focusing on the cases of Afghanistan and Iraq, he argues that the labeling of these states as failed by US policy-makers was as much a product of political considerations and agendas as it was an analytical assessment of the two polities. The discourse of state weakness was employed for purposes of waging invasions. The invaders—the United States and its Coalition of the Willing—correctly targeted cities as the primary sites of political power and state-building. Where they went wrong, Esser argues, is when they ignored the urban centers' "sub-national politics and practices" and instead focused on cities as sites of violence and terrorism. Pre-determined rulers were imposed on local populations; indigenous urban actors were excluded from the political process and ignored, replaced instead by imported technocrats who had resided in the West; donor money poured in to buttress fledgling security apparatuses; and old, statist patterns of centralized rule, albeit with new garb, began to re-emerge, this time with a decidedly pro-Western hue. Historic opportunities to reinvent "space of governance" in both countries were squandered and were sacrificed for the benefit of Western—US—hegemonic control of the region.

Frederic Wehrey chronicles the travails of post-revolutionary state-building in Libya, focusing specifically on the interplay between institutional fragility on the one hand and societal fissures on the other. The breakdown of political order in the lead-up to and following Qadhafi's ouster from power has given rise to multiple, previously suppressed fissures in Libyan society. Wehrey maps out these fissures, demonstrating that the most important ones are beginning to emerge along geographic and ideological lines. The Qadhafi state had rather successfully employed a combination of institutional coercion and patronage to foster, and in instances to forcibly impose, political and societal homogeneity. The weak and contested institutions that have appeared in the wake of his overthrow have been ill-equipped to pull together the centrifugal forces that the civil war had unleashed. Perhaps the most heavily contested of the political institutions has been the security forces. In addition to the ensuing "security gap", the tensions and at times open conflict among competing armed groups and militias has done little to deepen public confidence in the fledgling institutions of the state or, for that matter, to help remedy state weakness.

Weak states create space and opportunities for non-state actors to pursue opportunities and agendas they would not have otherwise been able to pursue had the state's capacities not been eroded. This is particularly the case with one of the Middle East's chronically weak states—Lebanon—and one of the comparatively more powerful, better-backed non-state actors in the region, the Hezbollah. Mikaelian and Salloukh examine the political space created by the weak Lebanese state within which the Hezbollah has operated with relative impunity. The group, in fact, owes its establishment to another state altogether, Iran, and has almost consistently found its domestic and regional strategies in line with those of either Iran or Syria, or both. In the process, the group has tied its own fortunes as much to the vagaries of regional military and diplomatic developments as to the shifting power balances of Lebanese politics and the state's ability to enforce its agendas and rule on the country's heterogeneous society.

Sudan's weakness is neither new nor a recent discovery. A number of Sudanese writers and intellectuals, in fact, have been exploring its genesis and lamenting its consequences from the earliest days of the republic's birth. Rogaia Abusharaf explores the work of one such Sudanese intellectual, the anthropologist Abdel Khaliq Mahgoub (1927–71). Zeroing in on one of his books, *Rectifying the Wrongs in Working with the Masses*, Abusharaf explores Mahgoub's thoughts on what she calls "the shared ideology of othering", an earnest attempt to understand "the enduring predicament of margin and center" in relation to the state's performance. *Rectifying* more than anything else is a cautionary analysis of the conflict that engulfed Sudan shortly after its independence in 1956. It offers a detailed examination of the historical, and specifically colonial, roots of the weakness of the Sudanese state. Mahgoub also presents pathways to state strength, seeing the essence of a successful state in a forward-looking, democratic political system. A product of his times, he warned against the lurking dangers of fanaticism, sought to subvert marginality, and called for political and cultural democratization. As the secession of South Sudan in 2011 and the ongoing turmoil in the Darfur region attest, Sudanese leaders have yet to come up with viable solutions for the problem of marginality, assuming solving it was a priority. In fact, South Sudan's secession demonstrates the Sudanese state's continued weakness.

In some ways, the very fact that Sudan continues to exist today despite deep-seated, structural dynamics that pull it in different directions, and a string of leaders committed more to their own political endurance than to the national project, is in itself a remarkable political achievement. Alex de Waal demonstrates how Sudan's endemically weak state can stay in power despite consistently failing to deliver essential public goods such as functioning institutions, peace and security, or social and economic development to its population for the last three decades. Relying on patrimonial governance, Sudanese political leaders in general and President Omar al Bashir in particular, in power since 1989, have relied on a finite "political budget" to dispense with favors, jobs, and rewards. Loyalties are bargained over, and a modernized patronage system resembling a "political marketplace" has emerged in which "loyalties are regularly auctioned off to the highest bidder".

Sudan is also explored in the chapter by Babar and Osman, here in comparison with Pakistan, another state located at the periphery of the greater Middle East. Babar and Osman focus specifically on these two weak states' neglect of rural women, who in both cases are among the most neglected of the marginalized communities. State inattention, or incapacity, to affect change to the conditions of rural women opens up space for the non-governmental sector to step in and fill the void. NGO efforts at social mobilization do usually bear fruit, as the women involved achieve a degree of autonomy and agency they are unlikely to have had otherwise. At the same time, however, the impact of NGO efforts tends to be limited by two undercurrents, one having to do with prevailing, and resilient, social norms and constraints, the other due to the continued power and relevance of the lingering state. Even in situations of state neglect and weakness, and even in instances where long-active NGOs have impacted social conditions, the magnitude of that impact has been mitigated by the continued perseverance of the state. NGOs can achieve grassroots empowerment on a micro level. But macro-level change that facilitates the social inclusion of women in a given society is something that needs the active involvement of the state. Limited state capacity and uneven delivery of services means that social inclusion of marginalized groups is greatly hindered. In fact, Babar and Osman maintain, in the cases under review NGO efforts help "reproduce and reinforce the hegemony of the state". Even for the most marginalized of peoples in weak states, the state, as a set of institutions with attached practices and symbols, continues to have relevance and salience.

Closer to the geographic heart of the Middle East is Palestine, which today exists as a form of hybrid nation-state ruled mostly by the Israeli occupation authorities, somewhat also by the Palestinian National Authority, in cantons that are not easily accessible to one another. Glenn Robinson examines the history and travails of institution-building in Palestine. The continued dispossession and dispersion of the Palestinian nation makes any potential Palestinian state fraught with dysfunction. According to Robinson, the Palestinian march toward statehood has been shaped by the dynamic interplay of three developments: institution-building under an over-bearing, in fact suffocating colonial rule; a rentier political economy; and the legacy of Arafat's personalist rule, which Robinson aptly calls "the politics of the antithesis". If Palestine were ever to become a fully-fledged state, it is likely to suffer from profound structural weaknesses, as well as, no doubt, territorial and economic ones.

Laurie Brand identifies four critical gaps in weak states—gaps in capacity, security, legitimacy, and national identity—and examines the relationship between these gaps and the potential role of diasporas in state and nation (re)building. Often, but certainly not always, diaspora communities come about as a result of state failure or conflict situations. Similarly, they often play important and changing roles in conflicts back home, functioning as peace-wreckers or peace-makers depending on changing circumstances. In relation to the MENA region, diaspora communities have emerged as a result of colonial linkages (across the Maghreb), ethnic cleansing and communal tensions (Palestine), sectarian strife and civil wars (Lebanon and Iraq), revolutions (Iran), and limited domestic economic opportunities and perceived regional opportunities (Yemen, Egypt, and elsewhere). Brand looks at the emergence of linkages between these and other MENA countries on the one hand and their respective diaspora communities on the other in the two critical areas of remittances and development projects and political development and state-building (as in civil society organizations and overseas voting). The nature of the relationship, Brand argues, is far from unitary or unidimensional, changing according to evolving historical and political circumstances.

Brand's focus in her chapter is on the relationship between diaspora communities and state-building and on how remittances and long-distance politicking contribute to state weakness or strength. Insofar as nation-building and/or social change are concerned, diaspora communities can also play salient roles in the diffusion of cultural norms and values, both in terms of the symbolic aspects of cultural communication—language, music, the arts, dress—as well as internalized codes of behavior and commonplace or accepted values. This potential role of diaspora communities is particularly important in instances, as in contemporary Iran, in which the state relies on highly pronounced ideological and normative tenets from which sizeable swathes of middle-class urbanites are disconnected.[96] In the case of Palestine, a non-state

---

[96] For the normative disconnect between the Islamic Republic state and large swathes of middle-class Iranians, see Samih Farsoun and Mehrdad Mashayekhi, eds., *Iran: Political Culture in the Islamic Republic* (London: Routledge, 1992).

vulnerable to multiple exogenous influences, cultural forces emanating from the diaspora have for decades been directly consequential for shaping social currents in Palestinian society in the Occupied Territories.

The volume ends with a critical analysis of weak states to absorb the international development assistance coming their way from donor agencies and countries. Weak states often face absorptive capacity constraints and diminishing returns on the aid they receive from abroad. More specifically, aid effectiveness may be curtailed due to capital constraints, policy and institutional constraints, macroeconomics limitations, donor factors, and social and cultural forces. An important first step, argues Mark McGillivray, is to identify the various dimensions of absorptive capacity and to devise a composite index of individual recipient countries. Within the Greater Middle East, Afghanistan is receiving more aid than its absorptive capacity would suggest. In Afghanistan and elsewhere, McGillivray argues, it is important for donors to identify and understand the drivers of absorptive capacity, to identify which drivers they can actually drive and how, and actually to begin to drive the identified driver. Only then will aid effectiveness increase.

Collectively, the chapters in this volume enrich our understanding of the nature and functions of weak states in general and those in the Middle East in particular. State weakness, the volume demonstrates, is essentially a matter of eroded or diminished capacity, in turn opening up space for non-state actors that can capitalize on the growing spread and rise of localized identities and loyalties. As the examples of Lebanon and Sudan illustrate, state weakness is often historically rooted. Weak states are vulnerable to foreign machinations. Additionally, diaspora communities could and often do play influential roles in the economic, political, and even cultural lives of weak states. Ultimately, however, insofar as the lives of their own societies or their relations with other states are concerned, even weak states matter. Domestically, they continue, at the very least, to frame the larger context within which operate marginal social groups and the NGOs helping them. Internationally, they constitute juridical entities which, at least theoretically, enjoy the benefits accorded to sovereign states. Finally, repairing weak states requires more than enhancing the capacity of their coercive and security institutions. It also means ensuring that they have the necessary absorptive capacity to channel donor assistance into capacity-enhancing venues.

The 2011 Arab uprisings shook and weakened supposedly strong Arab states, breaking some and greatly bending others. As of this writing, into 2014, the dust of what started as the Arab Spring is far from settled. So the question of the uprisings' ultimate imprint on Middle Eastern states is far from clear. What is clear is that weak states—whether in their pre- or post-revolutionary varieties or in their condition of political normalcy, whether touched by the Arab Spring or not, and no matter where in the Middle East they are located—are likely to remain prominent features of the greater Middle East.

2

YEMEN

FAILING STATE OR FAILING POLITICS?

Charles Schmitz

The academic literature on failing states focuses on the domestic capability of states: failing states are incapable of serving domestic needs. Beyond the scale of the nation-state, the literature argues that states provide stability for an amorphous international community. Yet, just as in the domestic arena where the literature on failing states obscures politics by reducing the state to a functional apparatus that delivers goods to citizens, the literature is silent on the international and transnational politics that shape domestic state institutions. The origins of states in the post-colonial world lie in the global colonial projects of imperial powers and, as in the Yemeni case, foreign interests have been critical in determining the course of domestic politics, including the historical development of key political institutions, in the post-independence period. The British introduced the concept of the modern state to the Arabian Peninsula in order to secure British interests. The transformation of tribesmen into citizens and sheikhs into heads of state was done to guarantee the security of British trade routes. When Yemeni nationalists attacked the palace of the Zaydi Imam in September 1962 and founded the modern Yemen Arab Republic, Saudi Arabia and Egypt fought a proxy war inside Yemen that was critical in determining the course of Republican politics.

Throughout the modern period, Saudi Arabia jealously guarded its influence in Yemen by making payments to domestic actors of all kinds in order to maintain Saudi influence over Yemeni politics. Then in 2011, when Yemenis revolted against the rule of Ali Abdalla Saleh and Yemen began a descent into civil war, the United States and Saudi Arabia intervened to shepherd a political settlement that led to the current transitional government. Both the US and the Kingdom of Saudi Arabia were concerned primarily with threats to their own countries emanating from Yemen.

This chapter traces the historical evolution of the Yemeni state, showing that it is a complex blend of foreign pressures and domestic interests. The state's forms, its policies, its institutions are all outcomes not only of "domestic" struggles, but regional and global political struggles and contests. Thinking of the state as a set of institutions that serves a domestic natural political community and defends it against an external foreign world is fictitious. Thus the designation of state weakness or strength may have more to do with the political interests of those claiming the power to label states weak or strong than some measure of state capacity.

Foreign state-building in Yemen: creating states and citizens in the nineteenth century

The notions, concepts, expectations, and behaviors of the modern state were first introduced by the British in the southern portions of Yemen. Tribal social relations were transformed by the British to conform to their notions of the functions of a modern state, or more particularly, to certain concepts of state that served British interests at the time. British intervention created a patchwork quilt of emirates and sultanates whose primary purpose was to protect British security, both "domestically" by making the emirs and sultans responsible for the actions of their "citizens", and internationally by making the British solely responsible for the sultanates' "foreign relations". The British were initially keen to limit Egyptian expansion, but later the British worried about the influence of the Ottomans. In the twilight of the British Empire, Nasser's Arab nationalism threatened the British in Aden.[1]

The British Empire first came to the Arabian Peninsula not in search of natural resources to exploit as in India or the West Indies, but to secure communication routes. The waterways surrounding the Arabian Peninsula pro-

[1] J. Gavin, *Aden Under British Rule* (London: Hurst and Co., 1975).

vided key routes for the transport of goods from India to the Mediterranean, and the British were keen to secure these communication routes. Napoleon's invasion of Egypt in 1798 sparked a long period of European geopolitical competition over the region, a struggle that continued throughout the nineteenth and twentieth centuries.

When the British attacked and took Aden in 1839, the Qassimi Imamate of Yemen was in decline. In the eighteenth century, Yemen's near monopoly of commercial production of coffee was ending due to Dutch competition in the East Indies. The Imam's revenues declined and local emirs and sultans in the southern and eastern regions of what would become modern Yemen broke away from the control of the northern Imams. The Abdali Sultanate became the dominant power in the western regions of the south. The Sultanate controlled rich agricultural lands in Lahj along one of the powerful washes, Wadi Tuban, that cut through the narrow alluvial plain on the southern and eastern coasts of Yemen. The Abdali augmented their power through their control of the port of Aden.

Aden is located on a natural breakwater formed by a caldera, a sunken volcano, whose rim protects an extraordinary deep water harbor from the wind and rough seas. In the era of coal-powered ships, the British Navy saw the strategic importance of Aden, but the British were also interested in limiting the extent of French and Egyptian power in the region. In the first half of the nineteenth century, Mohammed Ali had built Egypt into a regional power that threatened British dominance. Egypt expanded into what is now modern Syria and was expanding its presence in the Red Sea. The British responded to Napoleon's invasion by forcing the Abdali to sign a treaty making Aden a free port; and then when Muhammed Ali's forces moved south in the Red Sea, the British attacked and took Aden from its Abdali rulers.[2]

While British military wrested Aden from its Abdali rulers, the British quickly came to terms with the Abdali Sultanate. For the British the Abdali were key interlocutors with the rest of the southern "hinterland" of Yemen. The Abdali were the indigenous allies, native rulers, that the empire sought. The Abdali sultans gladly took advantage of the new British power in southern Arabia to bolster their own power relative to rival tribes and emirates.[3]

Although the British liked to believe they were merely making alliances with local leaders, in fact the British transformed local political relations.

[2] Ali al-Sarraf, *South Yemen: from colonialism to unity* (London: Riad El-Rayyes Books, 1992).

[3] Gavin, *Aden Under British Rule*.

Political relationships in southern Arabia and the Arabian Peninsula were tribal, a vague and rarely clearly defined term, but it suffices to say that tribal relations were built more upon personal loyalties than on territorial states. Tribal leaders ruled through consensus rather than coercion, and their power rested on personal ties of kinship, fictive kinship, rather than control of territory. Tribal groups did have territories, or places that were considered the tribe's land, but authority did not stem from control of territory in the sense of a modern state.[4]

In tribal society the "people" maintained a monopoly over the means of coercion rather than the state. Tribesmen prided themselves on their martial abilities and their ability to defend their family honor. Tribal leadership rested on leadership abilities; the ability to mobilize tribesmen depended upon the "carrots" of charisma, effective political strategy, and/or economic payoffs such as provision of payments, promise of war loot, or provision of weapons. Tribal leadership could not use coercion against tribesmen as a means of control. Power in tribal societies grew out of channeling wealth and assets to tribesmen, rather than authority's ability to coerce or tax tribesmen. Tribal leaders used assets and sources of wealth outside their tribal relations to provide resources to their followers, thus reinforcing their personal loyalties. Sheikhly families in the north of Yemen controlled agricultural tracts on the alluvial plain of Hodieda and in the "middle regions" of Taizz and Ibb. Tribal sheikhs could also gain access to resources by allying with powerful outside rulers, as the Abdalis did with the British.[5]

The Abdali Sultans acquired wealth from their control of the Port of Aden and revenue from agricultural land in Lahj worked by slaves. This wealth enabled them to "buy" the loyalties of tribesmen and to reinforce relations of dependency with other tribal leaders in the area. When the British arrived, the Abdali Sultans initially resisted British advances on Aden but quickly came to see in the British the resources which could substantially increase Abdali power.

The British saw in the emirates and sultanates small territorial states rather than tribes. "A tribe as it was constituted through the field of state ethnography was less a community organized according to common patrilineal descent than a complex of ruling houses, the men they ruled, and the geographical

---

[4] Paul Dresch, *Tribes, History and Government in Yemen* (Oxford, 1990); Shelagh Weir, *A Tribal Order: politics and law in the mountains of Yemen*, 1st edn (Austin, TX: University of Texas Press, 2007).

[5] Dresch, *Tribes, History and Government in Yemen*; Weir, *A Tribal Order*.

space they inhabited."[6] John Willis argues that British policy on the Arabian Peninsula followed their innovations with native rule in India. Aden was ruled through India until 1937 and British policy in the "hinterland" of Yemen followed closely the strategies of British indigenous rule in India. What the British called paramountcy, or "Princely" rule, amounted to the creation of princely states. For the British the new institutionalization of the princely state had the purpose of furthering British interests, principally controlling the countryside and preventing hostile imperial powers from intervening.

The British created an elaborate ritual to signify the relative status of each of the heads of state in the hinterland and signed treaties with each that stipulated that a British political agent would control the "foreign" relations of each state. The emirs and sultans were expected to maintain rule in their territories, meaning that, like a modern state, the head of state was responsible for events and people in his territory. The nine tribes of the hinterland recognized by the British were a mixture of Yemeni society and British imagination. Some powerful tribes were not recognized as tribes and other tribes were more or less created by the British.[7] Here the key point is not that the British created new tribes inasmuch as the convention of the proto-state was being instituted in Yemen. Yemeni tribal relations were subtly transformed into relations between leaders of proto-territorial states and citizens. The primary driver of this transformation was British interest in securing its power in Aden and the hinterland. Statehood was not the political project of a natural citizenry but of tribal elite and an imperial power, and the institutions that resulted reflected these relationships of power.[8]

State-building and state destruction in Cold War Yemen

State-building is not a natural process, it is a social one, and the emergence of a modern state is not the end result of a natural historical progression. The literature on failed states assumes that states are the "modern" form of government and that their strength is not only a moral good, but the natural goal of human

[6] John M. Willis, "Making Yemen Indian", *International Journal of Middle East Studies* (2009), 23–38.

[7] Ibid.

[8] al-Sarraf, *South Yemen: from colonialism to unity*; Sulaiman Faraj bin Azuun, "The Tribe in Yemeni Society", in *Tribes in Yemeni Society: Past, Present and Future* (Aden, 1997); Gavin, *Aden Under British Rule*; Willis, "Making Yemen Indian".

political endeavor.[9] The assumption of a world of states is not only an intellectual fallacy but also a political project. The failed state literature assumes that the post-colonial world lacks stateness and that world peace and progress depend upon the development of stateness in the post-colonial world. Proponents of the concept of state failure have the power to shape behavior in the post-colonial world. Aid, weapons, and political backing are conditioned on "good governance", the synonym of strong state in the failed state literature.

In the Yemeni case during the 1960s, the state builders, the people who wanted to establish state authority and institutions as envisioned in the state failure literature and had the ability to do so, battled the political forces that claimed to defend Yemeni tradition and custom. "Foreign" interests backed both sides. In the north, the Yemen Arab Republic, the state-builders backed by Nasser's Egypt confronted those who wanted to rely upon personalistic ties and tribal custom, supported by Saudi Arabia. In reality, the lines of battle were not so clearly divided. Tribal leaders were lined up on both sides of the conflict between republicans and royalists, those loyal to the Imam. The Saudis and Egyptians fought each other for influence in Yemen, and though the Egyptians stood for Arab nationalism and the transformation of Arab society, Yemeni society in the north, particularly the far north where the war was largely fought, is tribal. Thus, both sides became embroiled in tribal politics.

Similarly, Saudi Arabia backed "traditional" rulers, but they were not particularly attached to the rule of the Imam in Yemen. The Saudis were, and are, interested in maintaining their influence in Yemen and, if necessary, they would back even ideological enemies such as socialists, as the Saudis eventually did in the war of 1994, in order to maintain their influence. In the case of the civil war in the north in the 1960s, the Saudis attacked republicanism because it was associated with the Egyptians and Arab nationalism. The Saudis backed royalist tribes and they harbored the Imam, but they were partial to a modern, "Islamic" form of government proposed by a rebel faction of the Imam's family. It wasn't monarchy or tradition the Saudis backed in Yemen, it was Saudi interests. Saudi power was crucial in shaping the institutions of state that would emerge in the north and that provide the foundation for the Yemeni state today.[10]

[9] Pinar Bilgin and Adam D. Morton, "Historicising representations of 'failed states': beyond the cold-war annexation of the social sciences?" *Third World Quarterly*, Vol. 23, No. 1 (2002); Charles Call, "The Fallacy of the 'Failed State'", *Third World Quarterly*, Vol. 29, No. 8 (2008): 1491–507.

[10] Robert D. Burrowes, *The Yemen Arab Republic: The Politics of Development, 1962–*

After WWII, the Yemeni state became a battleground in the regional and geopolitical contests of the conflicting Cold War powers. Nasser's Arab nationalism competed with Saudi interests inside Yemen. The battles of the competing "foreign" powers shaped not only the state institutions of Yemen but also the notions of citizen and state. Far from reflecting the preferences of an independent and a priori citizen, the Yemenis were mobilized by competing factions with competing visions of good, community, and self. Power, foreign power, shaped Yemeni citizenship, the preferences of the citizen, the notion of the citizen, and the citizen's relationship to the state. The institutions and conceptions of the state that emerged in the Yemeni Arab Republic in the north reflected the outcome of political victories and defeats on the battlefield.

In September 1962, Imam Ahmed, the son of the founder of the modern state in the north, Imam Yahya, finally died. Within a week, high military officers in the Imam's army turned their guns on the Imam's palace in an attempt to kill Ahmed's successor, Imam Badr, to end the thousand-year rule of the Zaydi Imams and proclaim republican government. These officers were inspired by the Egyptian "Free Officers" and Arab nationalism. For these officers, the Imam's government was traditional and backward. The Imamate kept Yemenis in a medieval era of oppression and poverty. Arab nationalism stood for the creation of a new Arab person, a modern person, educated in the modern world and guided by rational principles of science, progress, and humanistic government. The vision of government proposed by the republican Free Officers had much in common with the vision of the strong state in the failed state literature.

Opponents of the republic's forces were the Imam, and much of the Zaydi religious aristocracy, with tribal and foreign backers in Saudi Arabia, the United Kingdom, and even Israel. Their vision of government was based upon tradition, on maintaining personalistic ties, meaning government by personal relationship

---

1986 (Boulder, CO: Westview Press, 1987); Paul Dresch, *A History of Modern Yemen* (Cambridge, New York: Cambridge University Press, 2000); F. Gregory Gause, *Saudi–Yemeni Relations: domestic structures and foreign influence* (New York: Columbia University Press, 1990); J. E. Peterson, *Yemen: The Search for a Modern State* (Baltimore: Johns Hopkins University Press, 1982); B. R. Pridham and University of Exeter, Centre for Arab Gulf Studies, *Contemporary Yemen: politics and historical background* (New York: St Martin's Press, 1984); Dana Adams Schmidt, *Yemen: The Unknown War* (New York: Holt, Rinehart and Winston, 1968); Robert W. Stookey, *Yemen: the Politics of the Yemen Arab Republic* (Boulder, CO: Westview Press, 1978).

rather than rule-making and bureaucratic procedure. The royalists fought for the traditional rule of tribal and religious elites. Their vision of the world was one based on religion and an eternal constancy, not social transformation.

The contest between these two camps shaped the institutions of government, but also the conceptions of Yemeniness, of citizenship and political community. In their arrogance, Egyptian-backed republican forces saw themselves as powerfully modern and assumed that they would quickly subdue the backward Yemeni tribal forces opposing them. Yet, Yemeni tribesmen proved to be much tougher than the Egyptians and their republican allies expected. Egyptian tactics and attitudes of superiority quickly alienated even allied Yemeni forces, and what was expected to be a short war turned into a protracted conflict. Egypt's defeat by the Israelis in 1967 precipitated the withdrawal of Egyptian forces from Yemen, and most people believed that the republic was doomed without Egyptian support. Royalist forces gathered around Sana'a and besieged the city for the final battle of the republic in late 1967. To the surprise of many, republican forces held and the siege was broken. The outcome on the battlefield determined the institutional form of the Yemeni state. Republicans survived the royalist siege and could insist upon a republican state.

The fact that the Egyptians were no longer backing Yemen's republicans certainly made republicanism more palatable for the Saudis. In 1970 Imam Badr renounced the Imamate from his residence in Saudi Arabia and left for London. Though republicanism may not have been the Saudi first choice of forms of state in Yemen, Saudi interests were not in Yemen's particular form of government but in having strong influence in Yemeni affairs, greater influence than anyone else. Thus, within the republican framework, the Saudis worked with their Yemeni allies to shape Yemeni affairs in a manner to Saudi liking.[11]

After the royalist siege was broken, the republican forces fought amongst themselves to determine who would lead the new republic. The conflict was not just a question of republican leadership; it was more about a vision of Yemeni nationalism. The republican forces included a variety of backers of different political stripes and social backgrounds. Left-leaning political leaders and their followers led the defense of Sana'a, but it was the more conservative republican forces, particularly those led by tribal leaders, who won the internecine battle for leadership of the new republican government. This explains one of the key characteristics of the Yemeni state: republican government with conservative social politics. The new Yemeni republic had a parliament with

[11] Gause, *Saudi–Yemeni Relations.*

elected officials, but most of those elected were tribal sheikhs and traditional rulers. The political compromise that ended the conflict after the siege of 1968 guaranteed the inclusion of royalist leaders in the new government, but even within the republican side, their internal conflict brought to power the tribal sheikh, among other traditional forces.

Never before in Yemeni history had tribal sheikhs had such power. Under the Imamate social hierarchy was constructed by a religious aristocracy that placed itself over tribal leadership, though the Zaydi aristocracy had little independent means of coercion and lived immersed in tribal life rather than geographically or socially separated from the tribes. In the aftermath of the civil war and the fall of the Imamate, tribal sheikhs became the leading power in Yemen, along with a nascent national military and a group of merchants connected to the military and state. These three social groups became the mainstay of the Yemeni state. This social constellation was, and is, convenient for Saudi interests in Yemen because it allows the Saudis to manipulate Yemeni politics.[12]

Gregory Gause argues that Saudi influence in the Yemen Arab Republic (YAR) was much greater than its influence in the People's Democratic Republic of Yemen (PDRY) because the state in the YAR did not have the capacity, or the strength, that the state in the PDRY possessed.[13] By strength, Gause means the ability to regulate society, to transform and control society. Gause uses the term "state strength" not in the sense of ability to deliver services to citizens as the state failure literature understands strength, but more like the strength that Huntington understood: the ability to create political authority and organize society.

As Gause argues, society and the state in the YAR were divided, fractured among many different competing powers. These divisions gave the Saudis the ability to develop Yemeni clients without interference from the Yemeni state. The Saudis were also able to manipulate the divisions in Yemeni society, so they supported tribal clients against the state when they did not like what was happening in Sana'a, and they supported the central state in Sana'a when Sana'a supported Saudi interests.

However, the fractured nature of the state in the YAR was not a "natural" phenomenon. South Yemeni society was also "fractured", as shown in the

---

[12] Elham Manea, "Yemen, the Tribe and the State", paper presented to the International Colloquium on Islam and Social Change at the University of Lausanne 10–11 October 1996, www.al-bab.com.

[13] Gause, *Saudi–Yemeni Relations*.

analysis of the British colony and its Yemeni hinterland. Yet in the south, the socialist state of the PDRY transformed the fractured nature of political relations by destroying the tribal elite and incorporating the tribesmen into a military/state bureaucracy that monopolized power in society. Divisions did appear, but they appeared as "regional" divisions within a socialist bureaucracy. Lahj fought Abyan, two regions, in the conflict of 1986; it was not the Abdali and Fadhli, two tribes, fighting.[14]

In the YAR, the ascendance of the tribal sheikh to a prominent role in the republican institutions ensured that tribal society would remain influential. The Yemeni state paid (and after the Arab Spring still pays) subsidies to tribal leaders who distribute the funds among their followers. In the region north and east of Sana'a, and in the eastern regions of al-Jawf and Marib, they are well armed and often provide leadership in the Yemeni military. The Yemeni state in these regions has been constructed around and through tribal order. The administrative districts of the state usually conform to tribal territories and tribal social order remains dominant, meaning that tribal custom and tradition govern social relations. The Yemeni regime makes alliances with key tribal leaders and groups such as the Hashid and Bakil tribal federations, whose power the Yemeni regime in Sana'a always takes into consideration.

This does not mean that tribes are the state. The Yemeni regime in Sana'a sometimes plays on tribal divisions in order to weaken tribal influence. Tribal order by its nature is divided into competing sections and units. The regime in Sana'a can fuel tribal feuds and competition to weaken tribal influence.[15] However, by playing on tribal divisions, the regime in Sana'a is reinforcing tribal order rather than destroying it. Thus tribes retain autonomy from the state in the sense that they are governed not by state law but by tribal law and custom. At the same time, the regime in Sana'a can exert influence in the tribal regions either by providing support for tribal leaders or by causing disruptions between tribal sections. In the end, tribal relations are reinforced and the continuance of tribal social order guarantees a degree of autonomy for tribal leadership.[16]

[14] Dresch, *A History of Modern Yemen*; Fred Halliday, *Revolution and Foreign Policy: the case of South Yemen, 1967–1987* (Cambridge, New York: Cambridge University Press, 1990); Helen Lackner, *P.D.R. Yemen: outpost of socialist development in Arabia* (London: Ithaca Press, 1985).

[15] Manea, "Yemen, the Tribe and the State"; Muhammad Muhsin al-Dhaheri, *Society and State in Yemen: a study of the relationship of the tribe to political pluralism* (Cairo: Maktaba Matbuli, 2004).

[16] Muhammad Muhsin al-Dhaheri, *Society and State in Yemen*.

The preservation of some degree of tribal independence and power enhances the Saudi abilities to manipulate Yemeni politics, as Gause argued. Saudi policy consists largely of "riyal politics", the subvention of various clients to ensure Saudi interests in Yemen. In the case of some tribes then, both the Yemeni state and the Saudi state pay for their allegiance. The Saudis like tribalism because it represents the preservation of custom and tradition as opposed to modernism and social transformation, but the Saudis also like tribal social order because it is centrifugal and disperses power rather than concentrates power.[17]

Institutional forms of the state are crystallization of power relations, the results of battles and contests for power, and the institutional form reflects relations of power. The continued salience of tribalism in Yemen is not a result of the failure of a state-building project or the inability of the central state to control its territory; it is the result of the particular strategies of the political elite in Yemen and the balance of power within Yemeni society and within the region. The Saudis play a key role in preserving this particular form of Yemeni politics.

Saudi ambiguity towards the state in Yemen

The Saudis were and are the most powerful "foreigners" in Yemen. The relationship between the Saudis and the Yemenis is similar to the relationship between the United States and Mexico. The United States is wealthy, and businesses in the United States want to take advantage of Mexican labor, yet the government of the United States fears the "failure" of the Mexican state, meaning that the Mexican state does not have the capacity to "contain" its citizens in Mexico. Violence and poverty in Mexico may spill over into the United States; therefore, the Mexican state is "failing" in the eyes of the US security analysts.

Similarly, the Saudis fear chaos from Yemen.[18] Saudis are wealthy and capital rich, while the Yemeni are poor and labor rich. Yemenis were the principle source of labor for the Saudis during the initial construction boom following the OPEC bonanza of the early 1970s. But Saudis also fear the Yemenis because they are poor and the Yemeni state does not "contain" Yemenis inside Yemen. Yemenis slip across the border, and Yemeni political currents also come with them. The Yemeni bring ideas of republicanism, political parties, and elections that are an anathema to the Saudi monarchy. However, the greatest fear the Saudis harbor against the Yemeni is not so much their politi-

[17] Ibid.
[18] Gause, *Saudi–Yemeni Relations*.

cal ideas as much as the fact that Yemenis are culturally close to the Saudis. Saudis are still dependent upon "foreign" labor. Though there are no precise figures, it is generally accepted that the Saudi population consists of about 16 million Saudis and 10 million non-national laborers. Saudis and the other Gulf States prefer labor that has no aspirations for staying on the Arabian Peninsula but only desires to work and send money back home. Home is elsewhere for South Asian or Southeast Asian workers in the Gulf States. Yemenis could quite well claim to be at home in Saudi Arabia and make claims on the Saudi state as "citizens". The great fear of the Saudi state is that poor neighboring Arab states contest the arbitrary division of the Arab lands into states that grant some great wealth and others poverty. Saudis and Yemenis are Arab brethren. By what right do the Saudi claim ownership of Arab oil?

Thus, the Saudi leadership does not really consider Yemen a foreign country. Saudis spend a lot of money buying influence in Yemen, and they jealously guard against the influence of other regional or global powers in Yemen. In Yemen, it is commonly understood that Saudi Arabia wants a "weak" state in Yemen but not a failed state.[19] The Saudis want a Yemeni state that cannot threaten the Saudi state, but one that possesses the capacity to control its own citizens. The relative balance of wealth between the United States and Mexico is similar to the inequalities between Saudi Arabia and Yemen, but the potential balance of military power is not. While the Mexican military cannot threaten the United States, the Yemeni military is potentially a huge threat to the Saudis. In spite of massive arms purchases, the Saudis do not have confidence in their armed forces and thus the Saudis fear a strong, united Yemeni state.

The Saudis were opposed to Yemeni unity and they tried to scuttle the unity agreement.[20] Abdalla bin Hussein al-Ahmar, leader of the most powerful tribal confederation in Yemen, the Hashid tribal confederation, and the Saudis' closest ally in Yemen, opposed the unity agreement. For al-Ahmar, there was no room for agreement with the Yemeni Socialist Party in the south, a position that the Saudis shared, probably less out of fear of communists than out of fear of the state-building capacities of the Yemeni Socialist Party. Were the YSP to introduce into the northern YAR their state-building capacities demonstrated in the PDRY, the Saudi ability to influence Yemeni society would diminish.[21]

[19] Ibid.
[20] Ibid.
[21] Jamal S. al-Suwaidi and Michael C. Hudson, *The Yemeni War of 1994: causes and consequences* (London: Saqi Books, 1995).

Thus, strange as it may appear, the Saudi support for the Yemeni Socialist Party and its allies in the Yemeni war of 1994 follows from Saudi pursuit of its interests in Yemen. The Saudis had no love for socialists, of course, but the secessionist leadership included long-time Saudi allies in the Yemeni elite from the days before the PDRY, precisely to signal the YSP's embrace of its former class enemies and their Saudi supporters. Abd al-Rahman al-Jifry, head of the League of the Sons of Yemen, was vice president of the short-lived southern state in the spring of 1994. However, Saudi motives were not so much to support the southern secessionist state as to tear apart the newly united Republic of Yemen in a Saudi version of the policy of mutual containment. The Saudis would rather deal with two smaller states with mutual animosities than one larger state with internal cohesion.[22]

On the other hand, the Saudis do not want Yemen to collapse entirely.[23] The Saudis sometimes back the Yemeni state and strengthen Yemeni state capacities. When Saudi al-Qaeda members crossed into Yemen and helped form al-Qaeda in the Arabian Peninsula, the Saudi state became very active in assisting and cooperating with Yemeni security to pursue al-Qaeda. Al-Qaeda in the Arabian Peninsula came very close to killing Prince Mohammed bin Nayef in a suicide attack, and the Saudis feared Yemen's chaos would allow al-Qaeda to launch further attacks against the Saudi elite from Yemen. In this, Saudi security support of Yemen strengthens the Yemeni state's capacities.

The Saudis were also instrumental in brokering the agreement that removed Ali Abdalla Saleh from power and established an interim government to resolve Yemen's multiple political crises. The agreement was signed not in the Yemeni capital, but in Riyadh where Saleh spent three months recuperating from severe wounds sustained in a bomb attack on the regime's top leadership. The agreement was not a victory for the street protesters in Yemen; the street movement saw the agreement as a betrayal of the revolution. Indeed, if the street movement represents revolutionary change, dramatic change in the Yemeni state and leadership, then the Gulf Cooperation Council (GCC) agreement is a betrayal. The GCC agreement allowed the Yemeni elite to retreat from the brink of civil war. The agreement created an interim government of half opposition members and half ruling party members and gave the presidency to Saleh's vice president, Hadi. In the two-year interim period, a national dialogue was convening with representatives from all of the various

---

[22] Ibid.
[23] Gause, *Saudi–Yemeni relations*.

factions of Yemeni society to write a new constitution under which new elections would be held in 2014. The GCC agreement is essentially a mechanism for the divided Yemeni elite to create a new elite pact.

Maintaining the cohesion of the Yemeni elite was very important for the Saudis and Americans who were frightened by the very real prospect that Yemen would be torn apart by civil war. In the view of US and Saudi governments, the GCC may have betrayed the street revolution, but it prevented the Yemeni state from "failing". The warring factions returned their troops to the barracks and the Yemeni military quickly refocused its efforts on the south where al-Qaeda's Ansar al-Shari'a held an entire province under its domain. Saudi support, not only in brokering the elite agreement, but also in supporting the Yemeni economy during the year of paralysis, prevented much greater dislocation and distress, but at the cost of maintaining the power of the old Yemeni elite, whose means of dominance led to the political crisis in the first place.

Saudi pursuit of their interests in Yemen sometimes "strengthens" the capacities of the Yemeni state, as in the GCC agreement and the massive economic support of the Yemeni state. The Saudis regularly place billions of dollars in the Yemen Central Bank and they provided 3 billion dollars' worth of crude oil to Aden's refinery to supply Yemen's domestic needs when Yemen's oil pipelines were destroyed in the fighting. The Saudis have often supported the central state over the past decades when it suits their needs.

At the same time, the Saudis have "weakened" the Yemeni state by supporting the tribes' independence from the central state, fomenting dissension with the Yemenis, attempting to keep the two Yemens from uniting.

Citizen preference, state construction, and foreign interests

The failed state literature assumes a state-centric posture. The states of the world already exist, their existence is considered a requirement of the modern world, and challenges to the state are seen as an indicator of state weakness. Political problems are the result of poor governance in existing states, and the principal blame for state failure lies in corrupt leadership. These assumptions stem from the view that individual citizen views and preferences are set and that the role of the state is simply to aggregate these preferences. Poor governance represents a failure to reflect citizen preferences and produces citizen protest and unrest; good governance accurately reflects citizen preferences and produces social harmony.

However, the boundaries of political community and state jurisdiction are constructed and contested. People's views of politics and their understandings of what the political community stands for and consists of are built upon the shared conceptions of the moral order and understandings of the self, but these understandings and conceptions are always constructed broadly. Political organizations and leadership claim to represent the moral good, the political community, but the leadership's representations are always partial and relational. Political positions are taken in relation to others. The statement, "we represent the true aspirations of the nation" always carries the implied but unstated assertion, "but those others do not represent the true aspirations of the people". The boundaries of who is included in the political community, as well as what is the nature of the political community, are constructed and do not exist naturally.[24]

In the current transitional government of Yemen, perhaps the most difficult issue is the southern movement, precisely because the southerners represent a political challenge to the framework of the Yemeni state. The southern movement itself is divided along many different lines; their definition of a common political community is a matter of great dispute within the movement. The biggest dispute is about secession. Who are the southerners, who represents them, and whether the southerners are a nation are all politically contested at different geographic scales. It is not a matter of citizen preferences, but of the politics of statehood.

The United States declared southern aspirations for statehood illegitimate and engineered a Security Council resolution that declared that Ali Salem al-Beidh, the most important leader of the secessionist faction, was impeding the political process in Yemen and therefore subject to UN sanction, along with former president Ali Abdalla Saleh.[25] The United States was trying to limit the influence of Iran in Yemen, perceived the southern secessionists as tools of Iranian designs, and therefore strongly rejected secession[26]

However, secession remains popular and those backing secession in the south are having some success in steering southern political imagination towards "breaking all ties" with the north. In response, the Saudis are taking a slightly different approach from the Americans. Saudi Arabia has been host to

---

[24] Lisa Wedeen, *Peripheral Visions: publics, power, and performance in Yemen* (Chicago: University of Chicago Press, 2008).

[25] Marib Press, "Feierstein to Marib Press: There is a Possibility of International Sanctions on al-Beidh and the Door is Still Open for the Southerners", on Marib Press (2013).

[26] al-Masdar Online, "The American Ambassador in Sana'a Says that Iran Plays a 'Negative Role' in Yemen", on al-Masdar Online (2013).

many southern Yemeni elites, including socialists, during their periods of exile, and thus the Saudis have extensive contacts and influence in the south. The Saudis along with UN special representative to Yemen, Bin Omar, are attempting to resolve the question of representation of political community in the south by convening as broad a coalition of southerners as possible, but within the bounds acceptable to the Saudis.[27] In the event that the southerners do succeed in forming a new political community, the Saudis and the GCC want to ensure that the new southern state will be amenable to Saudi interests. Thus political community and authority are constructed and not based on natural communities, natural rights, or a pre-existing citizenry.

The Arab Spring

The southern movement was one of the issues that brought the Saleh regime to its knees, along with the Huthi movement in the north. Although the Arab Spring is characterized as a popular revolt against corrupt dictatorship, the Yemeni case does not fit this mold. The street protests outside the University of Sana'a were important, but the Saleh regime fell because it lost its authority in the south and in the far north, and because the inner circles of the Saleh regime split. It was not the street protests, but the massacre of the street protesters that provided the final straw that split the very center of the Saleh regime. More importantly, it wasn't even the split in the inner elite that forced Saleh to turn power over to a transitional government; it was pressure from Saudi Arabia and the United States. The split in the inner circle of the Saleh regime divided the armed forces of Yemen into two military camps, but with Saleh still maintaining the military advantage. The capital of Sana'a was divided into zones of control between these two armed contingents, not of irregular insurgents, but regular military units. Military units across the country squared off against each other and many units were redeployed to the capital city and its environs in preparation for a final battle. Fighting erupted multiple times in the late spring of 2011 between the two camps during which missiles, aircraft and other heavy weaponry were used. Saudi Arabia intervened and the United State followed.

For the Saudis and the Americans, the Yemeni state was in danger of failing, meaning that it had taken its eye off its critical task—the pursuit of al-Qaeda

---

[27] al-Masdar Online, "Unpublicized Meeting Joins Bin Omar with Attas, Salem Saleh, and al-Jifri in Dubai to Discuss the Results of Their Last Meeting", ibid.

in Yemen. As if orchestrated, as many in Yemen argue, a group called Ansar al-Sharia appeared in the south of Yemen in the wake of security redeployments away from the rural periphery towards the major cities. Al-Qaeda's Ansar al-Sharia was not a terrorist organization, but a broad-based insurgency focused upon holding territory and forming an alternative government. Cities and entire provinces in the south of Yemen came under the jurisdiction of al-Qaeda's government. On this basis alone, Saudi Arabia and the United States declared the Yemeni state a failure and intervened to steer the political process towards its reconstitution. State structures, institutions, and power are not simply aggregations of citizen preferences, but constructed by politic interests. Conflict may not be a sign of state failure, but of struggling powers.

The Southern Movement

The southern movement is complex because the history of the south of Yemen over the last half century is ripe with factional political conflict that created layers of animosity between different social groups in the south. On top of the southern divisions, the relationship between the north and the south is not clear in the political imaginations of Yemenis, which lends an additional layer of complexity to southern politics. The modern division between north and south Yemen emerged from the struggle between the Ottoman and British Empires in the late nineteenth and early twentieth centuries. The Imamate that ruled north Yemen after the collapse of the Ottoman Empire contested the border with the British to no avail. Both the republican movement in the north that overthrew the Imam in 1962 and the independence movement in the south that began in 1963 saw themselves as Yemeni and understood that Yemen was one country. But Cold War politics, both domestic and international, prevented unification of the two Yemeni states. When the Soviet Union withdrew its support of the PDRY, the two Yemeni states unified in 1990, but tensions between their respective leaderships quickly deteriorated into war in 1994.

In the aftermath of the war of 1994, the northern regime, led by Ali Abdalla Saleh, attempted to reconstitute politics in the south in order to consolidate the unification of the two states. Under the auspices of an IMF structural adjustment program, Yemen Socialist Party property in the south was privatized, which in reality meant merely a new round of confiscations and political redistribution of property, but this time the beneficiaries were mostly northerners loyal to Saleh. The Saleh regime encouraged the re-emergence of tribal groups and tribal customs in the south and it supported new Islamist groups in the south as a means of guaranteeing the destruction of the social basis of socialism.[28]

However, the northern regime failed to establish political authority in the south. The northerners treated the south as war booty, not a political wound to be mended. Many northerners descended upon the south in search of quick riches. Land and property was simply taken by force.[29]

Southern animosity was channeled into the idea that the northerners had occupied the south, and a political movement emerged to address the grievances of the southerners. In 2007, a group of southern military officers dismissed from the military in the aftermath of the civil war in 1994 demanded the reinstatement of their positions and pensions. A civil disobedience movement quickly grew to include the grievances of all southerners, not just military men. The Saleh regime responded to this movement with a combination of attempts to buy key leaders and repress other leaders as well as the rank and file movement. Neither tactic worked. The southern movement grew and took root in much of the south.

The southern movement anticipated the Arab Spring by a number of years. The southern movement was peaceful, not an armed insurrection, because the south had already lost a war of secession. When the Arab Spring came to Yemen, the southern movement initially reacted by supporting the protesters in the streets of Sana'a. They saw a reflection of their own movement in the street protests against Saleh's regime in Sana'a. As the political situation developed in Sana'a, and the GCC agreement became the basis of the resolution of the political crisis in Sana'a, the southern movement began to split and fracture. When the southern movement was simply about southern grievances, there was unity, but when the time came for political proposals and solutions, the movement splintered into many different factions.[30]

Initially, former military officers of the PDRY dominated much of the movement, but as the grievances of the south reached far beyond the former socialist military, leaders from many different social groups in the south emerged. The past animosities of the south fractured the southern movement.

---

[28] Serge D. Elie, "State–Community Relations in Yemen: Soqotra's Historical Formation as a Sub-National Polity", *History and Antropology* 20 (2009), 363–93.

[29] Bashir Bakr, *Harb al-Yaman: al-qabilah tantasiru 'ala al-watan* (Bayrut, Lubnan: al-Mu'assasah al-'arabiyah lil-Dirasat wa-al-Nashr, 1995).

[30] International Crisis Group, "Breaking Point: Yemen's Southern Question", in *Middle East Report* (International Crisis Group, 2011).

Even among the members of the former socialist military and state there were divisions. The major division appeared between those who supported the re-emergence of the independent southern state and those who argued for accommodation of southern demands within the Yemeni state.[31]

Ali Nasser Mohammed and Abu Baker Attas, two exiled leaders, built support for accommodation with the Yemeni state after the fall of Saleh, while Ali Salem al-Beidh argued for secession. The interim President, Hadi, and his supporters built a faction of the southern movement that tried to rally the movement around the idea of participation in the National Dialogue. Muhammad Ali Ahmed, former governor of Abyan province the south and a close associate of President Hadi from their days in the PDRY, emerged as a major political force in the southern movement that supported Hadi. As a national political party and key component of the interim government, the Yemeni Socialist Party rejected secession and argued that the problems of the south were caused by the Saleh regime. Since the regime fell, the YSP argued, the southern issue could be resolved within the framework of the political process in Sana'a.

However, the idea of secession is popular in the south. The secessionist slogan, "break the ties" with the north is heard throughout the south. While secessionist arguments have captured the imagination of much of the south, it is important to emphasize that there is nothing native or innate in southerners that differentiates them from northerners. Yemen is culturally diverse and has strong regional differences, but whether these differences delineate "nations" or natural political communities that form the basis of a state depends upon the outcome of political struggle and contests.

As a result of the popularity of secession, many local members of the YSP in the south quit the party and joined the secessionist ranks. There are also people who support secession from other political orientations. The League of the Sons of Yemen, a Saudi-supported group of the pre-socialist period, support secession. Members of the Islah Party, the major opposition party in the north, also broke ranks with the party because of its rejection of secession. In the Hadhramawt there are many who support secession, but they do not want to join a movement dominated by former socialists.

The southern issue came to a head with the convening of the National Dialogue to solve Yemen's political problems and write a new constitution for elections in 2014. The secessionists rejected participation in the National

[31] Ibid.

Dialogue, arguing that the dialogue was a northern affair. Others from the south argued that southern issues could be resolved in the framework of the National Dialogue. However, even many of those southerners who chose to participate in the National Dialogue supported some of the demands of the secessionists. Members of the southern representatives to the National Dialogue asked that the committee charged with looking into the southern issue be transferred to a "neutral" state outside Yemen.[32]

The United States and Saudi Arabia both rejected the idea of resurrection of the southern state. Whereas in 1994 the Saudis wanted to cause disruption and divide the Yemeni state, in 2013 the Saudis rejected the division of Yemen and supported sovereignty of the Yemeni state in the south. The Saudis reversed their earlier position and the United States strongly supported them because they feared that secession would allow enemies of the United States and Saudi Arabia to gain influence in Yemen.

Iran gave support to many different groups in Yemen in an effort to gain Arab allies and to harass the Saudis. Iranian Saudi competition for influence in the region is a major element in regional politics in the Gulf region and the United States strongly backs Saudi Arabia. The Iranians seek Arab allies since the Iranians find themselves politically isolated in the region. The Iranians gave moral support to the al-Huthi rebellion in the north of Yemen because the al-Huthi argued for the right of religious freedom for the Zaydi sect, a Shi'a sect.[33] Since the victory of the al-Huthi movement, or Ansar Allah, the Iranians have given material support in addition to political support. The Iranians reached out to other groups in Yemen as well, not just Zaydi activists. The Iranians offered support to student protesters in Yemen, flying many of them to Tehran for conferences and workshops.

Ali Salem al-Beidh, the leader of the most strident secessionist faction, accepted Iranian support. He broadcast a television station called Aden Live from Beirut, and distributed funds in south Yemen to build a rejectionist front.

In response, Saudi Arabia and the United States strongly rejected the idea of secession. The southern secessionists petitioned the UN Security Council

---

[32] al-Masdar Online, "Representatives of the Southern Movement at the Dialogue to President Hadi: Six Demands or Our Participation Will End", on al-Masdar Online (2013).

[33] Barak A. Salmoni, Bryce Loidolt and Madeleine Wells, *Regime and Periphery in Northern Yemen: the Huthi phenomenon* (Santa Monica, CA: RAND).

and the Gulf States to create an independent political process for the southern region of Yemen, apart from the GCC program for the Yemeni state. The US and Saudi Arabia strongly rejected the southern secessionist overtures and as a result both the representatives of the UN Security Council and the GCC states rejected a separate political framework for the south, though the persistence of demands for secession is forcing the Saudis to cultivate favor even among secessionists.

In essence, politics define the question of political community. There is no natural community of southern citizens. In the south, the widespread perception is that southern problems stem from the imposition of northern rule on the south, and people accept the idea that the solution to southern problems is to create a political entity governed by southerners. For southerners, the idea of a separate southern state (either independent or federated with northern Yemen) carries great legitimacy. However, whether the southerners will form a separate political community with their own state depends upon politics. It is not only a question of the legitimacy of the southern demands for statehood among southerners; it is a matter of political power. Southerners may agree on the legitimacy of their demands, but others do not. Northern Yemenis generally do not consider the demands of the southerners for a separate state to be legitimate. Northerners argue either that southerners are traitors of the united Republic of Yemen or, more reasonably, that southern claims of discrimination are similar to claims of discrimination within other regions of Yemen and that the solution to southern demands is reform of the government in Sana'a, not secession. More importantly, the regional geopolitical conflict between the United States, Saudi Arabia, and Iran shapes the question of how to resolve southern demands. The US and Saudi Arabia insist that Yemen remain united, and both countries have tremendous power over the course of political events in Yemen. Thus, what may be legitimate in southerners' eyes may not be legitimate in northerners' or American eyes, and the relative power of these different actors determines the outcome, not the preferences of southerners.

Conclusion

The conception of the state in the state failure literature rests on weak foundations. In essence, state failure means the failure to conform to expected models of behavior derived from an idealized, functional model of the state. The actual social and political foundations of states, even in the context of Europe from which the idealized form of state is derived, are ignored. The state in this conception is a moral and political imperative rather than an empirical reality. The state is stripped of the struggle for power that is the essence of the state and replaced with a set of institutions that provide services to a domestic political community and to the international community.

Reducing states to functional structures whose success is measured in quality of services delivered to citizens and to international states obscures rather than reveals the dynamics of politics in places like Yemen. The very idea of a state came to Yemen in the form of an imperial British project to subdue the Arabian Peninsula to British power. The state failure literature understands the origin of the state as the social contract of an egalitarian community that revolted against tyrannical monarchs in Europe and America, yet in Yemen the state came in the guise of a foreign imposition, not the striving for freedom of a natural political community.

In the 1960s, a group of military leaders led a movement to instill in Yemen the model of the state that the failed state literature proposes. Yet the geopolitical struggle between competing blocs of the international community frustrated the state-building project of the Yemeni free officers. Saudi Arabia, Britain, and Israel wanted to undermine Nasser's influence in Yemen. The resulting war and political compromise in 1970 created a particular constellation of power in Yemen that persists to this day. An essential characteristic of the Yemeni state is its fractured nature, which facilitates Saudi influence in Yemen. The state is not a functional apparatus serving a domestic political community; rather, the state reflects the struggle for power between domestic actors and between "foreign" actors seeking influence in the country.

Finally, the state failure literature rests on the fundamental element of the autonomous citizen, an individual with a set of preferences shared to some degree with others in a prescribed geographical territory, and the state aggregates these preferences into a happy political blend, the Wilsonian ideal. In fact, individuals' political subjectivity is constructed in society. Peoples' ideas of politics are formed in relation to ideas and projects of groups vying for power. In the south of Yemen, the definition of the political community is contested. The idea of a separate political community defined by being "southern" has gained wide currency. The demographically much larger north of Yemen rejects any notion of a separate southern political community and insists that southern political aspirations will be met by reform of the government in Sana'a rather than the formation of a separate political entity. The international community rejects any notion of a separate political community, not as a result of an examination of the political reality of the south, but because the UN, the United States, and Europe fear instability in Yemen and they presume that secession will contribute to instability rather than stability. The formation of a southern political community depends upon the power of local southern groups to provide leadership, the actions of the Yemeni leadership in Sana'a, and the decisions of the United States, Europe, and Saudi Arabia. Group identity and political community are constructed in overlapping geographic circuits of power at the local, regional, and international levels. Political communities are not predetermined, naturally distinct groups of people, as the state failure literature presumes.

By failing to grasp the empirical dynamics of power, the failed states literature becomes a collection of particularistic political and moral imperatives rather than an investigation of the realities of power.

3

QUESTIONING FAILURE, STABILITY, AND RISK IN YEMEN

Sarah Phillips

Western scholarship often unintentionally frames a narrative of state "failure" and state "weakness" that is then used by policy-makers to construct specific policy objectives, many of which are informed by security issues and military concerns. This has been especially the case since 9/11 and more recently since the Arab uprisings of 2011, with much of the academic and policy concerns about weak and failing states revolving around the security threats emanating from them. The role of external actors is often obscured in these narratives, which tend to focus more narrowly on the internal security problems of "weak" states. This chapter seeks to counter this analytical inclination by examining the impact that Western conceptions of stability and state failure—particularly those of the United States government—have had in Yemen, and the way that these may have fed the insecurity they intend to eliminate. Narratives of state weakness and failure can thus do more than simply describe political conditions; they can also shape political outcomes.

The chapter begins by questioning the usefulness of the orthodox failed states narrative from which international policy to "stabilize" Yemen has largely drawn its intellectual justification. It will then analyze the implications of this for understanding processes of rapid political change and responding to them more effectively. To make this case the chapter places USAID's (United States Agency for International Development) *Yemen Country Strategy 2010–2012: Stabilization Through Development* within the context of Yemen's contemporary political and security dynamics.[1] This strategic document is particularly relevant to the issue of "weak" statehood in the Middle East because it articulates the perceived causes of, and solutions to, this condition as understood by the US government's development agency. The chapter will first examine some underlying assumptions of American stabilization strategies before analyzing the unintended consequences of framing rapid political change as an external security threat. It will conclude by suggesting that while Yemen desperately needs development, assistance that is given in the explicit expectation of receiving political or security benefits is likely not to be targeted at the areas of greatest need, and is thus perceived as self-serving. From the outset, therefore, this risks undermining the intention of winning "hearts and minds" and encouraging pro-Western sentiment. The chapter will also suggest, however, that there is a performative objective to Western stabilisation strategies: to establish for a domestic audience that complexity can be domesticated, and that power can outmaneuver uncertainty. As the anthropologist Carolyn Nordstrom writes, "power rests in part on the very illusion that power exists",[2] and stabilisation strategies are, in part, about protecting that illusion by being seen to take the risk out of political change.

Finally, the chapter situates al-Qaeda in the Arabian Peninsula (AQAP) within narratives of state failure and stabilization, arguing that because orthodox views of both shy away from explicitly engaging with the complexities of political power, both overlook key sources of resilience for militant movements. AQAP is adept at articulating narratives of injustice; theirs is a highly political narrative about Yemen's power structures and the injustice contained within them. Rightly or wrongly, it is widely believed within Yemen that factions of the old regime are entangled with AQAP and the fight against it is thus partly seen as a political game of one faction against the other. The US's

---

[1] USAID, *Yemen Country Strategy 2010–2012: Stabilization Through Development*, 2010, http://pdf.usaid.gov/pdf_docs/PDACP572.pdf. It is important to note that other donors—particularly the United Kingdom, Canada, and Australia—use the concept of stabilization in their state-building and peace-building programs. While the UK government's *Stabilisation Unit* is currently engaged in Yemen, the United States remains by far the most influential Western actor in Yemen in this regard and is thus the focus of this chapter.

[2] Carolyn Nordstrom, *Shadows of War: Violence, Power and International Profiteering in the Twenty-First Century* (Berkeley, CA: University of California Press, 2004), 233.

failure to grapple with these nuances leaves it not only apparently taking AQAP at face value to a Yemeni audience (which causes many Yemenis to think them naïve), but also being seen to take sides in a domestic confrontation that they misunderstand. This view carries weight in Yemen, and when combined with ongoing American military intervention through air and drone strikes, it is given even greater sting.

Failing at What?

The orthodox view of state failure benchmarks developing states against indices derived from Western liberal concepts of the state, particularly regarding their ability to provide security and other services to their citizens. It takes liberal institutions as its starting point and works backwards, judging failure to reside in those states that fall so far behind that they risk falling off an awful, though undefined, precipice in which anarchy becomes all consuming. In 2012, the only African states assessed by the Failed States Index to be "borderline" were South Africa, Botswana, and Ghana. A further nine African states were said to be merely "in danger" of failure while all remaining African states were "critical" (the worst ranking available). No African state was considered by the authors to be either "stable" or "most stable". Similarly, in the Middle East, the only state deemed by the Index to be "stable" was the UAE; Oman was "borderline", while all other states were considered either "in danger" or "critical" as well. The widespread nature of such apparently dire categorizations in developing states thus begs the question of what is really being measured: is it the breakdown of a system that once existed, or a symptom of the processes by which these states were formed? This is not to suggest that all states form in similar ways and that some are simply "less complete" than others, although it is the case that some states are far newer than others. Rather, it is to emphasize that the international political context in which a state emerges has a very significant bearing on its internal power configurations. As international power structures shift, so too does the imprint they leave on domestic political settlements. Those states that exist as internationally recognized sovereign entities but which never had, for example, a monopoly on the legitimate use of violence exhibit fundamentally different political compositions from those that have had, or still have, this capacity.

Western liberal states did not emerge as the result of their ability to provide services to their citizens effectively, but rather through profoundly disorderly processes that occurred gradually over centuries and were marked by ruthless violence, elite racketeering,[3] informal economies, colonial expansion, and unpredictable political transformations. By overlooking the relationship between the development of contemporary liberal institutions and the turbulent (and profoundly illiberal) politics that colored their evolution, the conventional notion of state failure assumes that all states should look roughly the same—and at the same time.

A second failing of conventional narratives of failure is their tendency to focus on the often massive flaws in a state's domestic structures while brushing aside the structural imbalances in international political and economic systems that disadvantage later forming, and usually post-colonial, states. This chapter argues that by overlooking important historical and international factors that influence state formation, these indices fail to capture the multifaceted drivers of political violence, exclusion, and economic malaise in developing states, particularly those that exist beyond the borders of the state in question. Instead they characterize rapid political change, and its attendant unpredictability and (often) violence, as signs of failure as these circumstances may lead a state closer to anarchy. This is not to suggest, of course, that the human rights abuses, political violence, or economic exclusion that the narrative highlights are desirable or worthy of defence as the birthrights of development; only that the pathway beyond them is unlikely to occur in a stable, linear, or predictable manner. Change necessarily involves uncertainty and risk, and in a globalized world where security threats can easily spread across borders, that risk is now perceived to be borne by those outside the "failing state" from which it originated. As US President George W. Bush stated in the 2002 National Security Strategy, the United States is "threatened less by conquering states than we are by failing ones". Later forming states are thus burdened with a pervasive view that their internal problems are also the problems of wealthier and militarily superior states.

Yemen's uprising was understood as an impediment to the counter-terrorism efforts that were already underway and was thus framed by Western donors and the Gulf Cooperation Council (GCC) as a situation that required urgent "stabilization" rather than one that demonstrated the popular urgency of genuine change. Stabilization is an ambiguous, open-ended concept that combines humanitarian programs, development programs, and often coercive or military operations in countries that are experiencing widespread violence,

---

[3] Charles Tilly, "War Making and State Making as Organized Crime", in Peter B. Evans, Dietrich Rueschemeyer, and Theda Skocpol, eds., *Bringing the State Back* (Cambridge: Cambridge University Press, 1985), 169–91.

complex political emergencies, or the withdrawal of popular legitimacy from an internationally recognized authority.[4] Based on a foundational assumption that underdevelopment and the lack of public services can generate instability that can spill over to other states, stabilization has essentially become short-hand for a politicized approach to development assistance with an explicit aim of achieving greater security for the implementing state. Moreover, it is based on an inherent assumption that the inability of the host state's institutions to provide goods for its citizens is correlated with the likelihood of terrorism occurring beyond the borders of the state. As the US Army Peacekeeping and Stability Operations Institute notes:

> Terrorists, transnational organized crime syndicates, local warring factions, war-lords, and petty thieves have all found common cause in states and regions in con-flict... The required response is a comprehensive one that brings together specialized organizations to stabilize extremely dangerous and hostile environments while laying the foundations for a sustainable peace... Stabilization aims to prevent the renewal of violent conflict; conflict-sensitive development seeks to enable a long-lasting peace.[5]

Applications of the concept vary between target states and between donors.[6] However, the overall aim is to reduce levels of conflict and increase social cohesion by providing valued services (and institutional reforms that may sustain such services) to those who may have incentives to challenge the authority of the state.

By conceptualizing the Yemeni uprising as a symptom of the state's institu-tional failures, "stabilization" strategies were implemented as a counter-insur-gency-inspired model of development programming. These policies were intended to fortify a central government that was being widely challenged by

---

[4] A useful analysis of the dilemmas that stabilization strategies raise for humanitarian actors can be found in Sarah Collinson, Samir Elhawary, and Robert Muggah, "States of Fragility: Stabilisation and its Implications for Humanitarian Action", *Disasters*, Vol. 34, No. 3 (2010), 275–96.

[5] United States Army Peacekeeping and Stability Operations Institute, *Guiding Principles for Stabilization and Reconstruction* (Washington, DC: United States Institute of Peace, 2009), 1.

[6] Sultan Barakat, Sean Deely, and Steven A. Zyck discuss the historical experiences of stabilization strategies in "'A Tradition of Forgetting': Stabilisation and Humanitarian Action in Historical Perspective", *Disasters*, Vol. 34, No. 3 (2010), 297–319. They argue (p. 297) that the lack of historical success with stabilization "raises the likelihood that it is not solely the design or implementation of individual stability operations that require modification but perhaps the entire concept of stabilisation itself".

its citizens in the hope that this would achieve an external security dividend. This overlooked the most important underlying grievance—namely that politics underpinning the state's institutions required urgent change, not external reinforcement. The logic driving the stabilization strategy in Yemen (and elsewhere) was that the stakes of a political transition were too important to be left to chance and that disorderly power struggles between competing interests, elites, and ideas must move to the post-conflict transition phase before unpredictability could become entrenched.

The Dilemmas of Late(r) Forming States

State formation is a fluid and ongoing process; states are not formed at a specific moment but evolve on the basis of negotiations, consensus, and conflict between the politically relevant actors within them. For this reason, understanding the political bargains and power im/balances that uphold a state's formal and informal institutions gives better analytical purchase than simply understanding their structural capacity to deliver goods and services. Statehood is more than a set of institutional rules and organizational capacities that dictate legitimacy. It is also the fluid outcome of complex, unstable negotiations over domestic power relations.[7] In other words, state institutions should not be mistaken for the substance of a political settlement, but rather as symptoms of it.

State formation in Yemen is a particularly contemporary phenomenon. The Yemen Arab Republic and the People's Democratic Republic of Yemen (North and South Yemen, respectively) only unified in 1990; it was not a "re-unification" as it is sometimes called, but the merger of two very different political, economic, and social systems, each containing very different internal tensions and lines of division. The Republic of Yemen has never exercised a monopoly on legitimate force. As is quite common in states where this monopoly is lacking, the regime of former president Ali Abdullah Saleh actively discouraged the formation of strong formal institutions and instead distributed power and local security through a patronage system, in which the key enforcers and beneficiaries were selected members of the tribal and military elite.

---

[7] Marleen Renders and Ulf Terlinden, "Negotiating Statehood in a Hybrid Political Order: The Case of Somaliland", *Development and Change*, Vol. 41, No. 4 (2010), 724.

Newer states have had to contend with several structural and normative circumstances that profoundly influence domestic political possibilities and power struggles. First among these is that there was already "a large number of sophisticated and wealthy states" that were willing and "able to project their influence well beyond their borders".[8] This influence has created expectations over what constitutes a legitimate domestic political order among external actors. Having experienced the ruthless violence of their own creation in the wars that ravaged Europe, the Americas, and parts of Asia for centuries, the industrialized states that emerged from World War II worked to establish safeguards to prevent such ruthless violence from continuing to occur in and between states. These states had by this time established relatively effective domestic political settlements concerning the management of violence (and the desirability of limiting domestic violence) and the political desirability of achieving at least relatively inclusive economic growth.[9] Their formal institutions had evolved to embody the underlying political settlement, not the other way around: the formal institutions did not forge the political settlement, but rather evolved as an expression of it.

Contemporary state-formation is an increasingly internationalized endeavour. In the post-WWII era there are far greater opportunities for domestic elites to extract resources internationally (through resource exports, strategic rents, international loans, or overseas development assistance), which reduces the relative importance of extracting resources domestically.[10] Newer states thus have relatively easy access to external sources of revenue and political support for the domestic political elite. Like other states under scrutiny in this book, Yemen has had access to a steady stream of international loans, credit, and strategic rents from the GCC states, and now Iran (though funds from Iran do not flow to the formal state per se), and of course from Western states,

---

[8] Antonio Giustozzi, *The Art of Coercion* (London: Hurst & Co., 2011), 17.

[9] Robert H. Bates, *When Things Fell Apart: State Failure in Late-Century Africa* (Cambridge: Cambridge University Press, 2009), 5.

[10] Paul Collier, "The Political Economy of State Failure", *Oxford Review of Economic Policy*, Vol. 25, No. 2 (2009), 223; Nicholas van de Walle, "The Economic Correlates of State Failure: Taxes, Foreign Aid and Policies", in Robert I. Rotberg ed., *When States Fail: Causes and Consequences* (Princeton, NJ: Princeton University Press, 2004), 108; William Reno, "Persistent Insurgencies and Warlords: Who is Nasty, Who is Nice, and Why?" in Anne Clunan and Harold Trinkunas, eds., *Ungoverned Spaces: Alternatives to State Authority in an Era of Softened Sovereignty* (California: Stanford University Press, 2010), 60.

although the latter source is small by comparison. In 2009, for example, the Yemeni government received at least $US2.2 billion from Saudi Arabia and a further $US700 million from the UAE—an amount that was equivalent to about three-quarters of what it earned from oil when revenues peaked in 2008.[11] The following year, the Yemeni government received at least another $US1 billion in untied funding from Saudi Arabia, though informal estimates put the figure at perhaps double that.[12] Saudi Arabia has continued to make public contributions to the Yemeni government, such as the 3 million barrels of oil that it contributed in 2011,[13] and a $US1 billion transfer to the Central Bank in 2012.[14] The amounts that have been given in private remain a matter of speculation, but if history serves as a guide, they are likely to be considerably more than what has been publicly announced. Saudi Arabia also contributes a tremendous amount of money to state and non-state political actors and social forces in Yemen. A Yemeni newspaper published a list of senior politicians, academics, sheikhs, military figures, and journalists whose names were among the 2,700 Yemenis who receive regular payments from the Kingdom. The paper reported that the budget, which had once reached as high as $US300 million per month, had recently dropped to $15 million a month.[15] As one source who received regular payments told me in 2008: "everybody can get money from Saudi Arabia if he knows someone there, or if he is a sheikh or even just a tribesman ... they give money to Hashid, Bakil, Madhaj, everybody, all tribes of Yemen receive money from Saudi Arabia."[16] The fact that this person was by no means a figure of tribal significance confirmed the truth of his observation.

These payments reinforce a political economy that is predicated on weak institutions. The politically relevant elites use their lack of capacity and/or

[11] Sarah Phillips, *Yemen and the Politics of Permanent Crisis* (London: Adelphi Series, 420, 2011), 130.

[12] Ibid.

[13] al-Ahram, "Saudi donates 3 million oil barrels to Yemen: minister", 8 June 2011, http://english.ahram.org.eg/NewsContent/3/12/13920/Business/Economy/Saudi-donates—million-oil-barrels-to-Yemen-minist.aspx

[14] Yemen Post, "Saudi Fund to Deposit $1 Billion in Yemen, Minister", 29 August 2012, http://yemenpost.net/Detail123456789.aspx?ID=3&SubID=5903&MainCat=3

[15] Jamal Jubran, "Naming Names: Senior Yemenis in Saudi's Pocket", 11 June 2012, http://english.al-akhbar.com/content/naming-names-senior-yemenis-saudi's-pocket

[16] Conversation with a source that receives regular payments from Saudi Arabia, Sana'a, November 2008.

lack of willingness to provide services to large groups of citizens (or even their lack of territorial control) as a resource for extracting more external revenue. This dilemma raises an important question: to whom is the state weak or failing, and at what is it failing? As the above suggests, circumstances conventionally described as weak or failing statehood can actually strengthen local elites, play to the interests of other states (including Western ones) that prefer illiberal regimes purporting to maintain stability, and can even be used strategically by ordinary citizens pursuing livelihoods in the absence of regulation.[17] However, for most citizens the deleterious humanitarian and developmental consequences outweigh any benefits produced by such a political economy.

The insecurity derived from "state failure" is not exclusively derived from domestic circumstances either, despite the characterization in orthodox narratives, with military intervention conducted in Yemen also causing civilian casualties and widespread fear. In early 2013, the Bureau of Investigative Journalism estimated that in the past ten years between 95 and 181 Yemeni civilians had been killed by American covert military operations in Yemen, including from drones and airstrikes.[18] The vast majority of these deaths occurred in the period from late 2009 as the campaign against AQAP intensified.[19] In May 2010, an American airstrike killed the Deputy Mayor of Marib (Jabr al-Shabwani) while he attempted to mediate with AQAP—on the basis of what appears to have been intentionally false intelligence from the Yemeni side.[20] Members of Shabwani's tribe responded with a series of intermittent attacks on a major oil pipeline which, by 2011, forced its closure for several months and reportedly cost the Yemeni government over a billion dollars in

---

[17] Tobias Hagmann and Didier Peclard, "Negotiating Statehood: Dynamics of Power and Domination in Africa", *Development and Change*, Vol. 41, No. 4 (2010), 540; Pierre Englebert, "Why Congo Persists: Sovereignty, Globalization and the Violent Reproduction of a Weak State", QEH Working Paper Series—QEHWPS95 (2003), 8–9.

[18] Bureau of Investigative Journalism, "Yemen: reported US covert actions 2013", http://www.thebureauinvestigates.com/2013/01/03/yemen-reported-us-covert-actions-2013/

[19] The Bureau reported that the total number of people during this period was much higher (between 603 and 1,134) though it is beyond the scope of this paper to analyze how civilians are distinguished from non-civilians.

[20] Adam Entous, Julian Barnes, and Margaret Coker, "U.S. Doubts Intelligence That Led to Yemen Strike", *Washington Post*, 29 December 2011, http://online.wsj.com/article/SB10001424052970203899504577126883574284126.html

lost revenue.[21] While this is clearly an amount that the "failing" country could not afford, this consequence of an American air strike was never, to the author's knowledge, placed within the context of American efforts to stabilize the Yemeni economy through development projects.

"Stabilization" and Concepts of the State

When the youth-driven protests began in Yemen in January 2011, the country was already a focal point for Western counter-terrorism and counter-radicalization efforts. The capacity and ambition of Yemen's militant jihadis had been steadily increasing since January 2009, when al-Qaeda in the Arabian Peninsula (AQAP) formally announced its establishment. In the space of just fourteen months AQAP conducted a number of high-profile, albeit failed, attacks on targets outside Yemen. These included the August 2009 attempted assassination of Saudi Arabia's Deputy Minister of Interior, Prince Mohammed bin Nayef, who is responsible for counter-terrorism operations in the Kingdom; the attempted bombing of a US-bound passenger jet on Christmas Day 2009 by the so-called "underpants bomber"; and the placement of sophisticated explosive devices disguised as printer carriages on passenger and cargo jets bound for the United States in October 2010. Each of these operations fuelled concerns that the deteriorating political and economic conditions in Yemen were driving not only AQAP but also two other unrelated movements that were challenging the foundations and legitimacy of the Yemeni state: the secessionist movement in parts of the south (al-Hirak), and the al-Houthi insurgency in the northern governorate of Sa'da and its surrounds. Then, in early 2011, the discontent that was evident not only in these three anti-regime movements but also in the population more broadly erupted onto the streets after the removal of the Tunisian and Egyptian presidents.

Like other leaders in the region, President Ali Abdullah Saleh experimented with various mechanisms of control, ranging from promises of reform, salary increases for civil servants, cash handouts and free lunches for anti-regime protesters; to pro-regime protests by men with military haircuts, the detention of protesters and oppositionists, and violence against protesters. His balance between co-optation and coercion soon strongly favored the latter, however,

---

[21] According to Yemen's Oil Minister, the closure of the Ras Isa Pipeline cost the country $15 million a day. Al-Sahwa, "Yemen's Aden refinery resumes output", 6 August 2012, http://www.alsahwa-yemen.net/arabic/subjects/5/2012/8/6/21360.htm

and the first massacre of peaceful protesters occurred on 18 March 2011, when snipers killed more than fifty unarmed civilians on the streets of central Sana'a. The massacre provided the stage for the defection of the second most powerful man in the Saleh regime—the Commander of the First Armored Division, General Ali Muhsin. Muhsin's defection was not simply a response to the murder of protesters, as he claimed, but was built on long-standing tensions within the regime's inner circle over the distribution of resources and the inheritance of power.[22] These tensions continue to shape Yemeni politics despite the removal of President Saleh from office in February 2012.

Speaking in the days following the massacre, then US Secretary of Defence Robert Gates said that: "Instability and diversion of attention from [al-Qaeda] are my primary source of concern in Yemen."[23] US Ambassador to Yemen Gerald Feierstein reiterated the al-Qaeda-centric stance regarding the protests: "We believe that the uncertainty and the instability is helpful to al-Qaeda."[24] Days later, a journalist asked Secretary Gates: "How dangerous is ... a post-Saleh Yemen to the United States?" Gates replied: "We've had counter-terrorism cooperation with President Saleh and the Yemeni security services ... So if that government collapses, or is replaced by one who is dramatically more weak, then I think we'd face some additional challenges out of Yemen, there's no question about it."[25]

That same month, as Yemenis seethed in anger over the ongoing atrocities against civilian protesters and also over the broader political context that fuelled the protests, the American Deputy Assistant Secretary of Defense for Special Operations and Combating Terrorism, Garry Reid, went on the record as saying that President Saleh's regime was: "the best partner we're going to have ... and hopefully it will survive because I certainly would hate to start over again in what we've tried to build."[26] The Assistant Secretary was referring

---

[22] Sarah Phillips, "Who Tried to Kill Ali Abdullah Saleh?" *Foreign Policy*, 13 June 2011.

[23] Cited in J. Fleishman, "Yemen President's Ouster May Deal U.S. Huge Setbacks", *LA Times*, 23 March 2011, http://www.latimes.com/news/nationworld/world/la-fg-yemen-dangers-20110323,0,3343598.story?track=rss

[24] Cited in Erik Stier, "Will Yemen Protests Boost Al Qaeda?" *Christian Science Monitor*, 25 March 2011, http://www.csmonitor.com/World/Middle-East/2011/0325/Will-Yemen-protests-boost-Al-Qaeda

[25] Agence France Presse, "US Says Post-Saleh Yemen Would Pose 'Real Problem'", 27 March 2011, http://www.france24.com/en/20110327-us-says-post-saleh-yemen-would-pose-real-problem

[26] Cited in Associated Press, "US and Israel Behind Unrest: Yemeni Leader", 2 March

to his desire not to have to rebuild mechanisms to contain the threat posed by AQAP. However, on the diplomatic front, the US government was also reiterating that removing President Saleh was no panacea for the country's broader troubles. Ambassador Feierstein had stated shortly before the massacre: "We've also been very direct with our friends in civil society and in the street protests, that the idea of 'isqat al-nitham' [the fall of the regime] is not really the answer to the problems."[27] In December 2011, Ambassador Feierstein caused considerable controversy by a calling a planned protest march from the city of Ta'izz to Sana'a "provocative". The Yemeni news agency al-Masdar quoted the Ambassador as saying that: "Being peaceful isn't just about not carrying weapons. If 2,000 people decided to march on the White House, we wouldn't consider it peaceful and we wouldn't permit it."[28] Regime forces later killed three people during the march.

Throughout much of 2011, therefore, the United States positioned itself against the indigenous calls for systemic change being made by the protesters and reinforced the idea that the regime of Ali Abdullah Saleh would continue to receive its support. By choosing this course, the United States asserted that the failure of the institutions and individuals that constituted the formal Yemeni state posed a greater risk than did the fact that they were no longer considered legitimate by a groundswell of ordinary citizens.

Securing the State from its Citizens

In January 2009, when AQAP formally announced itself, the group was primarily located in several poor and underdeveloped governorates where tribal structures are strong markers of identity and social organization. The fact that AQAP's cells were located in impoverished rural areas contributed to the view that the group's traction was linked to the lack of development in the areas in which it had found refuge. As USAID described its strategy throughout 2003–9, the agency had "focused on development initiatives in the five

---

2011, http://www.news.smh.com.au/breaking-news-world/us-and-israel-behind-unrest-yemeni-leader-20110302–1bde5.html

[27] United States Embassy, Yemen, "Ambassador Feierstein's interview with Saba, March 07, 2011", http://yemen.usembassy.gov/fis.html

[28] The original citation appeared in the Yemeni news outlet al-Masdar but has since been taken down. The quote is available from Mohammed Ghobari, "Street fights hit Yemen as US mulls letting in Saleh", Reuters, 27 December 2011, http://www.reuters.com/article/2011/12/27/yemen-idUSL6E7NR0KV20111227

remote, very poor, rural governorates most at-risk of generating political instability and providing possible refuge for terrorists".[29] The perception within
Washington and London was that the rising tension within Yemen was being
given form by three insurgencies against the state (the southern secessionist
movement, the al-Houthis, and AQAP). USAID characterized the drivers of
these movements as outcomes of underdevelopment:

> The development hypothesis of the USAID/Yemen Strategy postulates that
> addressing the development needs of underserved communities is causally related
> to improving political and social stability. The foundation of political opposition
> [to the state] and extremist ideologies is, to a great extent, based on people's level
> of satisfaction with the services their government provides, and whether there are
> real opportunities...
>
> [the solution to which lies in] addressing people's basic needs and opportunities at
> the local level by improving their access to basic services, by expanding economic
> opportunities and by prompting political/civic empowerment.[30]

The document conceptualizes development assistance as responding to the
population's needs in order to achieve greater security. However, while development was seen as the key to greater stability, there was apparently little
critical analysis about what stability actually meant or who its intended
recipients really were, although the centrality of homeland security was made
clear by the proviso that: "USAID projects must collaborate closely with
DOD [Department of Defense] where feasible."[31] A later document provides
slightly more clarification, when it notes that stability in the Yemeni context
"is characterized as reduced support for violent means of resolving conflicts
and grievances and increased support for the central government to prevent
fragmentation of the state and continued conflict"[32]. However, there is no
obvious consideration of the possibility that the central government might
be—or at least might be widely perceived to be—a source of insecurity for
segments of the Yemeni population. Also not mentioned in this later document is the possibility that "support for non-violent means of resolving conflicts" might already be embedded in traditional legal norms and in popular
preferences. The state-centric view of what constitutes stability is also

[29] USAID, *Yemen Country Strategy*, 1.
[30] Ibid., 2–3.
[31] Ibid., 12.
[32] USAID/Egypt, Risk Assessment of USAID/Yemen's Major Activities (Report
No. 6–279–11–001-S), 30 March 2011, 2; http://gopher.info.usaid.gov/oig/pub-
lic/fy11rpts/6–279–11–001-s.pdf

reflected in the way that USAID defined "vulnerable" persons in the 2010 strategy document:

> The term "vulnerable", unless otherwise defined in this document, describes individuals, entities, or groups that are needy, poor, and/or susceptible—because of social, cultural, political, and/or economic characteristics—to being subjected to violence or extremism, or engaging in illegal and/or rebellious activities against widely accepted religious leaders or ideologies, traditional governing bodies, elected or appointed local representative bodies, local government entities, and/or the central government. Distrust of seemingly distant, disconnected central authority is a defining characteristic of this descriptor.[33]

The USAID strategy to bring greater stability to Yemen thereby defines people who distrust the central government, because of its apparent disconnection from their lives, as being vulnerable to "engaging in illegal and/or rebellious activities". This is a profoundly different definition of "vulnerable" to what is usually found in development literature, where an individual's vulnerability is a function of having insecure access to the goods required for basic subsistence and security, not the possibility that they might resist that which they believe contributes to their insecurity. In USAID's strategy, therefore, the primary concern is for the vulnerability of the "seemingly distant, disconnected central authority" (the state) that is at risk of being challenged by its citizens.

If underdevelopment is seen as posing a security threat beyond the borders of the state, then development assistance drifts from being about poverty reduction and supporting basic education, healthcare, and infrastructure[34] to simply becoming a means of containing risk. Stabilization strategies use the language of human rights and empowerment, but are essentially about strengthening foreign state institutions to a sufficient degree that their citizens do not take up arms in resistance to it. Development assistance is deployed as a means of promoting the security of the donor state by increasing citizens' satisfaction with the performance of their own state authorities. Both stabilization and the concept of failed states have trouble imagining the possibility that security can exist beyond—or despite—the formal state. As a result of the perceived need to strengthen the formal apparatus of the state, stabilization

---

[33] USAID, *Yemen Country Strategy*, 2, footnote 1.
[34] Mark Duffield, *Global Governance and the New Wars: The Merging of Development and Security* (London: Zed Books, 2001), 15–16; David Chandler, "The Security–Development Nexus and the Rise of 'Anti-Foreign Policy'", *Journal of International Relations and Development*, 10 (2007), 365–6.

strategies attempt to create the perception that the host state is driving the development initiatives that are in fact being funded by external donor/s. USAID's strategy is explicit about this:

> Through development assistance tailored to communities' defined needs, people can see their government responding and improvements in their economic environment that open up opportunities to better their personal, family and community situation... USAID's assistance is specifically designed to provide support in areas where the Government of Yemen (*ROYG*) does not have the resources or expertise to execute, organize or manage such activities.[35]

Questions of the government's willingness to "execute, organize or manage such activities" are not addressed, however, which leaves unanswered the critical question of what to do if the country's power elites do not perceive an incentive to tackle these matters. If interventions by donors are based on an assumption that all states are primarily inclined toward providing services to their citizens or to improving standards of living, then they may fail to account for the entrenched political blockages to reform.

Carried to its logical conclusion, stabilization strategies are based on the implicit notion that changing the political status quo can be threatening, and that long-term developmental change and social cohesion can be engineered through the containment of short-term risks. It therefore suggests that change can be stimulated in the longer term—and in a specific direction—by preferencing stasis in the short term. The comments reproduced above by the US Ambassador, Secretary of Defense, and the senior counter-terrorism official all demonstrate America's reflexive desire to maintain the incumbent elite in the face of widespread calls for systemic change. Stabilization strategies provide the policy space for implementers to promote their desired ability to control the unknown, predict chance occurrences and render them harmless using apolitical technical solutions. This necessarily entails several important assumptions about how change occurs and how legitimate institutions are forged, some of which are questionable upon closer examination.

Assumptions: That Stabilization Programs Meet Recipients' Expectations

The programs that flow from USAID's assumption that stability is "characterized as reduced support for violent means of resolving conflicts and grievances and increased support for the central government"[36] necessarily makes an even

---

[35] Ibid., 2.
[36] USAID/Egypt, *Risk Assessment of USAID/Yemen*, 2.

more basic assumption about the nature of instability and the ability of external actors to decrease it. One of these is that the outputs generated by its development programs are perceived by their recipients to satisfy their expectations. However, even partial effectiveness requires that the program outputs are able to address all critical constraints to improving the targeted factors. In the Yemeni context, access to land and/or access to irrigation are critical constraints in almost all, if not all, of the areas targeted by USAID's Community Livelihoods Project. As such, considerable importance is placed by USAID on training farmers in sustainable farming practices for the local area, providing seed for farmers to use, or strengthening agricultural cooperatives.[37] However, providing local communities with access to training or to quantities of seed may be of marginal benefit at best when the real constraint lies elsewhere, such as in the limited availability of arable land and water, incentives to overuse water due to artificial pricing linked to diesel subsidies (which are kept in place by elite diesel smuggling rings), or by the power elite having strong incentives to maintain a weak regime of land tenure law enforcement. Resolving these issues requires lengthy negotiations between local communities, the central authorities and those with vested interests in the status quo both within and outside the state. The security-driven immediacy of stabilization strategies can be at odds with the contingency and patience required to work with (or against) the incentives of some in power not to devolve power and resources. If these larger barriers are not dealt with, however, grievances targeted by the program are likely to remain in place regardless of the program's other outputs.

A second related assumption to that of fulfilling the expectations of recipients is that the programs do not inadvertently create expectations that are frustrated in the medium to longer term. For example, short-term program assistance intended to have a "quick impact" or to "jump start" government service delivery is likely to create expectations of follow-through, particularly if the initial phase is reasonably successful. Even if the initial process is effective, temporary benefits may ultimately create further frustrations and grievances. Vocational training programs may appear to have created opportunities for recipients, but if these recipients are unable to find work due to broader

---

[37] Unpublished USAID documentation for the Community Livelihoods Project seen by the author. These figures are also indicated in USAID's Request for Applications, "Community Livelihoods Project: Project Guidelines", RFA 279–10–006 (2010), 12–14.

economic problems, then the "stabilizing" effects of the programs (understood in USAID's own terms) are also at risk.

The possibility of frustrated expectations is particularly likely when the underlying program rationale is based outside the target community and in the foreign policy objectives of the donor. As one employee at a USAID contractor in Somalia commented: "I hate to say it but much of [the stabilisation strategy and its budget] is in line with US foreign policy so it can change very quickly if US interests change." This person went on to note that because stabilization is inextricably linked to external priorities, funding for programs is highly unpredictable, which makes long-term planning difficult.[38] A USAID contractor in Pakistan commented along similar lines: "if the US government's driving mandate is to provide stability then there is no way this will happen in six months. It will take 25–30 years but they want results in six months or they change strategy entirely. The strategy is changing fortnightly because the US still does not know what it really wants to achieve."[39] The unpredictability of the short-term "quick impact" programs that are a signature of stabilization strategies, therefore, risk working against the stability of the target areas, if the livelihood of the area is viewed beyond the life of the project. Again, this derives from the flawed belief that the effectiveness of host state institutions has a linear relationship to the likelihood of external security threats being either generated or extinguished.

Assumptions: That Increasing Program Recipients' Satisfaction with Services Increases "Stability"

The second major underlying assumption of stabilization programs is that satisfying the recipients of the programs will in fact generate greater stability particularly when, as noted, the deeper meaning of this is largely unexplored in USAID's program literature. It has not been proven that activities such as building basic infrastructure, establishing cooperatives, or training in sustainable agricultural production necessarily generate support for the central government or even that they necessarily reduce conflict or increase social cohesion. For stabilization programs to be successful, members of society who may engage in "destabilizing" activities would need to perceive the programs'

---

[38] Interview with staff member at a USAID contractor: Hargeisa, Somaliland, June 2013.
[39] Phone conversation with a USAID contractor: Islamabad, Pakistan, August 2010.

FRAGILE POLITICS

benefits as sufficient to remain engaged with them. In the Yemeni context, this relates particularly to young men—the segment of society deemed most vulnerable to radicalization by militant jihadi groups. At the most obvious level, programs that claim to be addressing the concerns of this large group need to demonstrate that they have influenced enough members of that group to impede the activities of militant groups significantly. If only a small percentage of "at risk youths" are targeted (and influenced) by these programs, then militant jihadi groups may experience no real decline in their ability to attract followers as the result of these programs.

USAID's youth programming has a focus on diversionary activities, but the number of people targeted by the programs raises questions about its likely efficacy. A piece placed by USAID in the local Yemeni media notes, for example, that "340 boys and 80 girls within the age of 18 and 25 participated in the sports tournaments with eight teams participating in both volleyball and soccer".[40] With about 70 percent of Yemen's population of nearly 25 million people being under the age of twenty-five, the broader impact of programs of this scale is questionable. Moreover, other than the possibility of diverting time away from possible militant activity, the link between volleyball, soccer, political stability, and support for the central government is unclear. One might argue that such programming is more about "hearts and minds" than any more specific political objective, but other programming suggests the desire to fortify the status quo against dissent; one of USAID's implementing partners, Creative Associates, writes of its support for a talent show in Sana'a that:

> These activities [talent competitions, civic engagement courses, and a sports tournament that aims to foster peace through volleyball and soccer] are an attempt to *redirect youth's energies from exploding into violence* as a consequence of the current and recent political events in Yemen. Those taking part in these contests show the resilience of Yemeni youth when provided support from programs such as USAID's CLP [Community Livelihoods Program]; these youth exemplify that they are more than willing to cooperate and redirect their energies in a positive way.[41]

---

[40] USAID Staff, "Sports Tournaments Help Foster Understanding and Team Work Among Youth in Sana'a," *National Yemen*, 8 April 2012, http://nationalyemen.com/2012/04/14/sports-tournaments-help-foster-understanding-and-team-work-among-youth-in-sanaa

[41] Creative Associates, "Yemen: From Change, Tahrir Squares, Redirecting Youths' Energies Constructively", *Creative* (an online magazine by Creative Associates International), Summer 2012, http://creative-associates.us/2012/05/yemen-from-change-tahrir-squares-redirecting-youths-energies-constructively

The basis for Creative Associates' conclusion that participating in one of its events makes a person less likely to engage in protest activity is unclear. It also seems to imply that the protesters were the perpetrators rather than the victims of the "explosions of violence" at the protests. Moreover, the diversionary component of such programming contains the suggestion that Yemen's young people protested against the Saleh regime—which is portrayed as undesirable behaviour—at least partly due to boredom or for want of somewhere to "redirect their energ[y]". Protesters calling for change are thus presented as a nuisance to the stabilization strategy and its efforts to bolster the formal institutions of the state and prevent collapse.

Another critical assumption upon which the link between stabilization programs and service provision rests is that perceived injustices that are beyond the scope of the program do not outweigh or negate the perceived benefit of the program. For example, providing transparency training to government employees, community organizations and local leaders[42] who are not paid a living wage (and may thus be expected to supplement their income through corruption) may do little to disincentivize the targeted behaviour. Likewise, providing agricultural training to farmers who have had land appropriated by members or clients of the regime or central government may anger recipients more than it may appease them. More importantly, people who have suffered (or fear suffering) casualties from government or American military action may not be receptive to the influence of improved government services or greater government involvement in their communities. If it is the nature and the presence of the regime that militant jihadis are preying on, then reinvigorating that presence may have an unwanted effect. This effect is discussed in greater length shortly.

There is also the risk that the benefits from a program may either perpetuate the inequitable distribution of resources, or generate the perception that this is occurring. For example, if resources are targeted towards the "least stable" areas or populations, then others may regard this as rewarding instability, thereby encouraging destabilizing activities as a means of accessing resources and exacerbating the political economy of instability. USAID's *Yemen Strategy* has targeted its assistance at "the eight governorates of greatest priority to USAID ... Amran, Al Jawf, Marib, Shabwah, Abyan, Al Dhale'e, Lahj, and Aden".[43] The logic of targeting these eight governorates was that the most serious external

---

[42] USAID, *Yemen Country Strategy*, 8, 10.
[43] Ibid., 11.

security concerns were based there—largely due to the presence of AQAP. However, if the World Food Programme's (WFP) statistics on household food security are used as an indicator of vulnerability, only Amran appears on both USAID and the WFP's list of most at risk areas.[44] USAID's list of targeted areas, therefore, directly linked the ability of communities to access development funding to their perceived ability to pose a security threat.[45] This approach risks tacitly incentivizing both militancy and loot-seeking among the population without necessarily addressing the root causes of AQAP's traction or the marginalization of these areas. At the same time, the securitization of development can provide the intellectual justification for military intervention in the country if the stabilization strategy is viewed to have failed.

Assumptions: Domestic Drivers of Instability can be Isolated from their International Context

As discussed above, later forming states face a number of structural disadvantages against wealthier and militarily superior states. While it is beyond the scope of this chapter to examine this in detail, the conditions under which Yemen's liquid natural gas (LNG) is sold internationally provides a powerful example of the interplay of domestic corruption and external complicity. The international companies and governments that benefit from this deal (particularly the French, American, and South Korean) remain beyond the conceptual framework of the stabilization strategy, which frames destabilizing factors as domestic. Details are difficult to ascertain with certainty because neither the Yemeni government nor the international Yemen LNG (YLNG) consortium[46] adhere to transparent processes, but the contracts allow Yemen's natural gas to be sold at either fixed prices or with caps on sale prices to its shareholders. In 2010, for example, Korea Gas paid a fixed price of $3.2 per 1 million BTUs (British thermal units), which meant it paid about $193 per ton for Yemeni gas, compared to an average of $689 per ton the company paid for Qatari gas.[47]

---

[44] World Food Programme, *Comprehensive Food Security Survey: Republic of Yemen*, March 2010, 40, http://home.wfp.org/stellent/groups/public/documents/ena/wfp219039.pdf

[45] Oxfam, "Whose Aid is it Anyway? Politicizing Aid in Conflicts and Crises", *Oxfam Briefing Paper* 145, 10 February 2011.

[46] The state-owned Yemen Gas Company is a 16.73% shareholder in the YLNG consortium. The French company Total holds nearly 40%, while the American Hunt Oil company has 17.22%.

[47] Dinakar Sethuraman, "Yemen LNG to Honor Supply Deals with GDF, Total,

An analyst who works closely on corruption within the Yemeni resources sector argues that if the YLNG contracts met international standards, the country would make an additional one-third of its annual budget each year[48]—an amount that pales in comparison to what has been delivered in Western aid to Yemen through the stabilization strategy or otherwise. This has a substantial impact on Yemen's ability to control its own budget and to industrialize its economy. Moreover, it means that Yemen effectively pays twice for its power supply: once in what it loses by selling its gas below market rate through YLNG, and a second time because it is forced to generate power using diesel, which is vastly more expensive. The Yemeni government buys its diesel at international market rates and then subsidizes it for sale on the local market. Large quantities of the subsidized diesel is then smuggled back out of the country to be re-sold at international market rates by regime cronies for personal profit. In an effort to compensate high-energy consuming industries like steel smelters from the exorbitant costs of diesel-generated electricity, a decree was issued to ban the export of scrap metal, thereby reducing the production cost for smelters. This caused the scrap dealers to protest that the decree had forced their prices lower.[49] The outcome is that Yemen is less able to afford to produce the electricity and steel that it needs for industrial development, is more reliant on diesel imports, and more reliant on the unfavorable terms that the Saleh regime negotiated with foreign companies for natural gas exports.

Stabilization and Justice

Because the logic of the stabilization strategy defines under-development (instead of the domestic and international politics that have entrenched under-development) as the driver of instability and thus radicalization, it overlooks the importance of perceptions of injustice as a driver of instability. Perceptions of injustice in Yemen are rife—and undoubtedly fuelled the protest movement—and AQAP has proven adept at articulating this in its propaganda.

Korea Gas, CEO Rafin Says", *Bloomberg*, 18 June 2010, http://www.bloomberg.com/news/2010–06–18/yemen-lng-to-honor-supply-deals-with-gdf-total-korea-gas-ceo-rafin-says.html

[48] Interview, Sana'a, Yemen, February 2013.

[49] Conversation with a senior Yemeni politician: Sana'a, Yemen, February 2013.

To take one of many examples, an article in the eighth edition of al-Qaeda's Arabic language magazine, *Sada al-Malahim*, argued:

> The people of Yemen are suffering from the decline of living standards, the rise of costs, and the discriminatory practices with which the government deals with them in employment, the distribution of wealth and its looting, the misappropriation of lands, and the absence of someone to defend their rights.[50]

This is an astute narrative of injustice, not of poverty and livelihoods, except that the latter are symptoms of the greater problem of injustice—injustice that is argued to emanate from the political processes that are entrenched in the regime's core, not in its institutional or administrative failings. The reference to the misappropriation of lands hits a raw nerve among the Yemeni population and sits at the heart of the disjuncture between USAID's stabilization strategies and realities on the ground. Neither a foreign government nor its aid agencies can stop the state from stealing land (or acquiescing to the theft of land by favored elites) by funding the state's technical capacity to stop stealing land. Land theft is not a matter of administrative capacity but a symptom of the inequitable distribution of power and resources upon which Yemen's elite political settlement rests. This is first and foremost a matter of power, politics, and human agency rather than a matter of weak structural constraints.

While there is a fine line between poverty and injustice, that fine line is the difference between targeting the source of the problem and targeting its manifestations. If poverty and livelihoods are the key drivers of radicalization and recruitment to militant networks, then assisting target states to improve their ability to deliver services may be the most appropriate starting point. However, the framing of AQAP's propaganda suggests that the drivers of radicalism in Yemen are densely interwoven with the political characteristics of the regime—characteristics that the protesters have also challenged but that Western governments explicitly supported in the face of the protests.[51] Poverty

---

[50] Al-Qaeda in the Arabian Peninsula, *Sada al-Malahim*, No. 8, March 2009, 27. Cited in Alistair Harris, "Instrumentalizing Grievances: Al-Qaeda in the Arabian Peninsula", in Christopher Boucek and Marina Ottaway, eds., *Yemen on the Brink* (Washington, DC: Carnegie Endowment for International Peace, 2010), 36.

[51] Support was eventually withdrawn from President Saleh in late 2011 and transferred to his deputy and successor, Abd Robbu Mansour Hadi. In early 2013, Saleh and former vice president Ali Salim al-Beidh were singled out by the UN Security Council as interfering in the country's political transition, but the Council refrained from criticizing others. The suggestion that Ali Abdullah Saleh and Ali-Salem al-Beidh were the only spoilers smacked to some as partisan-

seems to be neither the key point that AQAP (or its offshoot Ansar al-Shari'a) has emphasized nor the most salient factor in its ability to gain traction. It was also not the main point that the protesters were emphasizing. Rather, injustice—specifically, the state's unwillingness to apply the rule of law equally and its propensity to privilege access to economic resources on a discretionary basis—was the intersecting theme.

Local Perceptions and Stabilization

When the single candidate elections in February 2012 formalized Vice President Abd Rabbu Mansoor Hadi's ascent to the top job, he landed in the middle of a factional struggle over who would inherit the real spoils of power in Yemen. This struggle revolved around the political ambitions of three main groups: former President Saleh and his family; General Ali Muhsin (Saleh's long-time ally who defected after the first major massacre of protesters in 2011) and his supporters; and the al-Ahmar tribal family, the late patriarch of which was a pillar of the modern Yemeni state.

The suicide bombing that killed nearly 100 members of the Central Security Forces in central Sana'a in May 2012 provided a graphic indication of how far reality was diverging from the linear transition that was symbolized by the international community's timetable for transition. Particularly revealing were the accusations and counter-accusations that flew over who was "really" behind the attack (which was claimed publicly by Ansar al-Shari'a—a group with still murky affiliations to AQAP). Local media outlets affiliated with General Ali Muhsin claimed that Saleh's loyalists masterminded the attack, while outlets affiliated with the former president maintained that Ali Muhsin had recruited the bomber.[52] Neither side seemed willing to acknowl-

---

ship, so real are the fears about the power of Ali Muhsin, the al-Ahmar family, and the Islah party.

[52] The titles of some local news articles give a sense of this polarization, such as: Anas Zaki, "Yemen: Saleh Officer Accused of Masterminding the Saba'een Explosion in Sana'a", Yemen Press, 23 May 2012, http://yemen-press.com/news9466.html; Asrar Press, "Important Information on the Bombing at Saba'een Square", 21 May 2012, http://www.asrarpress.net/news_details.php?lng=arabic&sid=7381; Hashad Net, "Ali Muhsin al-Ahmar was Involved in the Suicide Operation at Saba'een—New Information About the Bomber", 22 May 2012, http://hshd.net/news15306.html; Nashwan News, "100 Dead and Charges that Saleh and his Relatives are Behind the Bombing", 21 May 2012, http://nashwannews.com/news.php?action=

edge that AQAP/Ansar al-Shari'a could have acted without assistance from some part of the old regime. The level of distrust contained within these conspiracy theories illustrates the complexity of local perceptions surrounding the existence of al-Qaeda in Yemen (the group that USAID's stabilization programs are all directly or indirectly attempting to rout) and their perceived entanglement with factions of the political elite, including those whom the stabilization strategy has sought to maintain.

In Yemen it is always difficult—probably impossible—to know precisely where to draw the line between autonomous acts by AQAP and its affiliates, and those that could, at least conceivably, be attached to power struggles within the regime.[53] These suspicions about the connections between Yemeni elites and AQAP have some basis in fact, although it is important not to overstate these and deny agency to al-Qaeda-affiliated actors. Under President Saleh there were a number of dubious "escapes" from prison by al-Qaeda figures, the most audacious of which was when twenty-three members walked out of a high-security prison in February 2006. Included in this group of twenty-three were two of the men who now lead AQAP—Nasser al-Wahayshi and Qassem al-Raymi. Other prominent examples include the release of Jamal al-Badawi, the convicted architect of the USS Cole bombing, to house arrest in 2007 after he surrendered to President Saleh. The reason al-Badawi needed to surrender was that he too he had walked out of prison the previous year. In 2007, Saleh also pardoned Fahd al-Quso for his role in the USS Cole attack in 2000. In 2010, al-Quso re-emerged in an AQAP video, apparently unrepentant, and threatening to attack US interests. He was killed in 2012 by an American air strike. In March 2011, and as the protests gathered pace, the regime quietly granted around 70 al-Qaeda suspects their freedom from a political security prison in Sana'a.[54]

---

view&id=17649. All sources are in Arabic and some links contain very graphic images.

[53] For discussion of these links see Phillips, *Yemen and Politics of Permanent Crisis*: 13–14, 41–4, 139–40.

[54] Originally revealed in ibid.,14. The release was reported on the Islah party's Suhail satellite channel, and was believed by some within Yemen to have been fabricated by Islah. It was confirmed, however, by a security source who attended the Political Security Organisation (PSO) prison in Sana'a shortly after the release, and was subsequently confirmed by a ranking GPC official. Author's personal communications, March 2011.

These beliefs about al-Qaeda and the regime go right to the top, and sources close to former President Saleh have recounted conversations where he reassured his audience that he remained "in control" of AQAP and that the group did not, therefore, pose a threat to his regime.[55] Judge Hamood al-Hitar, the former Minister of Religious Affairs under Saleh, who led the government's dialogue committee with al-Qaeda, publicly stated in 2011: "Saleh uses Al-Qaeda to blackmail foreign countries so that he can get more financial support from them. But the reality of Al-Qaeda's existence in Yemen doesn't exceed even 10 percent of what the official Yemeni media promotes."[56] Likewise, a ranking official within Yemen's intelligence apparatus told his subordinates in mid-2012 that AQAP's key leaders are "still talking to both sides" (that is, to President Saleh and Ali Muhsin)[57]—in other words, that in his view AQAP remained at least partly an embodiment of elite intrigue.

Most of the English language analysis of AQAP focuses on the structure, strategy, and ideology of the group and not on the shadowy links that some members have (or have had, or are widely believed to have) with segments of the old regime. The former are clearly important, but in focusing on them exclusively one overlooks an important, if elusive and largely unprovable, part of the story. This more elusive part of the story is, however, the talk of the Yemeni qat chews, minibuses, and streets, and broadly posits that elements of the regime and elements of AQAP exhibit (varying) degrees of symbiotic co-dependence. Regardless of the level of truth contained in these discourses, the rampant conspiricism benefits both sides: AQAP seems more entrenched than it perhaps is, and the incumbent elite seems the last line of defence against something truly awful, particularly in front of an international audience. US efforts to stabilize the country need to be seen through a lens of local perceptions because this lens highlights how intensely politicized is the debate surrounding the organization they are trying to destroy. Al-Qaeda cannot be defeated through technical fixes and poverty alleviation because its existence does not express a glitch in Yemen's otherwise rational–legal politics. Al-Qaeda,

---

[55] Interview with source close to President Saleh, other details of which cannot be given, to maintain their anonymity. Informal conversations with others close to Saleh have contained similar accusations.

[56] Cited in Shatha al-Harazi, "Special from Yemen: Tribal sheikhs expel Al-Qaeda from their land", *Al-Masry Al-Youm*, 15 April 2011, http://www.egyptindependent.com/news/special-yemen-tribal-sheikhs-expel-al-qaeda-their-land

[57] Interview with security source, other details of which cannot be given, to maintain their anonymity.

as both an organization and a mythology, draws part of its resilience from its entanglement in the malignance of Yemen's opaque elite politics.

In Yemen, "al-Qaeda" is not only a network of ruthless militants but it is also an accusation that can be levelled—with varying degrees of credibility—against members of the regime who have previously had connections with some of its members or have even facilitated them. In this sense, al-Qaeda is more than just a terrorist organization; it is so often evoked as a domestic political pejorative that it has become enmeshed in mythologies about how national power functions. In becoming part of the narrative that sustains squabbling of Sana'a's elites, al-Qaeda is also widely viewed as a symbol of the regime's (and the central government's) detachment from ordinary Yemenis.

Foreign efforts to confront AQAP, whether through programs to strengthen the central government or through military engagement, need to consider how this debate is refracted within the population, whose support is so central to USAID's overall stabilization strategy. If the population does not believe that the strategy correctly frames AQAP, the strategy is lost. Perceptions that the US has helped to perpetuate not only an oppressive incumbent elite but also that this elite is responsible for the perpetuation of AQAP (a group that has now killed hundreds, if not thousands, of Yemenis) builds the view that ordinary Yemenis are paying the price for what is now widely referred to as a political game. The presence of AQAP is widely seen as having been exacerbated by the Yemeni regime to manipulate the United States[58]—a narrative on which other dissenting groups within the country have capitalized. Graffiti by the al-Houthi movement states, for example:

> Al-Qa'ida is manufactured by America... America focuses on removing some Qur'anic verses from the curriculum and is trying to control the education system to distort our sons and their morals... The American Initiative [i.e. the GCC Initiative] is trying to change the curriculum, and this is the biggest crime of the government against Yemeni citizens.[59]

By casting al-Qaeda as a product of America, the al-Houthis are trying to undermine their rivals' Islamic credentials and thereby portray themselves as the real Islamist insurgents. However, they are also reflecting the widespread view that al-Qaeda is entangled in the politicking of a Yemeni government

---

[58] Mona El-Naggar and Robert F. Worth, "Yemen's Drive on Al Qaeda Faces Internal Skepticism", *New York Times*, 3 November 2010.

[59] Graffiti around the town of Kawkaban—about a 90-minute drive from Sana'a—observed by the author in July 2012.

that sold out the country to the myth of al-Qaeda, a group cast as actually representing American imperial power. Here, al-Qaeda is framed as symbolizing American imperial power in a country that is under attack from US air strikes and drones: that is, they are both part of the same problem. In March 2011, an opinion poll of 1,005 Yemenis suggested that 86 percent of respondents viewed AQAP as being either "very" or "somewhat" unpopular in their local area, while 96 percent of respondents disapproved of the Yemeni government's cooperation with the United States.[60] If this is an accurate representation of popular views, it suggests that al-Qaeda's ideology is unpopular and that much of the traction the group enjoys is founded in people's disapproval of the relationship between the Yemeni government and the United States over counter-terrorism issues. This raises important questions over the degree to which the orthodox failed states narrative—which provides the intellectual justification for military intervention in so-called ungoverned spaces to prevent terrorism—can in fact become a self-fulfilling prophecy through which militancy gains new avenues for acceptance.

That the presence of al-Qaeda has brought American drone attacks, air strikes, civilian casualties and the destruction of property only sharpens the symbolic connection between the elite power struggles in Sana'a and the violence that is either experienced or feared by other Yemeni citizens. AQAP/Ansar al-Shari'a has seized upon this in its propaganda; in a video released in March 2012, prisoners from the military are shown being lectured by their captor, Jallal Baladi:

> Today we are occupied, and you are occupied. American airplanes and Saudi airplanes are in our skies. American, British and French ships are in our seas. Who is responsible for the security file in Yemen today? The Americans... And who is responsible for the guarding and securing President Hadi? The Americans. And who will write our constitution? ... The French. Did you know that? ... Today we are occupied and today you are occupied.[61]

Again, the issue of complaint is not one of livelihoods and underdevelopment—those aspects of "state failure" most directly targeted by the stabilization strategy—but justice, independence, and resentment that Yemen's political destiny is not in the hands of Yemenis. The problem of al-Qaeda in

---

[60] Glevum Stability Assessment, "2011 Yemen Stability Survey", Glevum Associates, March 2011, pp. 19 and 26 respectively, http://www.fpri.org/pubs/2011/glevum. yemen2011stabilitysurveyvi.pdf

[61] Video appearing on Ansar al-Shari'as Madad al-Akbariah channel (posted to Youtube, 11 March 2012), translated by the author.

Yemen is deeply political and is much more complex than simply the "jihadis versus the state" model that USAID's strategy—and indeed the drone strikes—rest upon. Fighting AQAP with air strikes, "Special Operations Forces who are as comfortable drinking tea with tribal leaders as raiding a terrorist compound",[62] and development initiatives that are perceived to have external security objectives as their primary goal are both strategies that carry risk in the longer term. First, by so explicitly tying development assistance to political and security objectives, the sincerity of purpose required to win "hearts and minds" is probably sacrificed from the outset. Second, by viewing the massive changes underway in Yemeni society as a threat to be contained, USAID enacted a policy to secure the "vulnerable" Yemeni state from its "rebellious" citizens. Perhaps inadvertently, this framing of the crisis made political passivity and stasis the core components of the desired stability, the contradiction and self-serving nature of which risk entrenching a level of anti-Western sentiment that may prove difficult to unmake.

Carried to its logical conclusion, the notion of stabilization that now predominates in Western donor engagement in so-called weak and failing states is based on the implicit notion that changing the political status quo can be threatening, and that long-term developmental change and social cohesion can be engineered through the containment of short-term risks. But state formation is an inherently risk-laden process, in which some coalitions gain power and influence while others lose it. As such, the very notion of stabilization seems to be at odds with the massive upheaval that is inherent to the disorderly and non-linear process of state formation and consolidation.

---

[62] Karen DeYoung and Ellen Nakashima, "U.S. Uses Yemeni Web Sites to Counter al-Qaeda Propaganda", *Washington Post*, 24 May 2012, http://www.washington-post.com/world/national-security/us-hacks-web-sites-of-al-qaeda-affiliate-in-yemen/2012/05/23/gJQAGnOxlU_story.html

4

INTERVENTIONISM AND THE FEAR OF URBAN AGENCY IN AFGHANISTAN AND IRAQ

Daniel E. Esser

This chapter investigates "state weakness" as a hegemonic discourse which eclipses state-building through sub-national non-violent collective action in countries in the greater Middle East that are emerging from externally induced regime change. I posit that this eclipse is the result of a level-of-analysis problem grounded in a predominantly statist conceptualization of governance, reiterated most recently by Francis Fukuyama,[1] which operationalizes governance "as a government's ability to make and enforce rules, and to deliver services, regardless of whether that government is democratic or not".[2] This characterization is anchored in global norms rather than local realities. Moreover, conceiving of governance as primarily state-led is also rooted in post-9/11 hegemonic concerns about state weakness and failure, which according to Fukuyama constitute "the single most important problem for international order".[3] This conceptualization precludes an appreciation of

---

[1] Francis Fukuyama, "What Is Governance?" *Governance: An International Journal of Policy, Administration, and Institutions* (Early View; no issue/page numbers yet).

[2] Ibid.

[3] Francis Fukuyama, *State-Building: Governance and World Order in the 21st Century* (Ithaca, NY: Cornell University Press, 2004), 92.

sub-national dynamics as building blocks for both human security and improved service delivery. It ignores evidence from cities in developing regions in the global South which suggests that a de facto absence of functioning state structures does not automatically translate into anarchy. One year after the US-led regime change in Iraq, Wilcke posited that "[l]ocal events and dynamics—in city councils and in the provinces—are key to understanding how the US botched its occupation".[4]

In this chapter, I probe this proposition by first examining how the underlying discourse on statist governance dovetails with an increasingly salient depiction of cities in developing countries as breeding grounds for organized violence and terrorism. I then juxtapose these two converging discourses with an investigation of the extent to which sub-national collective action in cities in Afghanistan and Iraq factored into hegemonic strategies for both warmaking and post-invasion state-building. While counterfactual reasoning does not suggest that the consideration of urban dynamics would necessarily have altered post-invasion realities in either of the two countries, it does illustrate how the negation of and, in many cases, active interference with local political agency ultimately limited the options available to both national and international actors in their quest for pacification and stability. At the same time, states like Afghanistan and Iraq have thus not only been failed internationally, as a result of global power politics, but also locally, as their citizens have endured lengthy occupations, resource exploitation, and resurgent violence.

Over a decade ago, the United States and its so-called Coalition of the Willing invaded Iraq based on what former British MP George Galloway termed a "pack of lies".[5] Prior to the invasion, the United States and its allies had deployed "resonant language in an effort to mobilize support"[6] by labeling Iraq a "state which has utterly failed its citizens".[7] This recourse to a then

---

[4] Christoph Wilcke, "Castles Built of Sand: US Governance and Exit Strategies in Iraq", *Middle East Report*, Vol. 34, No. 232 (Fall 2004), http://www.merip.org/mer/mer232/castles-built-sand-us-governance-exit-strategies-iraq (accessed 26 August 2013).

[5] *The Guardian*, "Galloway defends himself at US Senate", 17 May 2005, http://www.guardian.co.uk/world/2005/may/17/iraq.usa (accessed 26 August 2013).

[6] Ronald Krebs and Patrick Jackson, "Twisting Tongues and Twisting Arms: The Power of Political Rhetoric", *European Journal of International Relations*, Vol. 13, No. 35 (2007), 38.

[7] *The Guardian*, "Full text: Jack Straw's speech", 21 February 2003, http://www.guardian.co.uk/politics/2003/feb/21/foreignpolicy.iraq (accessed 26 August 2013).

already decade-old terminology of state weakness and failure[8] was designed to help legitimize international aggression despite contemporaneous concerns about "opportunities for a nonviolent solution [...] being missed"[9] and that "post-Saddam Iraq could, ironically, become a failed state along the lines of pre-2001 Afghanistan".[10] Indeed, nearly identical language had been employed two years earlier to help justify the US-led invasion of Afghanistan in the immediate aftermath of 9/11.[11] The concepts of state weakness and failure "open[ed] the way to political and even military intervention",[12] and in concrete terms to "impose US interests on less powerful nations"[13] based on a "new normative, institutional and operative regime which far transcends the traditional method [of international diplomacy] and which can be used, at least temporarily, to substitute for a collapsed system of governance".[14]

By assigning a label-as-policy, the determination of "state failure" has thus primarily constituted a political (as opposed to analytical) process.[15] Its application has altered the prospects for state sovereignty, especially in the greater Middle East, where US energy and security interests are most acutely at stake. Resulting international invasions are supposed to create opportunities for

[8] Pinar Bilgin and Adam D. Morton, "Historicising representations of 'failed states': beyond the cold-war annexation of the social sciences?" *Third World Quarterly*, Vol. 23, No. 1 (2002), 55–80.

[9] Peter Ford, "Is it too late for a popular uprising inside Iraq?" *Christian Science Monitor*, 27 January 2003, http://www.csmonitor.com/2003/0127/p14s01-usmi.html (accessed 26 August 2013).

[10] Philip H. Gordon and Michael E. O'Hanlon, "Should the war on terrorism target Iraq?" Analysis Paper #11 (Washington, DC: Brookings Institution, December 2001).

[11] *Boston Globe*, "Making a distinction over Iraq, Kosovo", 18 December 2003, http://www.boston.com/news/nation/articles/2003/12/18/making_a_distinction_over_iraq_kosovo/ (accessed 26 August 2013).

[12] Martin Khor, "Failed States Theory Can Cause Global Anarchy", 2002, http://www.twnside.org.sg/title/et0125.htm (accessed 26 August 2013).

[13] Elliot Ross, "Failed states are a western myth", *The Guardian*, 28 June 2013, http://www.theguardian.com/commentisfree/2013/jun/28/failed-states-western-myth-us-interests (accessed 26 August 2013).

[14] Daniel Thürer, "The 'failed state' and international law", 1999, http://www.icrc.org/eng/resources/documents/misc/57jq6u.htm (accessed 26 August 2013).

[15] Bilgin and Morton (2002); Edward Newman, "Failed States and International Order: Constructing a Post-Westphalian World", *Contemporary Security Policy*, Vol. 30, No. 3 (2009), 421–43; Dan Halvorson, *States of Disorder: Understanding State Failure and Intervention in the Periphery* (Burlington, VT: Ashgate, 2013).

"jump-starting battered economies, re-introducing the rule of law, and rejuvenating civil society"[16] by way of "strengthen[ing] the capability of the [newly installed government] not only to provide security, eliminate violent conflict and find ways to reconcile conflicting ethnic or religious factions, but also to protect human rights, generate economic opportunities, provide basic services, control corruption, respond effectively to emergencies and combat poverty and inequality".[17] According to this logic, international interventions constitute unprecedented "opportunit[ies] for some of these [invaded] countries to rebuild their societies, economies and polities and to start reforms and restructuring that may have previously proved unattainable".[18] A central concern in this context is the mode of "establish[ing] a sovereign authority capable of enforcing a hegemonic peace upon all the fearfully contending parties".[19] In the light of this line of reasoning, it is essential to understand which societal processes are most promising in terms of producing state legitimacy in post-invasion settings and at which level (or levels) of the political system these processes have most commonly occurred.

Conceptual[20] as well as empirical research on the potential of state-building from below in the context of fragile statehood, specifically in the cases of

---

[16] Robert I. Rotberg, "The Failure and Collapse of Nation-States: Breakdown, Prevention, and Repair", in Robert I. Rotberg, ed., *When States Fail: Causes and Consequences* (Princeton, NJ: Princeton University Press, 2004), 33.

[17] Dennis A. Rondinelli and John D. Montgomery, "Regime change and nation building: can donors restore governance in post-conflict states?" *Public Administration and Development*, Vol. 25, No. 3 (2005), 19.

[18] Reginald H. Green and Ismail I. Ahmed, "Rehabilitation, sustainable peace and development: towards reconceptualization", *Third World Quarterly*, Vol. 20, No. 1 (1999): 189–90.

[19] Barbara F. Walter and Jack Snyder, *Civil Wars, Insecurity, and Intervention* (New York, NY: Columbia University Press, 1999), 17; cf. Roland Paris, *At War's End: building peace after civil conflict* (Cambridge: Cambridge University Press, 2004), 227; Georg Klute and Trutz von Trotha, "Roads to Peace: From Small War to Parasovereign Peace in the North of Mali" in Marie-Claire Foblets and Trutz von Trotha, eds., *Healing the Wounds. Essays on the reconstruction of societies after war* (Oxford: Oxford University Press, 2004), 109–43.

[20] Sandra L. MacLean, "Contributions from civil society to building peace and democracy", in Ann L. Griffiths, ed., *Building Peace and Democracy in Post-Conflict Societies* (Halifax: Centre for Foreign Policy Studies, Dalhousie University, 1998), 31–50; Bruce Stanley, "City Wars or Cities of Peace: (Re)Integrating the Urban into Conflict Resolution", *Globalization and World Cities Study Group and Network (GaWC) Research Bulletin* 123 (October 2003).

Yemen,[21] Somalia[22] and Sierra Leone,[23] suggest that by virtue of human proximity, resulting density of interaction, and easier access to information, social dynamics in cities are constitutive of state-building as "creative and auto-dynamic [sites] to 'modernise' or reconstitute order beyond the state".[24] State institutions are located predominantly in cities,[25] and while "a politics of spontaneous conciliation hardly seems plausible at the national level in complex modern states", as Moore[26] conceded early on in the case of Tunisian colonial

---

[21] See Charles Schmitz's contribution in this volume.

[22] Green and Ahmed, "Rehabilitation, sustainable peace and development", Vol. 20, No. 1 (1999), 189–90; Jutta Bakonyi and Ahmed Abdullahi, "Somalia—Land ohne Zentralstaat, aber dennoch funktionsfähig" [Somalia—country without central state, yet capable of functioning], *Entwicklung und ländlicher Raum*, Vol. 39, No. 5 (2005), 14–16.

[23] Daniel E. Esser, "'When we launched the government's agenda…': aid agencies and local politics in urban Africa", *Journal of Modern African Studies*, Vol. 50, No. 3 (2012), 397–420.

[24] Trutz von Trotha, "Der Aufstieg des Lokalen" [The rise of the local], *Aus Politik und Zeitgeschichte* 28/29 (2005), 32–8; cf. Gordana Rabrenovic, "Urban Social Movements", in Jonathan S. Davies and David L. Imbroscio, eds., *Theories of Urban Politics* (Los Angeles: Sage, 2009), 239–54; Stephen D. N. Graham, "Postmortem city: Towards an urban geopolitics", *City*, Vol. 8, No. 2 (2004), 165–96; Roberto M. Unger, "False Necesity: Antinecessitarian Social Theory in the Service of Radical Democracy", Vol. 2 of *Politics: A Work in Constructive Social Theory* (Cambridge: Cambridge University Press, 1987), 563–4; John Walton, "Urban Conflict and Social Movements in Poor Countries: Theory and Evidence of Collective Action", *International Journal of Urban and Regional Research*, Vol. 22, No. 3 (1998), 460–81; Iris M. Young, "The Ideal of Community and the Politics of Difference", in Gary Bridge and Sophie Watson, eds., *The Blackwell City Reader* (Malden, MA: Blackwell, 1986), 228–36; Barry Hindess, "Actors and Social Relations", in Mark Wordell and Stephen P. Turner, eds., *Social Theory in Transition* (London: Allen and Unwin, 1986), 113–26; Peter C. W. Gutkind, "From the Energy of Despair to the Anger of Despair: The Transition from Social Circulation to Political Consciousness among the Urban Poor in Africa", *Canadian Journal of African Studies*, Vol. 7, No. 2 (1973), 179–98; Joan Nelson, "The Urban Poor: Disruption or Political Integration in Third World Cities?" *World Politics*, Vol. 22, No. 3 (1970), 393–414.

[25] Daniel E. Esser, "The Political Economy of Post-Invasion Kabul, Afghanistan: Urban Restructuring beyond the North–South Divide", *Urban Studies*, forthcoming (November 2013).

[26] Clement H. Moore, "Politics in a Tunisian Village", *Middle East Journal*, Vol. 17, No. 5 (1963), 527–40. I thank Matthew J. Buehler for alerting me to this source, as well as to literature on state consolidation in North Africa.

liberation, smaller units of governance such as towns and municipalities hold promise for spontaneous collective action to be successful. Drawing from a comparative study of Jerusalem, Belfast, Johannesburg, Nicosia, Montreal, Algiers, Mumbai, Beirut, Brussels, and Baghdad, Bollens has proposed that "the city is important in peace-building because it is in the streets and neighborhoods of urban agglomerations that there is the negotiation over, and clarification of, abstract concepts such as democracy, fairness, and tolerance".[27]

Cities serve as arenas for citizens to encounter realities of the state; they are thus training grounds for the practice of democracy, which in turn renders them sites of state-building via local governance. For instance, recent research on leadership hierarchies in Delhi's contested slums[28] shows that over time, "primordial attachments"[29] wane in urban settings; as a result, the relative importance and influence of ethnic and interfamilial relationships decrease and are replaced by educational achievement and evolving political–economic networking as primary determinants of slum leadership. More diverse city-based civil societies that emerge from such dynamics are characterized predominantly by informal communal organization, which is often highly effective locally but remains invisible to the international development industry.[30]

These observations of cities as sites of state-building from below problematize arguments by scholars of the Arab region positing that kinship-based societies appear more prone to experiencing difficulties associated with weak statehood due to inherent tensions between tribal identities rooted in rural areas and centralized power structures in cities.[31] Notably, their analytical framework, which highlights "the relationship between tribe and state [as] a

[27] Scott A. Bollens, "Urban planning and peace building", *Progress in Planning* 66 (2006), 67.
[28] Saumitra Jha, Rao Vijayendra, and Michael Woolcock, "Governance in the gullies: democratic responsiveness and leadership in Delhi's slums", *World Development*, Vol. 35, No. 2 (2007), 230–46.
[29] Clifford Geertz, "The integrative revolution: primordial sentiments and politics in the new states", in Clifford Geertz, ed., *Old Societies and New States: the quest for modernity in Asia and Africa* (New York: Free Press of Glencoe, 1963).
[30] Willemijn Verkoren and Mathijs van Leeuwen, "Civil Society in Peacebuilding: Global Discourse, Local Reality", *International Peacekeeping*, Vol. 20, No. 2 (2013), 159–72.
[31] Mounira M. Charrad, *States and Women's Rights: the Making of Postcolonial Tunisia, Algeria, and Morocco* (Berkeley, CA: University of California Press, 2001); Paul Staniland, "Cities on Fire: Social Mobilization, State Policy, and Urban Insurgency", *Comparative Political Studies*, Vol. 43, No. 12 (2010), 1623–49.

key, at times controlling, element in the process of regime construction and maintenance",[32] has been applied to the case of modernizing Afghanistan as well.[33] While there is no reason to believe that tribal, ethnic, and religious identities have not been important catalysts of political behavior in countries such as Afghanistan and Iraq and their urban centers, we should try to understand the specific conditions under which city-based local political agency did or did not take place.

Before we delve into an investigation of actual events, we should first examine why the aforementioned virtues of urban life in the context of contemporary state-building are not the ones foregrounded in contemporary international policy-making on cities. Here, we ought to consider that the narrative of ethno-religious determinism in the Middle East resonates strongly with recent characterizations of cities as battlegrounds of terrorism. Such images of urban-centric low-intensity conflict have been perpetuated by development agencies' warnings against a "dark side" of urban growth driven by mushrooming slums, deteriorating health conditions, and resulting instability.[34] The Asian Development Bank (ADB), for instance, has highlighted urban poverty and resulting mass mobilization as "a potentially explosive social and political issue".[35] Similarly, the United Nations (UN) attributed urban violence partly to "the combination of a surging youth population, poverty, urbanization and unemployment"[36] and emphasized that "urban insecurity is gaining importance on the international stage not only because of terrorist attacks but because of the daily violence that dominates many people's lives—further fuelled by the rapid growth of cities".[37] Yet the most acute warning to date in this regard has been uttered by the United Nations-

[32] Charrad, *States and Women's Rights*, 61.

[33] Hasan K. Kakar, *Government and Society in Afghanistan. The Reign of Amir 'Abd al-Rahman Khan* (Austin, TX: University of Texas Press, 1979); Richard S. Newell, *The Politics of Afghanistan* (Ithaca, NY: Cornell University Press, 1972).

[34] Cf. Caroline Moser and Dennis Rodgers, *Change, violence and insecurity in non-conflict situations* (London: Overseas Development Institute, 2005), v.

[35] Asian Development Bank, *Urbanization and Sustainability: Case Studies of Good Practice* (Manila: Asian Development Bank, 2006), 31.

[36] United Nations, "Poverty, Infectious Disease, and Environmental Degradation as Threats to Collective Security: A UN Panel Report", *Population and Development Review*, Vol. 31, No. 3 (2005), 595.

[37] UNOCHA, "Global: Urban conflict—fighting for resources in the slums", IRIN In-Depth, Nairobi: IRINnews, 8 October 2007, http://www.irinnews.org/Report.aspx?ReportId=74687 (accessed 26 August 2013).

led agency for urban development, UN-HABITAT. Its former Executive Director Anna Tibaijuka[38] went as far as suggesting that "globally rapidly growing slums [constitute] an urban social time bomb that is soon going to explode".

Rather than leverage the proven ingenuity of urban actors collectively to create and maintain basic systems of service delivery even in the absence of an organizing central state, global policy-makers have thus chosen to focus on cities' presumed propensity to foment and sustain large-scale insurgencies and violent conflict. This, in turn, has resulted in explicitly anti-sub-national policies and resulting practices in the aftermath of international invasions. Despite their obvious structural and historical differences, the cases of Afghanistan and Iraq provide evidence in support of this diagnosis. In both cases, hegemonic military invasions legitimized a previously selected ruler chosen primarily on the basis of his perceived loyalty to US interests through national ballots while stalling sub-national elections in order to stifle the emergence of a domestic opposition. In striking similarity to other cases of forced regime change during the past decade, "[t]he international community's priority was the restoration of the state because they saw the conflict as a breakdown of authority at the national level".[39] As a result, political stability rather than multi-party governance promised the greatest returns on the political as well as economic investment of invasion. According to Johnson and Leslie, in the case of Afghanistan,

> If the international community imagined a peace agreement, so too it imagined a state; both with what it was (a *terra nullis* on which they could set to work from scratch) and what it should become (a liberal democracy), [thus ignoring] a territory staked out by powerful players who have their feet in the past and their eyes on the future.[40]

In hindsight, "pressing forward with elections without having first begun the process of building these institutional foundations—including a central government with authority beyond Kabul"[41] indeed proved to be "a recipe for

---

[38] Anna Tibaijuka, "Schwierige Neue Welt" [Difficult New World], *Internationale Politik*, Vol. 11, No. 6 (2006), 10–14.
[39] Sara Hellmüller, "The Power of Perceptions: Localizing International Peacebuilding Approaches", *International Peacekeeping*, Vol. 20, No. 2 (2013), 219.
[40] Chris Johnson and Jolyon Leslie, *Afghanistan—The Mirage of Peace* (London: Zed Books, 2004), 158–9.
[41] Paris, *At War's End*, 127.

continued instability", as Paris[42] had predicted correctly early on in the process. With state-building instrumentalized as a tool for safeguarding regional control and global hegemony, the stakes were stacked against local collective action from the very beginning of both occupations. In Afghanistan as much as in Iraq, any leeway for local actors was feared to exacerbate "centrifugal" dynamics.[43] Tribal and religious fault lines in both countries were considered too volatile to allow for genuine democracy to arise. While this concern was clearly not without merit, it reflected general "donor reluctance to support political activities and emancipatory civil society, in settings where peace [and state-]building is all about changing state–society relations",[44] and resulted in almost complete disregard of indigenous approaches to state-building from below.

In Afghanistan, calls by Afghan intellectuals to seize the historical momentum for reinventing the "space of governance" as a core function and virtue of cities[45] therefore went unheard. Kabul was considered too risky an experiment for genuine local democracy; as Giustozzi notes, "[w]hile it may appear odd that the capital of a collapsed state could be the object of much desire, everybody has always been aware that whoever is in control of Kabul will be better positioned to claim international recognition and receive a greater share of power in the event of a settlement".[46] Instead, international stakeholders' efforts focused on rural areas. The resulting National Solidarity Programme's (NSP) declared purpose was to weaken the link between rural dwellers and traditional local power-holders in order to reorient villages toward the central state (an almost identical scheme had been rolled out unsuccessfully in East Timor).[47] However, although the NSP arguably increased local decision-making capacity and also, at least in less fervently

---

[42] Ibid.

[43] Jonathan Goodhand, "Aiding violence or building peace? The role of international aid in Afghanistan", in Sultan Barakat, ed., *Reconstructing war-torn societies: Afghanistan* (London: Palgrave Macmillan, 2004), 52.

[44] Verkoren and van Leeuwen, "Civil Society in Peacebuilding", 164.

[45] See, for example, Ashraf Ghani, presentation at Chatham House, London, 26 September 2005.

[46] Antonio Giustozzi, "Respectable warlords? The politics of state-building in post-Taleban Afghanistan", Crisis States Research Programme working paper 33 (London: London School of Economics and Political Science, 2003), 6–7.

[47] Tanja Hohe, "Developing Local Governance", in Gerd Junne and Willemijn Verkoren, eds., *Postconflict development: meeting new challenges* (Boulder, CO: Lynne Rienner, 2005), 62–8.

conservative areas of the country, broadened local participation in the process, Johnson and Leslie have argued that the NSP ultimately served to weaken the central state because of its failure to incentivize and institutionalize accountability.[48] Funded by donor dollars, the program was never designed to be fiscally sustainable in the first place;[49] in fact, it undermined the emergence of a capable multi-level state by circumventing provincial- and district-level authorities. All the while, local power hierarchies survived the NSP largely intact, with elders, landowners, and mullahs ranking among the most common electees to village-level NSP councils.[50]

Meanwhile in Afghanistan's urban centers, donors created an artificial layer of local technocrats recruited from the ranks of Afghans returned from exile in Europe and North America and hailed for their "potential in terms of their contribution to the reconstruction of Afghanistan".[51] Derogatively called "dog washers" (sing. *sag shoy*) by their Afghan subordinates, they had, in the majority of cases, little to no experience in managing governmental affairs. However, their aspirations to partake in the modernization of their homeland coupled with their bilingualism made them perfect collaborators to the international donor community: easy to manipulate and equipped with at least a rudimentary understanding of "Western" processes and customs, their central involvement in the reconstruction efforts "offered important opportunities to recruit expertise and solicit information for development programmes".[52] Conversely, there was no strategy of political inclusion for lower-level former resistance fighters, despite the fact that such shared experiences constitute a critical condition for political legitimacy in tribal political culture.[53] Likewise, former

[48] Johnson and Leslie, *Afghanistan—The Mirage of Peace*, 189–91.
[49] Astri Suhrke, "The Limits of Statebuilding: The Role of International Assistance in Afghanistan", paper presented at the International Studies Association Annual Meeting, San Diego, 21–24 March 2006.
[50] Inger W. Boesen, "From Subjects to Citizens: Local Participation in the National Solidarity Programme", Working Paper Series (Kabul, Afghanistan: Afghanistan Research and Evaluation Unit, August 2004), 58.
[51] Liesl Riddle and Valentina Marano, "Homeland Export and Investment Promotion Agencies: The Case of Afghanistan", in Jennifer M. Brinkerhoff, ed., *Diasporas and Development: Exploring the Potential* (Boulder, CO: Lynne Rienner, 2008), 140.
[52] Jennifer M. Brinkerhoff, "Digital diasporas and international development: Afghan-Americans and the reconstruction of Afghanistan", *Public Administration and Development*, Vol. 24, No. 5 (2004), 409.
[53] David Isby, *Afghanistan: Graveyard of Empires: A New History of the Borderland* (New York: Pegasus, 2010), 220.

Communist administrators and politicians were systematically excluded from the country's political reconstruction.[54]

In the subsequent elections for an Afghan Parliament (*Wolesi Jirga*) in September 2005—welcomed by international actors as the "conclusion of the Bonn agreement political transition plan"—partisan candidacies were possible, but considering the troubled history of party politics prior to the Soviet invasion, almost all candidates chose to run on individual tickets backed by ethnic or tribal loyalties.[55] With 53 percent voter participation, the turnout was markedly lower than during the previous year's presidential election when 75 percent of Afghan voters, according to official statistics, had participated.[56]

The most commonly cited reasons for this reluctance was an oversupply of candidates, including suspected war criminals; an undersupply of information on candidates' programs (where they existed); and, especially among the urban electorate, a general sense of frustration—"a palpable air of disillusionment"[57] as an ICG report put it—fed by the visibility of and spatial proximity to the riches that the reconstruction process had generated for a small minority.[58] Provincial councils were elected at the same time as the national parliament, but their responsibilities had been curtailed to "participating in development" and "advising administrators", as the national constitution laid out opaquely in article 138, thus bearing the "risk that a potentially effective mechanism for local government might be forever marginalized".[59] Deliberate neglect went so far that a reporter of a leading international news agency suggested that candidates had "no idea of their role, responsibility of powers once they [were] elected".[60] Not surprisingly, during the first meeting of provincial council members for Kabul Province in March 2006, protest against this premeditated powerlessness was vociferous. The head of the provincial council explained that in addition to inappropriate meeting facilities—two

---

[54] Ibid., 221.

[55] US State Department, "Ambassador Bolton issues statement on situation in Afghanistan", 23 August (Washington, DC: States News Service, 2005).

[56] BBC News, "Afghan women still suffer abuse", 30 May 2005.

[57] ICG, "Afghanistan's New Legislature: Making Democracy Work". Crisis Group Asia Report No. 116, 15 May (Kabul: International Crisis Group, 2006), 4.

[58] Soutik Biswas, "Puzzle of the stay-away voters", Kabul: BBC News, 19 September 2005.

[59] Amin Tarzi, "What will become of the Provincial Councils?" *Afghanistan Report*, Vol. 4, No. 28 (Prague: Radio Free Europe/Radio Liberty, 2005).

[60] BBC News, "Twin bombings kill three in Kabul", 14 November 2005.

rooms for up to thirty delegates in the case of Kabul Province were the norm—there were no provisions to grant members genuine oversight over provincial policies. Furthermore, they had not been given the right to appoint and remove district-level personnel; nor did they have effective control over provincial budgets.[61]

Much like Afghanistan, where cities from the 1950s to the early 1970s had served as sites of cautionary democratic experimentation,[62] Iraq's history is dotted with democratic experiences reaching back to the 1950s[63] and, in case of associational life, even farther back into the late nineteenth century.[64] However, this aspect of Iraqi history was overlooked entirely in the run-up to the US-led invasion in 2003. Instead, policy wonks in Washington, DC and London engaged in an exercise of Orientalism by drawing a direct line between reductionist depictions of ancient Middle Eastern history and contemporaneous despotism under Saddam Hussein,[65] arguing that regime change in Iraq would be impossible without foreign intervention and conveniently ignoring the "culture of clandestine dissent and opposition"[66] that had been prevalent under Saddam Hussein.

Once intervention had occurred, however, it became clear that the occupiers were interested primarily in exerting direct control over Iraqi economic assets "rather than to foster and encourage genuine democratic reform".[67]

---

[61] IWPR, "Provincial councils demand power", *Afghan Recovery Report* 207, 19 March (Kabul: Institute for War and Peace Reporting, 2006).

[62] Karl-Otto Hondrich, "Verfassungsentwicklung, politische Stabilität und sozialer Wandel. Die Modernisierung des traditionellen politischen Systems in Afghanistan" [Constitutional development, political stability and social change. The modernization of the traditional political system in Afghanistan], yearbook of *Verfassung und Verfassungswirklichkeit*, 1 (Köln: Opladen, 1966), 226; Jan-Heeren Grevemeyer, *Afghanistan: sozialer Wandel und Staat im 20. Jahrhundert* [Afghanistan: social change and the state in the 20th century] (Berlin: Verlag für Wissenschaft und Bildung, 1990).

[63] Muhsin J. Al-Musawi, *Reading Iraq: Culture and Power in Conflict* (London: I. B. Tauris, 2006), cited in Benjamin Isakhan, *Democracy in Iraq: History, Politics, Discourse* (Burlington, VT: Ashgate, 2012). I am grateful for Benjamin Isakhan's pointers to helpful additional literature on the Iraq case.

[64] Eric Davis, "History matters: past as prologue in building democracy in Iraq", *Orbis* 49 (2005), 229–44.

[65] Isakhan, *Democracy in Iraq*, 2012.

[66] Ibid., 110.

[67] Benjamin Isakhan, "The Streets of Iraq: Protests and Democracy after Saddam", in

Mirroring the fate of Communists in Afghanistan, the purge of Baathists both from formal politics and the military ranks aimed to create a political scene whose ideological pillars were considered acceptable by the occupying forces and conducive to their strategic objectives. Although less widely reviled than former exiles in Afghanistan, Iraqis returning from abroad were similarly installed as advisers and program managers by the occupying forces in an attempt to mobilize them as "resources for reconstruction".[68]

Members of the Iraqi diaspora had, of course, already played a role in helping frame US foreign policy objectives prior to the 2003 invasion. In the immediate aftermath of the overthrow of Saddam's regime, the cultural and language skills of this group were again in high demand. Much like international forces in Afghanistan, the Coalition Provisional Authority of Iraq (CPA) adopted a "greenfield approach" to municipal governance based on virtually no available intelligence on how cities were actually governed under Saddam.[69] In May 2003, CPA administrator L. Paul Bremer dismissed the members of the Baghdad City Council and declared the establishment of a new council a priority, which would assume an advisory role to the CPA. He contracted an American–Iraqi from an influential Baghdadi family to lead this effort. The project leader "relied initially upon coalition forces to assemble Iraqi citizens for meetings regarding [these] councils".[70] Although participation in these meetings was usually limited to a few dozen urban dwellers, in late June 2003 the CPA heralded the formation of 88 so-called neighborhood advisory councils, nine district advisory councils, and the new Baghdad Interim City Advisory Council.[71] Despite the latter's powerlessness-by-design—it had only an advisory role to the CPA—Bremer hailed its first meeting as "the resumption of a democratic system for Baghdad".[72] Preceding

---

Benjamin Isakhan and Stephen Stockwell, eds., *The Secret History of Democracy* (Basingstoke: Palgrave Macmillan, 2011), 203.

[68] Ninna Nyberg-Sorensen, Nicholas Van Hear, and Poul Engberg-Pedersen, *The Migration–Development Nexus: Evidence and Policy Options* (Geneva: International Organization for Migration, July 2002), 39.

[69] Derick W. Brinkerhoff and Samuel Taddesse, "Recruiting from the Diaspora: The Local Governance Program in Iraq" in Jennifer M. Brinkerhoff, ed., *Diasporas and Development: Exploring the Potential* (Boulder, CO: Lynne Rienner, 2008), 77.

[70] Ibid., 78.

[71] CPA, "Establishment of Baghdad Interim City Advisory Council", 30 June, press release (Baghdad: Coalition Provisional Authority, 2003).

[72] Quoted in *Seattle Times*, "Despite troubles, U.S. plan for Iraq forges on", 8 July

this coalition-led municipal restructuring in the capital city, local collective action in secondary urban centers unfolded with vigor, "typically [led by] a few courageous men or women who had decided to do something for their communities".[73]

Instead of articulating ethnicity-based political demands, these spontaneously formed groups sought to address acute public-service shortages in the immediate aftermath of the invasion through "a series of spontaneous elections".[74] "[I]n northern Kurdish cities such as Mosul, in majority Sunni Arab towns like Samarra, in prominent Shia Arab cities such as Hilla and Najaf and in the capital of Baghdad," Isakhan reports, "religious leaders, tribal elders and secular professionals summoned town hall meetings where representatives were elected and plans were hatched for local reconstruction projects, security operations and the return of basic infrastructure."[75] Likewise, the *Seattle Times* observed at the time that "city councils have been emerging around Iraq, with councils in Mosul and Basra, among other cities. Fallujah and other cities have mayors, [and] a 22-member city council took its seats in the southern city of Najaf".[76] Yet these initiatives were "largely being ignored by the Western media".[77] They also failed to secure approval by the CPA, which feared that emerging local constellations would be politically unwieldy and therefore viewed such agency as a problem rather than as a potential component of a functioning multi-level governance structure.[78]

Hegemonic policy towards democracy promotion emphasized manageability and stability over local accountability and pluralism. This fear of realities on the ground and the resulting focus on forging a national political elite while stifling local politics sent a signal to the various tribal and ethnic factions in the country: in post-2001 Iraq, local power-brokering would at best be challenging and at worst considered part of the growing insurgency movement. This is not to suggest that ensuing ethnic mobilization, which also played out mainly in Iraq's cities, was fueled primarily by the Coalition's dis-

---

2003, http://community.seattletimes.nwsource.com/archive/?date=20030708&s lug=iraq08 (accessed 26 August 2013).
[73] Brinkerhoff and Taddesse, "Recruiting from the Diaspora", 81.
[74] Isakhan, *Democracy in Iraq*, 133.
[75] Isakhan, "The Streets of Iraq", 193.
[76] *Seattle Times*, "Despite troubles".
[77] Davis, "History matters".
[78] Isakhan, "The Streets of Iraq", 194.

trust in local politics. But in conjunction with anti-Baathist policies, this stance amounted to a de facto "strategy of coercive urban governance suiting American ideological preconceptions and Shiite political ambitions".[79] Meanwhile, the CPA was determined to create municipal governance structures fully dependent on its political support and revoked the results of ad hoc local elections, culminating in a stand-off in Najaf where an Islamic candidate would probably have prevailed.[80] Where local elections were eventually allowed to go forward, such as in the northern Iraqi cities of Tallafar, Zumar, and Al-Eyaldia a few months later, the new procedure was hardly in compliance with accepted practices of free elections:

> Authorities would select a panel of nominees beforehand, then the nominees would vote amongst themselves. Then between Oct. 15 and Oct. 22 [2003], the 187th Infantry Regiment of the 101st Airborne Division (Air Assault) teamed with Iraqi citizens to conduct the first democratic elections held in Iraq since coalition forces have been in the country. The cities of Tallafar, Zumar and Al-Eyaldia in northern Iraq now have the first popularly elected city councils in the country.[81]

Such official enthusiasm among the occupying forces did not, however, necessarily imply growing faith that Iraqis would actually succeed. "Democracy remains highly misunderstood among council members", the news source goes on to assert by quoting one of the regiment's officers, echoing the discourse created by Western spin doctors and media pundits prior to the invasion.[82] In Mosul as well as several other Iraqi cities, a CPA-funded local governance program subsequently facilitated "democracy dialogues" with local dwellers[83] without giving them an actual political voice. Soon after, Baghdad, Ramadi, Fallujah, and Shia cities in the south turned into major post-invasion battlefields between occupying forces and local insurgents. Even where protests remained largely peaceful, such as in the case of Kurdish cities in 2005, cities remained the epicenters of protest and resistance against the occupation.[84] There is, of course, no ex post facto guarantee that greater initial attention to facilitating city- or neighborhood-level alliances could have prevented the bloodshed. But it is important to point out that this option was

---

[79] Staniland, "Cities on Fire", 1638.

[80] Naomi Klein, *The Shock Doctrine: the Rise of Disaster Capitalism* (Toronto: Alfred A. Knopf, 2007), 437.

[81] US Army News Service, "Democratic elections begin in Iraq", 28 October 2003.

[82] Ibid.

[83] Brinkerhoff and Taddesse, "Recruiting from the Diaspora", 82.

[84] Isakhan, *Democracy in Iraq*, 138.

never seriously considered. The international state-building machine's reliance on foreign expertise and technical leadership co-opted and instrumentalized potential local political actors to an extent that rendered political activism outside the national context both operationally challenging and potentially suspicious,[85] thus narrowing the "political spaces"[86] that are necessary for legitimate representation to emerge.

We have so far focused on tensions between local and international realms of political agency. But the notion of global hegemony compels us also to consider global dimensions of collective action in the context of liberal interventionism and its local impacts. In the face of massive *trans*national collective action—defined as "coordinated international campaigns on the part of networks of activists against international actors"[87]—against the wars in Afghanistan and Iraq, the decision by the United States and its allies to focus on minimizing platforms of dissent in the countries that they invaded becomes even more strategically plausible.[88]

This tension between the inability to control collective action at home and the desire to do so in countries under hegemonic control constitutes a fundamental conceptual schism of externally induced regime change and democracy promotion. To some extent, this reflects convictions that well-established democracies can weather more peacefully the dissent resulting from ever more interconnected geographic spaces of political contention. But it calls into question the extent to which there is faith in organically emerging democracies in the global south. As long as statist national governance continues to be portrayed in rosy terms while urban cradles of democratic pluralism are reduced to spaces of latent or acute insurgencies, there is little hope that post-invasion democracy assistance can do much good.

---

[85] Athena Vongalis-Macrow, "Rebuilding regimes or rebuilding community? Teachers' agency for social reconstruction in Iraq", *Journal of Peace Education*, Vol. 3, No. 1 (2006), 112.

[86] Wendy Larner, "C-change? Geographies of crisis", *Dialogues in Human Geography*, Vol. 1, No. 3 (2011), 319–35; Pal Anirban, "Political space for the civil society: The work of two community-based organizations in Kolkata", *Habitat International*, 32 (2008), 424–36.

[87] Donatella della Porta and Sidney Tarrow, "Transnational Processes and Social Activism: An Introduction", in Donatella della Porta and Sidney Tarrow, eds., *Transnational Protest and Global Activism: People, Passions, and Power* (Lanham, MD: Rowman & Littlefield, 2004), 2–3.

[88] Cf. Anthony F. Lang Jr., "The violence of rules? Rethinking the 2003 war against Iraq", *Contemporary Politics*, Vol. 13, No. 3 (2007), 273.

Hegemonic policies' flat-out dismissal of cities as sites of concrete state-building dynamics was thus driven by a wariness of local politics. In both Afghanistan and Iraq, city-level experiments on reinventing participatory local governance burgeoned but were either ended by occupying forces or mainstreamed into the latter's imposed political structures. Democracy suppression rather than democracy promotion characterized the early period of both occupations and was justified by a characterization of cities as cradles of instability that threatened the vision of unified national governments as key components of the liberal international order. Yet by denying urban dwellers political space in the early days following the invasion, the US-led occupations created a self-fulfilling prophecy: their fear of political agency in cities eventually rendered cities hotbeds of increasingly violent opposition and infighting. It is against the backdrop of this trend that we need to re-examine discourses on governance performance in the Greater Middle East, as well as in other regions of the global periphery. If indeed "international policies dissolve in local realities", as van der Lijn[89] acidly summarizes a lost decade in post-2001 Afghanistan, then we must reconsider the possibilities of a different kind of internationally supported state-building, one that puts local priorities, coalitions and institutional legacies first. Although this is likely to be a messy affair, its outcomes will be more viable in the long run than what the current top-down model could ever produce.

[89] Jaïr van der Lijn, "Imagi-Nation Building in Illusionstan: Afghanistan, Where Dilemmas Become Dogmas, and Models are Perceived to be Reality", *International Peacekeeping*, Vol. 20, No. 2 (2013), 185.

5

LIBYA AFTER QADHAFI

FRAGMENTATION, HYBRIDITY, AND INFORMALITY

Frederic Wehrey

Libya after Qadhafi is a country facing a dizzying array of challenges. A weak central government, gutted of institutions by the dictator's personalistic and idiosyncratic rule, has struggled to assert its authority over vast expanses of the country's territory. The restive eastern region of the country—long marginalized under Qadhafi—has witnessed a worsening spiral of violence between rival tribal factions, Islamists, and remnants of the old regime, as well as calls for greater political autonomy. Porous and ill-policed borders have become veritable thoroughfares for arms smuggling, illicit trafficking and the movement of armed militants across Africa and the Middle East. Deep and historic political divisions between Tripoli, Misrata, and the east continue to obstruct the formation of a broad-based consensus government and the drafting of an effective constitution. Long-suppressed grievances by ethnic Tabu, Tuareg, and Amazigh have surfaced along the country's southern and western periphery. In short, post-revolutionary Libya has seemed to display all the hallmarks of a failing or failed state: a state that is unable to control its territory, cannot provide basic security and other goods for its citizens, and exports its problems to its neighbors.[1]

[1] Robert Rotberg, "The Failure and Collapse of Nation-States: Breakdown,

99

Yet beneath this grim narrative, there are a number of structural factors that, when examined more closely, present a more balanced picture and even grounds for guarded optimism. First, Libya has a mostly urban, relatively homogenous population that is concentrated in a narrow territorial strip. Second, it has relatively high GDP and an infrastructure that was largely unscathed by the NATO campaign. Related to this, its oil production has nearly returned to pre-war levels. In contrast to Iraq or Syria, it is not afflicted by serious meddling by ill-meaning and more powerful neighbors. Finally, and perhaps most importantly, a robust civil society and networks of informal actors (tribes, religious figures, merchant elites, and militias) have stepped in to fill the shortcomings of the feeble state institutions, providing an array of goods and services.

In this sense, Libya seems to validate much of the criticism of the failed state literature that places too much emphasis on the Weberian ideal and ignores the wide variation of state-like functions within a given political community.[2] This is particularly the case regarding the security sector, where much Western commentary has adopted a rather simplistic Weberian framework for analyzing militias as antithetical to the state, discounting much of the literature on hybridity and warlordism that has arisen in sub-Saharan Africa and Southeast Asia.[3] That said, the longer the institutional vacuum in Libya persists, the greater the strains on this informal and hybrid arrangement, exacerbating dangerous fissures that either existed under the Qadhafi era or arose during the Revolution.

These fissures are varied and complex. Contrary to popular assumptions, the Islamist–secular divide is not the country's principal fault-line. Rather, it

---

Prevention, and Repair", in Rotberg, ed., *When States Fail: Causes and Consequences* (Princeton, 2004), 1–45.

[2] For a review of this criticism, see Jonathan Di John, "The Concept, Causes and Consequences of Failed States: A Critical Review of the Literature and Agenda for Research with Specific Reference to Sub-Saharan Africa", *European Journal of Development Research*, 22 (2010), 10–30.

[3] See Ariel Ahram, *Proxy Warriors: The Rise and Fall of State-Sponsored Militias* (Stanford University Press, 2011); V. Boege, A. Brown, K. Clements, and A. Nolan, "On Hybrid Political Orders and Emerging States: What is Failing—States in the Global South or Research and Politics in the West", in M. Fischer and B. Schmelzle, eds., *Building Peace in the Absence of States: Challenging the Discourse of State Failure* (Berlin: Berghof Conflict Research, 2009). Also, T. Debiel and D. Lambach, *Hybrid Political Orders in Fragile Environments* (Duisburg: Essen University Institute for Development and Peace, no date).

is tension between several regional loci of power in Libya that have each produced their own constellation of militias. As a result, a sort of stalemate has ensued, with none of these armed groups strong enough to dominate the others. Overlaying this contest, a fierce struggle has emerged over the mantle of revolutionary legitimacy, between factions and individuals that were long persecuted by Qadhafi, those who collaborated with the regime but then defected at the eleventh hour or during the Revolution, and those who joined the uprising after years abroad. The struggle has taken on a zero-sum quality because the hollow and ineffective institutions of coercion—the army and police—have been unable to play an arbitrating role.

This chapter will focus on the interplay in Libya between institutional fragility and societal fissures. It will focus specifically on how tensions between the center and the periphery and the rise of Islamism have been intensified by the dearth of political institutions (functioning ministries, a competent parliament, municipal government, and a constitution) and formal security entities (the army and police).[4] It will apply the concept of hybridity to characterize the Libyan security landscape, analyzing how the central state has created new security bodies that embody elements of militias and formal security entities. In tandem, it explores the way Libya's civil society and informal actors who exert traditional and charismatic forms of authority have tried to compensate for this institutional vacuum.[5] Finally, the chapter will conclude with a discussion of the implications of Libya's burgeoning oil sector for bolstering formal institutions.

Center–Periphery Tensions: A Legacy of Qadhafi's Divide-and-Rule Policy

Libya is moderately heterogeneous and geographically concentrated—the majority of its Sunni, Arabic-speaking population live along the Mediterranean seaboard. Unlike other countries confronting post-conflict recovery—Bosnia, Kosovo, Somalia, Iraq, or Afghanistan—the country's diverse fighting groups did not fight each other. Despite the plethora of armed groups currently in the country, none has mounted a violent insurgency against the central government. But if Libya is not Bosnia or Iraq, neither is it Norway. Long-suppressed fissures and identities are emerging in the wake of Qadhafi's ouster.

---

[4] This chapter makes use of interviews conducted in Tripoli, Zintan, Benghazi, and Misrata from mid-2012 to mid-2013.

[5] Max Weber, *Economy and Society: An Outline of Interpretive Sociology* (New York: Bedminster Press, 1968).

Many of these conflicts are between rival towns on the southern and western borders battling over power and resources in the post-Qadhafi order. In other instances, the roots were related to Qadhafi's long-standing policies of ethnic discrimination. Ethnic Amazigh (Berbers), who comprise roughly 4 to 10 percent of the total population, have begun to assert their identity and language in their north-western strongholds of Zawya and Jabal Nafusa.[6] Clashes have erupted between Amazigh and local Arabs over control of smuggling routes on the Tunisian borders. In the historic oasis town of Ghademes on the Algerian border, Tuareg residents have been subjected to a campaign of ethnic cleansing because of their support for Qadhafi. Far to the south, violent fighting has simmered between minority African Tabu and ethnic Arab tribes favored by Qadhafi.

In Kufra, the conflict has been especially violent, with over 200 people killed since the beginning of 2012. At its core, the fighting is about re-establishing social equilibrium and, more importantly, control of the illicit border economy. Under Qadhafi, the government deprived the Tabu of citizenship, employment, and access to medical care, condemning them to serf-like status under the local Arab tribe, the Zway. The country's interim governing authority, the National Transitional Council (NTC), eager to control the border, handed authority and power to a local Tabu leader, effectively granting him control of the region's lucrative smuggling networks. The proliferation of heavy weaponry has made the ensuing conflict especially violent. So far, the government's response has relied on informal tribal mediators or the dispatch of brigade coalitions—many of whom displayed overt partisanship toward the Zway, which ended up inflaming the situation even more.

Crucially, the continued marginalization of these southern communities is inextricably linked to the broader problem of border control—an issue of intense scrutiny from both the EU and the United States because of concerns about African migrant influxes and al-Qaeda. Bereft of access to the national economy, cross-border smuggling of illicit contraband developed into a deeply entrenched way of life among the southern Tabu, Tuareg, and Arab tribes, whose kin networks extended across the Sahara and Sahel. Contrary to popu-

---

[6] Militias from Jebel Nafusa played a critical role in liberating Tripoli, yet the new cabinet contained no Amazigh representatives—an exclusion that sparked several protests in front of the prime minister's office. François Murphy, "Libyan Berbers Vent Rage Over Cabinet Exclusion", Reuters, 27 November 2011. Also, WAL (Libyan News Agency) via BBC Worldwide Monitoring, "Libyan Amazigh Demonstrate Against Marginalization, Exclusion", 27 November 2011.

lar belief, this trafficking industry was never really controlled under Qadhafi, but rather exploited and managed. While much of the border control focus has been on manpower and surveillance technology, the human security dimension is ultimately central. These communities must be given alternative sources of income and allowed access to long-deprived political capital.

The Restive East

Among the aggrieved regions in Libya, none is more pressing than the eastern region of Cyrenaica (known in Libya by its Arabic name, Barqa). The historic seat of authority in Libya during the Sanussi monarchy, the east suffered a precipitous decline in its political relevance and living standards after the 1969 coup. Although many of his co-conspirators in the 1969 coup hailed from eastern families, Qadhafi realized that future resistance to his rule would ultimately emanate from the east, given the influence of the Sanussi monarchy and the area's powerful Saadi tribes. Shortly after seizing power, he began purging Sanussi officers from the army, dismantling Sufi orders, and expropriating land from Saadi notables and granting it to tribes of lesser status. Although he did not officially declare a capital, he began moving the bulk of government offices from Benghazi to Tripoli, and later, in 1977, to his home town of Sirte. Other institutions of economic and symbolic value were moved: the oil ministry, Olympic committee, and the Libyan national airlines.[7] The development of Libya's hydrocarbon sector added another irritant into the already combustible mix of eastern grievances. Roughly two-thirds of Libyan oil production comes from the Sirte Basin and the eastern Benghazi region, but the east saw little benefit to its living conditions or infrastructure from oil revenues.[8] In the post-Qadhafi era, there are widespread concerns in the east that the political and economic marginalization will continue.

Eastern economic and political grievances provided the grist for a small but vocal federalist movement in the run-up to the 7 July 2012 parliamentary elections. The federalists, represented by the so-called Barqa Council, called for an election boycott and instigated sporadic acts of violence with their armed wing, to include briefly shutting down oil production. But ultimately,

---

[7] Author interview with a Libyan parliamentary candidate, Benghazi, Libya, 1 July 2012.
[8] For background, Paul Rivlin, "The Libyan Economy and Oil Prospects as the War Ends", *Iqtisadi—Middle East Economy*, Vol. 1, No. 6 (October 2011).

the movement for eastern autonomy was the dog that did not bark. When the Barqa Council was mounting pro-autonomy demonstrations, there were simultaneous counter-demonstrations in both the east and Tripoli, with placards reading "No to *Fitna* [Sedition], No to Secession, Yes to National Unity". Voters in the east ignored the federalists' calls for boycotting the July elections, and the Barqa Council suffered a devastating blow from which it has not fully recovered. Many Libyan citizens, even in the east, still believe in the idea of Libya as a unitary state, but appear to be navigating a careful course between the hyper-centralization of the Qadhafi era and the break-up of the state. That said, the issue of eastern grievance and possible mobilization is not dead, and may yet rear its head again if political and economic power is not equitably distributed.

Aside from the division of oil revenues, a crucial litmus test for the new government is re-establishing security in the east. Since the summer of 2012, the east—particularly Benghazi—has witnessed a precipitous decline in security, with near-daily assassinations of Qadhafi-era officials, attacks on Western interests, kidnappings, and bombings of court houses and security headquarters.[9] The perpetrators of these attacks remain unknown. Some have attributed them to Islamist groups. Others speculate that local militias are striking at the state security apparatus, which are staffed by Qadhafi-era officials. Regardless of origin, the attacks point to the urgency of addressing the security situation in the east within the framework of broader security sector reform in the country.

A Fractured Islamist Field: Between the Muslim Brotherhood and Salafis

In contrast to neighboring Tunisia and Egypt, Libya's political scene has not been dominated by Islamist parties or witnessed polarizing debates between secularists and Islamists. In part, this stems from the legacy of Qadhafi's 42-year rule, but also the nature of Libya's generally conservative society.

---

[9] In late July, two separate improvised explosive devices were uncovered at the headquarters of the Benghazi Criminal Investigations Department (CID) and the National Security Directorate. A 40-kg bomb was also discovered in the basement of the Tibesti Hotel in Benghazi, which frequently hosts visiting NTC officials. On 28 July, General Khalifa Hiftar, the commander of Libyan ground forces, narrowly escaped an assassination attempt. On 1 August, the military intelligence headquarters in Benghazi was bombed. Most recently, the Iranian Red Crescent delegation in Benghazi was kidnapped, reportedly by an Islamist militia. *Al-Manara*, 28 July 2012.

Libya's interim constitution preserves Islamic law as the "principal source of legislation" (*al-masdar al-ra'isi lil tashri'*), while at the same time guaranteeing rights for Libya's minorities, offering full electoral participation to women, and establishing an independent judiciary.[10]

Throughout his long tenure, Qadhafi had an ambivalent, troubled relationship with Islamism. As noted, when the Libyan dictator came to power, he began systematically destroying the bases for Sufi power in the east. Ideologically, the quixotic political philosophy embodied in the *Green Book* tried to appropriate Islam while at the same time denigrating it as the organizing principle for governance. In the mid-1990s, the country faced a concerted insurgency from the Libyan Islamic Fighting Group (LIFG)—a Salafi-inspired movement that grew out of the east's dire political marginalization and the experiences of hardened Libyan veterans of the anti-Soviet jihad in Afghanistan. Although Qadhafi crushed the uprising with brutal force, he later attempted to "rehabilitate" many LIFG prisoners using a form of quietist Salafism that emphasized unconditional loyalty to the state. This brand of Islamism also informed the pronouncements of the state-sponsored clerical establishment and the Grand Mufti during the latter years of his rule.

The Muslim Brotherhood

Throughout all of this, the Libyan Muslim Brotherhood remained a banned organization whose members resided abroad, mostly in Europe. During the Revolution, Brotherhood and Islamist actors received a significant boost from Qatari funding and support. It is inaccurate, however, to say that the Revolution handed the country over to the Brotherhood—the actually strategic and battlefield contributions of the Islamists are a matter of continued contention and debate.

The collapse of the Qadhafi regime and the sudden opening of the country to participatory politics proved a disorienting, dizzying experience for many Islamist actors, who were unaccustomed to grass-roots organizing and political campaigning. For the Brotherhood-affiliated Justice and Construction Party (JCP), the new political scene was especially vexing. In the run-up to the July 2012 parliamentary elections, the party failed to articulate a coherent agenda that addressed the country's key challenges, focusing instead on moral-

---

[10] National Transitional Council of Libya, "Draft Constitutional Charter for the Transitional Stage", 2011, http://www.al-bab.com/arab/docs/libya/Libya-Draft-Constitutional-Charter-for-the-Transitional-Stage.pdf

ity and social issues. "They got lazy," noted one Libyan academic in the summer of 2012. "They assumed that just because everybody shouted 'Allahu Akhbar' during the war, they would vote Islamist."[11] In voting for party lists, the Muslim Brotherhood lost significantly to the more technocratic National Forces Alliance led by Mahmud Jabril. But it is inaccurate to characterize the election as "win" for liberals and "lose" for the Brotherhood: the NFA itself has since enacted a number of socially conservative laws, and the Brotherhood rebounded in voting for independent seats and in Cabinet positions. According to several observers close to the JCP, it has shifted its ethos to *bina'* (reconstruction) rather than dogma and morality, drawing lessons from a number of its Islamist counterparts across the region: technocratic know-how from the AKP in Turkey, grass-roots campaigning from the Egyptian Muslim Brotherhood, and elite consensus-building from Tunisia's Ennahda.[12]

The Salafis

Salafism in Libya is not a uniquely eastern phenomena but it has strong roots in the east, given the area's commingling of religion and politics under the Sanussiya. Partly as a result of developments in neighboring Egypt, the Muslim Brotherhood developed a strong influence in the area in the 1950s and 1960s. The industrial seaport of Darnah emerged as an especially active hub of Islamism in the eastern region. Here, growing religiosity combined with mounting economic woes and the collective memory of the town's prominent role in the anti-colonial struggle to produce a trend of jihadi volunteerism that sent thousands of young men to Afghanistan in the 1980s. A similar dynamic was at work in the poorer sections of Benghazi, particularly the Laythi neighborhood, which earned the nickname "Little Kandahar".[13] Returning veterans of this war formed the Libyan Islamic Fighting Group (LIFG), which had the explicit goal of bringing down the Qadhafi regime.

With the fall of Qadhafi and the holding of parliamentary elections, a significant portion of the LIFG's cadre—known in local parlance as *muqataleen* (fighters)—had adopted democratic participation. Yet the move into politics also produced splits among the *muqataleen*. One faction, led by 'Abd al-Hakim Bilhaj, the LIFG's former emir and the ex-commander of the Tripoli Military Council, formed the *al-Watan* party. But many more *muqataleen*

---

[11] Author's interview in Benghazi, Libya, 4 July 2012.
[12] Author's telephone interview with Libyan activists, February 2013.
[13] Author's interview in Tripoli, Libya, 29 June 2012.

joined a separate party, the *Umma al-Wasat*, led by Sami al-Saadi, the LIFG's key ideologue who once authored a seminal anti-democratic tract. Al-Saadi was joined by another key figure in the LIFG, 'Abd al-Wahhab al-Ghayid (the brother of the late Abu Yahya Libi, widely regarded as al-Qaeda's number two), who ran successfully as a parliamentary candidate in the southern city of Marzuq.[14]

At the same time as this current was entering politics, a parallel faction was forming, representing the second generation of Salafi jihadists. These are the sons and nephews of the first generation, who witnessed the 1990s crackdown and torture of their fathers or were incarcerated themselves and radicalized by it. Some went to Afghanistan and Iraq, post 2001, were imprisoned by coalition forces and repatriated to Libya by British and American intelligence services. In the tumult of the 2011 revolution, they re-emerged as leaders of revolutionary brigades in Benghazi, Darnah, and other eastern cities.[15]

Unlike Bilhaj and his cohort, though, this group never relinquished their militant view. Since early 2012, this faction has asserted itself in a number of attacks on Western interests, such as World War II graves, the International Committee for the Red Cross, the US consulate, the convoy of the British ambassador, and, most notoriously, the killing of the US ambassador and three of his colleagues in September 2012. At the center of much of the focus is the Ansar al-Shari'a. The organization made its most visible entrée into eastern politics in early June, when it organized a "seminar" in Benghazi for like-minded Islamist militias in support of Islamic law.[16] On the morning of 7 June, over 150 vehicles representing 15 militias (11 based out of Benghazi) paraded along the city's cornice. Many of the participants wore the Afghan dress that is fashionable among Salafi-jihadists. According to one of the com-

---

[14] Author's interview in Benghazi, Libya, 3 July 2012.

[15] For background on the Islamists' role in the defense of Benghazi, see the interview with Fawzi Bu Katif, *al-Manara*, 14 February 2012, available at http://www.alma-naralink.com/press/2012/02/10675, accessed 1 August 2012.

[16] According to several interlocutors, the rally in Benghazi was patterned along the lines of a similar event in Karouian, Tunisia. This protest highlights an important transnational link between Ansar al-Sharia and Salafi groups in Tunisia. On 18 June, armed Ansar al-Sharia members reportedly protested in front of the Tunisian consulate in Benghazi against an art show in Tunisia that was deemed an affront to strict Salafi sensibilities. See *Tunisia Live*, 18 June 2012, http://www.tunisia-live.net/2012/06/18/tunisian-islamist-violence-spills-across-libyan-border/, accessed 1 August 2012.

manders of the participating militias, the parade was "meant to intimidate those who do not want God's law".[17] Yet the rally met with fierce opposition. By late afternoon, groups of civil society activists, including large NGOs and women's groups, had appeared on Benghazi's cornice to oppose the rally. Many bore flags and placards emblazoned with "Libya is Not Afghanistan".[18]

Importantly, the Benghazi counter-demonstration was not an isolated incident. Across the east, there has been burgeoning opposition and outreach to Salafi rejectionism from a range of civil society actors. Nowhere was this more evident than in the wake of the killing of the US ambassador on 11 September 2012. The tragic event was a wake-up call for many Libyans that the Faustian bargain the country's provisional government had made with the country's revolutionary brigades was no longer tenable. It was time for the government to rein in the numerous armed groups that had filled the security vacuum left by the collapsed national army and anaemic police. In Benghazi, crowds stormed the compounds of the Ansar al-Shari'a and other Islamist brigades. The protests soon spread to Tripoli in a remarkable display of civic action against a transitional government that seemed unable to deliver one of the most basic goods of governance: security. Yet by early 2013, the government had still not acted on its promises to evict the militias and restore security. Many Islamist brigades in the east still provided security, albeit under the nominal authority of the Ministry of Defense.

Civil Society Counterweights to Salafi Militancy

In the wake of this vacuum, policing and regulating the challenge from radical Salafism fell to an array of non-governmental, informal actors. In each of the enclaves where it has enjoyed support, the Salafi rejectionist current has also encountered opposition from civil society activists, tribes, and religious figures.[19]

This opposition has been particularly evident in Darnah, a city which, despite its long-standing notoriety as a hotbed for Islamism, has a robust educated class and a thriving NGO scene. Voter turnout in Darnah was relatively high and Islamists did not make strong gains. Over 140 NGOs operate in Darnah, of which 60 are women-led. A number of liberal theater groups have

---

[17] *Libya al-Youm*, 14 June 2012.

[18] *New Quryna*, 14 June 2012.

[19] Author's interview with Ashur Shamis, Tripoli, Libya, 25 June 2012.

also sprung up to challenge the Islamic orthodoxy of Ansar al-Sharia.[20] Darnah's university has become a particularly contested area in the struggle, with Salafi groups attempting to impose social restrictions on students.

Aside from these interlocutors, there are religious mediators. These are clerics who hail from the same Salafi milieu as the rejectionists and were perhaps themselves incarcerated at Abu Salim prison, but who evince a more moderate outlook.[21] Chief among these is the Grand Mufti of Libya, Shaykh Sadeq al-Gharyani. Appointed as Grand Mufti by the NTC in May 2011, al-Gharyani has emerged as one of the NTC's foremost conflict mediators, not just on religious issues, but also on tribal fighting in the south and west. On the Salafi issue, he has played a central role in condemning the desecration of Sufi shrines.[22] Former *muqataleen* who have joined Bilhaj's *al-Watan* party have also played a role in outreach. According to a member of *al-Watan*: "We try to talk to Ansar al-Sharia. We tell them: 'You can protest, but bring your women and children, not weapons. Don't wear Afghan clothing.' We tell them, you should talk to the media."[23] The Libyan Muslim Brotherhood is a third counterweight; it maintains a robust media network in the east through the popular *al-Manara* website, which frequently posts condemnations and counterpoints to Salafi militancy. Yet it has been the tribes who have proven the strongest counterweights to Salafism in the east. Tribal elders—known in the local dialect as *wujaha*—have engaged in outreach to the Salafists, attempting to woo them into local councils and incorporate their militias into the formal security services.[24]

The net effect of these efforts has been to place the Salafi rejectionists on the defensive and to contain them. By many accounts, the movement's vociferous rhetoric against elections, attacks on Sufi shrines, and shrill calls for jihad in

---

[20] Author's interview with a Libyan civil society activist, Benghazi, Libya, 2 July 2012.

[21] For a representative example see the article by Sa'ad al-Na'as, "Ansar al-Shari'a wa Islam" (Ansar al-Sharia and Islam), *al-Watan* (Libya), 28 June 2012.

[22] *Libya Herald*, 9 July 2012. At the same time, some observers have criticized him for ambiguity on the desecration of shrines and for not being forceful enough. For a video of his rulings on Sufi shrines, see http://www.youtube.com/watch?v=-8OZv lDvCkI, accessed 1 August 2012.

[23] Author's interview with a parliamentary candidate from *al-Watan*, Benghazi, Libya, 1 July 2012.

[24] In an April 2012 interview, Qumu stated that he would obey the dictate of the *wujaha* to integrate Ansar al-Sharia into the national army or SSC. See the interview posted on the jihadist web forum, http://tamimi.own0.com/t97883-topic# 686380, accessed 1 August 2012.

Gaza and Syria are not signs of strength and potency, but rather just the opposite. "I met with several of the Ansar al-Sharia members," noted one local activist. "They seemed scared. They are constantly under fire because of the Sufi attacks and grave desecration."[25] The results of the elections have further put them on the defensive by revealing the majority of the Libyan electorate, even in eastern Islamist enclaves like Darnah, to be focused on pragmatic, technocratic agendas for developing the country, rather than piety, charity, and social justice—the traditional selling points of the Islamists. In many respects, the Salafis have yet to find a niche or a compelling cause. Much of this has to do with Libya's already conservative social foundations and religiosity.

Weak and Contested Political Institutions

Under Qadhafi's rule for the last 42 years, Libyans lack any real experience with participatory politics or liberal democratic culture. Despite a multi-tiered bureaucracy of Popular and Revolutionary Committees which, in theory, was supposed to solicit consensus on policy, Qadhafi maintained tight control on virtually every aspect of state affairs. Decision-making was confined to Qadhafi and a close inner circle of advisors and confidants, the so-called "men of the tent" (*rijal al-kha'ima*), who were either related to Qadhafi by blood or were part of his original 1969 cadre of "Free Officers".[26]

The country's provisional governing body, the 31-member National Transitional Council (NTC), was formed in Benghazi in late February 2011 and quickly gained the support of defecting military units, tribal leaders, and provincial officials. International recognition followed and the NTC has won high marks for setting forth a speedy timeline for the forming of an interim cabinet, promulgating an election law, appointing an election commission, holding elections for a 200-member constituent assembly in 2012 and presidential elections in April 2013.

An important bright spot in Libya's revolutionary journey was the 7 July 2012 elections, or the General National Congress. Voter turnout was relatively high, with the majority of voters showing their preference for technocratic candidates rather than dogmatic Islamists. It was a remarkable democratic

[25] Author interview with a Libyan civil society activist, Benghazi, Libya, 4 July 2012.
[26] See Amal Obaidi, *Political Culture in Libya* (London: Curzon, 2001); and Ronald Bruce St John, "The Ideology of Mu'ammar al-Qadhdhafi: Theory and Practice", *International Journal of Middle East Studies*, 15 (1983), 475–7.

experiment in a state that had had no experience in any sort of participatory politics or civic action for over four decades. That said, an important, last-minute measure which secured the participation of the east was a unilateral decree by the NTC that the Constitutional Drafting Committee, the so-called Committee of 60, would be elected from Libya's three regions rather than appointed by the GNC. For the east, this was an important gesture that helped temper their misgivings about the lack of parliamentary representation in proportion to the east's demographic weight.

A cornerstone of bolstering the state's institutional strength is the constitution, which will delineate local and central powers, define the role of Islam in political life, and lay the framework for disarming the brigades. There has been no shortage of outside advice and technocratic expertise on constitutional processes. But Libyans are looking to their own experience of drafting the 1951 constitution, reviving—with remarkable immediacy—this important episode of political participation. While few Libyans advocate a whole return to this document, there have been vigorous discussions about its merits and drawbacks as they pertain to present-day challenges.

More recently, there have been signs of a disturbing polarization inside the parliament and indications of the public's steadily decreasing patience. Among these, debate over the so-called Political Isolation Law has been the most deleterious and paralyzing. First drafted on 19 February 2013, the bill would ban Qadhafi-era officials from positions of government, listing 36 different categories of Libyans. Decried by critics as a sort of "de-Baathification redux", the Political Isolation Law suggests that national reconciliation will be an iterative process that is likely to buffet the country's political trajectory for some time to come.

More generally, there has been growing frustration in the east with the pace of the GNC's legislation. In the run-up to the two-year anniversary of the Revolution, this dissent coalesced into plans for massive demonstrations that came to be known as the "Correction of the Path". Encompassing a broad spectrum of groups from Islamists to federalists, the movement demanded the immediate passage of the Political Isolation Law, the passage of a decentralization law, the disbandment of militias, the removal of President Muhammad Magarief and Chief of Staff Yusuf Mangush, the relocation of the headquarters of the National Oil Company (NOC) to Benghazi, and the reinstatement of Tripoli and Benghazi as the two capitals of Libya in accordance with the 1951 constitution. At the eleventh hour, however, negotiations with the GNC averted the demonstrations and the federalists pulled out of the protests for fear that they might spark acts of violence by Benghazi's well-armed citizenry.

The Hybrid and Contested Security Sector

Among the country's security challenges, none has gathered more attention than the proliferation of armed groups outside the government's control. In many respects, their presence and continued power is the outgrowth of both the unique course of the Revolution and the peculiar pathologies of the Qadhafi regime. Libya's plethora of armed groups occupies an important nexus between civil society, regional marginalization, growing Islamism, and the weakness of the central state. In the more than two years since the Revolution, they have been brought into a tenuous and fluid relationship with the state, resulting in a hybrid security architecture that defies simplistic and dichotomous characterizations.

Much of the current security situation in Libya stems from the unique course of the Revolution. Unlike Afghanistan or South Sudan, there was no long-standing armed opposition that could commandeer the anti-regime forces. It was truly a grass-roots, diffuse revolt by the periphery against the centre. Its currency was the *katiba* (plural, *kata'ib*; literally, brigade)—the armed fighting groups ranging from 20 to 200 young men, formed along neighborhood, town, or tribal lines. Gradually, as the Revolution progressed, these diffuse units fell under loose regional commands on the war's three fronts: the western Nafusa mountains, the coastal city of Misrata, and the east. With the fall of the Qadhafi regime, these groups naturally stepped into the void. Meanwhile, the soldiers of the national army had all but disappeared—either through defections, deaths, or simply shedding their uniforms and fading away. In truth, the army had always been neglected, ill-equipped, and underfunded by Qadhafi, who feared a repeat of the coups that had rattled his grip on power in the late 1980s and early 1990s. A similar neglect afflicted the national police.

For a while, the public welcomed the revolution brigades as a sort of local constabulary: manning traffic stops, guarding key installations, patrolling the harbors and airports. At the same time, another type of brigade arose in the chaotic aftermath of the war: the so-called "rogue" brigades who had actually never fought in the Revolution but were formed purely for opportunistic financial gain. These groups entered the black market. In tandem, the powerful brigades from Misrata and Zintan, who had fought the bloodiest battles en route to the liberation of Tripoli, descended on the capital to claim the spoils of their hard-won sacrifice. The well-armed Misratans and Zintanis pillaged automobiles, took over ministries, and encamped at key institutions like the airport and oilfields.

To address the militia issue, the revolutionary brigades must be integrated into the regular police and army, and young *thuwwar* must be given opportunities for job training or further education. Much of the work will have to focus on dismantling or institutionalizing the ad-hoc and temporary security bodies that have been created or tolerated by the NTC.[27] It is these bodies that have given the security sector its unique quality of hybridity that has confounded outside donors and security patrons who, by bureaucratic protocol, are used to dealing with official institutions.

Among these bodies, the most troubling is the Supreme Security Committee (SSC), which falls under the Ministry of Interior. Numbers of the force remain murky, with some estimates ranging from 90,000 to 100,000. Ostensibly, the force is comprised of revolutionary fighters and is meant as a temporary harness to their zeal and fighting experience in the service of transitional security, particularly during the election period. Most ominously, the Committees have left the brigade structure intact—entire brigades have joined en masse and their commanders have simply switched hats. Paradoxically, then, the Committees are perpetuating the very militia system that the NTC is trying to dismantle, running at loggerheads with other demobilization programs under the offices of the Prime Minister and Minister of Defense.[28]

Among Libyan citizens, the SSCs have hardly engendered confidence or trust. While the local police (who also fall under the Ministry of Interior) are derided as Qadhafi-era hold-outs, the SSC are feared as unruly thugs or derided as misfits. Accusations of torture, kidnapping, and murder are widespread. Increasingly, there are signs of a worrisome formality—the uniforms have become more standardized and the SSC now has a website—which suggests that the SSCs are not going away any time soon.[29] Ironically, many Libyan commentators in social media are now referring to the SSCs as the

[27] For background on these structures, see Frederic Wehrey, "Libya's Militia Menace". *Foreign Affairs*, 15 July 2012.

[28] Author's interview with US and European defense officials: Tripoli, Libya, July 2012.

[29] *New Quryna*, 24 July 2012, available at http://www.qurynanew.com/38949, accessed 1 August 2012. See also the Facebook page for the Benghazi SSC: http://www.facebook.com/#!/ssc.benghazi, accessed 1 August 2012.

new *"lijan thawriya"* (Revolutionary Committees), demonstrating that escaping from the pernicious shadow of Qadhafi's security state will not be easy.

Even more problematic than the SSC over the long term are the so-called Libyan Shield Forces, coalitions of brigades from the east, Misrata, and Zintan which effectively function as a parallel to the anemic National Army. In many respects, the Shield Force is a bottom-up initiative by brigade commanders themselves, designed to resist the incorporation of their fighters into the official army or police departments and preserve the structure of the brigades—albeit under a different, more official-sounding name.

In the east, many of the Islamist brigades have joined the Shield divisions, but have continued to pursue agendas that are seen by many local residents as overbearing, parasitic, and antithetical to the larger task of state-building. From the Islamists' perspective, the unwillingness to surrender their arms and fully integrate into the army reflects endemic suspicion about the trajectory of the central government and the absence of a constitution that delineates civil–military relations. In early June 2013, these tensions came to a head when local Benghazi residents stormed the headquarters of the Libya Shield One division, headed by a well-known Islamist and war veteran, Wissam bin Ahmayd. In the ensuing clashes, thirty-one people died and over a hundred were injured. The incident sparked widespread outrage and renewed calls by the public that the government had to take immediate steps to disband the militias and replace them with the regular army and police.

In the latter months of its tenure, the NTC took some steps to demobilize the brigades and integrate their young fighters into society. At the forefront of this task is an initiative from the Prime Minister's office called the Warriors' Affairs Commission for Development (known locally as the WAC). The WAC has conducted an exhaustive registration and data collection on nearly 215,000 revolutionary fighters, and functions as a sort of placement service, moving these young men into the police and the army, or sending them on scholarships abroad, furthering their education at home, or giving them vocational training. After vetting and screening, roughly 150,000 are now eligible for placement; what happens to the other 65,000 remains to be seen. The implied goal of the WAC is to break up the brigades by appealing to individual interest: "We need to appeal to the *thuwwar*'s ambitions and desire for a better life. We need to tell him that the brigades cannot offer you anything."[30] Unsurprisingly, the reaction from the brigades has been tepid.

[30] Author's interview with a WAC official: Benghazi, Libya, 4 July 2012.

Increasingly, the problem of the *thuwwar* is having a disruptive effect on the country's nascent political institutions. On 3 February 2012, war-wounded revolutionaries and their supporters stormed the Congress building and a small group staged a sit-in in the main debating chamber, demanding that the government pay for their medical treatment abroad. On 3 March, government forces tried to evict the protesters but were unsuccessful. In the face of this armed presence, the country's newly elected parliament, the General National Congress (GNC), has been unable to meet regularly, exacerbating an already rocky start to the country's political life.[31] In May, the country faced its most serious political crisis when a coalition of Misratan and eastern-based militias (co-led by the aforementioned Wissam bin Ahmayd) laid siege to the parliament demanding that the sweeping Political Isolation Law be passed. When it was, the pressure didn't stop there: the militias next demanded that Prime Minister 'Ali Zeidan be ousted. The entire episode set a dangerous precedent for collusion between armed groups and disgruntled political factions and individuals.

Aside from the issue of demobilization of the militias, Libya faces serious challenges in its police and judicial system. Under Qadhafi, the police were a hollow and marginalized force that lacked even basic communication equipment (which was hoarded by the omnipresent domestic intelligence services). In the post-revolutionary period, the police have suffered from the perception of being hold-outs from the Qadhafi era. Efforts at recruitment have been mixed; a program to train new policemen in Jordan collapsed after a near-mutiny by the trainees. Across Libya, the police face an uphill battle against the better-armed and more pervasive brigades who have meted out their own justice, against both criminals and political opponents. Relatedly, the new government faces the vexing challenge of thousands of detainees being held in militia-run prisons without due process. Gradually, the judiciary has sought to create a warden force that will oversee these facilities, with the eventual goal of transferring all the prisoners to government control.

The Oil Sector and the Nascent Economic Recovery

Although the tens of billions of dollars in recently released frozen assets will aid the country's short-term reconstruction, the oil industry holds the key to

[31] http://www.libyaherald.com/2013/03/03/security-guards-injured-trying-to-evict-congress-occupiers/

its long-term economic growth and political stability. With over 46.5 billion barrels of oil reserves (the largest in Africa) and 55 trillion cubic feet of natural gas reserves, Libya possesses a tremendous economic asset not found in other Arab Spring countries.[32] Remarkably, production has already exceeded pre-war levels (1.8 million barrels a day).[33] That said, the Paris-based International Energy Agency (IEA) noted that although the Libyan oil infrastructure emerged from the war largely unscathed, the country still faces "many logistical, operational and security related challenges" to fully capitalize on its oil wealth and attract much-needed foreign investment.[34]

Oil accounts for a staggering 95 percent of export earnings and 80 percent of government revenue.[35] In the light of this dependence, Libyan officials have recently stressed the importance of diversifying the economy to other sectors, such as the untapped tourism market, but have also acknowledged the shortcomings in infrastructure and capacity (roads and hotels) needed to support this expansion.[36] A number of other factors have limited the full utilization of oil to aid Libya's post-war recovery. First, security conditions at or near the country's major oilfields have acted as a major deterrent to foreign oil companies returning en masse. Much of Libya's reserves are located in the south and in the east, where government control has been tenuous and where militias have frequently clashed. The oil-rich Sirte basin, in particular, has been a major concern for foreign oil companies contemplating moving their foreign staff into the country. Consequently, these companies—whose expertise is in some cases sorely needed to restart operations at Libya's refineries and terminals—have focused their efforts primarily on Libya's offshore fields in the Mediterranean.[37]

A second major obstacle to the development of the oil sector and the economy more broadly is the country's general lack of infrastructure and con-

[32] Paul Rivlin, "The Libyan Economy and Oil Prospects as the War Ends", *Iqtisadi—Middle East Economy*, Vol. 1, No. 6 (October 2011), 2.
[33] Anon., "IEA: Many Months to Restore Libya's Oil Output", Voice of America News, 20 October 11.
[34] Ibid.
[35] Richard Anderson, "Libya Oil: The Race to Turn the Taps Back On", BBC News, 8 September 2011.
[36] Clifford Krauss, "Spared in War, Libya's Oil Flow is Surging Back", *New York Times*, 15 November 2011.
[37] Anon., "IEA: Many Months to Restore Libya's Oil Output", Voice of America News, 20 October 2011.

struction capacity. Specifically, the transitional government has thus far been unable to effect the full reconstruction of damaged towns such as Sirte and Bani Walid—and not for lack of foreign financing, but rather construction capacity. "There aren't even enough cranes in the country to start anything near the level of construction needed," noted one Libyan consultant to the NTC. "On every level, from ability to construct, labor, the capacity of the ports, to the amount of machinery, we are not able to absorb the amount of investment we'd like to."[38]

Finally, economic development and foreign investment will be stunted by Qadhafi's legacy of endemic corruption and a sclerotic system of state-controlled businesses. A key priority for the country's new leadership, therefore, will be overturning the former regime's heavy-handed business regulations. These included foreign currency exchange limits and a law stipulating that Libyan employees had to be shareholders in private enterprises.[39] On the whole, the energy question and economic development in general will be inextricably linked to political stability and security.

Conclusion

This chapter has canvassed the key societal and political fault-lines in post-Qadhafi Libya with a view toward understanding how the absence of formal institutions is reshaping the landscape. Libya today is characterized by a high degree of paralysis among a number of regional-based political factions. The security sector is no longer defined by a static, dichotomous division between militias and society or militias and the state. Rather, militias have ingratiated themselves into civil society and, more recently, with political factions. For its part, the formal state has cooperated and co-opted with the militias, leading to the growth of fragmented security bodies, with fluid lines of authority and overlapping responsibilities.

Moving forward, the country faces a range of perils and potential setbacks. Formalizing the security sector, securing the country's borders, rebuilding the judiciary, drafting an effective constitution, and delineating the roles of federal, provincial, and municipal government are all formidable challenges.

---

[38] Quoted in Bradley Hope, "Libya Economy: Outside Investment Vital for Growth", *The National* (UAE), 27 December 2011.

[39] Margaret Coker, "Hurdles to Economic Rebuild Remain as Libya Oil Output Picks Up", *Wall Street Journal*, 11 November 2011.

Relations between the center and the periphery must be repaired. The towns, tribes, and ethnic groups that fell victim to Qadhafi's divisive patronage politics must be reconciled and brought into the new political order. Libya's non-Arab ethnic groups like the Tabu, Tuareg, and Amazigh must recover a measure of cultural autonomy and escape from the pervasive discrimination that marked the Qadhafi years.

As Libya continues its post-revolutionary journey, the powerful pull of Qadhafi's 42-year rule will be difficult to escape. The Libyan despot's personalized, hyper-centralized style of rule left the country bereft of many of the basic bureaucratic structures needed for government—to say nothing of depriving the citizenry of any sort of political participation. Diplomats and NGOs report all-too-common stories of dealing with ministries that are staffed by two or three senior officials but devoid of competent lower-level staff. Decision-making is ponderous and rarely delegated to middle or lower levels. Added to this, there is still the residual distrust of outside parties as predatory, which stems from four decades of Qadhafi's paranoid rule and the country's international isolation. The longer the institutional vacuum continues, the greater the likelihood that the country will succumb to Qadhafi-era practices and processes, spurring greater fragmentation and dimming the hopes for a truly functioning democracy.

6

STRONG ACTOR IN A WEAK STATE

THE GEOPOLITICS OF HEZBOLLAH

Shoghig Mikaelian and Bassel F. Salloukh

Since its formal independence in 1943, the Lebanese state has suffered from chronic weaknesses and diminished capacity in relation to the country's rich and vibrant confessional mosaic. Throughout its short history, multiple confessional groups, among the most notable of which have been Christian and Shi'a militias, have in fact capitalized on the weakness of the central state to push forward their own, much more narrowly defined, confessional or sectarian agendas. Depending on domestic and regional developments, the weakness and strength of the central Lebanese state have varied over time. But non-state actors of various colors and loyalties, often nurtured by powerful patrons at home and abroad, continue to remain constant features of the Lebanese political landscape.

One of the more powerful of these groups has been Hezbollah, which in the past three decades has transformed itself from a little-known, secretive security apparatus founded by Iran's Revolutionary Guards into one of the most powerful non-state domestic actors in Lebanon and a major player in regional politics. The party's geopolitical agenda also changed in parallel with this metamorphosis. Hezbollah evolved from a resistance movement preoccupied by liberating Lebanese territory from Israeli occupation to a powerful domestic political actor, yet one assuming also a central role in Iran's regional strategy and deterrence posture. After the 2006 war with Israel, Hezbollah marketed itself as Lebanon's only viable deterrence against a future Israeli military operation. By the time the Arab uprisings made their way to Syria, and the country was engulfed in a violent war between the regime and a mix of domestic rebels and external Salafi-jihadi groups, Hezbollah crossed the Lebanese–Syrian borders in support of Bashar al-Assad's besieged regime and in defense of the "axis of resistance".

Hezbollah's domestic and regional transformations transpired in the context of an institutionally weak and externally penetrated Lebanese state. The party capitalized on the state's disregard of the socioeconomic underdevelopment of Shi'a areas and its inability to liberate occupied Lebanese territory or deter future Israeli incursions into southern Lebanon. Moreover, and like other Lebanese sub-state actors, Hezbollah finds itself bandwagoning with external regional players to balance against the latter's regional and international opponents but also its own domestic adversaries. The Lebanese state often finds itself a weak and hapless bystander in this overlapping domestic–regional contest over control of the country's local politics but also its geopolitical orientation.

This chapter traces the impacts of these transformations on the party's geopolitical calculations. It opens by situating Hezbollah in the context of Lebanon's perpetually weak state structure. The chapter then unpacks Hezbollah's transformations and concomitant geopolitical considerations in four main temporal periods. The first covers the period from the party's formal birth in 1985 until the end of the Lebanese civil war in 1990–91. This is followed by an examination of the party's domestic and geopolitical positions from the onset of *Pax Syriana* in 1991 until Israel's 2000 withdrawal from Lebanon. Hezbollah's geopolitics during the period between Israel's withdrawal until the 2005 Syrian exit from Lebanon is tackled next. The chapter then turns to an analysis of the domestic and geopolitical exigencies created for the party by Syria's withdrawal from Lebanon followed by the Arab uprisings. It closes by spelling out the possible implications of regime change in Syria on Hezbollah's domestic and geopolitical agenda.

Hezbollah in Lebanon: A Non-State Actor in a Perpetually Weak State

Since its creation by the French mandatory authorities in 1920, Lebanon was born a weak state.[1] The country's historical process of state formation produced a society deeply divided along vertical cleavages, strong sectarian actors, and concomitantly weak state institutions. Joel Migdal's model of state–society relations for developing polities best captures these infrastructural features of the Lebanese political system.[2] Migdal depicts the state as one, among many other, social organizations locked in "an active struggle for social control of the population".[3] State efforts at social control through a monopoly over the stipulation of social rules governing people's social behavior are actively resisted by existing social organizations—families, clans, tribes, sects, patron–client dyads. These organizations control the available resources and manipulate the symbols that make up people's "strategies of survival", the blueprints that guide people's actions and beliefs in a conflictual social environment.[4] However, sociopolitical organizations other than the state deploy their own strategies of survival— myriad forms of sanctions, rewards, or symbols—to make people behave according to predefined rules and norms. Hezbollah is one of the most powerful such sociopolitical organizations in Lebanon, possessing not only material and symbolic capital, but also a formidable military arsenal.

The structural features of Lebanon's weak state were institutionalized in multiple pre- and postwar power-sharing formulae—namely the 1943 National Pact and the 1989 Ta'if Accord—that shielded the country's eighteen sects from state intervention, depositing in them the administration of their personal and cultural affairs. Articles 9 and 10 of the Lebanese Constitution institutionalized sectarian group autonomy; the Personal Status Law (*nizam al-ahwal al-shakhsiya*), which covers all issues relating to family, marriage, divorce, child custody, adoption, kinship, lineage, and inheritance relegated personal matters to the jurisdiction of sectarian rather than civil courts; and Decree 60 of 13 March 1936 recognized sectarian groups as cor-

---

[1] See Michael C. Hudson, *The Precarious Republic: Political Modernization in Lebanon* (Boulder, CO: Westview Press, 1985); and Fawwaz Traboulsi, *A History of Modern Lebanon* (London: Pluto Press, 2007).

[2] See Joel S. Migdal, *Strong Societies and Weak States: State–Society Relations and State Capabilities in the Third World* (Princeton, NJ: Princeton University Press, 1988).

[3] Joel S. Migdal, "A Model of State–Society Relations", in Howard J. Wiarda, ed., *New Directions in Comparative Politics* (Boulder, CO: Westview Press, 1985), 48.

[4] Migdal, *Strong Societies and Weak States*, 27.

porate entities.[5] In many respects, then, almost all of Lebanon's sects are invariably strong communal actors in an otherwise institutionally weak state. They possess their own peculiar "visions of Lebanon",[6] their own social service institutions and clientelist networks financed either by state resources, private, and/ or foreign funding,[7] and their own external, regional, and international patrons. With the exception of the interventionist Shihabist administration (1958–70), all other Lebanese administrations respected the prerogatives and autonomy of the different sectarian actors.[8] This combination of an institutionally weak but centralized state and powerful sectarian actors with foreign patrons and sophisticated domestic clientelist networks empowers sub-state actors, obviates the possibility for the emergence of any semblance of rule of law, and exposes the country to external manipulations and geopolitical agendas.

In this respect, Hezbollah's uniqueness is a function of its elaborate security and military apparatuses.[9] Hezbollah's military and security capabilities far exceed those of any other sub-state actor, and are significantly more advanced in a number of sectors than those of the Lebanese Armed Forces (LAF). Its weapons arsenal includes conventional guerrilla warfare arms but also short-, medium-, and long-range rockets and missiles and any number of mortars, anti-tank weapons, anti-aircraft and short-range surface-to-air missiles, anti-

[5] See Suad Joseph, "Civic Myths, Citizenship, and Gender in Lebanon", in Suad Joseph, ed., *Gender and Citizenship in the Middle East* (Syracuse, NY: Syracuse University Press, 2000), 107–36; Marie Rose Zalzal, *Al-Nizam al-Qanuni lil-Tawa'ef wal-Hayat al-Monbathiqa 'Anha* (Beirut: CRTDA and IDRC, 2009); and Max Weiss, *In the Shadow of Sectarianism: Law, Shi'ism, and the Making of Modern Lebanon* (Cambridge, MA: Harvard University Press, 2010).

[6] See Albert Hourani, "Visions of Lebanon", in Halim Barakat, ed., *Toward a Viable Lebanon* (Washington, DC: Georgetown University Press, 1988), 3–11.

[7] See Melani Cammett and Sukriti Issar, "Bricks and Mortar Clientelism: Sectarianism and the Logics of Welfare Allocation in Lebanon", *World Politics*, 62 (2010), 381–421; and Nisreen Salti and Jad Chaaban, "The Role of Sectarianism in the Allocation of Public Expenditures in Postwar Lebanon", *International Journal of Middle East Studies*, 42 (2010), 637–55.

[8] See Michael C. Hudson, "The Problem of Authoritative Power in Lebanese Politics: Why Consociationalism Failed", in Nadim Shehadi and Danna Haffar Mills, eds., *Lebanon: A History of Conflict and Consensus* (London: I. B. Tauris, 1988), 225–39.

[9] For an overview, see Nicholas Blanford, *Warriors of God: Inside Hezbollah's Thirty-Year Struggle Against Israel* (New York: Random House, 2011); and Anthony H. Cordesman, *The Lessons of the Israel–Hezbollah War: A Briefing* (Washington: Center for Strategic and International Studies, 2008).

ship missiles, and unmanned aerial vehicles (UAVs) that serve the party's asymmetrical warfare strategy against Israel.[10] Its clandestine security apparatus is infamous for its stealth, immunity to enemy penetration, and effectiveness.[11] It operates both inside and outside Lebanon. The latter branch is accused of staging a number of attacks against Jewish targets, most recently against Israeli tourists in Burgas, Bulgaria on 18 July 2012.[12]

The party has also created a complex corporatist institutional structure that penetrates Shi'a communities in the south, the Ba'albak-Hermel region in the Beqa', and Beirut's southern suburbs.[13] An archipelago of institutions and social units was created to offer an array of socioeconomic services—ranging from the reconstruction of houses destroyed in multiple wars with Israel, the provision of financial support and social services to the families of injured and "martyred" Hezbollah fighters, the provision of health and educational services to the public, and the production of non-material, symbolic capital targeted at the party's constituency—in an effort to mobilize and bind large sections of the Shi'a community to the party.[14] This combination of a powerful military–security complex and a complicated corporatist structure in the context of an otherwise institutionally and coercively weak state rendered Hezbollah a very strong non-state actor with domestic as well as regional reach.

---

[10] See Aram Nerguizian, "U.S.–Iranian Competition in the Levant, Part I: Competing Strategic Interests and the Military and Asymmetric Dimensions of Regional Instability", Center for Strategic and International Studies, January 2013, at http://csis.org/files/publication/121212_Iran_VIII_Levant_report_Part_1.pdf

[11] See Carl Wege, "The Hizballah Security Apparatus", *Perspectives on Terrorism* 2 (2008), at http://terrorismanalysts.com/pt/index.php/pot/article/view/42/html

[12] See Benjamin Weinthal, "Bulgaria Names Hezbollah Suspects Behind Bombing of Israeli Bus in Burgas", *Jerusalem Post*, 25 July 2013, at http://www.jpost.com/International/Bulgaria-names-2-suspects-in-Burgas-bus-bombing-321017

[13] See A. Nizar Hamzeh, *In the Path of Hizbullah* (Syracuse: Syracuse University Press, 2004), 44–79; and Judith Palmer Harik, *Hezbollah: The Changing Face of Terrorism* (London: I. B. Tauris, 2004), 81–94.

[14] See Catherine Le Thomas, "Socialization Agencies and Party Dynamics: Functions and Uses of Hizballah Schools in Lebanon", in Myriam Catusse and Karam Karam, eds., *Returning to Political Parties? Partisan Logic and Political Transformations in the Arab World* (Beirut: Lebanese Center for Policy Studies, 2010), 217–49; and Roschanack Shaery-Eisenlohr, *Shi'ite Lebanon: Transnational Religion and the Making of National Identities* (New York: Columbia University Press, 2008).

The Geopolitics of Hezbollah

Hezbollah's geopolitical calculations have passed through a number of phases mirroring transformations within the party, Lebanon, and the wider region. The main constant throughout these phases is the weakness of the Lebanese state. Once an ideological–political–security apparatus created by the Iranian regime during the revolution's export phase, Hezbollah later transformed itself into a national liberation movement in the 1990s, preoccupied by resisting Israel's occupation of south Lebanon, to an elite advanced commando unit in the Iranian–US confrontation after Israel's withdrawal from Lebanon in 2000, to a self-described deterrence force against Israel after the military successes of the 2006 war.[15]

Yet the party that one day was celebrated as a pan-Islamist resistance movement that expelled Israel from Lebanon finds itself after the Arab uprisings mired in sectarian accusations because of its involvement in the Syrian civil war. These transformations in Hezbollah's geopolitical roles parallel similar ones in its domestic incarnations. The party has gone from being a shadowy organization to a national hero after the 2000 liberation, back to being a pariah after the sectarian battles following the February 2005 assassination of the late Prime Minister Rafiq al-Hariri. More significantly, and after shunning the formal political arena, Hezbollah took a strategic decision after the end of the civil war to participate in parliamentary and municipal elections, and then, following Hariri's assassination, to enter cabinet.

While Lebanon was and remains a weak state since its founding, it has nevertheless undergone several transformations—in no small part linked to regional developments—that have largely shaped Hezbollah's responses and policies. Different periods presented a different set of challenges and opportunities, and provided Hezbollah with a different set of tools and resources to respond to them. It is therefore necessary to examine each of these periods and the manner in which domestic and regional developments and their position and strength vis-à-vis domestic and regional actors have shaped the party's actions. This strategy controls for several factors such as domestic dynamics and distribution of power during a specific period, and allows for diachronic comparisons.

---

[15] See Jihad al-Zayn, "Qira'a la Munaqasha li-'Hizbullah' Muwathiqan", *al-Nahar*, 3 December 2009.

From the Party's Birth until the End of the Civil War (1982–91)

Geopolitics was an organic part of Hezbollah's birth and later transformation. The party's explosion into Lebanon's domestic political scene with the promulgation on 16 February 1985 of its first public communiqué, the so-called "Open Letter to the Downtrodden in Lebanon and the World", was itself a consequence of changing geopolitical dynamics.[16]

Israel's 1982 invasion of Lebanon created a new balance of power in the country and the region. The decision by Nabih Berri, leader of the Shi'a Amal Movement, to join a National Salvation Committee formed by President Elyas Sarkis in the wake of the invasion triggered a split within the party. Cadres gathered around Hussein al-Musawi condemned Berri's move, considered it akin to recognition of Israel, an Iranian taboo, and subsequently broke away from Amal and established their own Islamic Amal (*Amal al-Islamiya*). This schism within Amal overlapped with Tehran's decision, part of an Iranian–Syrian concerted effort to thwart US plans in the region, to send in June 1982 some 1,000 Iranian Revolutionary Guards troops to Ba'albak via Syria to provide military training and religious indoctrination to an ever-growing group of Amal defectors who espoused the concept of *wilayat al-faqih* (guardianship of the jurisconsult). Syria blessed Iran's move into Lebanon, partly because it was geopolitically weak and to counterbalance attempts by Berri's Amal Movement to improve relations with Washington.[17]

Hezbollah would later coalesce as the merger of Islamic Amal with other Islamist Shi'a groups, namely the Lebanese branch of the Da'wah Party, the Islamic Revolutionary Committees (*al-Lijan al-Thawriya al-Islamiya*), the Muslim Youth (*al-Shabab al-Muslem*), and the Lebanese Union of Muslim Students (*al-Ittihad al-Lunbani lil-Talaba al-Muslemin*). It focused primarily on resisting Israel's occupation in south Lebanon, undertaking a number of spectacular suicide attacks against the IDF (Israel Defense Forces) without however claiming responsibility for them. For example, only in 1985, after the Israeli forces had withdrawn to a 9-mile wide security zone along the border, did Hezbollah disclose the identity of one of its cadres: Ahmad

---

[16] For a detailed analysis, see Bassel F. Salloukh and Shoghig Mikaelian, "Hizbullah in Lebanon", in John L. Esposito and Emad Shahin, eds., *The Oxford Handbook of Islam and Politics* (Oxford: Oxford University Press, forthcoming).

[17] See Augustus Richard Norton, "Lebanon: The Internal Conflict and the Iranian Connection", in John L. Esposito, ed., *The Iranian Revolution: Its Global Impact* (Miami: Florida International University Press, 1990), 132.

Qassir, the perpetrator of the 1983 suicide attack against the headquarters of the Israeli Military Governor in Tyre.[18]

Domestically, the party remained aloof from the then raging civil war, opting to make public its political opinion, for example its opposition to the US-brokered Lebanese–Israeli 17 May 1983 treaty, through popular demonstrations in Beirut's southern suburbs under the mantle of its then ideologue Sayyed Mohammad Husayn Fadlallah. Hezbollah is accused, however, of undertaking in this phase—albeit under the shadowy label of the Islamic Jihad Organization—a number of terrorist attacks against Western targets, most notoriously the 1983 suicide attacks against the US Embassy in Beirut and the US Marine and French contingents of the multinational forces, the 1985 hijacking of the TWA airliner, as well as the kidnapping of a number of Westerners in Beirut, all of which were masterminded by Imad Mughniyeh.[19] During this period, when the Lebanese state lost any semblance of control and institutional autonomy, Hezbollah followed Iran's geopolitical script as the latter sought to create a foothold in Lebanon, even when this brought it into direct confrontation with Syria's interests and its Lebanese allies, namely Amal.[20] For example, to the dismay of the Amal leadership, a number of hijackings were traced directly to orders from Tehran.[21] Nor did Hezbollah participate in the bloody War of the Camps between Amal and Fateh (1985–December 1987); it rather opted to serve as a buffer between Amal's fighters and those of Fateh in the environs of Sidon.

Damascus began clipping Hezbollah's influence after 1984, once it succeeded in defeating a US–Israeli attempt to snatch Lebanon away from its sphere of influence.[22] Amal–Hezbollah competition in Beirut's southern suburbs and in the south reflected both local but also proxy Syrian–Iranian turf wars. One of the first violent acts Syrian troops undertook when they re-entered West Beirut in February 1987, after weeks of fighting between its own putative allies, Amal and the Druze Progressive Socialist Party, was a massacre against some eighteen Hezbollah cadres in the party's headquarters

[18] See Blanford, *Warriors of God*.
[19] See Mark Perry, "The Driver", *Foreign Policy*, 29 April 2013, at http://www.foreignpolicy.com/articles/2013/04/29/the_driver; and Norton, "Lebanon".
[20] See the excellent discussion of this period in Norton, "Lebanon".
[21] See ibid., 129.
[22] See Patrick Seale, *Asad of Syria: The Struggle for the Middle East* (Berkeley, CA: University of California Press, 1988), 394–420.

at the Fathalla barracks.[23] The February 1988 kidnapping of US Marine Lieutenant Colonel William Higgins, then on duty with the UN contingent in south Lebanon, finally triggered an Amal assault on Hezbollah in the south, to which the latter responded by overrunning Amal's positions in Beirut's southern suburbs.[24] The gruesome war ended only after Syria and Iran succeeded in negotiating an agreement that delineated new spheres of influence for their respective allies. Nevertheless, Hezbollah–Amal skirmishes continued for some time, and when the US, Saudi Arabia, and Syria pushed through a new power-sharing agreement to end the Lebanese civil war, the Ta'if Accord, Amal accepted it with reservations. Hezbollah categorically rejected the accord, however. After all, it collided with the party's objective of an Islamic state in Lebanon and its rejection of the pre-war and wartime Lebanese state as an unjust one,[25] but also because the accord ran counter to Iran's regional interests.[26]

Hezbollah's relation with Damascus improved only after Iraq's invasion of Kuwait in the summer of 1990 created new geopolitical exigencies. Washington was determined to include Syria in a US-led coalition gathered to expel Iraq from Kuwait.[27] Hafez al-Assad agreed but only in exchange for a free hand in Lebanon. The long era of *Pax Syriana* had commenced, albeit in coordination with Washington and Riyadh. Consequently, Iran deferred its Lebanon policy to Syria, and Hezbollah's resistance against Israel was now a function of its own raison d'être but also part of a coordinated strategy to serve Syria's foreign policy choices vis-à-vis the Arab–Israeli conflict.

From Pax Syriana to Israel's Withdrawal (1991–2000)

Hezbollah's shunning of the domestic political scene and the Lebanese political system in the 1980s was replaced by a willingness, post-Ta'if, to take part in the political system. Nonetheless, suspicions regarding Hezbollah's vision for Lebanon and its political system were rife. Its aforementioned views on the

---

[23] See As'ad AbuKhalil, "Syria and the Shiites: Al-Asad's Policy in Lebanon", *Third World Quarterly*, 12 (1990), 1–20.

[24] See Norton, "Lebanon", 130–33; and Robert Fisk, *Pity the Nation: Lebanon at War* (Oxford: Oxford University Press, 1990), 584–627.

[25] Augustus Richard Norton, *Hizballah of Lebanon: Extremist Ideals vs. Mundane Politics* (New York: Council on Foreign Relations, 1999), 14.

[26] See Norton, "Lebanon", 135.

[27] See James A. Baker, III, *The Politics of Diplomacy: Revolution, War and Peace, 1989–1992* (New York: G. P. Putnam's Sons, 1995), especially 295.

Lebanese political system and its leaders' subscription to the idea of the *wilayat al-faqih* rendered it the target of accusations of loyalty to a foreign state—in this case Iran—rather than to Lebanon.[28] With the signing of the Ta'if Accord which put an end to the fifteen-year civil war in Lebanon, and the cementing of Syria's position in Lebanon, Hezbollah found itself compelled to accept the legitimacy of the postwar political order, and to move gradually towards participation.

Domestic and regional changes in the early 1990s created an unfavorable atmosphere for the violent pursuit of Hezbollah's domestic agenda. Hafez al-Assad's attempts to gain control over Lebanon and his success in doing so meant that elements of Hezbollah's political agenda—those that did not pertain to the armed resistance to Israeli occupation—would now clash head-on with Syria's geopolitical interests in Lebanon. As such, despite the mere revamping of the Lebanese confessional system, Hezbollah accepted the new order as cemented by the Ta'if Accord, and adopted a policy of cooperation with Syria.[29] Concomitantly, it reached out to other segments of Lebanese society to build a broader support base.[30] From then on, Hezbollah sought recognition as a legal political party and a resistance movement against the Israeli occupation in the south.

To what extent Hezbollah's shift to a pragmatic position was due to domestic constraints alone is a matter of debate. Thus, for example, Nizar Hamzeh argues that the party's gradual pragmatism was largely linked to Iranian pragmatism in the wake of Ayatollah Khomeini's death in 1989.[31] Nonetheless, even if Iran had not adopted a pragmatic agenda, it is questionable to what extent Hezbollah could have sustained non-pragmatism, considering Syria's direct control over Lebanon and the inability of Iran to provide arms and logistical support to the party. These logistical limitations therefore arguably account, at least in part, for Hezbollah's acceptance of a system that was in direct opposition to its ideological predilections. This postwar policy shift highlights how both the structural weakness of the Lebanese state and regional developments shape Hezbollah's choices, and how both domestic and external actors abuse the weakness of the Lebanese state to pursue their own

[28] See Amal Saad-Ghorayeb, *Hizbu'llah: Politics and Religion* (London: Pluto Press, 2002).
[29] See Hamzeh, *In the Path of Hizbullah*, 109.
[30] See Norton, *Hizballah of Lebanon*, 34.
[31] See Hamzeh, *In the Path of Hezbollah*, 109.

local and geopolitical agendas. This, in turn, perpetuates the state's weakness and penetration.

With the demobilization and demilitarization of all wartime militias, Hezbollah stood out as the only major armed group from the civil war period to receive official endorsement to maintain its weapons arsenal.[32] This not only underscored the party's importance in Syrian calculations, but also the weakness of the postwar state—under Syrian tutelage—and the inability or unwillingness of other actors to challenge this status quo. Moreover, it also underscored the importance, in Hezbollah's calculations, of liberating south Lebanon from the Israeli occupation. With Assad's and Hezbollah's objectives coinciding on the question of armed struggle against the Israeli occupation of southern Lebanon, Hezbollah's continuity as an armed group and a relevant political actor in postwar Lebanon was guaranteed. Nonetheless, this did not mean that Hezbollah did not find itself walking a political tightrope. Relations between it and Syria hardly suggested ideological and political agreement, but rather an alliance born of necessity; in the 1990s, Syria sought to limit the party's electoral clout by engineering, in some cases, a cross-confessional electoral alliance against it.[33]

Hezbollah's participation in the 1992 elections—the first since the end of the civil war—yielded significant results. The party captured eight out of twenty-seven seats allocated to the Shi'a. With its increased electoral weight and the widening of popular support for it, Hezbollah demanded an increase in the number of its own candidates on the Hezbollah–Amal coalition list for south Lebanon. Amal's rejection of this demand threatened to undo the coalition, an eventuality that greatly concerned Hafez al-Assad. As a result, leaders of both parties were summoned to Damascus. Amal was forced to accede to Hezbollah's demands, thanks to Syrian weakness in the wake of Operation Grapes of Wrath and the collapse of Syrian–Israeli negotiations, and al-Assad's fear that pressuring Hezbollah would damage the much-valued relationship with Iran.[34] In this manner, Hezbollah utilized regional realities to achieve gains at the expense of its domestic political rivals, as well as to secure virtually

---

[32] See Traboulsi, *A History of Modern Lebanon*, 230.

[33] See Bassel F. Salloukh, "The Limits of Electoral Engineering in Divided Societies: Elections in Postwar Lebanon", *Canadian Journal of Political Science*, 39 (September 2006), 635–55.

[34] See Hamzeh, *In the Path of Hizbullah*, 114–15; and Nqoula Nasif and Rousana Boumonsef, *Al-Masrah Wal-Kawalis: Intikhabat 96 fi Fusuliha* (Beirut: Dar al-Nahar lil-Nashr, 1996).

unhindered access to occupied south Lebanon in pursuit of its resistance activities. Concomitantly, it entered into cross-ideological and cross-sectarian electoral alliances with the aim of strengthening its domestic influence and ensuring the continuation of its armed activities and its monopoly over resistance to the Israeli occupation.[35]

Hezbollah's resistance activities coincided with Syria's geopolitical interests and foreign policy in a post-Madrid Conference regional environment. Both parties placed this new relationship at the service of their own interests. Indeed, Syria considered the party as an appropriate conduit to exert pressure on Israel to liberate the Golan Heights. It is therefore not surprising that rather than putting an end to violence in South Lebanon, the end of the civil war heralded an era of increased military operations by Hezbollah against Israeli armed forces and Israel's proxies in South Lebanon.[36] The assassination of Sayyed Abbas al-Mussawi and the subsequent election of Sayyed Hassan Nasrallah to the position of Secretary General marked the beginning of a new chapter in Hezbollah's resistance activities. The most important change came in the form of, as Sheikh Na'im Qassem puts it, a strategy of rocket attacks against northern Israel in response to the targeting of Lebanese civilians, cities, villages, or civilian infrastructure by Israel, which amounted, in the words of Simon Murden, to a "policy of retaliation" rather than a "policy of resistance".[37] The decision was significant: it signaled the adoption of a new strategic outlook that aimed at creating parity between Israeli and Lebanese civilians. The cumulative effect of tit-for-tat rocket attacks would, it was hoped, create a "balance of terror", which in turn would serve as deterrence

---

[35] See Ahmad Nizar Hamzeh, "Lebanon's Hizbullah: From Islamic Revolution to Parliamentary Accommodation", *Third World Quarterly*, 14 (1993), 321–37; Hamzeh, *In the Path of Hizbullah*; and Salloukh, "The Limits of Electoral Engineering in Divided Societies".

[36] Immediately following the assassination of Sayyed Abbas al-Mussawi, Israeli officials were quick to point out that over the course of a year and a half prior to the appointment of al-Mussawi as Secretary General of Hezbollah, only sixteen attacks had been recorded against the Israel Defense Forces (IDF) and the South Lebanon Army (SLA) resulting in the death of two soldiers. By contrast, in the five months following his appointment, the number had jumped to fifty-one attacks and ten fatalities. See Chris Hedges, "Killing of Sheik: Israel Waited for Months", *New York Times*, 22 February 1992, 1.

[37] Simon Murden, "Understanding Israel's Long Conflict in Lebanon: The Search for an Alternative Approach to Security during the Peace Process", *British Journal of Middle Eastern Studies*, 27 (May 2000), 37.

against Israel, preventing the latter from carrying out further attacks against Lebanese civilians and civilian targets, thereby keeping the struggle in the military realm where Hezbollah—despite being inferior in terms of capabilities, manpower, and resources—had an edge owing both to its nature as a guerilla force and to a terrain well-suited to the type of struggle it was conducting. The weak Lebanese state was absent from this strategic equation, however. Hezbollah assumed for itself a task that should have otherwise fallen to the Lebanese state: liberating occupied Lebanese lands and deterring future Israeli attacks against Lebanese civilians.

Nevertheless, Hezbollah's unrelenting quest for the establishment of a "balance of terror" as an alternative to an unattainable symmetry of power and its intensification of attacks in the "security zone" set the stage for an escalation of unprecedented scale. Yet while Hezbollah sought to portray itself as a national liberation movement, in stark contrast to its image as an extremist group during the early days of its existence, it was nevertheless accused of orchestrating several attacks on non-military targets, most notably the March 1992 attack on Israel's embassy in Argentina and the July 1994 AMIA building bombing in Buenos Aires, both of which were alleged to have been planned by Imad Mughniyeh, the party's security and military mastermind.[38]

On 25 July 1993, Israel launched Operation Accountability in response to month-long attacks against its soldiers. It commenced in the form of air strikes against Lebanese villages and towns as well as civilian infrastructure. Aware of Hezbollah's goal of establishing symmetry between the targeting of Israeli and Lebanese civilians and civilian infrastructure, and keen on preventing a change in the rules of the game, Yitzhak Rabin and his government opted to unleash massive firepower on more than seventy villages in south Lebanon, causing a flood of refugees fleeing northward towards Beirut. In fact, Israel made no secret of the deliberate targeting of villages and the rationale behind it. Shortly after Israel began its attacks, Rabin "vowed to flood Beirut with displaced people until the Lebanese and Syrian governments intervened to rein in the ... guerilla forces".[39] Hezbollah remained defiant in the face of the Israeli campaign, insisting that it would halt its rocket attacks only if and when Israel ended its shelling of Lebanese villages, civilians, and infrastructure, an offer that Israel dismissed. Israel's refusal, however, did not fundamentally alter the

---

[38] See Perry, "The Driver".

[39] Chris Hedges, "U.S. Brokers Truce to Halt Fighting in South Lebanon", *New York Times*, 1 August 1993, 12.

outcome of the confrontation. After seven days of continuous bombardment and perennial rocket fire, a ceasefire based on an oral "understanding" put an end to the fighting on 31 July 1993. Operation Accountability demonstrated clearly the limits of military power in the face of a well-equipped and well-trained armed non-state actor operating with the blessing of a third party state. This denouement underscored yet again the relative weakness of the Lebanese state's diplomatic and military capabilities: Damascus assumed the role of the negotiator while Hezbollah, and not the grossly under-equipped LAF, maintained a continuous rocket barrage against Israel.

This reality was cemented in 1996 with Israel's Operation Grapes of Wrath. The ceasefire agreement—which came in the wake of a massacre of civilians in the village of Qana—was an historic "understanding" that would, in the words of the current Israeli Minister of Domestic Security Avigdor Kahalani, effectively turn IDF soldiers into "sitting ducks" for Hezbollah attacks.[40] In this manner, Operation Grapes of Wrath was a decisive turning point in Hezbollah's decade-long struggle for the liberation of south Lebanon. The 1996 understanding marked the beginning of the end of the Israeli occupation of south Lebanon. It set the stage for a radical increase in attacks in the security zone. This, along with domestic political considerations within Israel, convinced the Israeli leadership of the futility of holding on to the security zone. With Ehud Barak basing much of his (successful) electoral campaign on the promise of a withdrawal from south Lebanon, Hezbollah found it opportune to increase its resistance activities.[41] With the severe demoralization of the SLA, Israel was forced into making a swift departure from Lebanon, which dealt a severe blow to its prestige, and provided a massive boost to Hezbollah's image and position both in Lebanon and in the Arab world.

In the Eye of the Regional Storm (2000–2005)

With the end of the Israeli occupation, and the international recognition that Israel had satisfied the requirements of UN Security Council Resolution 425, Hezbollah sought a justification that would give its weapons a new lease of life. The need to preserve Hezbollah's status as an armed group was recognized by both Hafez al-Assad and Bashar al-Assad, who saw in the end of the Israeli

[40] Avraham Sela, "Civil Society, the Military, and National Security: The Case of Israel's Security Zone in South Lebanon", *Israel Studies*, 12 (Spring 2007), 67.
[41] See Dalia Dassa Kaye, "The Israeli Decision to Withdraw from Southern Lebanon: Political Leadership and Security Policy", *Political Science Quarterly*, 117 (Winter 2002–3), 561–86.

occupation of south Lebanon the retraction of a trump card for the return of the Golan Heights. Given Syria's hegemony in Lebanon, Hezbollah could easily acquire official blessings to maintain its weapons arsenal. This was also aided by the party's popularity in Lebanon—especially within the Shi'ite community—and in the region as a whole. This is not to say, however, that there existed no domestic resentment over, or opposition to, this new arrangement. As such, in order to justify the need to keep its weapons arsenal, Hezbollah and Syria insisted that the total liberation of Lebanon had not been achieved due to the continued presence of Israeli forces in the Shebaa Farms.[42] This was supplemented by the demand for the release of Lebanese prisoners who remained in Israeli jails as well as the return of remains of dead fighters. Additionally, not long after the Israeli withdrawal, Nasrallah stated that "[a]s long as Israel threatens Lebanon every day with air strikes, attacks, and punishment, Lebanon has the right to maintain all elements of strength that can confront these Israeli threats".[43] The new modus operandi served both Hezbollah and Syria's interests. For Hezbollah, it justified its weapons arsenal. For Damascus, however, Hezbollah's operations in the Shebaa Farms were a convenient reminder of Syria's indispensable role in any prospective negotiations for the settlement of the Arab–Israeli conflict. In sum, a combination of a weak state and Syria's geopolitical calculations permitted Hezbollah to impose its own non-state agenda on postwar Lebanon.

Notwithstanding Israeli warnings about the dire consequences of any attack launched from Lebanese territory following its withdrawal, the first test of Israeli determination to retaliate came not long thereafter—in October 2000—in the form of a Hezbollah attack in the Shebaa Farms, which resulted in the capture of three Israeli soldiers. While Hezbollah continued its operations against Israel, these were relatively minor, and were concentrated on the Shebaa Farms. At first, Israel did not respond forcefully given its reluctance both to open a second front and to "broadcast to the public that its unilateral withdrawal from Lebanon had resulted in an escalation of violence on the northern border".[44] A change in policy soon came into effect with the election of Ariel Sharon as Prime Minister, however.

---

[42] See Asher Kaufman, "Who Owns the Shebaa Farms? Chronicle of a Territorial Dispute", *Middle East Journal*, 56 (Autumn 2002), 577.

[43] Steven N. Simon and Jonathan Stevenson, "Declawing the 'Party of God': Toward Normalization in Lebanon", *World Policy Journal*, 18 (Summer 2001), 33.

[44] Amos Harel and Avi Issacharoff, *34 Days: Israel, Hezbollah, and the War in Lebanon* (New York: Palgrave Macmillan, 2008), 40.

On two occasions, following attacks on IDF posts in the Shebaaa Farms, the IDF responded by targeting Syrian radar stations in Lebanon, refraining from targeting Lebanese infrastructure. If Hezbollah had successfully deterred Israel, it had paradoxically done so at Syria's expense. While the initial Israeli counter-attack did not elicit a response from Hezbollah, the second one did. The explicit message behind the Hezbollah response was that it would not accept a change in the rules of engagement between it and Israel in the Shebaa Farms. The two sides therefore reverted to a strategy of containment. This strategy was tested once more in 2002, at the height of Israel's Operation Defensive Shield. Having again sensed that Israel's preoccupation with military action in the Occupied Palestinian Territories would prevent it from opening a second front in response to relatively minor incidents on the Lebanese–Israeli border and in the Shebaa Farms, and feeling the need for a show of solidarity with the Palestinians, Hezbollah escalated its attacks on the Shebaa Farms.[45]

While Syrian influence in Lebanon and the intersection of Syrian and Hezbollah strategic interests guaranteed Hezbollah's continued access to arms, both Hezbollah and Syria were now under increased international and domestic scrutiny over their behavior: the continuation of the former's status as a state-sanctioned armed group, and the latter's continued presence in Lebanon. Domestically, Hezbollah's position on the Shebaa Farms was considered—especially by Christians—a pretext to maintain its arms.[46] These critics argued that Hezbollah's weapons arsenal was merely deployed at the service of Syria's and Iran's regional and geopolitical ambitions.[47] Simultaneously, starting in the middle 1990s and continuing into the 2000s, both Hafez and Bashar al-Assad restructured Lebanese state institutions and consolidated Damascus's control over the Lebanese security apparatus. These policies, however, could not stem the growing domestic opposition to Syria's presence in Lebanon, one that reached new heights after the May 2000 Israeli withdrawal from Lebanon.[48]

[45] See Nicholas Blanford, "Fears of a Second Front: The Lebanese–Israeli Border", *Middle East Report*, 223 (Summer 2002).
[46] See Rola El Husseini, "Hezbollah and the Axis of Refusal: Hamas, Iran and Syria", *Third World Quarterly*, 31 (2010), 808.
[47] See Bassel F. Salloukh, "Syria and Lebanon: A Brotherhood Transformed", *Middle East Report*, 236 (Fall 2005), 14–21.
[48] For a more detailed discussion, see Bassel F. Salloukh, "Remaking Lebanon after Syria: The Rise and Fall of Proxy Authoritarianism", in Holger Albrecht, ed., *Contentious Politics in the Middle East and North Africa* (University Press of Florida, 2010), 205–28.

In addition to these domestic pressures, there was growing pressure emanating from the United States and Europe on Syria, to force it to end its decades-long occupation of Lebanon. Following the US invasion of Iraq and overthrow of Saddam Hussein, neo-conservatives within the Bush administration aimed for Bashar al-Assad's regime, as part of a broader strategy of re-ordering the geopolitics of the Middle East.[49] Both the Syria Accountability and Lebanese Sovereignty Restoration Act of 12 April 2003 and UN Security Council Resolution 1559 of 2 September 2004 reflected the convergence of US and European—especially French—interest in the rollback of Syrian troops from Lebanon and the termination of Hezbollah's status as an armed group. These growing Lebanese and non-Lebanese pressures on Bashar al-Assad's regime transformed the relationship between Hezbollah and Syria. While in the past the latter had assumed leadership of the relation, after 2000 (but especially after 2004) the two acted as rough equals in pursuit of their mutual interests.[50] The dilemmas facing the party grew increasingly complex and perilous. In the light of these domestic and regional challenges, the party largely refrained from opening a "hot" battlefront on Lebanon's borders with Israel, all the while preparing for that eventuality. In many ways, then, Hezbollah's partnership with Syria in the post-2000 political upheavals defies the dominant characterization of armed non-state actors in the scholarly literature as mere proxy militias that always pursue the policies—and adhere to the orders—of supporting states.

Post-Syria Lebanon and the Arab Spring

The Hariri assassination on 14 February 2005, and Syria's concomitant withdrawal from Lebanon on 26 April 2005, unleashed an intense domestic and regional struggle over post-Syria Lebanon.[51] Lebanese politics fractured into two binary domestic political blocs: the 14 and 8 March alliances. Despite attempts to represent the conflict as a political–ideological one, involving disagreements over different visions of Lebanon's domestic and foreign poli-

---

[49] See John J. Mearsheimer and Stephen M. Walt, *The Israel Lobby and U.S. Foreign Policy*, John F. Kennedy School of Government, Faculty Research Working Paper Series, RWP06–011, March 2006, 37–8.

[50] See Blanford, *Warriors of God*, 312.

[51] For a detailed analysis, see Bassel F. Salloukh, "Democracy in Lebanon: The Primacy of the Sectarian System", in Nathan Brown and Emad El-Din Shahin, eds., *The Struggle over Democracy in the Middle East* (London: Routledge, 2009), 134–50.

tics, it was rather a crude Sunni–Shiʿa sectarian power struggle over who rules the post-Syria Lebanese state and in which regional camp will this state be located. This domestic clash overlapped with a wider regional geopolitical contest pitting Iran and Syria and allied non-state actors, namely Hezbollah, Islamic Jihad, and Hamas, against the United States and Saudi Arabia and their allies among the so-called 'moderate' Arab states, namely Egypt, Jordan, the UAE, and Tunisia. Unleashed on the morrow of the US invasion and subsequent occupation of Iraq, this geopolitical contest was played out in post-Syria Lebanon, but also in Iraq, the West Bank and Gaza Strip, and, to a lesser extent, Yemen and Bahrain.[52]

This overlapping domestic–external contest over post-Syria Lebanon further weakened state institutions, dividing them into sectarian fiefdoms organized along clientelist loyalties. It also exposed the country to penetration by a host of external actors each vying to relocate Lebanon to its own geopolitical camp. Rather than straining the relationship between Hezbollah and Damascus, these overlapping domestic and external pressures fortified it. The partnership between the two reached a point whereby Damascus outsourced its Lebanon policy to Hezbollah.[53] Instead of reducing Hezbollah's clout in Lebanese and regional politics, the concerted efforts on the part of Western states and their Lebanese allies after the Hariri assassination had the opposite effect. This was in no small part due to the weakness of the Lebanese state, Hezbollah's material and institutional resources and its substantial domestic support base, its enormous military experience, and its strategic regional role.

The shift in the party's domestic and geopolitical environments obliged Hezbollah to assume a direct role in managing post-Syria Lebanon's political arena.[54] Hitherto Hezbollah had reserved for itself a substantial parliamentary block without however claiming a share of the Shiʿa sectarian quota in state institutions, a privilege otherwise monopolized by Damascus and Berri's Amal movement. Instead, Hezbollah dedicated its military and security efforts to preparing for the next war against Israel. The seismic tremors unleashed by the Hariri assassination invited a new domestic role for the party, however.

Hezbollah consequently decided to participate in Fuʾad al-Saniora's cabinet formed on 19 July 2005. Henceforth the party tiptoed across Lebanon's sec-

---

[52] See Bassel F. Salloukh, "The Arab Uprisings and the Geopolitics of the Middle East", *International Spectator*, 48 (2013), 32–46.

[53] See Bassel F. Salloukh, "Demystifying Syrian Foreign Policy under Bashar", in Fred Lawson, ed., *Demystifying Syria* (London: Saqi Books, 2009), 159–79.

[54] For a detailed account see Salloukh, "Democracy in Lebanon".

tarian minefield, and in the process it lost much of its allure as a resistance movement as it found itself marred in sectarian squabbles. The overlapping domestic–external contest over post-Syria Lebanon brought Hezbollah—backed by Iran and Syria—into a collision course with Sa'd al-Hariri's Future Movement, supported by the US and Saudi Arabia. The two camps battled over a new electoral law; the implementation of UNSCR 1559 of 2 September 2004 mandating the "disbanding and disarmament of all Lebanese and non-Lebanese militias", in reference to Hezbollah's weapons arsenal; the preroga-tives of the international tribunal created to investigate Hariri's assassination; the implications of UNSCR 1701 of 11 August 2006 which ended the 2006 summer war between Israel and Hezbollah on the latter's weapons arsenal and the state's defensive policy vis-à-vis Israel; and the constitutional modalities shaping the next presidential elections. This sectarian contest brought the country, on multiple occasions, to the brink of an irreversible sectarian war, Hezbollah's nightmare scenario. The confrontation climaxed in May 2008, when Hezbollah and Berri's Amal Movement undertook a lightening military operation, occupying West Beirut and decimating the Future Movement's skeletal military structure. Albeit the Qatari-negotiated 21 May 2008 Doha Accord resolved the political stand-off between the two camps, it nevertheless was unable to heal the sectarian scar created by Hezbollah's military takeover of West Beirut. Hezbollah also faced the challenge of managing the geopoliti-cal implications of post-Syria Lebanon.

In the aftermath of the July–August 2006 war against Israel, Hezbollah rebranded the strategic utility of its weapons arsenal for Lebanon's security and hence its own geopolitical utility. Its peculiar form of hybrid warfare, blending a disciplined irregular warfare machine with an impressive conven-tional arsenal, was marketed as Lebanon's best deterrence against future Israeli military threats.[55] This position was announced obliquely in the 30 November 2009 party document entitled *Al-Wathiqa al-Siyasiya li-Hezbollah* (Hezbollah's Political Document).[56] Hezbollah insisted that its weapons arsenal was part of a trinity that also included the LAF and the Lebanese population—labeled *al-jaysh, al-sha'b, al-moqawama* (the army, the people, the resistance)—responsible for deterring any future Israeli attacks. Yet the logic of the *Wathiqa* assumed that Hezbollah's weapons arsenal served the cause of perpetual deter-

---

[55] See Frank G. Hoffman, "Hybrid Warfare and Challenges", *Joint Forces Quarterly*, 52 (2009), http://www.ndu.edu/inss/Press/jfq_pages/editions/i52/9.pdf

[56] See Hezbollah, *Al-Wathiqa al-Siyasiya li-Hezbollah* (Beirut: n.p., 2009).

rence against Israel, and that the party holds veto power over any discussion of the country's prospective defensive strategy and, concomitantly, any potential scenarios for its demobilization and disarmament.[57] Unperturbed by the impact this would have on the already weak Lebanese state and on its armed forces, Hezbollah continues to devise new military options and develops its weapons arsenal in anticipation of a future round against Israel.[58]

At the regional level, Iran claimed a more robust role in matters Lebanese on the morrow of Syria's withdrawal from Lebanon; it consequently replaced Damascus as the dominant partner in the Syrian–Iranian dyad in Lebanon. As Damascus outsourced its Lebanon policy to Hezbollah, the latter became responsible for ensuring that post-Syria Lebanon did not slip into the US–Saudi orbit, and that Washington and Riyadh's allies did not succeed in effecting a wholesale takeover of state and security institutions. Nor was Hezbollah's role in the regional confrontation between Iran and Saudi Arabia limited to Lebanon. Hezbollah's sophisticated military capabilities are part of a grander Iranian network of proxies aimed at balancing against Washington and Israel's threats to the regime in Tehran.[59] Hezbollah is also accused of aiding the advance of Tehran's geopolitical agenda in Iraq, the Gaza Strip, Yemen, and Saudi Arabia.[60] How Hezbollah will respond to an Israeli or a US military attack against Iran's nuclear facilities remains a matter of serious speculation. However, Iranian military commanders have declared repeatedly that Hezbollah constitutes Iran's "strategic depth", and that the party will respond militarily in the event of an attack against Iran.[61] Even if such discourse is deployed for mere rhetorical purposes, it places a heavy burden on Hezbollah's geopolitical calculations.

The Arab uprisings that commenced in Tunisia in December 2010 and avalanched across the Arab world altered Hezbollah's geopolitical environ-

---

[57] See Salloukh and Mikaelian, "Hizbullah in Lebanon".

[58] See Blanford, *Warriors of God*.

[59] See Nerguizian, "U.S.–Iranian Competition in the Levant".

[60] See Michael R. Gordon and Dexter Filkins, "Hezbollah Said to Help Shiite Army in Iraq", *New York Times*, 28 November 2006, at http://www.nytimes.com/2006/11/28/world/middleeast/28military.html?_r=0; Hassan Illeik, "How Hamas Gets its Weapons", *Al-Akhbar English*, 19 November 2012, at http://english.al-akhbar.com/node/13950; "Hamas, Hezbollah helping Iran in Yemen", *Jerusalem Post*, 25 March 2012, at http://www.jpost.com/Middle-East/Hamas-Hezbollah-helping-Iran-in-Yemen; and *al-Sharq al-Wasat*, 4 April 2013.

[61] See comments by Brigadier General Yahya Rahim-Safavi, senior military adviser to Khamenei, in *al-Safir*, 10 September 2012.

ment dramatically. At the outset, the party welcomed the popular uprisings. After all, they seemed to target regimes—such as Tunisia's Zine El Abidine Ben Ali, Egypt's Hosni Mubarak, and Bahrain's Hamad bin Isa Al Khalifa's— that were either part of the pro-US "moderate" Arab camp in direct geopolitical confrontation with the "axis of resistance" to which Hezbollah belonged, or, as in the case of Muammar Gaddafi's pariah regime, with which Hezbollah had a personal score to settle, one that dates back to the 31 August 1978 abduction of Imam Musa al-Sadr while on a trip to Libya. The popular uprising in Syria that commenced on 15 March 2011 as a call for democracy, social justice, and accountability, but later developed in part into a sectarian civil war, created a strategic conundrum for Hezbollah.

From Hezbollah's geopolitical standpoint, and despite its objective original causes and demands, the uprising in Syria became part of the regional–international geopolitical contest between Saudi Arabia—now supported by the US, France, Turkey, and Qatar—and Iran, supported by Russia and China.[62] Riyadh used the democratic aspirations of the Syrian peoples to serve its otherwise all-too-realist geopolitical objectives: namely, to undermine Iran's regional power by toppling the regime of an allied state and replacing it with another one allied to Riyadh; and, furthermore, to use regime change in Syria to recalibrate the pro-Tehran political balance of power in Iraq. Regime change in Syria could eventually deny Iran precious access to the territory of an allied state bordering Israel,[63] curtail substantially Tehran's ability to transfer weapons and military supplies to its geopolitical proxy Hezbollah, and deny the latter the use of Damascus as a logistical base for the procurement of military supplies and the movement of the party's cadres to train in Iran. All this would seriously undermine Hezbollah's deterrence capabilities vis-à-vis what it perceives as Israel's persistent threat to Lebanon, but also the role it plays in Iran's geopolitical calculations and ambitions.

Hezbollah also felt increasingly beleaguered by Riyadh's decision to deploy sectarianism as a tool to achieve geopolitical objectives, especially in Syria. Riyadh's tactics inflamed sectarian sentiments across the region, tarnishing Hezbollah's image as a pan-Islamist resistance movement, and placed the party

---

[62] See the texts of Hezbollah's Secretary General Hassan Nasrallah's speeches reproduced in *al-Safir*, 12 November 2011, 4 January 2013, and, more importantly, 27 May 2013.

[63] See Julian Borger, "Iran and Hezbollah 'Have Built 50,000-Strong Force to Help Syrian Regime'", *Guardian*, 14 March 2013, at http://www.guardian.co.uk/world/2013/mar/14/iran-hezbollah-force-syrian-regime

in a military confrontation with armed Salafi groups in its own Lebanese backyard. This sectarianization of regional dynamics has turned the conflict in Syria, in part at least, into a veritable Sunni–'Alawi civil war. With logistic assistance from Turkish intelligence, transnational Salafi-jihadi fighters, such as the al-Qaeda-affiliated *Jabhat al-Nusrah li-Ahl al-Sham* (Support Front for the People of Greater Syria), poured from across the Muslim world into the Syrian theatre to fight a putatively infidel 'Alawi regime oppressing the Sunni majority. This brought *Jabhat al-Nusrah* into direct confrontation with Hezbollah along the Lebanese–Syrian borders, and in control of territory considered strategic for the party's supply lines through Syria. Moreover, control of this border area by Salafi-jihadi fighters would enable the latter to cross the borders and link up with their counterparts either in the north of the country or in the Palestinian camps. This could potentially drown Hezbollah in a sectarian quagmire at home, and sandwich it between two enemies— Israel and Salafi-jihadi fighters—thus undermining its political and military power in Lebanon and its ability to resist a future Israeli attack aimed at destroying the party's military infrastructure. It could also curtail Hezbollah's role in Iran's deterrence strategy to prevent a potential Israeli or US strike against its nuclear facilities.

All these geopolitical and domestic threats converged as Hezbollah decided to intervene in its "necessary war of choice in Syria" in a bid either to forestall regime change in Damascus or cushion it to minimize its detrimental implications on both Iran and the party's strategic interests.[64] At the risk of inflaming sectarian sentiments even more, Hezbollah declared its public support of what was otherwise viewed across the region as an 'Alawi regime defending its parochial sectarian interests. This transpired at a time when Hamas, whose sanctuary in Damascus caused the regime much diplomatic headache in the past, disowned it and jumped swiftly onto the Qatari bandwagon. At the domestic political level, Hezbollah ensured that the Lebanese state assumed a neutral political stance vis-à-vis the Syrian crisis in Arab and international forums; it was unable, however, to obviate the country's use as a support base or a weapons route for the Syrian rebels. Hezbollah's material support to the Syrian regime mutated incrementally into a full-scale military operation, however.

[64] See Aram Nerguizian, "Assessing the Consequences of Hezbollah's Necessary War of Choice in Syria", Center for Strategic and International Studies, 17 June 2013, at http://csis.org/publication/assessing-consequences-hezbollahs-necessary-war-choice-syria

Hezbollah's direct military involvement in Syria first started in the form of strategic consultations with the Syrian regime on a range of non-conventional military tactics.[65] The party helped train some regime units in guerrilla warfare and restore control to a number of strategic sectors around Damascus and Homs lost to the Free Syrian Army (FSA). Hezbollah also deployed some of its own elite military units to defend the Sayyidah Zaynab shrine in southern Damascus, and provided logistic and military support to Shi'a villages along both sides of the Lebanese–Syrian border in the Hermel region against attacks by the FSA. Moreover, it assisted the Syrian army in protecting its scientific establishments and missile factories built during the last decade with Iranian funding. Hezbollah then took the lead in training an Iranian-financed "Peoples' Army", a paramilitary militia composed largely of minority groups loyal to the regime, founded with the objective of supporting the regime's 50–65,000 core loyal fighting force in the regular army, but also of protecting Iran's, as well as the party's, interests in Syria the day after regime change.[66]

Hezbollah's public military involvement in the Qusayr battles in April 2013, and its ability to assume control of this strategic corridor—linking Damascus to Syria's coastal cities, controlling rebel supply lines to the cities of Homs and Aleppo, and bordering the party's bases in north-east Lebanon and its supply line in Syria—underscored the extent to which Hezbollah was willing to proceed militarily to protect its geopolitical interests as well as Tehran's. For a resistance movement founded to liberate Israeli-occupied Lebanese territory, Hezbollah's military intervention in Qusayr marked a watershed in the party's history: its first offensive operation over the territory of an Arab country against Sunni armed groups.[67] Nasrallah's rhetorical attempt to justify the party's military involvement in Syria by characterizing the battle as one against the US, Israel, and Salafi-jihadi fighters rather than the Syrian peoples failed to contain the impact of Hezbollah's operation on sectarian relations in the region.[68] In fact, the Qusayr battle incurred upon the party and its supporters

---

[65] See Ibrahim al-Amin, "Hezbollah fi Suriya", *al-Akhbar*, 22 March 2013.

[66] See Borger, "Iran and Hezbollah 'Have Built 50,000-Strong Force to Help Syrian Regime'"; and Dexter Filkins, "The Thin Red Line: Inside the White House Debate over Syria", *New Yorker*, 13 May 2013, at http://www.newyorker.com/reporting/2013/05/13/130513fa_fact_filkins

[67] See Ali Shehab, "Al-Qusayr Isra'eliyan: Hezbollah min al-Difa' ila al-Hujoom", *al-Safir*, 6 June 2013.

[68] See the text of Nasrallah's crucial speech on Syria reproduced in *al-Safir*, 27 May 2013.

a number of terrorist attacks on its own security enclave in Beirut's southern suburbs, the wrath of Gulf regimes, served to demonize Hezbollah even further with Sunni Muslim public opinion, may have contributed to a change in Washington's position on the arming of Syria's moderate rebel groups, and, finally, elicited open protestations from elements of the Shi'a community in Lebanon and some of the party's rank and file.

Conclusion

Given Lebanon's chronically weak state, Hezbollah's resilience and expansive role so far as a central actor in the country's politics are likely to continue for the foreseeable future. Since 2011, the failing, or at the very least steadily weakening, Syrian state has provided Hezbollah with a new theater of operations, but this time in a rearguard action designed to maintain the failing Syrian state from total collapse. In fact, Hezbollah's geopolitical environment is in deep crisis. The party's contingency plan for the day after regime change in Damascus is a tightly-held secret. Invariably, it is *how* regime change transpires—whether through a sudden collapse or as part of an externally-imposed transition process—that will determine the extent of the damage done to Hezbollah's, and by implication Iran's, strategic interests in Syria and beyond. The party leadership repeatedly reiterates the claim that it has achieved a level of military self-sufficiency and preparedness for the next round against Israel. If anything, the Qusayr operation demonstrated just how important Syria's geography is to Hezbollah's operational plans and supply lines and, concomitantly, its ability to pursue its own geopolitical interests and, by proxy, those of Iran. Nor does the party underestimate the potential blow-back Salafi-jihadi effect which its military involvement in Syria may incur in the future. Fighting on three simultaneous fronts—against Israel in the south of the country, Salafi-jihadi groups in Syria, and domestic groups in Lebanon—is a scenario the party takes seriously and seems to be preparing for actively.[69] Only time will tell whether Hezbollah's intervention in Syria will prove to be a quagmire rather than a pre-emptive strike intended to protect the party's strategic environment and obviate a harder battle at home.

Hezbollah's future political role in Lebanon and the region is bound to be affected by its military intervention in Syria and the fortunes of the Lebanese state. As long as the Lebanese state is weak, unable to assert meaningful ter-

---

[69] See Ibrahim al-Amin, "Tamhidan lil-Harb al-Shamila", *al-Akhbar*, 30 April 2013.

ritorial and institutional sovereignty, and the LAF remains under-manned and under-equipped, Hezbollah will assume its socioeconomic and deterrence responsibilities vis-à-vis the Shi'a community and Israel respectively. Lebanon's political system will continue to be based on a delicate—but respected—sectarian balance of power between its different communities, but one that exposes the country to all kinds of overlapping domestic and external contests at the expense of Lebanese sovereignty. Only the emergence of a strong and non-confessional state in Lebanon, with substantial infrastructural capabilities and trans-sectarian appeal, can undermine Hezbollah's military and political clout.

Hezbollah's main political challenge in the near future is to avoid the pitfalls of its Lebanese precursors: namely, acting as a hegemon in a sectarian political system prone to perpetual crisis and external penetration. The contest over post-Syria Lebanon since 2005 demonstrated that no single sectarian community can control the country or, alternatively, impose its own "vision of Lebanon" on other communities. Hezbollah's vision of perpetual resistance is increasingly incommensurate with that of other sectarian communities, and has already alienated substantial sections of Lebanese society, including some in its own Shi'a community. Its military intervention in Syria reopened the domestic debate over the utility and legality of its weapons arsenal. Hezbollah's political opponents in the 14 March alliance and their regional patrons—but especially Saudi Arabia—no longer endorse the *al-jaysh, al-sha'b, al-moqawama* formula that allowed for a cohabitation in post-Syria Lebanon between overlapping domestic and external political nemeses. The party also faces the challenge of reconstituting its battered image and appeal across the Arab and Muslim worlds. Yet short of a regional grand bargain involving Iran, the US, and Saudi Arabia, Hezbollah will continue to defend the utility of its weapons arsenal for Lebanon's deterrence posture; it will also continue to deploy this arsenal at the service of its own geopolitical interests and that of Iran. And this, in turn, will further divide Lebanese and expose the country to overlapping local and regional battles at the expense of domestic stability.

7

MARGIN AND CENTER IN SUDAN

ON THE HISTORICITY OF STATE WEAKNESS

Rogaia Mustafa Abusharaf

The "Failed States Index" published in *Foreign Policy* magazine in 2013 identified fifty-nine states as "failed". Sudan, which is the focus of this chapter, ranked third. The map is color-coded to reflect the situation in different states, which range from being "critical", "in danger", and "borderline", to "stable" and "most stable". States are also scored according to the following indicators: "mounting demographic pressures; massive movement of refugees or internally displaced persons; vengeance-seeking group grievance; chronic and sustained human flight; uneven economic development; poverty, sharp or severe economic decline; legitimacy of the state; progressive deterioration of public services; violation of human rights and rule of law; security apparatus; rise of factionalized elites; and intervention of external actors".[1]

Besides ranking poorly on all these indices, Sudan has also recently experienced secession. Mediations between North and South attempting to avoid secession had systematically yielded broken promises and a reproduction of

---

[1] See *Foreign Policy*, "Failed States Index", 13 April 2013, http://www.foreignpolicy.com/node/1282061

marginality, and in 2011 South Sudan voted to establish itself as a separate country. In spite of the euphoria, the ululations, the festivities of chanting a new anthem, and the carnivals of victory that accompanied the secession referendum, however, this dream has turned into a living nightmare for both Sudan and the Republic of South Sudan. Talk of freedom from dominance, sharing of power and wealth, as well as of disarmament and repatriation of refugees, as avenues for creating an "attractive unity" proved to be empty words. Exceptionally problematic was the subject of repatriation of the millions of Southerners who lived in the North and across the border in neighboring African countries. Those Southerners who tried to return to their original villages were blocked or even murdered by their own compatriots. The tragedy of the killing of refugee families who tried to return to their home villages by the Jongli Canal was a dramatic but by no means an isolated incident. A valuable online resource, *Niles Editors*, which reports regularly on the current crisis in the fledgling Republic, has detailed numerous examples of inter-communal and ethnic violence.[2] These incidents together with other factors such as corruption have combined to depict South Sudan as a failing state, which its leadership resented.

Be that as it may, any attempt at unraveling the fundamental logic of weakness and failure must analyze it as a phenomenon that is as much about the past as it is about the present. It must also recognize that the world of international politics is one interdependent field, which must be anatomized and explored in detail as the struggle to determine the nuances of cultural and political life as they are experienced at the level of the quotidian continues in states depicted as weak or failed. The "Failed States Index" does not heed these nuances and thus remains of limited utility.

In the large body of literature that has been written since the 1990s, the concept of failed states has picked up momentum. As political destabilization and social upheavals took root in a wide array of states and societies around the world, the debate about failed states was expanded to highlight the likelihood that conflicts would extend beyond the frontiers of these newly carved "ungovernable spaces" into the most stable nations. In the words of former US Secretary of State Condoleezza Rice:

> One of the defining challenges in our world, now and for many years to come, will be to deal with weak and poorly governed states that are on the verge of failure, or

---

[2] See www.theniles.org, "South Sudan Detains Commander for Human Rights Abuses in Jongli", 26 August 2013.

indeed, states that have already failed. These crises create environments of anarchy, and conflict, and ungoverned space—where violence and oppression can spread; where arms traffickers and other transnational criminals can operate with impunity; and where terrorists and extremists can gather, and train and kill the innocent. In a world as increasingly connected as ours, the international system is only as strong as its weakest links.[3]

Rice's statement provides strong evidence of how stable governments produce knowledge about state failure without owning up to the burdens of history, since it leaves out these governments' support of repressive regimes, imposition of sanctions that prevent ordinary citizens' access to the bare necessities of life, and carrying out of measures of "anticipatory self-defense" in which infringements of innocent civilians' human rights are looked upon simply as "collateral damage".[4] It supplies a decontextualized, ahistorical narrative of the reasons behind state failure.[5]

In spite of the limitations of this essentialist representation of state weakness, foreign policy-makers, donor agencies, and politicians have embarked on a voyage of discovery for ways to fix the predicament of states' fragility, collapse, and ultimate failure. In the rhetoric generated on the subject so far, little is offered with respect to the politics of the language used to frame the debate on the classifications of states as stable or fragile. The significance of semantics, which is produced by donor agencies and foreign policy-makers, lies in their tendency to sidestep nuanced, historically-minded perspectives on international relations in an interlinked globalized universe. Language is particularly important as a pathway to knowledge and subsequently to specific political practices and policies. As David Palmer argues, "language is the stage on which consciousness makes its historical entrance and politics is scripted".[6] With a few notable exceptions, the language which stable states apply in their discussion of failed or fragile states fails to engage the effect of the increasing

[3] Stewart Patrick, *Weak Links: Fragile States, Global Threats, and International Security* (New York: Oxford University Press, 2011), 3.

[4] For a critique of this doctrine, see Noam Chomsky, *Failed States: The Abuse of Power and the Assault on Democracy* (New York: Metropolitan Books, 2006).

[5] Several examples with respect to Sudan's failure illustrate the convenience of shying away from the colonial roots of the problem. See J. Millard Burr and Robert Collins, *Sudan in Turmoil: Hasan al-Turabi and the Islamist State, 1889–2003* (Princeton, NJ: Markus Wiener Publishers, 2010).

[6] Bryan D. Palmer, "The Discovery/Deconstruction of the Word/Sign", in *Descent into Discourse: The Reification of Language and the Writing of Social History* (Philadelphia: Temple University Press, 1990), 3.

intermingling of national and international politics. These exceptions include the contributions of Charles Call,[7] Noam Chomsky,[8] and Stewart Patrick,[9] all of whom stress the importance of comprehending the underlying power structures of state failure and the ironies they embody.[10] The rest of the extant literature so far lacks such historical contextualization of the states included in the *Foreign Policy* "Index".[11] Situating the discussions about weak states in their proper historical, sociopolitical, and economic frames of reference on the world stage is by no means tantamount to exonerating the failed governments' dismal political behavior. It is obvious that weakness and failure as existential conditions experienced by large populations all over the world are unquestionably real.

In Sudan, evidence of failure abounds.[12] To the people of Sudan, incidents of state transgressions are not surprising; nor is the *Foreign Policy* ranking. In the face of the extraordinary suffering and sorrow that the state has inflicted on its people, Sudan has exhibited all the symptoms of a failed state.[13] The

---

[7] Charles Call, "The Fallacy of the 'Failed State'", *Third World Quarterly*, 29 (2008): 1491–1507.

[8] Chomsky, *Failed States*.

[9] Patrick, *Weak States*.

[10] Other writers, such as Daron Acemoglu and James Robinson, also engage with these issues. In their recent book *Why Nations Fail: The Origins of Power, Prosperity, and Poverty*, they raise probing queries about colonialism and postcolonial institutions that perpetuated colonial policy by proxy.

[11] Daron Acemoglu and James Robinson, "Understanding Prosperity and Poverty", in *Why Nations Fail: The Origins of Power, Prosperity, and Poverty* (New York: Crown Business, 2012), 428–63.

[12] The public flogging of a young woman robed in "Islamic dress" by police in full view of cavalier spectators in a Khartoum street shocked viewers and bloggers in the world of social media. This incident showed the impunity with which the state meted out corporal punishment to a female "with no articulable, reasonable suspicion" (language commonly used by police) to stop her in the first place. In the court of public opinion, the state not only failed this lashed young woman but also indicated an astounding license for perpetrating violence on a whim.

[13] Critiquing the current Islamic government that ascended to power in a *coup d'état* in 1989. Sudanese author Fathi Eldaw remarked in a recent book *Alkhandaq* (The Foxhole)—now removed from bookstores' shelves by the state—the following: Let's pause to consider the convoluted range of predicaments beleaguering the country: Authority, wealth sharing, marginality, theocracy, diversity, unity, secession, self-determination, federalism, confederacy, central versus state governance, constitutionalism, freedoms, health, education, revolution, security, war, borders

significant grievances incurred among its diverse populations from past and present experiences are enormous, but they too need to be infused, like the "Failed States Index", with a sense of history.

This chapter analyzes a text by the late Sudanese secular intellectual Abdel Khaliq Mahgoub (1927–71) that has been banned by both military and civilian governments.[14] This text is arguably among the best of what has been written on colonial governance and postcolonial forms of surrogacy. Analyzing it is vital for understanding the context of the highly fraught political environment in which those who inhabit these "ungovernable spaces" find themselves. The text, aptly titled *Rectifying the Wrongs in Working with the Masses* (henceforth *Rectifying*), allows for a methodical engagement with the historicity of failure in its totality to help spawn new ways of understanding this political phenomenon in its appropriate context and finding effective ways to heal and strengthen the nation. *Rectifying* was initially written in 1963, after independence, and was published by the author as part of a body of leftist underground literature that flourished at that time.[15] I have chosen this text because of its focus on the signs of weakness that Mahgoub recognized decades ago and that have now become reality. Had those in power heeded his warnings, so much of the social and political turmoil the country has experienced could have been pre-empted or resolved completely. At a critical political juncture in Sudan's history, Mahgoub managed to author a text "that sought to touch on the inner lives of individuals and communities".[16]

---

and refugees, social cohesion etc. etc. Is there a nation in the whole universe, whose political dictionary brims with such a mix or one whose ruling elites kept chewing on them without boredom or weariness? After all, Sudan has become the perfect illustration of a state with a sustained record of failure. Fathi Aldaw, *Al-Khandaq* (The Foxhole) (Cairo: Jazeerat Alward Publications, in Arabic, 2012), 37.

[14] Mahgoub was one of Africa's most important public intellectuals. He was a member of parliament 1965–6, when he was expelled from the government on charges that as a leftist he had a disdain for religion. He was executed by the government in July 1971.

[15] The book was re-published in Arabic by Azza Press in 2004.

[16] Anthropologist Sally Falk Moore describes these challenges when writing about the significance of trying "to place knowledge in larger-scale terms. Or to put scale in a temporal rather than a spatial frame, which involves attempts to understand the visible in terms of pasts and futures, local and supralocal." Sally Falk Moore, "Past and Future: Conclusion and Recapitulation", in *Anthropology and Africa: Changing Perspectives on a Changing Scene* (Virginia: University of Virginia Press, 1994), 130.

As soon as independence was declared, Sudanese society was riven by unspeakable violence, comparable to that the British had used in subduing "the natives", only now at the hands of Sudanese regimes whose lust for power and property reigned supreme. This state of affairs persists with terrible tenacity today. Since Mahgoub was among the first to articulate the magnitude of postcolonial violence and provided a theory and method for understanding it, reading him in great depth allows one to look at the roots of the quandaries besieging Sudan today. As I pondered the construction of knowledge that produced the "Failed States Index", Mahgoub's work raised several questions in my mind. I ask: What is in the label of "failed states"? Who owns the right to apply it, not only as an idiom depicting states with unsatisfactory performance towards their peoples, but also as an ahistorical designation suggesting a homogenous view on state and society characteristic of representational discourses on the "other"? What implications does the rather recent deployment of this idiom mean for states labeled as failed, fragile, or collapsing?[17] How can we begin to think critically about the localities and temporalities of the semantics around the thorny topic of accountability at both the national and international level? Are failed states autonomous entities endowed with full independence and sovereignty but performing miserably at keeping the good of their citizens at heart, or are they merely neocolonial bureaucracies which have failed the ultimate test of self-governance?

Further Purposes

Analyzing one example of Mahgoub's extensive work serves multiple purposes. The first of these is clarifying the concept of the "failed state". In his important critique of the scholarship and policy on failed states, Stewart Patrick writes: "despite this unprecedented recent attention, the concept of the 'failed state' remains vague and imprecise. Analytical shortcomings include the absence of clear criteria to measure 'weakness' or define 'failure,' and an inattention to the specific histories, trajectories, regimes of the countries so designated."[18] Mahgoub was aware of historical context and the politics of language as well as the contradictions they reflect. He paid considerable attention to the nuances and trajectories of Sudanese history, rendering his work of great value for circumventing the narrowly reductionist accounts upon which blame for

[17] Patrick, *Weak States*, 26–7.
[18] Patrick, *Weak States*, 21.

"failure" is commonly apportioned. Understanding his premises will prove important across disciplines and will have implications far beyond the borders of Sudanese society. His ideas on the reproduction of the colonial epistemes in relation to government and conservative right-wing politics illuminate the paradoxes of postcolonial Africa's pressing problems.

Another important element that lies at the intersection of philosophy and culture supports a consideration of Mahgoub's work on the weakness of Sudan in philosophical–anthropological terms. Mahgoub would concur with questions raised by Congolese philosopher V. Y. Mudimbe regarding the production of knowledge about colonial and postcolonial societies, such as "Who is speaking about it? Who has the right and the credentials to produce it, describe it, comment on upon it, or at least represent it?"[19] Mahgoub attempted to answer the conceptual and representational dilemmas these questions pose. His exploration of a Sudanese "order of knowledge" was central to his perspective on the complexities of Sudanese philosophies of independence and those of averting failure.

Second, Mahgoub presented significant insights on matters that lie at the heart of political and dialectical anthropology today. Mahgoub's attention to these matters further frames the issue of state weakness. Of pertinence to current debates in anthropology are his lessons on commodity circulation, secularism and religion, and the conditions and consequences of capitalist accumulation in its open and blatant form. Mahgoub engaged with economic issues, elaborating on ideas about the dialectics of politics and history, an effort that has figured prominently in various works on political anthropology. For instance, Thomas Patterson's invocation of the notion of anthropology as "the study of people in crisis by people in crisis"[20] resonates with Mahgoub's analysis of the intricacies of Sudanese political experience over time. Furthermore, Mahgoub saw the importance of Marx's theories of capitalism's expansion and monopoly and the labor aristocracy to African societal dynamics.[21]

Third, Mahgoub's writing deepens our understanding of the sense of "urgency" in dealing with complex emergencies. This sense of urgency has been long and deeply present in the African intellectual tradition. In the years

[19] V. Y. Mudimbe, "Introduction", in *The Invention of Africa: Gnosis, Philosophy, and the Order of Knowledge* (Bloomington: Indiana University Press, 1988), x. The two writers' views dovetail in a number of ways.

[20] Thomas C. Patterson, *Karl Marx, Anthropologist* (New York: Berg, 2009), 158.

[21] See Andrew Brewer, *Marxist Theories of Imperialism: A Critical Survey* (London: Routledge, 1990).

following decolonization, Africanist anthropologists hailing primarily from the world's most powerful nations produced a significant body of literature on a wide array of African cultural phenomena, including important ethnographies on such diverse subjects as law, gender, moral order and codes of conduct, land, kinship, magic, religion, proselytizing, and ritual symbolism. It is important to illuminate the powerful African intellectual tradition as developed in Mahgoub's analysis and theoretical accounts of urgency in anthropology.[22] Mahgoub's work provides greater precision and clarity to this theory, a more trenchant depiction of the maladies of the state, and a firmer grasp of the complex sociocultural contexts where past and present politics converge in most disruptive ways. Mahgoub's supple understanding of notions of culture, politics, and urgency recall the work of Raymond Williams, with whom he might be compared.[23]

Mahgoub immersed himself in the mastering of political anthropological literature as well as philosophical examinations crucial to an analysis of state and society and the disconnect that marks them. Weakness resides in this ruptured space between governors and the governed. Mahgoub viewed historical change through the lens of political economy and its intimate links to culture and society.[24] With attention to infinitesimal details that resist easy generalities, Mahgoub viewed the totality of the processes of change he aspired to through the needs of a diverse marginalized populace: women, youth, students, workers, peasants, national and religious minorities, and intellectuals who did not sell their souls to self-interest. Mahgoub's *Rectifying the Wrongs in Working amongst the Masses* was written with the purpose of drawing the attention of political leaders to problems plaguing the nation and forewarning them about the horrors to come. It examines the enduring pre-

---

[22] Urgency to Mahgoub is about linking abstract concepts to real-life situations to which ordinary people could relate, which is not what "urgency" usually means.

[23] See Raymond Williams, *Keywords: A Vocabulary in Culture and Society* (Oxford: Oxford University Press, 1976). Returning to Cambridge after service abroad, Williams took note of the frequency with which the term "culture" was used, often with vague and implicit meaning, and in *Keywords* set out to explicate its contemporary meanings. He went on to unpack its relevance to "urgent contemporary problems", culminating in the publication of *Culture and Society*. Mahgoub's preoccupations bear striking resemblance to Williams in this regard.

[24] This approach can help us relate his work to other powerful writings about marginalized populations. See analysis of the "Unhomely" in Homi K. Bhabha, *The Location of Culture* (London: Routledge, 1994).

dicament of margin and center in Sudan in relation to the state's performance. Understanding this historical and cultural situation will help us rethink the factors that lead to the weakness and failure of states.

Rectifying is an anthropological study of the conflicts that emerged in Sudan in the early years of independence. It emphasizes the inescapability of class analysis in relation to the continued struggle to bridge the gap between those trapped in the margins and those who blossomed as powerful elites occupying the center. Mahgoub's theory of building a progressive society was based on specific knowledge of both politics and economics and was exceptionally effective in presenting the dilemmas of carving out new spaces for intellectual inventiveness and creativity.[25] A theoretically informed search for the solid ground on which a just society could be built permeated his thinking throughout his life. Mahgoub was an able fieldworker. With both objectivity and sensitivity to the circumstances under which the Sudanese people were living, he theorized about and described in copious detail the urgency of dealing with the problems of accountability in the governance of the new nation. In a conservative society steeped in sectarian politics, a progressive culture, as Mahgoub came to understand it, would entail "a systematic critique of all that is unfavorable within society and the institutionalization of a transformative politics that would carefully renegotiate the relationship between state and society. It would require identifying measures for the formation of a strong culture that would open up possibilities for confronting authority and dismantling the arrogance of power."[26] If Mahgoub were to write his own index of the weakness of states, he would have put forward a different set of indicators.

If Mahgoub Were to Write the Index

Although Mahgoub was cognizant of all of the critical transformations that had taken place during the long history of the Sudan, he found the British colonial period to be the most consequential. In *Rectifying*, he outlined the major characteristics of colonial Sudan, as follows. The country had endured British colonization from 1898 to 1956, a sixty-year experience that engendered artificial rifts, social and ethnic boundaries based solely on British conjecture that militated against the development of a political imagination capable of supporting a commitment to transformative politics. Mahgoub

---

[25] See Samir Amin, *Eurocentrism* (New York: Monthly Review Press, 2010).

[26] Mahgoub, *Rectifying*, 40.

recognized how this history shaped the worldview of the new leaders who came to power in the postcolonial period, leaders who ignored the needs of the vast majority of Sudanese people.

To ensure their dominance and facilitate their governance, the British established a divide-and-rule policy that was more than the mere racist cliché characteristic of most colonial situations. Indifferent to the complexity of Sudanese society, the British saw their perceptions of race and ethnicity as biological facts and translated them into segregation of the citizenry. In the 1920s the British authorities established the Closed Door Ordinances, intended to keep apart what they perceived as two mutually exclusive groups of people. These ordinances banned interaction between "Arabs" and "Africans" by limiting communication and contact between North and South, despite the fact that these peoples had interacted for millennia.

The British aimed to protect the poor, benighted black Africans of the South from exploitation by Arab merchants and the insidious influence of Islam until they were literate, Christian, and capable of dealing with the modern world on terms the British thought proper. Sudanese missionary societies were encouraged to introduce healthcare and education. This was an important factor in the formation of a Southern Christian educated elite. The British also granted native leaders predominant roles in governance. Like their counterparts elsewhere in Africa, tribal chiefs were linked to colonial structures of power and authority and embodied the localized expression of this power.[27] Meanwhile, the British made major efforts to solidify the Northern elite by using as government functionaries the most reactionary elements of the traditional parties who then served as enablers of the colonial regime.

As a result of all these policies, the people of the Sudan lost the opportunity to embrace difference as inherent in the human condition, and create a collective vision capable of cementing a shared national consciousness. They also lost the chance to develop a sense of national belonging and the sort of citizenship that David Miller defines as "a set of rights enjoyed equally by every member of the society in question".[28] By the time the British left, colonialism had created legacies that seemed insurmountable, including favoritism for one group at the expense of others, unequal development, and unjust distribution of resources.

---

[27] For discussion on the Native Administration's link to colonial power in Africa, see Mahmoud Mamdani, *Citizen and Subject: Contemporary Africa and the Legacy of Late Colonialism* (Princeton, NJ: Princeton University Press, 1996).

[28] David Miller, *Citizenship and National Identity* (Oxford: Polity Press, 2000), 44.

Fragmented Nationalism

Mahgoub subsumed the problem of conservatism within the larger, more urgent issue of installing a public culture and a broad democratic front that would accommodate the difference necessary to build the just society to which he aspired. He clearly recognized that the complementarity of the myriad power structures that had been forged within colonial contexts was an early warning sign of weakness.

During the anti-colonial struggle, there was no such a thing as a single front against imperialism, and Mahgoub believed that in postcolonial Sudan different political factions among the elite as well as groups supporting social progress, such as working-class trade unions, peasants, and other progressive elements of Sudanese society, all needed to be recognized on an equal footing. He exposed the significance of colonial tactics and the alliances of colonial officials with right-wing and reactionary forces in Sudanese society. To him, these alliances were important factors impeding nation-building in Sudan and elsewhere in Africa. In Mahgoub's words:

> Of course, such a situation could have been an opportunity for positive change in our societies if it had inspired the development of dialogue among various segments of our people and had promoted among them a sense of empathy and connection with popular interests. We must make a conscious attempt to broaden the circle of advocacy by creating solid programs that will strengthen our people and further their interests.[29]

Mahgoub recognized that traveling such a path would be uneven and full of difficulties because of the presence of an elite linked to a set of aspirations that undercut those of ordinary people. Even after the colonial power had been forced to leave, colonialist policies had triumphed in creating an arrogant ruling class and isolating them completely from the rest of the populace.

Before making his case for how to fix Sudan's political economy, Mahgoub explained the anatomy of the post-independence body politic and the diminishing power of the concept of sovereignty as a slogan for self-rule. Mahgoub saw that invocations of independence were not a sufficient framework for governance; he saw the paradox that national sovereignty had become a road to power for those very individuals who had benefited from their allegiances and loyalties to the British.

Rectifying exposes the inability of Sudanese political leaders to propose a roadmap for the advancement of the people of Sudan or engage with the issues

---

[29] Mahgoub, *Rectifying*, 23.

of capital and labor in the agricultural sector. It reflects Mahgoub's effort to comprehend crucial anthropological predicaments vis-à-vis structures, transformation, and progress, not as predetermined evolutionary or linear phenomena to be contested, but as resources for improving the lot of a society that has fallen on hard times. His ability to navigate these essential processes conceptually identifies him as someone who could have been a valuable broker for change.

Hierarchy and the Reproduction of Colonial Epistemes

The shift from colonialism to independence has always occasioned special attention to what in the cultural and political life of a country has persisted or changed. Despite the boon of independence, Mahgoub became suspicious whenever the issue of the defense of sovereignty arose. His views on the constraints of local and global politics were analogous to the views of other public intellectuals such as Cameroonian philosopher Achille Mbembe's triangulation of boundaries, territoriality, and sovereignty.[30] These subjects were approached by them with marked trepidation. Nationalist governments, they felt, spoke glowingly of sovereignty while ironically exhibiting tendencies to profit economically at the expense of the citizenry.[31] Mahgoub further elaborated on these postcolonial political processes by drawing attention to the nationalist practices that failed to tackle the predicaments of constitutionalism, national minorities, and citizenship, leaving postcolonial Sudanese society to emerge as a fragmented social organization riven with unequal development and gaping disparities.[32] During the Sudanese struggle for independence, the nationalists promised the moon, but when the struggle was over, they delivered little.

Independence brought about new divisions and reinforced old ones in Sudanese society, creating new indices of exclusion and inclusion, margin and center, via new vocabularies, which often proved to be merely empty rhetoric. Marginalities and stratifications inherent in the colonial experience reappeared, newly veneered under the name of "sovereignty". At independence, it

[30] Achille Mbembe, "At the Edge of the World: Boundaries, Territoriality, and Sovereignty in Africa", trans. Randall Steven, *Public Culture*, 12 (2001), 209–84.

[31] Ibid.

[32] Mahgoub's deconstruction of colonialist knowledge and practice may be compared to that of Bernard S. Cohn, *Colonialism and its Forms of Knowledge: The British in India* (Princeton, NJ: Princeton University Press, 1996).

became clear that the new nationalist leaders had emerged not only as surrogates of colonial interests, but also as devout supporters of postcolonial politics. The ties that bound them to colonialist discourses and practices in relation to governance were to be upheld, and perpetuated at every turn. The new nation remained mired in a cycle of despotism, bureaucracy, and militarization. In his preface to *The Colonizer and the Colonized* by Albert Memmi, Jean Paul Sartre wrote: "[A] relentless reciprocity binds the colonizer to the colonized—his product and his fate."[33] For Mahgoub, the new/old epistemes in postcolonial Sudan masked vested interests and meant rejection of an authentic engagement with questions of a national renaissance.

> What is the mystery that lies behind our Sudanese leaders' total about-face and duplicity that our people would not understand? My modest experience, politically, intellectually, and personally has led me to recognize that these leaders do not carry within their chests a consistent political theory with which to challenge colonialism. While the colonists possessed their own advanced capitalist theories with which they subjugated and objectified entire populations in different parts of the world, Sudanese nationalists did not. Rather, they searched for ways to appease the colonizers, and further personal aggrandizement. If our beleaguered people are to be liberated in the fullest sense of the term, they too must be guided by a theory that will amalgamate their efforts and defeat the colonial project in Sudan. Under such a theory, no leader will reap the benefits of the toil and suffering of the people.[34]

Being among the first to critique the boundaries drawn by the British and the premises upon which they were based, Mahgoub believed in a strong leadership that could direct nation-building and fundamentally alter the emblems of hierarchy characteristic of colonialism.

At issue for Mahgoub were the ideologies of "othering" that render the suffering of the other invisible and unworthy of easing. Avram Bornstein described this process when he argued:

> Severe violence and oppression come not necessarily from those without an understanding of morality, but from systematic exclusion of particular people from empathy. We detach ourselves from the pain of others by placing them outside "our" community, which is often understood and identified by reference to overlapping distinctions of gender, class, race, ethnicity, or ideology.[35]

[33] See Jean-Paul Sartre, Preface to Albert Memmi, *The Colonizer and the Colonized* (New York: Orion Press, 1965), 3–17.

[34] Mahgoub, "*Rectifying*", 53.

[35] See Avram Bornstein, *Crossing the Green Line between the West Bank and Israel*

The state's persecution of a large swathe of the population consisting of the poor, the rural, the ethnically different inhabiting the periphery of society was the obvious corollary.

Rectifying demonstrates that the relationship between the right wing and colonialism was the result of a shared ideology of othering, which manifested itself in the structural violence that the postcolonial state had produced. When the Left addressed political culture, defied complacencies, and urged wisdom, the government attacked them brutally. Such is the fractured story of the independence of a people scarred by inherited absolutism and exploitation.

Militancy and Militarism

For over sixty years since independence, the Sudan has been caught in the grip of military dictatorships that waged war against their populace and applied some of the harshest laws to curtail their access to fundamental rights. These regimes imposed Sharia in 1983, and even during a short period of democratic rule, the civilian government that came to power could not summon the imagination to deal with the unfairness of applying this code to a diverse society. Moreover, the mobilization of religiosity as a discourse on governance was not totally divorced from economic interests. Mahgoub was able to gauge the winds and calms of Sudanese politics vis-à-vis secularist alternatives. In the spirit of explaining the possibilities of alternative solutions to the status quo, he attempted to alert the Sudanese public to the fact that economics and the state were even more indissolubly conjoined after independence than they had been before, with monopoly capitalism continuing, only under a different authority. With great effectiveness, he laid bare the increased centralization of production and capital in complex monopolies and exposed the spread of militarism, which he predicted would inevitably lead to recurring interferences in politics. Militarism, which as an institution received considerable support from stable states, was and remains exceptionally pertinent to the state's weakness because of the economic crises that it continually produces through warfare and division of Sudanese society.

Closely tied to the discussion of markets in *Rectifying* is Mahgoub's understanding of power structures in their manifold forms and political configurations. Enrique Dussel has shed light on the role that institutions play in the

---

(*The Ethnography of Political Violence*) (Philadelphia: University of Pennsylvania Press, 2003), x.

"fetishization of power", which he explains as a "will-to-power as domination of the people, of the majority, of the weakest, of the poor".[36] It is important to link this concept to the question of state weakness. Mahgoub, like Dussel, saw institutions as breeding grounds of dominance, the consequence of historically constructed asymmetrical structures and differentiations, inequalities, and residual interests, and hence to be contested. Institutions and the institutionalization of power through a concatenation of projects affecting economics and politics lead us to a discussion of Mahgoub's theorizing about the formation of elites, which warrants a comparison with C. Wright Mills's *The Power Elite*, even though Mills was writing in a completely different context. As Mills writes:

> The institutional trends that make for society of masses are to a considerable extent a matter of impersonal drift, but the remnants of the public are also exposed to more personal and intentional forces. With the broadening of the base of politics within the context of a folklore of democratic decision-making, and with increased masses of mass persuasion that are available, the public opinion has become the object of intensive efforts to control, manage, manipulate, and increasingly intimidate.[37]

Like Mills, Mahgoub deconstructed the institutionalization of right-wing politics:

> The ease with which the right wing achieved its massive influence on politics demonstrates its ability as the center of power to shape the political movement in the country. This influence is derived from its position within the state apparatus. There is absolute trust of senior bureaucrats who are connected with old colonialism and who are always prepared to create a front against the advancement of the democratic revolution in the country. The elite, which assumed power, viewed its role as a historical responsibility to keep the state apparatus in line with its predecessors. These are the social forces that are hostile to national liberation and to improving the lives of the majority.[38]

Mahgoub presented highly original ideas on democratization. He urged the building of a consensus about the need for a national–democratic movement that drew upon the expertise and input of diverse segments of the Sudanese people. In this context, he explained the usefulness of Marxist class analysis in

---

[36] Enrique Dussel, *Twenty Theses in Politics* (Durham, NC: Duke University Press, 2008).

[37] C. Wright Mills, "The Conservative Elite", in *The Power Elite* (New York: Oxford University Press, 2002), 310.

[38] Mahgoub, *Rectifying*, 20.

Sudan: "Marxism", he wrote, "is a distinguished epistemology in both its coherence and consistency in its unsurpassed capacity for the holistic analysis of multiple dimensions of culture and society, human rights, politics and aesthetics, literature, philosophy, and economy."[39]

Enforced Silences and Exclusions

Demonstrating the reflexivity and contemplative distance characteristic of the scholar, Mahgoub was nonetheless an anthropologist of his own society, toiling to introduce a measure of "multivocality" into a political culture besieged by burdensome, long-standing silences and exclusions. Nowhere was this effort more evident than in his probing of the mechanisms by which colonial discourse was reproduced in postcolonial Sudan. Mahgoub's frustrations over the absence of the collective body, however, did not prevent him from appreciating the theatricality present in the expressions of new nationalisms, in their various episodes, political emotionality, complicated characters, and crowded scenes. Sudanese independence, he understood, was a momentous rite of passage packed with ambiguity.

Drawing upon theory and praxis, Mahgoub was thus distinguished by his ability to recognize the impending failure of the state through a firm grasp of irony and the ability to explain the logic behind his formulations of a Sudanese national–democratic transformation. In a path-breaking literature that combined textual analysis, a deep knowledge of history, and a rigorous critique, he probed the iniquities that overwhelmed the Sudanese social scene. His reconstructions of the details of Sudanese politics reflect an extraordinary ethnographic imagination aided by in-depth comprehension of concepts such as framing, performativity, and tradition.[40] Mahgoub deployed these concepts to understand different chapters of Sudanese political life since independence. He recognized the role of the individual in igniting and sustaining any revolution. However, he also understood the diversity of opinions among the populations of the Sudan about the objectives they sought in the extraordinary bazaar of revolution. This insight into the role of individuals in igniting change is important for deconstructing the motives of the masses, whose reasons for participating in revolutionary actions are as different from those of

[39] Mahgoub, *By Virtue*, 161.
[40] For explanations of these concepts see Mieke Bal, *Traveling Concepts in the Humanities: A Rough Guide* (Toronto: University of Toronto Press, 2002).

self-conscious leaders as night is from day. Mahgoub recognized with great clarity that revolutions can encompass conflicting interests.

Thoughts on Creating a Just and Stable Society

So far, I have attempted to present the multiple opportunities that Mahgoub's meticulous tracings of Sudan's political trajectory in *Rectifying* has made available for comprehending the root causes of state weakness. But as its name suggests, *Rectifying* also presented a program for a just and stable society. Mahgoub's vision of a more equitable society necessarily involved a command of the language of knowledge and power as well as an understanding of the intermingling fields of culture and politics. Also, because such a society would introduce new ways of apprehending a political culture that had previously been treated as if carved in stone, two key matters had to be addressed: first, there was the myth of the Left as an enemy of religion; second was making a Leftist public culture comprehensible and relevant to the Sudanese masses. The latter required carefully thought-out strategies. The secularists including Mahgoub had to provide an image of transformation that recognized the specificity and complexity of Sudan's social configurations. If this effort was successful, Mahgoub understood that the resulting social order would have great potential for improving the lives of Sudanese people. To him, effecting and institutionalizing transformative politics required careful renegotiation of the relationship between state and society. This relationship had to be a dynamic one, and the state had to align itself with the people and acknowledge the primacy of a strong economy in transforming society.[41]

Differentiating Myth from Reality

Among the major philosophical dilemmas that commanded Mahgoub's interest and that have direct bearing on broadening the scope of study of the failed states, *Rectifying* articulates two broadly interrelated concerns: Sudanizing the Left and knitting together knowledge and perception, as Mahgoub reckoned with the deep cultural impasses and repressive politics that enveloped the country in perpetual crisis.

Rectifying highlights the ways in which the right repressed notions of change through its circulation of distorted, reactionary views via its well-oiled media

---

[41] For elaboration, see Abusharaf, *Marx in the Vernacular*, 484–500.

machine. Oral tradition and rumor also played a role in fomenting ideas about the Left's attempts to spread "a culture of atheism". Mahgoub clearly recognized the urgent need for fundamental alternatives to received wisdom about the conflation of secularism with atheism. Developing a public culture that recognized Leftist views on political life and society thus required unmasking the prevailing myth about religious belief as an ideological problem. Roland Barthes' comments give insight into how myth can work politically:

> Statistically, myth is on the right. There, it is essential; well fed, sleek, expansive, garrulous, it invents itself ceaselessly. It takes hold of everything, all aspects of the law, of morality, of aesthetics, of diplomacy, of household equipment, of Literature, of entertainment. Its expansion has the very dimensions of bourgeois ex-nomination...The oppressed is nothing; he has only one language, that of his emancipation; the oppressor is everything, his language is rich, multiform, and supple, with all the possible degrees of dignity at its disposal: he has an exclusive right to meta-language. The oppressed makes the world, he has only an active, transitive (political) language; the oppressor conserves it, his language is plenary, intransitive, gestural, and theatrical: it is Myth. The language of the former aims at transforming, of the latter at eternalizing.[42]

To deconstruct the very language with which mythical perceptions of the Left had been formulated and circulated on a large scale, Mahgoub first embarked on uncovering the right-wing propaganda that labeled the Left as atheistic, aiming to shake core religious beliefs in devout God-fearing communities. Mahgoub explained how during colonial rule these ideas were prevalent, with colonialism and its ideological allies promoting a view of Leftist politics as equivalent to a Leftist religion, since the Left did not incorporate religious beliefs within its economic framework. Attacks on this framework were promulgated aggressively during the colonial period in newspapers, mosque sermons, political speeches, and other conservative platforms. After the departure of the British, their surrogates, eager to create a climate of fear around the concept of secularism, continued to paint Leftists as apostates. Refuting these views, Mahgoub continued to emphasize the importance of respecting religion as a significant element in Sudanese society.

The question of religion in politics absorbed him deeply. In the context of conservatism, politics and religion touched a sensitive nerve concerning governability and legitimacy. Thus Mahgoub never expressed views on religion as an impediment to political understanding or a stumbling block in the quest

---

[42] Roland Barthes, *Mythologies*, trans. Annette Lavers (New York: Hill and Wang, 1972), 148–9.

for justice. Mahgoub's ability to distinguish between the conservative manipulation of Marxism and a Marxism that was Africanized vis-à-vis religion was extraordinary. Muslims, Mahgoub explained to a large audience in his writing, could still embrace the five pillars of Islam, attend mosque, fast, pray, give alms, and visit the Haj if they had the means to do so. Some imams and judges of Islamic courts, in fact, joined Marxist circles, as the philosophy did not tamper with their deeply held beliefs.

Mahgoub was able to explain to these communities of faith that the often-quoted Marxist nostrum about religion as the opiate of the masses had been uttered in a specific context and its meaning should not be detached from its particular historical referent. Mahgoub argued that Marxism was neither a dogma nor a creed exempt from interpretation. It was primarily a body of theory that lent itself to indigenous forms apposite to the conditions of a country riven by sectarian divisions. Religious belief, he felt, must be distinguished from a sustained struggle for a secular, democratic state for Muslims, Christians, and believers of indigenous African religions.

"The counter-revolution hides in the shadow of Islam," he wrote, "in order to prevent social cohesion through the exploitation of religion as a weapon; this means nothing but political bankruptcy leading them to abandoning secular political life and spreading right-wing hypocrisy that touch all aspects of life in our country. Ultimately, they seek to establish a conservative power in the name of religion."[43] To Mahgoub, this was clear evidence of deep-seated fanaticism among conservatives, who left no stone unturned in their effort to subvert opportunities for Sudanese people to be exposed to alternative views and possibilities.[44]

Mahgoub then turned to the task of building a successful state through a national democratic project. Neither dwelling on the conservatives' perspectives on politics and religion nor heeding their prejudices and hate speech, he ventured forth with a program for empowering communities and addressing exploitation, corruption, and profligate squandering of the country's resources. He worked to unionize diverse groups all over the country in order to break the siege of silence they had been living under for decades. When asked by the military judge who presided over the summary trial in which he

---

[43] Mahgoub, *Rectifying*, 54.

[44] In a paradoxical twist, Mahgoub's opponents frequently invoked the Jewish origins of his Marxist mentor, world-renowned activist Henri Curreil, as well as that of Karl Marx whenever Mahgoub addressed rallies on the subject of social justice.

was convicted of conspiracy to overthrow the regime in 1971 what his contributions were to Sudan, Mahgoub responded in a few succinct words: "consciousness, as much as I could".

Recognition of the "The Power of the Between"[45]

In 1964, during a brief period of civilian rule, Mahgoub was elected to Parliament. His efforts during this time to mediate among multiple parties in discussions about the future of Sudan have often been cited by scholars as evidence of his support of democratization. His reception as visionary for a democratic approach to decision-making was—and still is—unparalleled on the continent. His relationship with all parties has been described as amicable and respectful, while he also maintained his principled commitment to fairness for all. He was adept at demonstrating what anthropologist Paul Stoller called "the power of the between", that is, a power grounded in "deploying multiple layers of significations, complexities, intersections, and embodiments as a technique for weaving the world".[46] For Mahgoub, it was in the alchemy of multiple, often opposing, forces that solutions could be reached.

As he worked to establish a unified democratic front, Mahgoub was attentive to the nuances of the project, which involved diverse social groups who, to varying degrees, were convinced of the need for the Left and saw great possibilities in continued dialogue with it. Evidence suggests that Mahgoub was able to soften polarizing discourse about authority, politics, and religion during the brief interval of civilian rule and to gauge the calms and storms coursing through political factions while keeping in perspective the competing political interests in the country.

Democratization: An Urgent Anthropological Project

It is still possible today to look at *Rectifying*, written fifty years ago, to find a message that speaks with relevance to present-day issues in so many societies in North Africa that are experiencing political change. It is particularly important for Sudan, where at this moment there are protests from numerous and varied groups and an Islamist president who has waved his cane saying there

---

[45] Paul Stoller, *The Power of Between: An Anthropological Odyssey* (Chicago and London: University of Chicago Press, 2008).
[46] Stoller, *The Power of Between*, 126.

was no spring in Sudan but rather a hot summer that would burn those who dared to challenge him.

The notion of a broad front for change embodied in democratization as an urgent task for Sudan's political future was an idea original to Maghoub.[47] In foregrounding transformative discourses on social justice, Mahgoub's vision of new ways of reading political life necessitated drawing inspiration from successful international experiences while simultaneously recognizing home-grown versions of what works and does not. In today's complex, often chaotic, political situation, I suggest that intellectuals read Mahgoub to explore pathways through which democratization and emancipatory praxis can be set in motion.[48]

Subverting Marginality

"Marginality", according to sociologist Tony Bennett, "combines the idea of a dominating force with a spatial metaphor: to be marginal is both to have less power and to be at some distance from the center of power."[49] *Rectifying* demonstrates how essential the concept of marginality was in Mahgoub's thought, even as he was cognizant of how institutionalized power constrains free agency and subjectivity in a weak state. Mahgoub maintained that problems regarding borders, marginality, minorities, citizenship, gender, and ethnic discrimination were all symptoms of unequal accumulation, reinforced by a political culture steeped in authoritarianism and lacking transparency and accountability. By unmasking the mechanisms by which the political elite continued to wreak profound suffering upon the populace, Mahgoub exposed the winner-take-all mentality that enabled the post-independence government to reproduce the inequality and injustice of the colonial government. With his deep understanding of context and of the insidious abuses of power in postcolonial Sudan, Mahgoub's vision was informed by a creative application of Marxism, which as a political theory had been occluded by decades of misrepresentation. His views on democratization rested on the belief that revolu-

---

[47] Even before *Rectifying* was published Mahgoub spoke out against the myth that he was trying to destroy Sudanese culture and tradition by importing Western theories of Marxism:

[48] See Rogaia Mustafa Abusharaf "Introduction: Writing the Dialectic," *South Atlantic Quarterly* 109 (2010): 1–7

[49] See Tony Bennett et al., *New Keywords: A Revised Vocabulary of Culture and Society* (Oxford: Blackwell Publishing, 2005), 204.

tionary change cannot occur without a theory to inform it. The seemingly interminable ruminations in *Rectifying* and the reiteration of idea after idea are textual manifestations of these important views on the political relevance of theories of change that can effect positive political actions on the ground. The analysis developed by Mahgoub informed his approaches to structural change, especially his activism in unionizing women, workers, peasants, youth, and other segments of Sudanese society, both separately and jointly, as van-guards of meaningful transformation of society. He believed that "economic restructuring could not be achieved without strengthening local communities and economies, nor could it be done in a mechanical or perfunctory way".[50] Desired transformations must be apprehended as complex dialectical pro-cesses by both scholars and activists organizing for change. To him a robust theory of sociopolitical transformation and his advocacy on behalf of the silent majority were inseparable.

Current Resonances

The recent secession of the Republic of South Sudan from Sudan and the crisis in Darfur and the east are dramatic results of the perpetuation of marginality by the Sudanese national government. It is a situation which Mahgoub might have predicted: the nationalist government's attitude toward minorities within the country led to grievances seemingly so serious that they could only be resolved by separation. Indeed, the largest country in Africa has become the ultimate house of cards. Both its past and present are grim and desolate, and its situation reflects the urgent problems in fragile societies and weak states around the world who share similar historical experiences and present corrupt govern-ments. Heeding the historical context of the experiences of South Sudan leaves no doubt that secession, a critical factor in Sudan's present weakness, has deep historical roots in British colonial history and must neither be abstracted from this oppressive episode nor from the postcolonial environment that barred a viable nation-building project from successful implementation. Today the Republic of South Sudan, like the state from which it seceded, has found itself on the list of failed states. Fifty years ago, Mahgoub deciphered the writing on the wall, and now his worst fears have turned into dire reality.

Mahgoub understood what he was up against: elite ideology, feudal men-tality, existing relations of production, and the deeper impediments created

[50] Mahgoub, *Rectifying*, 37.

by those invested in the existing establishment. In the northern provinces of Khartoum, Kassala, and Darfur, semi-feudal exploitation abounded. In the South, a weakening of the subsistence economy and the failure to promote equality were, in Mahgoub's view, conscious attempts by the state to accumulate and circulate surplus among the wealthiest, thereby imperiling the entire country. These views were corroborated by nuanced ethnographic accounts that appeared after Mahgoub's death, when, despite considerable odds, the Left played an important role in advancing a social movement, raising national consciousness, and encouraging popular attention to economic and political matters. Nonetheless, as the years wore on, conservative forces maintained the status quo. In all of Mahgoub's philosophical debates on nation, class, and culture, he underscored the imperative of deep thinking. To him this activity was in and of itself a transformative act, confronting burning issues such as old colonial structures, postcoloniality, modernity, and traditionalism—issues that span national frontiers and are germinal to understanding the seeds of state weakness.[51]

Conclusion

In this chapter I have introduced questions that lie at the heart of the problems of representation and production of knowledge about weak societies. As I pondered these questions, I summoned Abdel Khaliq Maghoub's *Rectifying* to guide a discussion seen through a lens of political economy—one that engages the complementarity of national and global politics. I drew lessons from *Rectifying* to expand the debate on topics heretofore ignored, such as how to develop a new public culture that accommodates alternative ways of knowing. This task, which may seem impossible to some, was not so difficult for Mahgoub, who drew evidence from the devastating facts on the ground. He believed in a democratic process in post-independence Sudan, achieved through a closer attention to the subjects of citizenship, parity, and constitutionalism. These subjects, however, had been hijacked by his opponents, who had gained power during the colonial period and were able to maintain it after independence. Their control of the economy and their claims to religious orthodoxy seemed to have circumscribed Sudanese citizens' ability to embrace structural change. Open discussions about the consequences of these sectarian influences seemed to have circumscribed Sudanese citizens' ability to embrace

---

[51] Abusharaf, *Marx in the Vernacular*, 493.

structural change. Notwithstanding, Mahgoub believed that, in the end, the heterogeneity of the population would become a potential resource for recognizing difference as a valuable feature of Sudanese life. Mahgoub's openness was essential for excavating the latent potential for political change in pockets scattered throughout the margins of an Arab–African society.

Rectifying can provide researchers of weak states with rich resources for a nuanced interweaving of anthropology, politics, and philosophy. Besides showcasing an Arab intellectual writing within the progressive tradition, Mahgoub's work offers ways of grappling with the questions of how to deal with a failed state. Reading Mahgoub can show how Sudan's history has led to its present situation.[52] Mahgoub was murdered by the government forty years ago, but his comprehension of the complicated political scene can lead the way to making Sudan a stable state today. His writing provides a road map for future generations of activists. Non-Sudanese scholars and activists in countries that have also acquired the label of weak states will also stand to benefit from Mahgoub's explications of history and politics in their own societies. What scholars in stable states can glean is a lesson in the interweaving of theory with practice in order to remove the impediments in the path toward national belonging and equal citizenship.

The postcolonial government of Sudan might have provided a bridge linking the Arabs, the Africans, and the Afro-Arab populations living within its borders, but this bridge has collapsed. The collapse and the weakness that characterize the Sudanese state cannot be isolated from a deep understanding of the emergence of a privileged few who rose as the new epicenter of power and authority and who, instead of promoting a more democratic society, moved rapidly to acquire power and property in a market in which the Sudanese citizen was the cheapest commodity, to be ignored and flouted. State weakness and the discourse about it are emblematic of severe empathy and accountability deficits. Weak states are entangled in a web of intricate international politics in which their most stable counterparts often act to support

---

[52] The distinguished professor and former Lebanese ambassador Clovis Maksoud has observed that Mahgoub circumvented the crisis of the Arab's Left by recognizing the far-reaching influences of religion in society and has noted how his emphasis on political economy enabled him to mount powerful arguments about bridging the intellectual and political gaps in the debate on the place of Leftist thinking in Arab societies. Personal communication: Washington, DC, August 2012. Maksoud met Mahgoub in person when they attended a students' conference in Algeria sometime around the end of the 1950s.

their weakness at the same time that they establish a set of indicators that categorize them as failed. Empathy with the predicaments faced by the majority of the inhabitants of the world and recognition of the accountability of powerful states for their quandaries are conspicuously absent. Only by recognizing these political dynamics and the structures of transgression they helped engender can we crack the code of state weakness. We must, therefore, recognize the lasting intellectual legacy of Mahgoub, who summoned the courage to draw attention to the spectacular failure of the colonial and postcolonial state and to envision a public culture that holds innovation and renewal in high regard. With such an intellectual framework, fixing weak states will at least have a fighting chance.

8

SUDAN

A TURBULENT POLITICAL MARKETPLACE

Alex de Waal

This chapter describes and defines the political economy of Sudan and South Sudan in a manner that addresses the realities of how power is exercised. It argues that Sudan emerged from the political and economic crises of the first twenty-five years after independence as a polity run on the basis of a modernized patronage system, characterized by weak institutions and constant political bargaining. In this system, described as a turbulent political marketplace, the factions that comprise the ruling oligarchy bargain with one another and with provincial elites, who control local instruments of violence, to maintain sufficient cohesion and allegiance to maintain a political regime. With their political capital reduced due to the failure of the projects of Islamism and national unity, with their political budgets shrunk with financial crisis following the separation of South Sudan, President Bashir and the other members of the ruling group rely on their formidable political business skills for survival. The principal risk facing Sudan and South Sudan today is the descent of both countries into ungovernability.

For the last thirty years, successive governments in Sudan have conspicuously failed to produce public goods such as functioning institutions, peace and security, or social and economic development. They have intermittently delivered a broad spread of private goods through patronage systems, funded by borrowing, aid and oil revenues, but the state itself is widely despised by Sudanese citizens as corrupt and incompetent. For Sudanese, modernity has become a political project of the past, a subject for nostalgia.[1] However, despite their evident failures, Sudanese regimes have demonstrated a resilient and dynamic hybridity. This is notably the case for President Omar al Bashir, who seized power in June 1989. At the time, the Sudanese political class widely dismissed this little-known brigadier, with his vulgar public speeches and his conspicuous lack of political sophistication, as a puppet of the Sheikh of the Islamists, Hassan al Turabi, or as a transitional figure who would quickly be swept aside. Twenty-four years later, Bashir has proved to be a master of survival.

Bashir's particular talent is an extraordinarily detailed memory of individuals, their networks, and their material demands. He is a skilled manager of a political business plan that relies on retail patronage. Sudan's contemporary political system relies on patrimonial governance. Its institutions are run on patrimonial lines: political conflicts are managed by bargaining with individuals and not resolved by rules and procedures. Over the decades, Sudan's leaders have seen their political legitimacy wither, due to a succession of failed national projects. Lacking any credible hegemonic project and the political capital associated with it, they have relied instead on dispensing patronage through what in the vernacular is called the "political budget"—the system of dispensing rewards, favors, and jobs. Among the members of the ruling oligarchy, there is constant bargaining for position, and between those members and the provincial elites—many of whom command the local allegiance of armed men—a further process of bargaining over loyalties. In short, Sudan has modernized its patronage system so as to resemble a political marketplace in which loyalties are regularly auctioned to the highest bidder.[2]

Consequently, any attempt to measure Sudan's success or failure in terms of providing public goods—the conventional indicators of state fragility or failure—misses entirely the political processes whereby the regime maintains itself, adapting to changing circumstance, and managing violence and enrich-

---

[1] Cf. James Ferguson, *Global Shadows: Africa in the Neoliberal World Order* (Durham, NC: Duke University Press, 2006).

[2] Alex de Waal, "Mission without end? Peacekeeping in the African political marketplace", *International Affairs*, Vol. 85, No. 1 (2009), 99–113; idem, "Dollarised", *London Review of Books*, Vol. 32, No. 12 (2010), 38–41.

ment. Such conventional classifications of Sudan as strong, fragile, failing, or weak contribute neither to understanding the nature of the country nor to policies that respond to its predicament. Where Sudan stands in the Fund for Peace/*Foreign Policy* "Failed States Index", the Brookings Index of State Weakness in the Developing World, or the World Bank Country Policy and Institutional Assessment (CPIA) does not help us. (Sudan is not included in the Mo Ibrahim Foundation Index of African Governance.)[3] Without doubt, Sudanese citizens would prefer that their country resembled Sweden in terms of human development and human security, and those who have an opportunity to pursue their careers or seek personal safety in countries such as Sweden frequently do so. But that comparison has no other value, and indeed the dominant approach to "failed" and "fragile" states has not been short of critics. One alternative set of frameworks is the "Africa works" approach,[4] which argues that African states are run on the basis of deeply-entrenched and culturally-validated models of patrimonial or neo-patrimonial governance, which have proved remarkably resilient to shocks and global changes. This approach runs the risk of simply inverting its challenge to the overly normative paradigms and neglecting the genuine destructiveness of war, corruption, and limited-access governance typically based on ethnicity. A second framework, drawing on the work of Douglas North,[5] focuses on "the central role played by elite bargains embedded in wider political settlements in determining trajectories of violence and change in developing countries".[6] This approach provides for a rich analysis of the interactions between formal institutions and other forms of political power. However, despite avowing teleology, this framework is implicitly built on the assumption of a progression from older "limited access orders" to modern and progressive "open access orders". A third framework is that of imperial rule, and by extension the governance of some very large and diverse countries. An example is the Ottoman Empire,

---

[3] Mali is another country whose fate bears no relation to its performance by these indicators. Even after Mali's collapse in 2012, it continued to score better than its neighbors on the Fund for Peace/*Foreign Policy* index.

[4] Patrick Chabal, *Africa: The Politics of Suffering and Smiling*, 1st edn (London: Zed Books, 2009).

[5] Douglas North, John Joseph Wallis, and Barry R. Weingast, *Violence and Social Orders: A Conceptual Framework for Interpreting Recorded Human History* (Cambridge: Cambridge University Press, 2009).

[6] James Putzel and Jonathan DiJohn, "Meeting the Challenge of Crisis States", London School of Economics, Crisis States Research Centre (2012).

which endured a remarkably long time through a system whereby the imperial hub maintained a mediated authority through indirect rule, managing diversity through an accretion of ad hoc bargains with local powerbrokers, but therein sowing the seeds of its own demise by means of enabling local nationalisms and other centrifugal tendencies.[7]

Each of these approaches provides useful insights into Sudanese political life. However, none of them captures the specificities of a modernized, regionally- and globally-integrated competitive patrimonial order, financed by rents—what I term a "deregulated political marketplace". The construction of such a theoretical framework is beyond the reach of this chapter, but several of the key components emerge from a historical political–economic analysis of the Sudanese case. Additionally, none of the above approaches addresses the significance of political decision-making in determining outcomes. It is evident that the actions taken by political leaders, especially heads of state, can critically determine the trajectory that a country takes, but political science has little space for an approach that either privileges agency or places agency on a par with structure. The "political marketplace" framework adopted for this chapter tries to give full credit to political leaders' agency: they have "business plans" and associated skills, and use them to greater or lesser effect.

This chapter seeks to describe the "real politics" of Sudan, in the sense meant by Lenin when he pithily defined politics as "who, whom".[8] To understand Sudanese political life we should adapt Lenin's dictum to ask: who is buying, who is selling, how much is on offer, how are they bargaining? The following sections provide a political economic analysis of how Sudan became a highly deregulated political marketplace, an account of some of the major factors that determine the functioning of that marketplace, and a brief overview of how it is functioning today. One central concept that I bring to bear is the "political budget", namely the financial capacity of a ruler to rent allegiances within the political marketplace. This is the twin of "political capital", closely associated with legitimacy, which is the non-monetary resources that a regime brings to bear, such as nationalist sentiment. With the diminution of political capital in Sudan over many decades, the importance of the political budget and the management of the political marketplace become more signifi-

---

[7] Karen Barkey, *Empire of Difference: The Ottomans in Comparative Perspective* (Cambridge: Cambridge University Press, 2008).

[8] Cf. Raymond Guess, *Philosophy and Real Politics* (Princeton, NJ: Princeton University Press, 2008).

cant. This leads to a second concept, the "political business plan", which is a lens for studying the agency and skill of the leader.

Overall, Sudan is better characterized using the term "turbulent", borrowed from fluid dynamics, in which a system is subject to apparently random or chaotic changes in property, but nonetheless maintains its overall structure at a higher level. Just like the incessant moment-to-moment fluctuations in a stream of water, Sudan is unpredictable from week to week, but its basic character remains constant over a longer period.

Sudan: An Unstable Oligarchy

Since independence in 1956, Sudan's normal condition has been an unstable oligarchy. From the imperial reconquest in 1898 until the military coup of 1989, no single group ever managed to consolidate hold over the state.[9] Insofar as there were military dictators (Gen. Ibrahim Abboud, 1958–64; and Col. Jaafar Nimeiri, 1969–85), they were either weak or mercurial. Nimeiri stayed in power for as long as he did by continually shifting his alliances and changing his political colors. During the parliamentary periods, the two major sectarian parties (Umma Party, based on the Mahdist Ansar Movement, and the Unionist Party and its fragments, based on the Khatmiyya Sect) were constant rivals, neither able to dominate the other. Each sought to make inroads into what the Sudanese used to call the "modern forces", namely the institutionalized socio-political organizations—the trade unions, the professional associations, the civil service, and the army. Preoccupied with power relations among the oligarchs, governments neglected the problem of southern Sudan, and could not address the challenge of forging national identity in a diverse nation.

Within northern Sudan, all the social groups had some representation within the power blocs dominated by the two sectarian parties, and their secular rivals (such as the Communist Party). Tribal aristocrats in the east generally voted for the Khatmiyya/Unionists, and those in the west for the Umma. Their rewards were status in the sectarian hierarchies and the spiritual patronage of their leaders. Members of the orders dutifully provided their leaders with gifts.

One of the notable characteristics of Sudanese political life is the civility among the members of the political elite. Individuals who are bitter political

[9] Peter Woodward, *Sudan 1898–1989: The Unstable State* (Boulder, CO: Lynne Reinner Publishers, 1990).

enemies can be personally courteous and even warm to one another. It is a feature that has puzzled outsiders: Sudanese culture is marked by extreme charm and hospitality. Arguably, this is the other side of the coin of a system built on distrust: just as today's friend can be tomorrow's adversary, so today's rival might be tomorrow's ally. Possibly this characteristic preceded the pervasive distrust. It might have arisen because of the peculiarly tolerant nature of the Khatmiyya Sect, for example, which tends to regard those who abandon it as merely temporary prodigal sons who will return to the fold. Alternatively, this civility may be a structural characteristic that emerges in societies without enduring power hierarchies. Cause and effect is less important than the fact that these characteristics coexist.

Despite the history of domination by the ruling families, this system gradually became more inclusive over time. In the northern peripheries, ethnic-based political parties sprang up, notably the Beja Congress (eastern Sudan), the Union of the Fung (Blue Nile), the National Party (Nuba), and several manifestations of Darfurian revanchism. Southern Sudan always had its distinct political parties, mostly asserting an "African" identity, and the leaders of the northern marginalized groups persistently sought them as allies. Their leaders dreamed of a pan-Sudanese alliance of the marginalized, but as soon as such a coalition was put together, it fell apart. The parties of the marginalized never had the financial means to run campaigns and reward their followers. Most of their leaders compromised and joined the dominant parties, sometimes rising to high rank, but with their constituencies nonetheless in a subordinate position. Only with the emergence of the Sudan People's Liberation Army (SPLA), which combined a leadership committed to a national Sudanese alliance against the "old Sudan", a protean political agenda that simultaneously espoused democracy, "Africanism", and self-determination for southern Sudan, and which won regional and international standing, did a genuine challenge emerge to the patrimony of the Khartoum oligarchs.

In 1989, the National Salvation Revolution of the National Islamic Front and the army promised to put an end to the instability within the center. However, the new regime reproduced oligarchic competition within the new ruling group.[10] Although the trade unions and professional associations were crushed, and most of the sectarian elite fled to exile, the ruling coalition proved to have as many internal fissures as the old sectarian politics, and it

[10] Alex de Waal, "Sudan: The turbulent state", in Alex de Waal, ed., *War in Darfur and the Search for Peace* (Cambridge, MA: Harvard University Press, 2007).

absorbed many of the old fissures as well. By eliminating the middle ground in northern Sudan, the Islamist–military coalition strengthened the appeal of the SPLA. The Islamists were split internally and there was a division between civilians and military men, and between the army and the security services.[11] Those splits were spectacularly on show barely a year after they seized power, when President Bashir condemned Saddam Hussein's invasion of Kuwait, only to be overruled a few days later by Hassan al Turabi, sheikh of the Islamists who had no formal position in government, whose support for Saddam Hussein prevailed. Bashir emerged as the lynchpin of the system, rarely making decisions but rather engaging in a balancing act among the various factional leaders. The division of labor made at the time of the coup proved remarkably enduring: Bashir's task was to keep the regime in power; the tasks of the others were to make and implement policy. Bashir made one of his rare forays into decisive politics when the security services overstepped the mark and attempted to assassinate the Egyptian President Hosni Mubarak in 1995. He demoted several of his lieutenants and brought in some of his own closest aides to clean up the intelligence services. Later he expelled Usama bin Laden and some other foreign jihadists, but he never threw any of the Sudanese conspirators to the wolves. Only in 1999, when Turabi moved to assume power for himself, did Bashir make a countermove and expel Turabi from the circle of power, but even then many of Turabi's closest allies stayed in government.

The military–Islamist oligarchy has proven extraordinarily resilient, surviving financial crises, international isolation, and nearly continuous war. Even leading members of the regime confess to being puzzled as to how they managed it.

The Political Budget

The decline of the traditional sectarian families who ruled Sudan, and the failure of successive modernizing projects, has deprived Sudan's rulers of the political capital associated with that elusive concept, "legitimacy". In the 1990s, the declining credibility of sectarian and modernizing political projects left a vacuum that was filled by transformative political Islam, with Hassan al Turabi's project of building an Islamic state and society. By 1999, however, this

---

[11] Alex de Waal and A. H. Abdelsalam, "Islamism, state power and jihad in Sudan", in Alex de Waal, ed., *Islamism and its Enemies in the Horn of Africa* (London: Hurst & Co., 2004).

project was itself bankrupt and the Islamist–military coalition split in two. At that same moment, Sudan began to export oil, beginning a remarkable if short-lived economic boom that provided sufficient funds for the military junta to reconsolidate power using a suddenly enhanced political budget.

The single most important indicator of the health of a government in the political marketplace is the political budget, namely the resources that can be dispensed for patronage purposes without needing to be accounted for. The struggle to acquire these funds is one of the major activities of such a government. The political budget is the heartbeat of the system. This does not eliminate other elements in political life, such as nationalist sentiment, democratic representation, or political Islam, and indeed these do intermittently play a pivotal role in Sudanese politics. However, the political–economic trajectory of Sudan over recent decades has been towards the monetization and instrumentalization of political life.

The monetization of patronage in Sudan accelerated in the 1970s, when Nimeiri attacked the power bases of the existing sects and political parties, eliminated the Sudan Communist Party[12] and tried to build a new political constituency based on the promise of modernization and development. He did this by authorizing his ministers to borrow on their own account, which was a straightforward activity in the immediate aftermath of the oil boom.[13] Billions were borrowed and Sudan had little to show for it. When the payments became due in 1978, the Minister of Finance had to hire a foreign auditor to find out what had been borrowed from whom: the auditors described opening drawers in ministerial offices and discovering new loans in each one. Sudan was forced to swallow an IMF-designed austerity package.

Nimeiri managed the fiscal crisis through several mechanisms.[14] He invited the Muslim Brothers into government and encouraged them to set up Islamic banks that helped capture the vast remittance flows from the Sudanese diaspora in the oil-rich Gulf states. These finances largely escaped the supervision, let alone taxation, of the ministry of finance, but they provided money to Nimeiri's key allies. He continually appealed to the US for debt rescheduling, arguing that Sudan was a pro-Western bulwark surrounded by Communist

[12] Alain Gresh, "The Free Officers and the Comrades: The Sudanese Communist Party and Nimeiri Face-to-Face, 1969–1971", *International Journal of Middle Eastern Studies*, Vol. 21, No. 3 (1989), 393–409.

[13] Khalid Mansour, *Nimeiri and the Revolution of Dis-May* (London: KPI, 1985).

[14] Richard Brown, *Public Debt and Private Wealth: Debt, Capital Flight and the IMF in Sudan* (London: Palgrave Macmillan, 1992).

countries, at one point persuading the State Department to take out a commercial bridging loan to enable Sudan to be briefly up to date on its debt repayments to the IMF and World Bank, so that the Paris Club could meet and reschedule Sudan's debts, and from the new money, repay the State Department. (The treasury found out and prohibited further dealings of this sort.) Nimeiri cut secret deals with the CIA to facilitate a favorable hearing at the Paris Club. He allowed the Israelis to airlift Ethiopian Jews to Israel. He sold off state assets to private businessmen, and gave the army control of substantial economic sectors as a pay-off to keep military officers loyal. But the amounts simply grew too big, and in early 1985 the US Treasury acceded to the IMF complaints and put its foot down, denying another rescheduling. The gears of the patronage system began to grind to a halt. Nimeiri was forced to announce price rises for bread and other essentials. As street protests began, he flew to Washington DC to make a personal appeal to President Ronald Reagan. The appeal was successful: Nimeiri persuaded the American president to unlock enough money to keep him in power. But it was too late. As the *New York Times* remarked, the rug that was pulled from under Nimeiri had "IMF" written on it.[15]

Compelled to reverse some of Nimeiri's final austerity measures and faced with a fiscal crisis, the incoming Transitional Military Council had to economize in fighting the war, and the Minister of Defense decided that the cheapest way to confront the SPLA was to permit the Arab tribes on the North–South borderlands to arm themselves and pillage their southern neighbors. It was counter-insurgency on the cheap and the outcomes were predictably horrific. The month before Sudan's first free elections for eighteen years, the IMF suspended Sudan for non-payment of arrears. Thus the incoming democratic government of Sadiq al Mahdi was bankrupt from the start. Among the measures he took to manage the country without any cash in hand was to intensify the militia policy and to permit Gaddafi's Libya a free hand in Darfur. He also played the pro-Western card, and brought the US State Department round to assist in "managing the unmanageable", as running a state in official bankruptcy was described.[16] The Minister of Finance managed to persuade the IMF to run a "shadow program" in Sudan and kept its accounts liquid—just—by selectively paying the key creditors at the key moments.[17] Again, when the

---

[15] Ibid.

[16] Ibid.

[17] African Rights, *Food and Power in Sudan: A Critique of Humanitarianism* (London: African Rights, 1997).

US ran out of patience (January 1989) this latitude for borrowing dried up, this time for good. Sadiq conceded that he could not govern the country; and when the military coup came in June, it was no surprise.

Ten years of crisis in state finances had eroded government institutions and left the country run on the basis of a cluster of competing patronage systems, financed by illicit dealings, war-driven predation, and international Islamist networks. The following ten years were to be an exaggerated version of the same, as international assistance collapsed, and the Islamist government sought private money from the Gulf states, including from Usama bin Laden. National revenue collapsed to approximately $40m in 1993, expenditure to $100m. Ironically, the very collapse of the public sector and the growth of parallel financing mechanisms for the security services and army meant that the government could implement what appeared to be orthodox austerity measures such as eliminating subsidies, freezing salaries, and selling off the remaining public companies. For these actions the ministry of finance won plaudits from the IMF, which struggled to find a way to revise its rules so that it could deal with a country that was swallowing its medicine, but could not receive multilateral loans because its debt arrears were too great.

During the two decades of fiscal collapse at the center, Sudan's political budget became decentralized, controlled by a range of financiers, party leaders, security officers, and generals. The proliferation of parallel centers of authority resulted in the intelligence services running a plot to assassinate Hosni Mubarak without the knowledge of Bashir. Military campaigns in the war were often financed on an ad hoc basis by those with commercial interests in the areas of operation.

Sudan did recover from this near-total collapse. Revenue increased fivefold (in real terms) from SDG 237m in 1993 to SDG 2270m in 1999, still equivalent to less than $1bn. With oil, the budget increased a further tenfold to SGG 28bn in 2008 ($12bn). But as it recovered in the 2000s, the system that emerged did not resemble the preceding hybrid of institutions and patronage, and still less did it resemble any form of developmental state. Sudan re-emerged as a political marketplace, its political budget funded by rents, governed by a political business manager skilled in retail patronage—capable of remaining in power, but of little else.

With the prospect of oil exports coming close to realization in 1999, and with it the possibility of a political budget that was both centralized and much bigger than anything hitherto available, the internal political contest heated up. Turabi wanted the oil money to be handled by Islamic financial institutions. The Minister of Finance chose this time to expose corruption in Islamic banks associated with Turabist oligarchs. Bashir bided his time and then struck decisively, at a moment when it appeared Turabi was about to win. The oil money came mostly to the central government. Turabi was cut out, although there was an emergent capitalist group, chiefly Zaghawa business-men from Darfur with links to Chad, Libya, and the Gulf, who stayed with him and his allies. The Darfur war was fought in part over this commercial rivalry and the political funds associated with it.[18]

The oil boom saw the government supporting a vast expansion in public sector employment, in local government, security and defense.[19] The ruling National Congress Party (NCP) abandoned Islamism in all but rhetoric and became instead a coalition of commercial barons. Oil revenues first gave the government the financial capacity to threaten seriously the SPLA, and then to make a peace deal with the SPLA. Khartoum was suddenly flush with funds. At that time, Chad was friendly and Libya was inactive: the price of loyalty was low. This meant that the SPLA could be accommodated in the pay-off system without sacrificing members of the NCP, and Bashir could seriously contemplate renting southerners' commitment to unity bribing the leader-ship—underestimating the element of southern nationalism that simply could not be bought. This was the financial basis for the Comprehensive Peace Agreement (CPA) signed in January 2005.

After 2005, the political budget was squeezed from two directions. First, under the wealth-sharing provisions of the CPA, the SPLA—now a partner in government as the Sudan People's Liberation Movement (SPLM)—began to take a substantial slice, equivalent to 50 percent of the value of the oil extracted from southern Sudan. This was anticipated, but the second inflation-ary pressure was not: the Darfur war brought unwelcome external patronage, from Chad, Libya, and the United States, which pushed up the price demanded by provincial leaders.

The Sudanese government blundered into the Darfur war in 2003. It had good reason to fear the implications of an insurgency that was sponsored simultaneously by the SPLA and by its own rival Islamists. Then the rebels humiliated the armed forces, caught unprepared by a rebel attack on al Fashir air base. In mounting a response, the government found it no longer possessed a political and intelligence infrastructure in Darfur, because most of the Islamists had either defected to the opposition or simply stopped cooperating

---

[18] De Waal, "Sudan: The turbulent state".
[19] World Bank, "Sudan: Public Expenditure Review, Synthesis Report" (December 2007).

with the government. Without good information the party and security services did not know who was who and therefore who should be bought, rented, or eliminated. Philip Roessler[20] has convincingly made this argument to explain why the government could repress the 1991 Darfur rebellion quickly and with relatively little bloodshed—because it had its party apparatus intact and could quickly identify who was involved—whereas the 2003 rebellion was far bloodier. Without the option of retail patronage and individually targeted elimination, the army resorted to mass violence targeted principally on the basis of ethnicity. The military offensives of 2003–4 were successful in pushing the rebels back, but the army was unable to complete the job. However, by the time the Darfur peace talks began in earnest in late 2005, the government had rebuilt its security files and knew who was who, and how much they were demanding. The problem was that by this point the price of renting loyalty was, in their view, too high.

Center–Periphery Patronage and Bargaining

Sudan is one of the world's most unequal countries. Khartoum is a wealthy city. In 1993, when the government brought in a new currency, it discovered that more than 80 percent of the banknotes in circulation were in greater Khartoum. The outlying areas are poor. The financial base for organizing a political party in the provinces simply does not exist. Consequently, in the pre-1989 period, each of the main parties penetrated the peripheries and co-opted provincial leaders, in a manner similar to the "hub and spoke" model whereby imperial rulers broker relations with peripheral elites, while impeding those peripheries joining up to create a "rim".[21] In the post-1989 period, the National Islamic Front and its successor the NCP did the same.

Rural opposition tends to turn to ethnic–territorial rebellion with land as a central grievance. Guma Kunda Komey sums up the logic whereby provincial movements became ethnically particularist and armed:

> Four common features characterize the various ethno-political movements in Sudan. First, they arose in the regions whose populations are largely of African origin in response to persistent exclusion and marginalization by the central state. Second, in pursuing their political endeavours, these regions form a loose political solidarity in some national issues of common interest, particularly in their demand

---

[20] Phillip Roessler, "Political instability, threat displacement and civil war: Darfur as a Theory Building Case", Social Science Research Network, http://ssrn.com/abstract=1909228 (accessed 7 July 2013).

[21] Cf. Barkey, *Empire of Difference*.

for a federal system. Third, these movements pursue their demands to the central government on the basis of their ethno-territorial affiliations, with each region progressively becoming a spatial expression of belonging and attachment, a source of economic livelihood, and an icon for socio-cultural identification. Finally, in response to their persistent political marginality and socio-economic deprivation, these regional movements gradually shifted from peaceful and political to armed movements coupled with a change of loyalties from national to regional levels, with each region (land) being concretized as a political category with a specific character, image and status in the minds of its inhabitants.[22]

The logic of ethnic particularism leads to self-determination and ultimately secession, as has been the case with the independence of South Sudan in July 2011. However, Guma does not mention the fifth characteristic that all these provincial movements share: some of their leaders are bought off and join the ruling oligarchy. This imperial-style "divide and rule" strategy has been effective in negating the military and political capability of provincial movements. But it is more than a cunning maneuver by scheming security chiefs: the phenomenon of renting allegiance is the very stuff of peripheral governance in Sudan.

Indirect rule on the "hub and spoke" model is, however, a dangerous game for the center. By ruling through administrative tribalism, the ruler also cultivates ethnic particularism. Tribal "subjects" in such a system of decentralized despotism[23] are ready recruits to ethnically-based rebellion, and to separatism. In turn, to maintain its pretense of hegemony, the government is compelled to respond with a show of force.

The cheapest way for government to organize a counter-insurgency is to rent a militia. The drawback of this is that the militia may initially be ready to fight for payment in kind but will then realize the downside of committing atrocities against one's historic neighbors, and also then realize it can demand higher payment, and do so. The army is well aware of the perils of the militia strategy. Its response to this threat is to absorb the militia into the armed forces or official paramilitaries. This brings some control and detailed intelligence about who actually controls the militia, a prerequisite for efficiently buying them off.

The SPLA began, in the words of John Garang, as a "mob".[24] For its first eight years it was extensively supported by the then government of Ethiopia, and was one of the largest and most exclusively militarized rebel armies in

---

[22] Guma Kunda Komey, *Land, Governance, Conflict and the Nuba of Sudan* (Oxford: James Currey, 2010), 10.

[23] Cf. Mahmood Mamdani, *Citizen and Subject: Contemporary Africa and the Legacy of Late Colonialism* (Princeton, NJ: Princeton University Press, 1996).

[24] African Rights, *Food and Power in Sudan*, 61.

Africa. It was run entirely on a centralized basis by the commander in chief and possessed no political institutions outside the military high command. After losing Ethiopian backing in 1991, the SPLA simultaneously fragmented and its leadership embarked on a search for new sponsors. It never regained its centralized military command. The leadership reluctantly conceded the need for a convention (held in 1994) and for some political and administrative institutions, but these remained weak and contingent upon the personal decisions of the leader. The SPLA was actually de-institutionalized over its second decade, with the command preferring to organize military units specifically for particular operations, after which their members would be dispersed, remaining solely as SPLA fighters or commanders, with minimal unit coherence. The rationale for this was that organizational capability might threaten the supremacy of Garang, a position he retained through his function as the sole intermediary with foreign patrons.

On moving into government in 2005, the SPLM adopted much the same system of governance by renting allegiance. This was cemented in the January 2006 Juba Agreement, whereby Garang's successor, the President of the Government of southern Sudan, Salva Kiir, brought most of the non-SPLA militia into the fold with large payments. Among the consequences of this were that the defense payroll was over 200,000 people (many of them "ghost soldiers"), including more than 600 generals, each of whom had a personal retinue of somewhere between twenty and a thousand armed guards. The legislative assembly voted to increase the budget of the SPLA, paying each putative infantryman a salary of $150 a month, twice that of his counterpart in the Sudan Armed Forces. Unsurprisingly, the SPLA did not find it difficult to recruit over the border into northern Sudan, causing consternation in the Ministry of Defence in Khartoum.

The historic state-building trajectory in Europe was based on a pact between a ruler who controlled the means of violence, and provincial and commercial elites that controlled the resources, leading to the emergence of a "protection racket" as a precursor to an institutionalized state.[25],[26] In oil-boom Sudan and southern Sudan, this relationship was reversed: the state controlled the money and the provincial elites had the guns. This led to politics as an extortion racket,

[25] Charles Tilly, "War making and state making as organized crime", in Peter Evans, Dietrich Rueschemeyer, and Theda Skocpol, eds., *Bringing the State Back In* (Cambridge, Cambridge University Press: 1985).

[26] Mancur Olson, "Dictatorship, Democracy and Development", *American Political Science Review*, Vol. 97, No. 3 (1993), 567–76.

in which militia leaders, military entrepreneurs, rebels (with or without causes), and commanders of army and paramilitary units could—and did—threaten the governments and demand resources. Ironically, it is the leaders of the deprived peripheries that possess the fiercest means of coercion, but their competition for rents deriving from the political centers in Khartoum and Juba leave them incapable of achieving political change or contributing to state-building. Survival and personal advancement demands all their political–business skills. This is the contemporary Sudanese political marketplace.

The Regional Marketplace

Sudan's political marketplace has long stretched beyond the boundaries of the state. In the nineteenth century, Sudanese merchant adventurers ranged across wide swathes of central Africa. In the 1960s and 1970s, Sudan's famed hospitality to refugees has had, as its counterpart, security engagement with the affairs of neighboring countries such as Chad, Eritrea, and Uganda. Such cross-border engagement in renting loyalties in turn encouraged the rulers of neighboring countries to seek clients inside Sudan. Although this phenomenon has historical roots, notably in the case of Egypt, it was only from the outbreak of the second civil war in 1983 that the interpenetration of national governance systems in the region truly deepened. We can briefly sketch how each of Sudan's neighbors functions, moving from the north in an anti-clockwise manner.

Egypt historically dispenses patronage in a targeted and predictable way, through the state, army, and its favored political intermediaries (the Unionist Party). More than fifty years after Sudanese independence, the Egyptian government regards Sudan as a lost territory, and still cherishes dreams of a united Nile Valley.

Libya under Qadhafi was a binge shopper, intermittently spending large amounts on Sudanese clients and proxies, often indiscriminately. Since Qadhafi's overthrow, Libya has turned its back on sub-Saharan Africa, but enjoys close relations with Khartoum on account of the latter's support for the Transitional National Council in its hour of need in 2011.

For years Chad was a client state on Sudan's outer periphery, its rulers often dependent on Sudanese money and security expertise. This changed when oil was discovered in the 1990s. By the mid-2000s, President Idriss Déby had sufficient political budget to buy loyalties inside Darfur. Having achieved parity with Sudan, in 2010 he agreed to a truce whereby neither destabilizes the other.

The Central African Republic is a client state, subordinate to all its neighbors. President Ange-Félix Patassé (1993–2003) was subordinate to the Congolese rebel Pierre Bemba, and hence within the Ugandan axis. Consequently, with Sudanese cooperation, Chad installed François Bozizé in 2003 and removed him ten years later in much the same manner. The Democratic Republic of Congo's peripheries are contested marketplaces, in which the neighbors (notably Uganda, Rwanda, and Angola, but also Sudan) pay their clients or even intervene directly. President Yoweri Museveni of Uganda has skillfully instrumentalized the international outcry against the Lord's Resistance Army to establish forward bases for his army in South Sudan and Central African Republic, which Uganda uses both for commercial purposes and to support the northern Sudan rebels. By contrast, Kenyan oligarchs rarely venture into Sudanese affairs, except for specific commercial purposes.

Ethiopia's Meles Zenawi was the only leader in the region who theorized the political economy of rent and political budgets. During the last decade of his rule, Zenawi's attempt to build a developmental state involved the deliberate allocation of rent to productive sectors, minimizing his political patronage spending and maximizing public goods. When Ethiopia intervened in Sudan, it did so as a state, not a sponsor. This is manifest in Ethiopia's leading role in peace talks, and its provision of a mechanized brigade for the UN Interim Security Force for Abyei.

In Eritrea, the criminalization of the state gave it an occasionally significant budget to spend in internal Sudanese affairs. In 2006, Sudan dealt with the ongoing conflict in eastern Sudan by cutting a deal directly with Asmara, confident that enough of the Beja insurgents would comply that the remainder would be insignificant. It worked. Subsequently, most of President Isseyas Afewerki's external political budget has been dispensed in combating Ethiopia, through Somalia. Latterly, there is evidence of complicity between Eritrean and Sudanese security officers in the lucrative people-trafficking business up the Red Sea coast.

Saudi Arabia sporadically dispenses vast sums, usually as an act of personal largesse by the king or another member of the ruling family. Qatar saw an opportunity for cheaply buying influence in Africa and has used its funds accordingly. Iran has been engaged with Sudan since the early 1990s, when Turabi's Popular Arab and Islamic Conference tried to bridge the Sunni–Shia divide. It has supported the Sudanese military industries and has used Sudanese territory for shipping arms to Hamas. The financial pay-offs for the Sudanese army have been such that the government has been ready to pay the price in terms of cooler relations with Gulf states. Israel is an active sponsor of South Sudan and the northern Sudanese opposition. Israeli fighter jets have struck arms supply convoys in the Red Sea littoral, probably destined for Hamas, and in October 2012 Sudan blamed Israel for an air strike on a munitions factory in Khartoum.

The main government strategy for dealing with provincial insurgencies has been to neutralize their external sponsors. Thus Sudan made a deal with Eritrea in 2006 and removed the threat in eastern Sudan. It tried to overthrow the government of Chad in 2008 and failed, but was able to cut a deal with President Déby in 2010, minimizing Chadian interference in Darfur. In 2011, Sudan assisted in the overthrow of the Qadhafi government in Libya, removing the threats of military destabilization and patronage competition. It has not been able to cut a deal with South Sudan, both before and after secession. Independent South Sudan is a standing rebuke to President Bashir's repeated commitments to national unity, and the sacrifices made by northern Sudanese in pursuit of that failed enterprise. And it is also an ongoing sponsor of insurgencies within northern Sudan.

The regional integration of the marketplace complicates the business plans of the Sudanese oligarchs. It intermittently makes loyalty much more expensive, for example in Darfur during the period 2005–11. It provides provincial elites with alternative patrons and greater bargaining leverage, demanding that Khartoum expend greater efforts in information-gathering and make more complicated calculations.

Successive efforts at international mediation have been incorporated into this regional marketplace. The CPA was possible because of the threat and potential of oil revenues and the benefits that a stabilized Sudan promised for neighboring states. The Darfur peace negotiations in Abuja in 2005–6 were undermined by circumstantial dynamics in the patronage marketplace. The Eastern Sudan Peace Agreement of 2006 was based on a straightforward bargain with Eritrea, as was the 2010 accord with Chad. The Doha Document for Peace in Darfur was an experiment in an internationally validated template, backed by Qatari funds, to incentivize peace, but it was incompetently managed. The AU High Level Panel on Darfur (AUPD) sought an alternative approach, of exploring a public consensus for peace, reconciliation, and justice—generating political capital out of social capital, as it were—but this was obstructed by the Sudanese government, Qatar, and the UN.

Sudan after Separation

The secession of South Sudan was an immense political shock to the Sudanese establishment. In the aftermath, Sudanese politics are marked by demoralization and search for scapegoats. Political life is bitter, vengeful, and introverted. The CPA promised unity, peace, and normalization with the West, and delivered none of the three. When the southern Sudanese voted overwhelmingly for separation in 2011, all the civilian political leaders who were associated with the CPA kept their heads down, while those who preferred to reject compromise were ascendant.

The economic shock of separation also reverberated. In July 2011, Sudan lost 70 percent of its oil production and 90 percent of its hard currency. Most countries, faced with such a blow, would have been able to turn to the IMF for assistance, but under US-led financial sanctions, international financial institutions are debarred from lending to Sudan. Sudanese negotiators reached an in-principle agreement that the post-secession financial gap would be filled, approximately equally, by Sudan's own austerity measures, by international assistance (the precise mechanism unspecified, but the US indicated that it would permit Arab countries such as Saudi Arabia, Kuwait, and Qatar to assist Sudan without being held to be abrogating the financial sanctions), and by transitional transfers from South Sudan. The total figure, based on IMF estimates, was $9.1 billion over three and a half years.

However, Sudan received only modest and ad hoc assistance from Arab countries. The oil and financial agreements signed in September 2012 have been subject to interminable delays in implementation. The government only implemented its own austerity package in May 2012, after long delays created by near-paralysis of decision-making.

The same internal paralysis makes it very hard for Sudan to make the compromises necessary to establish peace with the South and normalize relations with the US. Vetoes are exercised by groups with special interests, such as the leaders of the Misseriya tribe who make seasonal use of the Abyei area on the border with South Sudan, and claim the major part of Abyei as their historic territory. Although Abyei is small and the Misseriya are a small factor in the calculus of national interest, they have been able to hold to ransom a matter of far greater national importance—resolving a bitter dispute that is a major obstacle to peace with South Sudan. Another argument, routinely used by hardliners to good effect, is why make a concession when we can be sure that the US will swallow it and simply ask for more? And that when faced with an adversary that will be satisfied only with regime change, the best strategy is to give nothing away.

Khartoum's paranoia is not wholly irrational, as influential groups in the US have consistently opposed any measure that would demonstrate good faith compromise, with the result that Sudan has received no positive response from Washington, D.C. despite a record of counter-terrorist cooperation, signing the 2005 CPA, the 2006 peace accord with Darfur, permitting a peaceful secession of the South in 2011, and cooperating extensively with the overthrow of Qadhafi that same year. Sudan's rulers discount Washington's promises very steeply, perhaps entirely. Additionally, the pinnacle of success of the US advocacy movement, namely the arrest warrant against President Bashir demanded by the prosecutor of the International Criminal Court in 2008, has meant that the US and the United Nations cannot deal with the President personally. This leaves the African Union to take the lead as negotiator. Nonetheless, the superpower makes the rules, and Sudan has continued to seek normalization of relations with America.

As the southern referendum approached in late 2010, negotiators from north and south committed themselves to a separation on the "overriding principle" of "two viable states", at peace with one another. Subsequently, this principle was honored in the breach, as each state endured hardship in an attempt to make the other collapse first. Neither was able to sustain the effort, in part because of international pressure on both. However, by the time the two presidents signed cooperation agreements in September 2012, each was sufficiently weakened internally that he could not instruct his subordinates to implement what had been agreed, but rather had to negotiate every detail with military commanders, tribal leaders, and other members of the national political elite. Repeatedly, unable to achieve a consensus, one leader or the other returned to the African Union mediator, the former South African president Thabo Mbeki, with a request to renegotiate some part of the agreement.

The paralysis in implementing the agreements is due largely to the weakness of the two leaders, who, lacking both political capital and political budget, must bargain with their own subordinates to achieve consensus before they can act. One consequence is that the AU facilitators and the international community's special envoys themselves become dragged ever deeper into the bargaining process, spending enormous amounts of time and energy on issues that are themselves trivial, such as the precise geographical definition of a remote border area no more than 14 miles wide, but which are the focus of ever more minute bargaining among the two countries' provincial elites. Implementation has staggered from crisis to crisis.

Sudan and South Sudan proved more resilient in the face of austerity during 2012–13 than was predicted. Nonetheless the economic shock to both was immense. South Sudan's GDP contracted by 55 percent during 2012 as a consequence of the government shutting down its oil production, which had represented 82 percent of GDP and 98 percent of government revenue. South Sudanese society survived chiefly because relatively little of the oil funds actually reached the general population, being creamed off by the oligarchs. Sudanese GDP also contracted, though by less. With a more educated and demanding citizenry, the Khartoum government faces more vocal opposition. Each government can handle popular protests and provincial rebellions. What poses a more systemic challenge to them is the drying up of the funds that rent the loyalties of intermediate elites. If the financial pressure on the two governments becomes even more severe, the basic pacts that keep the oligarchies together also come under pressure. In the north, what virtue in Bashir's proven efficacy at keeping the regime in power if it is as bankrupt as when he took power 24 years ago? In the south, Salva Kiir is a leader by default rather than an elite bargain, and the southern Sudanese polity has a history of dictatorship (under Garang) rather than oligarchy. However, regime change in north or south, or armed conflict between the two, is not the fundamental issue: it is whether either state remains governable or not.

Meanwhile, the maturing of the economic and fiscal crises in both Sudan and South Sudan leaves the two rulers with very modest political capital and political budgets. The oil boom is over and patronage pay-outs no longer suffice to maintain the bloated public service and security sectors. Soldiers are unpaid and, in the case of the SPLA's Eighth Division in Jonglei, have turned to provisioning themselves from a local population designated as insurgent—a recipe for atrocity and humanitarian crisis. The broader risk is that ongoing economic crisis will cause a crisis in governability in either or both of northern and southern Sudan.

The AU High-Level Implementation Panel (AUHIP) has sought to be a patient and persistent point of certainty amid the turbulence. It has neither a coercive capability (although Ethiopia has provided peace-keeping troops) nor funds for incentivizing its proposals, and so has pursued the option of stubborn suasion. Until the South Sudanese decision to shut down its oil production in January 2012, this formula was likely to work, as the default option for relations between Sudan and South Sudan was to cooperate just enough to maintain their shared economic lifeline, namely oil production. The South Sudanese decisions to close down its oilfields and invade the north shattered this fragile equilibrium and set both nations on a course towards ungovernability. The AUHIP has only been able to provide the two leaderships with every opportunity to revoke their suicide pact, but as the months pass and the systemic political–economic crisis deepens, the possibility of escape from the effects of the slow-motion "doomsday machine" reduces.

The Opposition

The grievances and capacity for sustained and even widened rural insurrection and urban protests should not be underestimated. However, the opposition in Sudan has recently relied chiefly on the mistakes and provocations of the government rather than a coherent strategy of its own. Rather than forming a new front with a common agenda of social justice,[27] the broad left or progressive forces in Sudan gravitated towards the SPLM, which failed to deliver on its "New Sudan" agenda.

The shortcomings of the opposition were starkly illustrated during the general elections of April 2010. The opposition parties failed to organize their constituents to register to vote in 2009, partly because some foreign commentators lulled them into believing that the elections would not take place on time. The NCP was, by contrast, very well organized. It was ready to concede a power-sharing arrangement with a range of opposition parties. But the NCP was not prepared to lose the presidency—in part because of the ICC arrest warrant against President Bashir. However, the electoral system meant that, if Bashir were to avoid a run-off for the presidency, he would need to win 50 percent plus one of the votes nationwide, including from among the approximately 25 percent of voters in southern Sudan, who could be relied upon to vote for the SPLM. So he needed to win about 70 percent of the northern vote. This required a high turnout for the NCP and additional manipulations.

Generally speaking, no such rigging was required for constituency elections. Most voters wanted a member of parliament who would deliver services and jobs. They wanted someone who would be close to the president. Consequently, voters predictably voted for the NCP. One commentator called it the "ugly election",[28] on the basis that no candidate could expect to be

[27] Al-Khatim Adlan, "It Is Time for Change", *South Atlantic Quarterly*, Vol. 109, No. 1 (2010), 117–46.
[28] Abd-al Wahab Abdalla, "Sudan: The Ugly Election", http://africanarguments. org/2010/04/22/the-ugly-election/ (accessed 7 July 2013).

elected who was better-looking than Sudan's famously ugly president, and so the NCP's electoral literature showed all its candidates scowling and frowning: "Political competition turned not into a free exchange of ideas and consideration of alternative public policies but instead a beauty contest of oaths of allegiance to our president and his debased slogans." This analysis echoes the framework of "competitive clientelism" that has been used to explain why elections in many Middle Eastern countries return pro-government candidates, even though the government is unpopular on most measures.[29] The same commentator further remarked that the real tragedy of the election was that the opposition incompetence—failing to register their voters, then dithering over whether to run or not, and finally boycotting—meant that the NCP did not even need to manipulate the vote.

One of the most revealing episodes in the 2010 elections occurred when the opposition parties were publicly debating a boycott. The NCP made two cash payments to the leader of the Umma Party, Sadiq al Mahdi, to persuade him to run. Sadiq's argument was that his party had no money to organize a campaign and there was no public financing for campaigns, so he was at a disadvantage. The NCP realized that Sadiq did not represent an electoral threat to Bashir, but were keen for there to be at least some Umma candidates elected on the party list. This would have given the elections some credibility, and would have meant that a multi-party coalition was ruling Sudan at the time of the referendum on self-determination in southern Sudan, just nine months away. Bashir wanted other political leaders to join him in shouldering the responsibility of allowing southern Sudan to secede. Sadiq took the first payment, and used it for personal expenses. He took a second, but then, pressured by a younger and more militant generation of party activists led by his daughter Miriam, still boycotted the election.

The election in southern Sudan was rigged in a more public and blatant manner even than in the north. The SPLM was running its political system on the same lines, but without the same skills, and had to resort to readily observable coercion and fraud. The international community, its attention focused on the January 2011 referendum, was ready to overlook the shortcomings of the elections in both northern and southern Sudan, treating the vote as fulfill-

---

[29] Ellen Lust-Okar, "Legislative Elections in Hegemonic Authoritarian Regimes: Competitive Clientelism and Resistance to Democratization", in Staffan I. Lindberg, ed., *Democratization by Elections: A New Mode of Transition* (Baltimore, MD: Johns Hopkins University Press, 2009).

ing an obligation laid down in the CPA rather than as a true exercise in democratization. Nonetheless, it is remarkable that the election passed off without violence or visible mass intimidation.

Since the disappointments of the 2010 elections, a significant part of the opposition is focused on the potential for non-violent popular uprising in Khartoum and other major cities, as occurred in Sudan in 1964 and 1985 and in Tunisia and Egypt in 2011. A diverse group, that includes politicians from quasi-derelict political parties associated with the pre-Bashir oligarchy, professionals and civil society organizations, and a disparate youth and student movement, lives in hope of such an uprising.

Another component of the opposition is the armed rebellion of the Sudan People's Liberation Movement-North (SPLM-N), in Southern Kordofan and Blue Nile, and the SPLM-N's alliance with Darfurian rebels, notably the Justice and Equality Movement (JEM) under the banner of the Sudan Revolutionary Front (SRF). Negotiations to resolve this conflict have been stalled since July 2011, when President Bashir repudiated a Framework Agreement with the SPLM-N signed by one of his most senior lieutenants, Assistant President Nafie Ali Nafie, in favor of the advice of army officers who advocated a military solution. The SPLM-N in southern Kordofan has shown that it cannot be defeated on the battlefield. The military setbacks suffered by the SPLM-N division in Blue Nile caused it to withdraw forces to South Sudan. If there is no credible move to resolve the conflict in these "two areas", any north–south security agreement will be at risk. An additional factor affecting the SPLM-N calculation is that the issue of the disputed area of Abyei is unresolved, with the government of Sudan refusing to implement a series of agreements, the most recent of which is an African Union proposal to hold a referendum in October 2013 to determine the future status of Abyei, namely whether it stays as part of Sudan or joins South Sudan. The prospect of indefinite delay in resolving Abyei is encouraging military officers in the South to support rebels in Sudan as a means of bringing pressure to bear.

A "Sudanese Spring" may yet happen, but much depends on whether a non-violent movement is able to bring a substantial sector of the Islamist movement into its camp, and win over enough of the army command to side with the people.[30] Most importantly, the two components of the opposition

---

[30] Abdelwahab El-Affendi, "Revolutionary anatomy: The lessons of the Sudanese revolutions of October 1964 and April 1985", *Contemporary Arab Affairs*, Vol. 5, No. 2 (2012), 292–306.

will need more than rhetorical coordination. Their fundamental difficulty is that the urban constituencies that would support an uprising, or stand aside to allow it to proceed, are deeply antipathetic to the provincial armed rebellions, especially insofar as they espy foreign sponsorship behind them. The insurrections provide ample pretext for the security services to repress the opposition without abandoning a credible claim to protecting the national interest. The fingerprints of South Sudan in the wars waged by the SPLM-N in southern Kordofan and Blue Nile mean that those rebellions are unlikely to gain constituents beyond their heartlands, and may indeed develop a separatist agenda which would further alienate them from the civil opposition. The fact that South Sudan has ambitious territorial claims on the north means that any party associated with it within northern Sudan—such as, by its very name, the SPLM-N—is open to a charge of being a traitorous fifth column.

The only extant mechanism for uniting the opposition is an umbrella that encompasses all the diverse agendas of the different groups under generic banners and disputatious leaders, which inspire nobody. Under these circumstances, the most probable political change would be mounted from within the regime itself, possibly led by army officers disappointed with what they see as the timidity and betrayal exhibited by their political masters. It's also possible that an uprising would be led by groups opposed to both the current NCP leadership and the SPLM-N, part of its critique being that the politicians didn't give the army what it needed to suppress the mutiny.

Conclusion

Sudan is a turbulent state, which tends to look different from one week to the next, but somehow remains remarkably unchanged over the years. The ruling oligarchy in Sudan has conspicuously failed to deliver on the public goods that are associated with a successful state. Nonetheless it has survived and—until 2011 at least—provided a sufficiently effective allocation of private goods to retain a degree of legitimacy.

Explaining Sudanese political life starts with the questions, "who, whom?" We need to add only the details of when, where and how much to cover the essential details that make the polity function. In this analysis, the state (as an entity and a concept) is subordinate to the regime (the political entities that constitute the ruling oligarchy) and the political marketplace (the power and patronage relations that link the regime to patrons and rivals, and intermediary elites who bargain allegiance for resources, producing systems of organized violence in the process). Note that the patrons, rivals, clients, and rebels overlap the categories "internal" and "external". We should not be mesmerized by the standard frameworks of international relations and political science or over-concerned with territorial boundaries, statehood, or legitimacy. State power and its accoutrements are wholly instrumentalized in pursuit of political power and personal enrichment.

The most important indicator for the viability of the regime is the political budget. Military power and security capability are primarily a function of the resources in that political budget. The political budget should be measured within the regional political marketplace, taking into account the competitors and subordinate elements making demands. Alongside this are non-financial components of political capital, such as the credibility of the regime's appeal to national and confessional sentiment. For the most part these are called upon in times of crisis, bringing only the transient capacity to mobilize popular sentiment against an insult. However, of greater interest is the value of those appeals to the individuals who control the means of violence: if military and security officers can be mobilized by sentiments of national or ideological loyalty, those elements of political capital are valuable.

The second important element is how effectively the political budget is utilized. This requires an assessment of the political–managerial skill of the ruler. Some individuals possess better political–business skills than others, and those capabilities and the goals to which they are deployed are a key determinant of political outcomes. From 1999 to 2011, President Bashir's political business plan relied on a well-supplied patronage budget, but as that has shrunk, he has relied increasingly on his political–business skills. His detailed knowledge of the country's political elite and sharp assessments of their respective bargaining positions are his best asset. However, his plan for managing the crisis has relied heavily on a divide-and-rule strategy of dispersing power so as to minimize the opportunities of internal rivals combining to challenge him, a strategy that multiplies veto-holders and leaves the government unable to take strategic decisions in the national interest.

Sudanese politics may surprise us in the coming years, for good or ill, but in either direction there is little indication of the political leadership needed, or the material resources required, for a transformative change. Sudan is unlikely to climb up the rankings of states that provide public goods to their citizens. When Bashir leaves office, willingly or unwillingly, his successor will face much the same challenges, and have much the same resources to call upon, or fewer. Whatever political capital the new leader may possess, part of it, simply because the Sudanese people are tired of Bashir, will soon be dissipated. Regime finances are unlikely to improve quickly. Much will depend on the political business plan of the new leader and the skill with which that can be implemented. Many Sudanese hope for a different future: a truly inclusive and frank national dialogue, which might establish national consensus as a public political good, and build an inclusive democratic constitution. The political leadership for such a logical step does not currently exist.

9

WOMEN, WORK, AND THE WEAK STATE

A CASE STUDY OF PAKISTAN AND SUDAN

Zahra Babar and Dwaa Osman

State failure need not be reserved for cases of complete state collapse, either into civil war or anarchy, but can also be understood as a process involving the weakening of a state's capacity to meet its responsibilities.[1]

In a weak state, the government has limited ability to provide adequate social protection for marginalized segments of society. Within this vacuum, non-governmental organizations (NGOs) can potentially begin to play an extensive role by providing a range of welfare programs, delivering human development and infrastructural projects, giving "voice" to the marginalized, and "empowering" the excluded. NGOs are often encouraged, supported, and even funded by the government in these endeavors. In weak states NGOs move beyond the space traditionally reserved for civil society and often replicate or replace some of the core functions of government.

[1] Donald Potter, "State Responsibility, Sovereignty and Failed States" (Paper Presented at the Australasian Political Studies Conference, University of Adelaide, Australia, 2004), 2.

In this chapter, we examine two weak states located at the periphery of the greater Middle East: Pakistan and Sudan, focusing in particular on how conditions within each have driven NGOs to play a dominant role in addressing the exclusion of one of society's marginalized groups, namely women. We draw on the experiences of two organizations that are delivering "empowerment" to women living in the Khyber Pakhtunkhwa in Pakistan and North Kordofan in Sudan, both areas located at the margins of each country where the reach of the state is particularly tenuous. We review and evaluate these attempts to provide for women's greater economic participation amidst a steady unraveling of the state's capacity and heightened conditions of insecurity and conflict.

Our argument is that within weak states, limited public capacity, the erosion of rule of law, institutional inefficiencies, and poor implementation of legislative protections leave marginalized communities at the mercy of an ever more threatening and disrupted social order. The function of providing adequate social protection is increasingly left to the non-governmental sector. Beyond serving as mere recipients of social welfare programs, through NGO support, women are engaging in their own development trajectories. It is precisely the limitations in the weak state that have opened up space for NGOs to promote women's participation in their own development, as well as that of their households and their communities. However, the NGOs included in our two case studies operate within the constraints of a prevailing social order, and their ability to deliver a "rights-based agenda" that addresses core issues of women's unequal status is curtailed.[2] Through involvement in NGOs' social mobilization efforts, women have achieved a degree of agency and partial autonomy, but their status within their homes and communities remains informed by the overarching cultural and social constraints that limit women's social inclusion in both Pakistan and Sudan. Moreover, while a degree of empowerment may be achieved through involvement in micro-level social welfare programs, women's social inclusion is contingent upon policy and institutional reform at the state level.

This chapter is divided into four sections. In the first section we discuss the social exclusion of women in and through the development process, especially in states that are weak and fragile. In the following section, we provide a rationale for this study's comparative case selection. The chapter then focuses

---

[2] For an overview on the rights-based approach to development, see Andrea Cornwall and Celestine Nyamu-Musembi, "Putting the 'Rights-Based Approach' to Development into Perspective", *Third World Quarterly*, Vol. 25, No. 8 (2004), 1415–37.

on Pakistan, outlining important political, economic, and social conditions which have restricted women's advancement in the country. We discuss the particular constraints of women's economic integration, and include a case study of a non-governmental organization working in the north-west of the country to deliver microfinance services to low-income women. We then review the conditions for women's inclusion in Sudan, focusing on the social and economic constraints they are exposed to in rural areas of the North Kordofan state. We review the initiatives being undertaken by an international NGO to enhance the economic inclusion of Sudanese women, and also provide them with increased participation in their communities and societies. In each case, we focus on women as a socially excluded group with limited access to state services, and highlight how NGOs have stepped in to address the palpable vacuum left as a result of state weakness.

Situating the Study

Social exclusion terminology initially developed within the European context in the 1960s, where the emerging welfare state model was found to be wanting in terms of providing adequate social protection for certain marginalized communities.[3] While much of the social exclusion discourse focused on issues of income disparities and unemployment, and was also grounded in the particular realities of post-industrial European nations, conceptually it began to expand thinking on poverty in a manner that was to have a global influence.[4] The language of social exclusion contributed to a nuanced understanding of the conditions reinforcing inequality, moving beyond traditional class stratifications to draw attention to other forms of group identity that could determine exclusion. Gender, ethnicity, religion, and language as markers of excluded social identities were considered critical to understanding marginalization and inequality.[5]

Social exclusion and poverty are not interchangeable concepts. While poverty is often understood as a static condition, social exclusion is a process. Also, while poverty is usually assessed in financial terms, social exclusion

---

[3] Gerda Jehol-Gijsbers and Cok Crooman, "Explaining Social Exclusion" (The Hague: Netherlands Institute for Social Research, 2007), 11.

[4] Ruhi Saith, "Social Exclusion: the Concept and Application to Developing Countries" (University of Oxford: Queen Elizabeth House Working Paper Series, 2001), 3–4.

[5] Floya Anthias, "The Concept of 'Social Division' and Theorising Social Stratification: Looking at Ethnicity and Class", *Sociology*, Vol. 35, No. 4 (2001), 838.

measures the unequal access to a host of rights that are also political and social in nature.[6] Important for the purpose of this chapter, while poverty is usually measured in absolute terms, social exclusion emphasizes the socio-cultural dimensions of exclusion, and posits that groups or communities are marginalized within particular contexts, and therefore need to be evaluated through a relational lens.[7]

Regardless of the debates in the literature, social exclusion has certainly had an impact on evolving conceptions of poverty, and has influenced poverty alleviation policy-making and programs in developing states. Its language has been adopted by the international development world, donors, governments, and non-governmental organizations. The adoption of social exclusion concepts has altered definitions of poverty, expanded the scope for how poverty is assessed and measured, and impacted on how the causes and consequences of poverty are addressed.[8]

In the analysis of social exclusion and gender, the state is considered to be a principal social actor, permeating society and structuring the dynamics of everyday life. Development interventions carried out by NGOs aim to reduce inequality by engaging in parallel and complementary processes that build the capacity of both the state and social communities. Formal and informal institutions manage and structure access to resources, networks, and capabilities, and accordingly determine the prevailing distributional rules within society.[9] NGO interventions aim to bring about social inclusion through policy reform, and building the incentives and capabilities within and across institutions in order to enable the state to respond effectively and equitably to the demands and needs of its citizens.[10] Development intervention at the micro or community level is primarily concerned with community empowerment, by enabling the socially excluded to gain equitable access to assets and capabilities and to have a more audible voice in society.

Since the 1990s, development institutions and NGOs have increasingly focused on community-level interventions in acknowledgment that grass-

[6] Jehol-Gijsbers and Crooman, "Explaining Social Exclusion", 13.
[7] Walter Bossert, Conchita D'Ambrosia, and Vita Peragine. "Deprivation and Social Exclusion", *Economica*, Vol. 74. No. 296 (2007), 778.
[8] Saith, "Social Exclusion: the Concept and Application to Developing Countries", 10.
[9] Lynn Bennett, "Using Empowerment and Social Inclusion for Pro-poor Growth: A Theory of Social Change", World Bank Working Draft of Background Paper for the Social Development Strategy Paper, Washington DC, 2002, 16.
[10] Ibid., 14.

roots empowerment is necessary for sustainable social change. Two key dimensions of empowerment have been recognized. The first emphasizes enhancing access to and control over resources and networks from which economic advancement can be attained. The second aims to transform beneficiaries of service delivery to citizens who are responsible for their own development and who will accordingly hold the state accountable.[11] NGOs facilitate social mobilization of marginalized groups by engaging them in participatory and locally-owned development projects.[12] This direct group engagement in development trajectories brings about solidarity and the heightened capacity to engage with, influence, and control the institutions that dictate the distributional rules within society.[13] While the first level of livelihood empowerment deals with fulfilling the practical needs of marginalized groups, the second dimension of mobilization empowerment is concerned with satisfying their long-term strategic needs.[14]

The prevalence of gender disparity across the globe and particularly in weak states has received global recognition. As indicated by the United Nations third Millennium Development Goal, which aims to "promote gender equality and empower women", gender disparity manifests itself in the forms of unequal access to education, the outnumbering of women in paid employment by men, the high concentration of women in the informal economy, the minimal presence of women in decision-making positions, and the limited presence of women in formal positions of political power.[15] In response, many development projects have incorporated gender mainstreaming in their strategy and project design.[16] While these interventions are meant to generate equality in access to assets and capabilities, achieving the strategic goal of gender equality is less conclusive. Mainstreaming gender has meant that the

---

[11] Sam Hickey, "The Government of Chronic Poverty: From Exclusion to Citizenship?" *Journal of Development Studies*, Vol. 46, No. 7 (2010), 1145.

[12] Ibid., 1140.

[13] Bennett, "Using Empowerment", 22.

[14] Ibid., 24.

[15] United Nations, "Millennium Development Goals 2015", http://www.un.org/millenniumgoals/gender.shtml.

[16] Gender mainstreaming is a public policy strategy in which the gender implications of a particular legislation, policy, or program are assessed during its design, implementation, monitoring, and evaluation. See Naila Kabeer, *Gender mainstreaming in poverty eradication and the millennium development goals a handbook for policymakers and other stakeholders* (London: Commonwealth Secretariat, 2003).

social embeddedness of productive resources is at times overlooked, consequently generating other avenues of exclusion.[17] While projects may specifically target women and encourage their direct participation and involvement in their own development, a gendered approach to policy and implementation is rarely taken. Women are seldom involved in either policy-making or project design. Additionally, the likelihood of women having a greater share in the distribution of assets, an increased role in decision-making (at the family, community, and societal level), and greater leverage over institutions is unlikely if men are not supportive of such strategic shifts.[18]

The power relations that generate horizontal inequalities are reinforced by the relations between the individual, society, and the state. Social exclusion analysis is at times criticized for considering economic integration as principal to inclusion.[19] For instance, exclusion from the labor market or political participation may be due to strong family integration.[20] This bias elides women's "exclusion" from society due to their excessive participation in the domestic sphere. Access to and control over resources for women is facilitated by NGOs and serves the purpose of minimizing the distance between a woman's place in society and the axial center of economic participation. Within the development discourse, experts suggest that increased public employment advantages women beyond the material benefits it accrues and benefits women individually as it places them in a position where they can exercise increased agency in the public sphere.[21] This may translate to progressive cultural change where women's heightened voice in the public sphere is a reflection of their own agency and works to correct the institutionalized gender disparity evident within their polity.

Going beyond access to resources and social networks and assessing the distance between particular groups and power centers in society informs the basis of horizontal inequalities. These power centers are not just present in the economic and political arenas but also include cultural and symbolic realms. Family is recognized as one of the most socially valued networks, one that highlights the blurring of the lines between the private and public spheres, and

---

[17] Nitya Rao, "Women's Rights to Land and Assets: Experience of Mainstreaming Gender in Development Projects", *Economic and Political Weekly*, Vol. 40, No. 44/45 (2005), 4702.

[18] Ibid., 4707.

[19] Daly and Saraceno, "Social Exclusion and Gender Relations", 98.

[20] Ibid., 99.

[21] Jackson, "Social exclusion and gender", 129.

one which is critical in either promoting or curtailing a woman's capacity, her ability to mobilize socially, and her access to and control over productive resources. Within the development discourse, there is increased recognition of the importance of the care economy and the interdependence of family and economic networks in improving women's status in society. Although the social exclusion discourse originally placed the most weight on the economic sphere, there is increasing recognition that multiple centers may exist within society, depending on the individual's identity and various group affiliations.[22] In the particular case studies of Pakistan and Sudan, the socio-cultural context and setting of women in rural areas that may be marked by conflict place familial and community relations at the core of women's integration in society.

Comparative Case Study

Located at opposite ends of the Greater Middle East, Pakistan and Sudan share similar historical, political, and social qualities that inform the position of women in their respective societies. Decades of corrupt, inefficient, authoritarian military rule, perforated by periods of similarly dysfunctional civilian rule, have generated prominent economic inequalities amongst the citizenry and protracted ethnic tensions in both countries. Since independence, the colonial legacy of Pakistan and Sudan has left behind surrogate, dysfunctional political leaders and political processes that have continuously marginalized certain groups and localities for decades. In the recent past of Pakistan, an escalation in ethnic conflict, sectarian tension, and terrorist activity by extremist groups has left the fate of many of its citizens in a tenuous security situation. The geopolitics of the region, particularly with Afghanistan's politically unstable state and the active presence of the Taliban in Pakistan's Federally Administered Tribal Belt, have left Pakistani citizens and vulnerable groups at the mercy of broader political agendas. In Sudan, President Omar Al-Bashir's National Congress Party has ruled for decades using political Islam and patronage politics to dominate much of the political scene. Mapping these exclusionary political practices onto Sudan's multi-ethnic and multi-religious make-up has led to decades-long internal strife within Sudan's geographic periphery: the Darfur states in the west, the Blue Nile states in the east, and South Korodfan in Sudan's recently receding southern borders. This has

---

[22] Cecile Jackson, "Social exclusion and gender: Does one size fit all?" *European Journal of Development Research*, Vol. 11, No. 1 (1999), 133.

diminished the Sudanese government's capacity to provide development services to its citizens as it seeks to curb insurgencies and maintain territorial and political control within its sovereign boundaries.

In addition, both states have experienced the challenges of failing to include minority ethnic and religious communities successfully within the larger whole; have experienced civil conflict as a result; and both have lost territory due to their inability to develop their provinces equally and their failure to create cohesive national identities. The states' failure in social inclusion is most clearly manifested in Pakistan's territorial loss of East Pakistan and the sovereign birth of Bangladesh more than four decades ago, and similarly in the secession of South Sudan from Sudan in 2011.

Against this backdrop of protracted conflict that has threatened Pakistan and Sudan's domestic security, their formal institutions, political forces, and social actors have sought morally and socially to regulate women's position in society in both countries. In the Islamic Republic of Pakistan, Islamist political parties as well as radical Islamist groups seek a moral regulation of society, particularly through the sanctioning of women's behavior. While Pakistan's legal code has been influenced by Sharia law, in contemporary Pakistan, instead of the state, it is the fringe extremist groups as well as more mainstream Islamic parties that have sought to enforce their moral codes on society and restrict women's social inclusion. In Sudan, the prevailing influence of Sharia law on the Sudanese legal code has codified gender inequalities (particularly in relation to Family Laws) and has accordingly limited women's access to economic resources, diminished their social and economic mobility, and reduced their participation in the public sphere.[23] Since the rise to power in 1989 of the ruling National Congress Party, it has placed women at the center of their vision of an Islamically moral society, accordingly basing policies and institutions on the image of morally bound women, thereby dictating the limits and extents of Sudanese women's social inclusion.[24] In both Pakistan and Sudan, women face limited access to resources and basic rights as a result of the failure of the countries' development trajectory, and additionally women face the hostility of a social discourse which terms women's participation and advancement as morally reprehensible.

[23] Balghis Badri, "Sudanese Women and Sharia Law" (Ahfad University: Regional Institute of Gender, Diversity, Peace and Rights, 2012).
[24] Sondra Hale, *Gender Politics in Sudan: Islamism, Socialism, and the State* (Boulder, CO: Westview Press, 1996), 143.

Thus, the historical context, weak institutional environment, the influence of more conservative interpretations of Islam on politics and society, all inform the degree and nature of women's constraints to inclusion in Sudanese and Pakistani society. The diminishing capacities of governments in both Pakistan and Sudan to provide basic services to their citizens have been further eroded through the need to maintain security and law and order. In such a context, examining how women are being impacted and how they are being assisted makes for a compelling comparative case study.

Women throughout Pakistan and Sudan do not constitute a uniform group and exhibit varying levels of economic empowerment, political engagement, and social inclusion. The regional province of Khyber Pakthunkhwa in Pakistan and the state of North Kordofan in Sudan have distinct social fabrics and security climates that influence NGO operations as well as rural women's ability to cope with economic hardship.

Conflict and violence have over the course of the past five years had a grave impact on security conditions in the Khyber Pakhtunkhwa province in Pakistan. As a spill-over from the war in Afghanistan, and with the active presence of the Taliban, in Khyber Pakhtunkhwa the security situation has restricted the presence and operation of NGOs, placing provincial women in a more precarious position. Women's development in Khyber Pakhtunkhwa has become increasingly politicized with the rise of Islamic fundamentalism.[25] The local NGO examined in this study, the Sarhard Rural Support Programme (SRSP), has been operating for decades in the region to alleviate poverty. While the SRSP may not have a clear mandate to empower women, their gender-focused projects are couched in terms of community development and income-generating programs that strategically facilitate women's access to productive resources while depoliticizing their status as targeted beneficiaries. Although local NGOs are politicized on a social level, they nurture a symbiotic relationship between themselves and the state. The resources channeled via the state from bilateral donors seek to fund the developmental activities of local NGOs and accordingly to fill the palpable vacuum left by the state.

In the Sudanese state of North Kordofan, drought and desertification since the 1980s have put pressure on the livelihoods of agriculturists, nomads, and pastoralists. While NGOs have been actively carrying out relief and rehabilitation projects aimed at enhancing food security in North Kordofan, economi-

---

[25] Asfahan Jafar, "Engaging Fundamentalism: The Case of Women's NGOs in Pakistan", *Social Problems*, Vol. 54, No. 3 (2007), 262.

cally empowering inhabitants through financing schemes, and particularly women, is a more recent endeavor.[26] One of seventeen states in Sudan, North Kordofan has not directly experienced conflict on the scale of neighboring South Kordofan or the Darfur states. North Kordofan is located closer to the geographic and political center of Khartoum, is regarded as one of the country's more stable areas, and is the agricultural heartland of the country's export of gum Arabic. Yet it continues to suffer from the state's uneven development trajectory and vast poverty.[27] Thus, while the day-to-day operations of NGOs in North Kordofan are not directly affected by Sudan's security situation, women's economic engagement and social inclusion continue to be influenced by infrastructural and developmental constraints as well as by social and political mores. Like Pakistan, where all NGOs are politicized, INGOs in Sudan are exceptionally politicized as they are viewed—and are occasionally treated as—an intrusive force.[28] Due to Sudan's fragile relationship with the West and more precisely since President Al-Bashir's indictment by the International Criminal Court in 2009, INGOs such as Plan International have trodden carefully to deliver needed development services throughout the country while maintaining political neutrality in the eyes of the ruling regime. In addition to threatening domestic security, INGOs may be regarded by both the state and various social actors as forces that seek to alter the cultural and moral fabric of society through their socially embedded developmental services. In this regard, INGOs must exercise political neutrality and social awareness in order to depoliticize their activities and continue their operations within Sudan.

Thus, women's social exclusion, which is exacerbated by the political atmosphere and weak government institutions of Pakistan and Sudan, is largely

[26] "A Consultancy Review of Village Savings and Loan (VS&L) Project—North Kordofan Program Unit—Plan Sudan", VSLA Report provided by North Kordofan Program Unit Manager of the Plan International Head Office Khartoum (2013), 14.

[27] Nawal El Gack, "Participation of Women in Grassroots Development Interventions: Reflections on experiences of development projects in Sudan", *Development Studies Working Paper* Series 1 (2009), 7.

[28] Following the ICC indictment of President Al-Bashir in March 2009, Sudan expelled ten foreign aid agencies and dissolved two local organizations. See "Sudan expels aid agencies after ICC warrant", *ReliefWeb*, 4 March 2009, http://reliefweb.int/report/sudan/sudan-expels-aid-agencies-after-icc-warrant, accessed 12 June 2013.

dealt with under the auspices of NGOs in Khyber Pakhtunkhwa (KP) and North Kordofan (NK). The operations of politicized local NGOs in a conflict zone (KP) versus International NGOs in a relatively stable area (NK) may offer valuable insight into how women are able to navigate social, political, and economic hurdles that obstruct their inclusion. Moreover, while financial support to women in the form of microfinance has been prevalent throughout Pakistan for decades, in certain areas of Sudan, and particularly in North Kordofan, it is a newly introduced service; whether or not decades of micro-finance have altered women's economic empowerment and social inclusion is also a valuable point of comparison in this study.

The Context for Pakistan

Women in Pakistan cannot be thought of as comprising a homogenous group. Pakistan stands as the first Muslim-majority country to have elected a female head of state, and along with Bangladesh, Indonesia, and Turkey remains amongst only four Muslim countries ever to have done so. Currently its lower house of government, the National Assembly, has 57 out of 342 seats occupied by women; its upper house of parliament, the Senate, has 18 out of 104 members seats for women.[29] Under its 1973 constitution, the state recognizes the equal rights of women to political, social, and economic participation, and over the past few years the country has adopted additional legislation aimed at ensuring gender-based equality and protection across different sectors.[30] However, despite an enabled judicial mechanism and frequent promises to ensure greater equality between the sexes, Pakistan has still not seen adequate progress on a range of gender measurements.

While women's position in society continues to demonstrate the influence of religious norms, cultural traditions, and social mores, gender-based forms of exclusion are experienced by women across the country to varying degrees. The rural–urban divide is a significant variable, as is the particular socio-cultural context.[31] The country is divided into four provinces, each with its own

---

[29] International Foundation for Election Systems, "Pakistan Fact Sheet: Senate of Pakistan" and "Pakistan Fact Sheet: National Assembly of Pakistan", http://www.ifes.org

[30] "Benchmarking National Legislation for Gender Equality: Findings from Five Asian Countries", Human Development Report Unit, UNDP Asia-Pacific Regional Centre, Bangkok (2010), 48.

[31] Farzana Bari and Mariam S. Pal, "Women in Pakistan", Asian Development Bank County Briefing Paper (2000), ix.

unique language, ethnicity, and set of social norms governing the role and status of women. In sum, social status, socio-economic background, and geographic location matter a great deal when we speak about Pakistani women.

Determining how poverty and gender align in Pakistan is a complex issue. In the absence of a universal understanding of poverty, multiple indices for measurement exist. According to levels of calorie consumption, 21 percent of Pakistan is poor, while income poverty impacts 30 percent.[32] The *Human Poverty Index*, a more multi-dimensional tool of measurement that looks beyond consumption and income levels, states that 47 percent of Pakistan is poor. And the most recent *Multidimensional Poverty Index*, developed in 2012, suggests that 49 percent of Pakistan lives in poverty.[33] According to the *Human Development Index*, Pakistan lies in the "Low Human Development Category" of countries, and ranks 145th out of 187.[34] At the national level, Pakistan lacks a comprehensive measurement for gender-based poverty.[35] This is principally a result of the lack of accurate data collected on gender and poverty from within the state.[36] As a result international indices must be relied on for establishing how gender and poverty converge within the country. According to the United Nations' *Gender-related Development Index*, out of the 146 countries that are regularly evaluated, Pakistan most recently ranked 120th.[37]

That there is a gender gap in Pakistan is both nationally and internationally recognized, as a range of human development indicators demonstrate that women in the country fall behind when compared to men.[38] Pakistan invests less than 1 percent of its GDP in education, and this critical lack of funding translates into a national literacy rate of 44 percent and a female literacy rate of 30 percent.[39] In addition to disadvantages expressed in lower achievements

---

[32] Ibid., ix.

[33] "Human Development Report 2011: Sustainability and Equity, A Better Future For All" (New York: United Nations Development Programme, 2011).

[34] Ibid., 127.

[35] Bari and S. Pal, "Women in Pakistan", 15.

[36] Ibid.

[37] Arab Naz and Hafeez-ur-Rahman Chaudhry, "Developing Gender Equality: An analytical study of socio-political and economic constraints in women's empowerment in Pakhtun Society of Khyber Pakhtunkhwa province of Pakistan", *Indian Journal of Health and Wellbeing*, Vol. 2, No. 1 (2011), 259.

[38] Bari and S. Pal, "Women in Pakistan", 16.

[39] Government of Pakistan Finance Division, "Federal Budget 2011–2012", http://www.docstoc.com/docs/94445687/Federal-budget-2011–12-government-of-Pakistan-finance-division-Islamabad.

in the social sectors of education and health, women in Pakistan have unequal representation in the economic and political sectors.[40]

Assessing women's participation in the economy is also challenging, as official sources of data collection, such as the regularly carried out Pakistan *Labour Force Surveys*, do not accurately reflect women's actual participation in the labor force.[41] Pakistan's 2010–11 *Labour Force Survey* shows a glaring disparity between male and female labor force participation rates at the national level, with 21.7 percent of the female population and 69 percent of the male population shown as being actively engaged in the labor force.[42] The rate of participation is much higher for women living in the rural areas, where 28 percent are engaged in the labor market, as opposed to the urban areas, where only 11 percent are deemed to be active.[43] The data also reflects significant regional differences, signifying both the variances in social and cultural environments, as well as the disparate economic conditions between the four provinces. In the more developed and most populous Punjab province, almost 27 percent of the female population is active in the labor force, while the figures for Sindh show a marked decrease to 16 percent, in the Khyber Pakhtunkhwa to 15 percent, and in Balochistan to 9 percent.

It has been suggested that weaknesses in data collection in Pakistan have falsely deflated women's economic contribution.[44] Surveyors are frequently men, who due to cultural constraints may often conduct their interviews with male members of households. Women's work is not always thought of as productive labor, and social constraints may prevent husbands and fathers from providing details on economic contributions of female members of the household.[45] Previously, the *Labour Force Survey* was also heavily criticized for excluding questions on the informal sector, but in recent years the surveys have dedicated sections on the informal economy. As in many other developing countries, a large percentage of the total Pakistani labor force is engaged in the informal sector. Recent data show that the informal sector employs

---

[40] Khawar Mumtaz, "Gender and Poverty in Pakistan", *Development*, Vol. 50, No. 2 (2007), 149.

[41] Bari and S. Pal, "Women in Pakistan", x.

[42] *Labour Force Survey 2010–11*, 30th issue (Islamabad: Government of Pakistan Statistics Division, Federal Bureau of Statistics, July 2011), http://www.pbs.gov.pk/content/labour-force-survey-2010–11

[43] Ibid.

[44] Bari and S. Pal, "Women in Pakistan", x.

[45] Ibid.

about 74 percent of the working male population and 71 percent of the working female population.[46]

Women's low socio-economic status in Pakistan is determined by both social and cultural constraints, as well as institutional and structural deficiencies. Religious, class-oriented, and cultural factors place restrictions on women's mobility in the public arena, and limit their activities to the family domain.[47] Micro studies that have examined the conditions of women in the rural areas of Pakistan indicate that very few women own material assets and control productive resources.[48] Additionally, poor investment in women's training and capacity building, their lack of access to formal credit institutions, and inability to access markets are some of the key structural constraints which hamper them from attaining economic success.[49]

The current cultural and religious norms that place women within the home as custodians of family honor do not easily lend themselves to enhanced formal employment for women. Over the past two decades there has been increasing support by the government to promote microfinance and home-based entrepreneurship as a means to assist rural, low-income women in developing economic traction through engagement in the informal sector. Across the country a number of Grameen Bank-like microfinance schemes have been launched, many specifically targeting female clientele in order to assist them with income-generating and vocational enterprises.[50] While currently the outreach of microfinance is still limited, with only 2 million recipients of microfinance loans to date, the government hopes that through its network of microfinance banks and NGOs it can expand such services to many more over the coming years.[51]

---

[46] *Labour Force Survey 2010–11*, 30th issue (Islamabad: Government of Pakistan Statistics Division, Federal Bureau of Statistics, July 2011), Table 17, http://www.pbs.gov.pk/content/labour-force-survey-2010–11

[47] Mumtaz, "Gender and Poverty", 150.

[48] Khawar Mumtaz and Meher M. Noshirwani, "Women's Access to Rights to Land and Property in Pakistan", *International Development Research Centre (IDRC) Scoping Paper* (Canada, 2007), 1–8.

[49] Bari and S. Pal, "Women in Pakistan", x.

[50] State Bank of Pakistan Microfinance Division, "Strategic Framework for Sustainable Microfinance in Pakistan" (Islamabad, January 2011), 1–7.

[51] Ibid., 1.

The Sarhad Rural Support Program: Development on Pakistan's Frontiers

The Khyber Pakhtunkhwa (KP) province, located in the north-west of the country, shares a long, porous border with Afghanistan and, in its most recent history, has served as a site of conflict and contestation.[52] Since 2005, the region has become the epicenter of political violence as a spill-over from the war in Afghanistan.[53] Rising Islamic fundamentalism, sectarianism, and the active presence of the Pakistani Taliban in the tribal belt of KP have shrunk the space for NGOs to engage actively on women's issues. KP is considered to be the part of the country most persistently resistant to the presence of women's NGOs.[54] Much of the antagonism towards women's development comes from the religious sphere, and from the clerics who view the agenda of women's NGOs with deep suspicion if not out and out hostility.[55]

Based in KP since 1989, the Sarhad Rural Support Programme (SRSP) is the largest multi-sectoral NGO delivering development programs to the province's poorer communities. While SRSP's poverty alleviation efforts are designed to assist both men and women, the organization has a specifically female-focused strategy when it comes to its microfinance operations. Project documents suggest that the microfinance program is driven by an overarching interest in "empowering" women.[56] Women are provided with access to both material and non-material resources in the shape of credit, training, skills development, and business management, in the hope that such inputs in the long run will lead to greater decision-making power for women, and enable them to "make strategic choices" about their lives.[57]

SRSP's microfinance strategy is to assist rural communities to develop group savings and to manage a community fund, through which internal lending can take place for the purpose of productive investment. These traditional

---

[52] Sohail Habib Tajik, "Analysis of Peace Agreements with Militants and Lessons for the Future", *Conflict and Peace Studies*, Vol. 4, No. 1 (Jan-March 2011), 2–4; and Jacob N. Shapiro, C. Christine Fair, and Rasul Bakhsh Rais, "Political Violence in Pakistan 1988–2010: Patterns and Trends", International Center for Growth Working Paper 12/0063 (February 2012), 4.

[53] Shapiro, Fair, and Rais, "Political Violence in Pakistan", 4.

[54] Jafar, "Engaging Fundamentalism", 262.

[55] Ibid.

[56] "Microfinance for Social and Economic Empowerment of Women", Programme Brief provided by the Programme Monitoring Evaluation and Research Unit of the Sarhad Rural Support Programme Head Office Peshawar (2012), 2.

[57] Ibid.

microfinance operations have been complemented by the development of a subsidized mechanism of credit delivery specifically for the poorest members of the community. Through an expansive network of 300 village-level community organizations over the course of the past decade, SRSP has delivered $8.5 million in small loans to 40,000 primarily rural households.[58] The loans typically range from $50 to $200 per borrower, and 98 percent of the loans so far have been accessed by women.[59] SRSP provides training and technical assistance as well as marketing support to increase the success of productive ventures undertaken.

SRSP's credit delivery services, combined with capacity building and marketing support, have had a demonstrated impact on increasing women's abilities to generate incomes and to operate successful microenterprises in the informal sector. SRSP's experiences add to the existing body of literature which states that access to micro credit for investment in productive purposes has a demonstrated positive impact on alleviating rural women's poverty.[60] What is harder to ascertain is whether this program has led to significant non-material gains for women in the rural areas of the Khyber Pakhtunkhwa. In 2008, an external assessment was carried out by consultants for the UK's Department for International Development (DfID) to determine the extent to which rural support programs in Pakistan are succeeding in women's empowerment through microfinance.[61]

The DfID study included a number of qualitative interviews with SRSP beneficiaries and provides some illuminating data on the linkages, or lack thereof, between economic inclusion and enhanced agency. Using a combined research methodology that included household surveys, focus group discussions, and cases studies, the external evaluators were able to ask informants a

---

[58] Ibid., 1.

[59] Ibid.

[60] See for example Ferdoushi Ahmed, Chamhuri Siwar, and Nor Aini Hj. Idris, "Improving Well-being of Rural Women Through Participation in Microcredit Programme: Evidence from Bangladesh", *Australasian Journal of Basic and Applied Sciences*, Vol. 5, No. 8 (2011), 857–62; and Ferdoushi Ahmed, Chamhuri Siwar, Nor Aini Hj. Idris, and Rawshan Ara Begum, "Impact of microcredit on poverty alleviation among rural women: A case study of Panchagarh District of Bangladesh", *African Journal of Business Management*, Vol. 5, No. 16 (2011), 7111–19.

[61] Shaheen Rafi Khan and Shahrukh Rafi Khan, "Women's Access to and Control over Micro Credit in Rural Support Programme Area", *DfID/Rural Support Programmes Network* (Islamabad, 2008).

range of questions on the impact that microcredit had had on their lives.[62] In addition to an assessment of the impact of micro loans on income levels, occupation, consumption patterns, family well-being, and social status, the survey included research questions specifically aimed at determining how the microfinance program had altered configurations of gender and empowerment within the family and within the community.[63] Sets of questions were asked to determine women's degree of participation in the loan process, changes to their status in the household as a result of the loan, and their perception of changes to their empowerment overall.[64]

Regarding women's control over and participation in the loan process, 89 percent of the female respondents stated that they had needed their husband or father's permission to take a loan; 58 percent stated that they had initially taken the loan at their male family member's urging; and 61 percent responded that male family members were involved in some way in the loan and microenterprise (i.e. through marketing assistance either for procurement of supplies or sale of goods). However, almost 90 percent of the women had an active involvement in managing the loan themselves and the associated productive venture.[65]

In order to ascertain whether engagement in income-generating activities had led to a greater degree of empowerment, a series of questions were asked related to perceived changes in household status, changes in household-level decision-making, and changes to political engagement.[66] In addition, women were asked questions relating to any perceived changes in the role taken on by male family members relating to household chores traditionally considered women's work.[67] When asked whether their engagement in economic activities had enhanced their status within their households, 30 percent of the women indicated that they felt there had been a high degree of improvement, 42 percent reported a moderate degree of improvement, while 28 percent stated that there had been no change to their status within the home.[68] On questions related to decision-making, respondents indicated a greater degree of improvement in areas related directly to their participation in project

[62] Ibid., 4–5.
[63] Ibid., 6.
[64] Ibid., 14–17.
[65] Ibid.,14–17.
[66] Ibid., 15–17.
[67] Ibid., 17.
[68] Ibid., 15.

activities, such as decisions related to business and financial matters. Regarding decisions pertaining to general financial aspects of the household, 51 percent of the women stated a moderate to high degree of improvement, while 57 percent reported greater participation in decisions related to personal savings. In addition, 65 percent of the women stated that they had experienced moderate to high levels of improvement in their personal mobility.[69]

More diffuse signs of empowerment within the family were less likely to be indicated by the female respondents: 54 percent of the women responded that they had experienced no change to decisions related to marriage; 56 percent responded no change to decisions pertaining to dowry; 72 percent responded no perceived change in their impact on electoral decisions; and 74 percent stated no change to their decision-making in regard to contraception. Women were also asked to indicate whether their male counterparts were contributing higher levels of input in terms of childcare, cleaning, shopping, and obtaining water and fuel for the home.[70] For the most part, there was not a great deal of change to male behavior perceived by the women in these areas.

Table 1: Decision-making Processes and Gender Configurations

Women's Control and Participation in Loan Process	
Husband/father's permission to take loan	89%
Male family member's urging	58%
Involvement of male family members	61%
Woman's active involvement in managing loan and microenterprise	90%

Finance-related Decisions			
Indicator	No Change	Moderate Improvement	High Improvement
Decisions pertaining to business	49%	29%	23%
General financial decisions	49%	25%	26%
Decisions pertaining to personal savings	43%	30%	27%

[69] Ibid., 16.
[70] Ibid., 17.

Family- and Community-related Decisions			
Indicator	No Change	Moderate Improvement	High Improvement
Marriage-related decisions	54%	28%	18%
Decisions pertaining to dowry	56%	28%	16%
Electoral decisions	72%	17%	11%
Contraception decisions	74%	18%	8%
Status in household	28%	42%	30%
Mobility	35%	27%	38%

Male household support			
Indicator	No Change	Moderate Improvement	High Improvement
Childcare support	62%	29%	9%
Cleaning support	73%	19%	8%
Shopping support	51%	32%	17%
Getting fuel/water support	61%	21%	11%

Source: Shaheen Rafi Khan and Shahrukh Rafi Khan, "Women's Access to and Control over Micro Credit in Rural Support Programme Area", *DfID/Rural Support Programmes Network* (Islamabad, 2008), 14–17.

SRSP's model of delivery credit and assorted resources to low-income rural women has certainly contributed toward addressing issues of economic exclusion and poverty in its project areas. Women's involvement in certain areas of household decision-making appear somewhat enhanced, and given the snail-like pace at which social change takes place, this can be considered a positive achievement. Visible change to gender dynamics at the micro level are demonstrated through the increased levels of influence experienced by women in managing the household's finances, traditionally an area where decisions are dominated by male family members. The enhancement of women's personal mobility also is an indication of the program's success. If social exclusion denotes a lack of access to material goods, infrastructure, and services, as well as a low capacity in partaking fully in the economic and political domain, then the focus of grass-roots development is not only to address the shortfall in material access but also to address issues of equity and rights. While SRSP's initiatives appear to address the former more successfully than the latter, and may not have led to a complete transformation of gender dynamics, they have created certain openings for women and enabled them to participate more fully in both their homes and communities.

SRSP's vision of gender development focuses on enhancing women's opportunities, while accepting the notion that women's core role and contribution is within the household, and it is within the household that they can advance. The NGO's stated vision has the family as the "principal unit of survival", and mechanisms for addressing women's well-being are framed within this understanding. SRSP holds that its programs are sensitive to the cultural and social values of KP, and implements a strategy to deliver gender-based development that does not take a combative approach to accepted social norms. In order to ensure the success of programs for women, male family members are encouraged to "allow their women to participate in development activities, with minimal of social disorder".[71] The NGO employs separate female staff to interact with women, so as not to jar local sensitivities which regard the mingling of the sexes with suspicion.

In sum, SRSP's concerns are to address the practical needs of women who have suffered from a lack of access to adequate resources and opportunities, economic and otherwise. In order to deliver its poverty alleviation program, while raising awareness on a host of rights-based issues is part of the NGO's agenda, it is not looking to alter society dramatically by tackling the complex web of social, cultural, and religious practices which continue to dominate gender relations in the rural areas of Khyber Pakhtunkhwa.

Similar to SRSP's services, the next section highlights the efforts of the international non-governmental organization Plan International to enhance women's economic activities and participation in public life.

The Context for Sudan

Sudan's complex political and cultural landscape has long created varying experiences and profiles of its citizenry. Much more pronounced are the differences evident in women's place within society vis-à-vis the formal and informal institutions that govern them, and the economic and security dimensions that characterize their space. The current ruling Islamist NCP party has placed "women's culture" as central to "Islamic culture", and has accordingly depicted targeted interest in the role of women in the family and

---

[71] SRSP, "Gender Policy" (2013), http://www.srsp.org.pk/srsp_new1/srsp-programmes/gender-policy

society at large.[72] Conflict, centralization of resources, and the domination of the public arena with Islamist voices of the NCP have all combined to create a divergence between different women's experiences of empowerment on the one hand and the state's rhetoric about social inclusion on the other. Since Sudan's independence, the country's constitution has enshrined giving "equal rights" to its citizenry irrespective of gender, race, or religion. However, the gap between the content of the constitution, and the practice of social, economic, and political inclusion of the citizenry has manifested itself in decades of conflict and struggle between the central government and marginalized Sudanese citizens. Vulnerable groups, including women, have had to contend with contradictory government policies and limited state capacity. Government attempts to empower women politically are illustrated in the Elections Act of 2008, which mandated a 25 percent quota of seats for women at federal and state legislative assemblies.[73] This is contrasted with the government's narrow attempts to secure the basic protection of women, as indicated by Sudan's non-ratifying of international protocols and conventions related to women, including the Convention on the Elimination of all Forms of Discrimination Against Women, and the Protocol on African Women's Rights.[74]

Gender equality within a state is usually assessed across the dimensions of equality of access to rights, resources, and voice.[75] According to the UNDP's Gender Inequality Index (GII), Sudan is currently ranked 128th out of 187 countries.[76] More specific indicators on education and economic and political participation reveal gender disparity across various facets of development and social empowerment. Evidence of gender disparity in education is indicated by the female literacy percentage compared with the male, and stands at 76 percent.[77] Gross primary school enrolment for females is 56 percent and stands at a

[72] Sondra Hale, *Gender Politics in Sudan: Islamism, Socialism, and the State* (Boulder, CO: Westview Press, 1996), 137.
[73] "The Paradox of Women's Representation in Sudan: Muslim Women's Diverging Agendas", *CMI Brief* 9 (2010), 2.
[74] Balghis Badri, *Sudanese Women Profile: Pathways to Empowerment* (Omdurman: Ahfad University, 2007), 16.
[75] World Bank, *World Development Report 2006: Equity and Development* (2006).
[76] United Nations Development Planning, "Human Development Report 2011: Sustainability and Equity: A Better Future for All" (2011), http://hdr.undp.org/en/reports/global/hdr2011/
[77] Data for 2005–10: UNICEF, "Sudan Statistics—Women", accessed 30 January 2013, http://www.unicef.org/infobycountry/sudan_statistics.html

ratio of 0.87 of male primary school enrolment.[78] The gender gap in education is mirrored in the economic sphere, where female labor force participation stands at 30 percent in comparison to the 73.9 percent labor force participation rate of males.[79] On the political front, representation of women in parliament has positively surged from 13 percent in 2010 to 25 percent in 2011, due to the Elections Act of 2008.

Social and economic institutions within weak states often exhibit systematic discrimination against women.[80] The lack of gender-aware policies and the predominance of gender-blind institutions have perpetuated structural sources of gender inequality in Sudan. According to some development practitioners, within fragile states the issue of mainstreaming gender issues in both state programs and policies is considered to be a question of "luxury" and not necessarily beneficial to establishing economic development and national security.[81] Increasingly, however, pressure by international donors and local activists to address gender dimensions in development and increased attention and resources toward empowering women have combined to result in explicit government action in this regard. Moving at a steady pace, there have been efforts by the government of Sudan to introduce programs and policies aimed at women's empowerment. The Ministry of Welfare and Social Security, for example, implemented a National Policy for Women Empowerment in 2007, which addressed health, education, human rights and law, economic empowerment, political involvement and decision-making, and peace and conflict resolution.[82] Within the area of economic empowerment, the initiative aims to incorporate gender issues within economic policies, provide increased opportunities to access social and economic resources, maximize women's integration in the economic sphere, and to ensure the coverage of social protection. In 2011, the government launched a similar measure aimed at enhancing the lot of rural women.[83] Despite these efforts, however, the informal

[78] Samia Satti, "Assessment of Gender Gap in Sudan" (United Nations University—Maastricht Economic and Social Research and Training Centre on Innovation and Technology, 2011), 7.

[79] Ibid.

[80] Wendy Harcourt, "Literature Review on Gender and Fragility", *European Report on Development* (2009), 5.

[81] "Gender-responsive Peace and State-building: Transforming the Culture of Power in Fragile States", *A Cordaid and wo=men Policy Brief* (2010), 6.

[82] National Policy for Women's Empowerment, Ministry of Welfare and Social Security (March 2007).

[83] "Rural Women Empowerment Project 2011–2015", Project Profile provided by

sector, in which state intervention to enhance women's position is most needed, remains as yet untouched, and overwhelmingly unpenetrated, by the government.

As part of its efforts aimed at empowering women, in 2008 the government passed an Elections Act that set a 25 percent women's quota in the national parliament. Consequently, in the 2010 elections to the National Assembly, 82 women from the ruling NPC Party and five women from opposition parties were elected.[84] These "official" gains are, nevertheless, only peripherally consequential insofar as women's overall position in Sudanese society and economy is concerned. Even inside the NPC, in fact, women's voices remain marginal. In the broader public arena, women are seldom heard. And, despite constituting some 78 percent of the agricultural labor force,[85] their ability to shape agricultural policy is practically non-existent.[86]

Education and social class are key determinants of access to government resources and institutions. Not surprisingly, it is among the more marginalized groups in society—especially women in the informal sector and in the country's periphery—where NGOs tend to be most consequential. NGOs can facilitate the active engagement of women in the development process and offer a way to "activate" a sense of citizenry amongst marginalized women. The next section highlights the efforts of the INGO Plan International to enhance economic activity and community participation of rural women in North Kordofan.

Work, Developmental Participation and Social Inclusion of Women in Damokia, North Kordofan

North Kordofan has not been directly involved or heavily impacted by the violence raging in its bordering provinces and states. Nevertheless, the region has been indirectly affected by the conflict due to the influx of internally displaced persons and ex-combatants from South Kordofan and the Blue Nile

---

Ministry of Welfare and Social Security—Women and Child Affairs Directorate (2013).

[84] "National Assembly's Elected Members in the 2010 General Elections from Geographical Constituencies and Women/Party Lists", National Commission for Elections, http://nec.org.sd/new/new/eng_doc/asmb.pdf, accessed 12 January 2013.

[85] Central Bureau of Statistics, "Sudan Labor Force Survey" (2009).

[86] El Gack, "Participation of Women", 5.

states into its main cities and towns.[87] This inflow of refugees has generated increased pressure on the existing, limited employment opportunities and the few social services that are accessible to indigenous inhabitants.[88] Rural areas in the state have been affected by recurrent droughts that hit the region in the 1980s and 1990s, and led to large-scale desertification. This has put added stress on the region's fragile resources, further impeding economic and infrastructural development.[89] North Kordofan's economy is largely agriculturally based and includes crop cultivation and livestock breeding. In the urban and semi-urban localities, non-agricultural activities in the services sector and activities in petty trade dominate. As in most regions throughout Sudan, women's political, social, and economic experiences differ between localities and between urban and rural areas. While women's economic participation in North Kordofan is amongst the highest in Sudan, registering at 51 percent,[90] the region also has one of the highest Human Poverty Indexes at 70.8, indicating extensive deprivation.[91]

Widespread poverty, poor education and health services, and limited infrastructure have increased the prevalence of NGOs in the region in an attempt to secure basic needs and improve living standards amongst the inhabitants. Plan International (PI), an INGO that has been operating in Sudan since the late 1970s, has been an active player in the development of basic infrastructure and poverty alleviation in North Kordofan. In the rural village of Damokia, located in the eastern part of the Sheikan locality, infrastructure and liveli-

---

[87] More recently in April and July of 2013, there have been isolated attacks on military bases and areas that produce gum Arabic (one of Sudan's chief exports) in North Kordofan by the Justice and Equality Movement—the Darfur-based rebels. See "Sudan Darfur Rebels attack North Kordofan Military", BBC News, 24 July 2013, http://www.bbc.co.uk/news/world-africa-23440721, accessed 25 July 2013.

[88] Abdel Rahman El Mahdi, "Youth Employment in Sudan. A Consolidated Report on Labor Market Survey Findings from Three Northern States: Blue Nile, North Kordofan, South Kordofan States", UNDP and SUDIA (August 2011), 11.

[89] International Fund for Agricultural Development, "North Kordofan Rural Development Project", http://operations.ifad.org/web/ifad/operations/country/project/tags/sudan/1045/project_overview, accessed 17 February 2013.

[90] As noted, their economic participation predominates in the agricultural sector and in the informal component of the services sector. El Mahdi, *Youth Employment in Sudan*, 19.

[91] Hamid Faki, Eltahir Mohamed Nur, Abdelaziz Abdelfattah, Aden A Aw-Hassan, "Poverty Assessment Northern Sudan Report", International Center for Agricultural Research in Dry Areas (2012).

hood development projects have been largely left to the efforts of NGOs. Within the village, a school for boys and girls, a healthcare center, and a drinking water well are the main infrastructures accessible to the villagers, of which PI has built the majority.[92] In Damokia, PI has introduced a Village Savings and Loan Assocation (VSLA) as part of its mandate to improve living standards, and to facilitate increased economic participation, the empowerment of women, and strengthening of social capital.

VSLAs entail a community-owned and managed approach whereby members of the group contribute their savings in the form of shares to a communal pot of savings (*sanduq*) from which participants can borrow. Borrowers repay the money with a 10 percent service fee, causing the fund to grow and allowing participants to attain a return on their saving investments that is much larger than those paid by commercial banks.[93] Formal and centralized microfinance institutions (MFIs) in Sudan have had limited reach in remote and rural areas of the country, and specifically in North Kordofan, where MFIs have only recently been introduced.[94] Since 2005, PI has implemented VSLAs in Damokia, encompassing nine associations of which 91 percent of the participants are women.[95] The educational profile of the participants reveals low levels of education, with only 15 percent having had any kind of formal schooling. In terms of the participants' marital status, 76 percent of the participants are married, which gives them access to diversified sources of income via family networks.

While the women in the village are highly active in economic activities such as handicrafts and *hina* production, their management of economic ventures is limited and lags far behind that of men.[96] Through VSLA, PI aims to propel women's economic participation and, more importantly, their management of economic activity as a means of empowerment and attaining a heightened sense of control over resources and production. A value-added component of the program is that the management of the VSLA projects in and of itself lends a venue for women to exercise management of their own development endeavors.

---

[92] "A Consultancy Review of Village Savings and Loan (VS&L) Project—North Kordofan Program Unit—Plan Sudan", VSLA Report provided by North Kordofan Program Unit Manager of the Plan International Head Office Khartoum (2013), 5.

[93] Ibid., 3.

[94] Ibid., 14.

[95] Ibid., 11.

[96] Ibid.

PI has faced several challenges in achieving its aims of enhancing women's economic participation and engagement in income-generating activities. Amongst the other localities (one urban and one semi-urban) that had the VSLA program introduced, Damokia exhibited the highest savings amount per cycle, as well as the lowest amount of loans taken out per cycle. Moreover, of the loans taken out, the debt–equity ratio (as an indicator of loan efficiency) was only 0.12 in Damokia. This is mainly attributable to the fact that the majority of spending was directed towards household assets, rather than income-generating activities. PI reports indicate that 32.4 percent have gone to home furniture, 26.47 percent to petty trade, 14.7 percent to handcrafts, 8.83 percent to building materials, 8.83 to school fees, 2.94 percent to agricultural practices, 2.94 to raising livestock and 2.94 percent towards travel expenses.[97] One of the main motives for saving by women in the group is to prepare for marriages and funerals in the family.[98]

Although commercial activities on the individual level are rare and sporadic in Damokia, a common business activity amongst the women is post-harvest price arbitration. This activity entails the process of participants pooling their produce and storing it until peak season in order to avoid low prices during the post-harvest season. Meanwhile, they often take loans from the VSLA fund in order to cover their expenses. The larger produce and size of crop would enable the group to arbitrate directly with urban-based vendors, cutting out the middle-men and thereby increasing their margin of profit.[99] Once the produce is sold, the VSLA group shares the profit amongst each other.[100] Thus, the majority of expenses are re-invested in fulfilling the basic household and village needs.

Overall, limited engagement in income-generating activities and entrepreneurship initiatives are due to two main impediments that rural women face. Firstly, within the village, there is limited cash flow amongst the inhabitants and thus the market for income-generating activities is restricted. The second obstacle is that, although the rural village of Damokia is not far from the semi-urban and urban localities of Al Regaiba and Al Dago, women's mobility and access to markets are limited due to social norms and cultural constraints

[97] Ibid., 18.
[98] Telephone interview by Dwaa Osman Sara Sinada, Youth Employability Coordinator, Plan International: Doha, Qatar, and Khartoum, Sudan, 27 February 2013.
[99] Ibid., 3.
[100] Ibid.

that informally institutionalize women's exclusion from geographic centers of economic resources, markets, and networks, by restricting their physical mobility and consequently their access to these spaces.

While enhanced economic participation at an individual level has not been achieved on a significant scale by the VSLA scheme thus far, participants have continued to benefit from the program by other means. For one, an increase in household assets increases the economic security of the women and their households. Moreover, a rise in assets lends itself to making participants more credit "worthy", should MFIs begin their operations in the locality of Sheikan. However, these spending habits also allude to the women's prioritization of spending on household assets over investment in entrepreneurial initiatives.

These household and communal activities, along with other similar responsibilities, have their gendered dimensions, where a woman's position in society is dictated by the formal and informal institutions that have long woven an image of women as agents of social rehabilitation and have placed them at the center of the domestic sphere. The "civilizing project" that the ruling regime introduced upon its rise to power in 1989 saw women's social position as one of its central ideological projects designed to create a society based on its vision of Islam.[101] The domestic sphere came to be romanticized. Accordingly, the ideal woman was judged by her ability to fulfill her traditional roles in upholding a "moral life" and in fulfilling her family obligations.[102] The value of the domestic sphere is altered in different settings, namely between rural and urban cash economies. In the latter, domestic labor becomes somewhat devalued as women's participation in income-generating activities is increasingly relied upon. Thus, women's level of entrepreneurial involvement in rural economies is largely a function of the setting where a woman's contribution to the domestic sphere remains highly valued at both the household and community levels, and her ability to maintain the image of a family-oriented woman informs her decision to engage in certain economic activities and dictates her spending habits.

Another factor that women benefit from through their participation in VSLA groups is the strengthening of their social capital and participation in community development projects. PI often interlinks different self-selected VSLA groups with each other, expanding the network to which women are exposed. This is generally done by integrating VSLA target groups with other

[101] Hale, *Gender Politics in Sudan*, 143.
[102] Ibid., 172.

areas of development intervention. Interventions such as the Integrated Management of Childhood Illness, and Community-Led Total Sanitation, use VSLA groups as institutional target groups.[103] This level of engagement enables the women to increase their effective participation beyond their immediate family network and to contribute at the village and community levels.

Thus, although VSLA groups have not directly translated to increased economic empowerment of women, they have provided a venue for women to exercise increased engagement at both the home and community levels. PI has not collected data indicating whether women's involvement in the VLSA projects has altered the gender dynamics in the home. Women's involvement in other community projects, however, has in fact led them to hold more explicit participatory roles outside the home. The type of community development interventions that women in Damokia are engaged in, such as Integrated Management of Childhood Illness and Community-Led Total Sanitation again, sheds light on the limitations of women's grass-roots empowerment in the face of broader exclusionary informal institutions and social norms. Much like their preference for securing household assets over engaging in more risk-prone economic activities, women's engagement in community-level projects also focuses on matters of survival. In the face of meager infrastructural support and diminished government capacity to provide basic resources, women's development trajectory is increasingly intertwined with the care economy. As NGOs seek to fill the gaps left by the state, so do women bear the burden of the state's inability to provide political goods by increasingly focusing their efforts on securing their own and their family's basic needs over longer-term needs that may enhance their overall economic profile.

Moreover, while their engagement in these community-level intervention programs may lock in women's familial and community roles as "care-takers", it nevertheless creates an opportunity for women to manage developmental processes that extend beyond the home. As Karin Willemse indicates in her account of working women in Darfur, the dominant Islamist discourse set by the ruling elite may create and perpetuate stereotypical identities.[104] However, these identities are not static, and individuals, particularly women, are constantly and actively involved in "negotiating their subject positions within those discourses".[105]

---

[103] "A Consultancy Review of Village Savings and Loan (VS&L) Project", 4.
[104] Karin Willemse. *One foot in Heaven narratives on gender and Islam in Darfur, West-Sudan* (Leiden: Brill, 2007), 450.
[105] Ibid.

Conclusion

While structural and cultural constraints have impeded women's social inclusion in Khyber Pakhtunkhwa and in North Kordofan, the presence of NGOs has created space for women's active involvement in community development processes, and contributed to their advancement in productive and social sectors. By involving women in the management of community development interventions, SRSP and Plan International have enhanced the degree of women's participation and decision-making related to family and community affairs without creating a backlash from communities. The NGOs have opted for a strategy which focuses on micro-level empowerment of women, without challenging the dominant moral discourse that classifies women as care-takers and custodians of the home. While this may not adequately contest the cultural constraints that impede women's social inclusion in these countries, and may not translate into advancing women's position vis-à-vis political and economic centers of power, it does create spaces where women can exercise increased control over development practices.

Despite these achievements, our case studies do not indicate that NGOs are able to play a transformative role in changing gender dynamics in society at large. In the current fragile, politically unstable, and dysfunctional environments of Sudan and Pakistan, it is unlikely that micro-level development projects will serve as catalysts for the sweeping socio-political transformation that are needed for the greater social inclusion of women. NGOS like SRSP and PI that step into the capacity-vacuum of weak states may serve to act as a release of pressure on the state, and keep people's dissatisfactions in check without any serious realignment of contested political goods. Rather than serving as agents of change, however, such initiatives, it could be argued, "reproduce and reinforce the hegemony of the state".[106]

As we stated earlier, NGOs principally address the social exclusion of the marginalized by enhancing people's capacity to engage with the state, and by creating or strengthening necessary linkages between the excluded and existing sources of power at the community and state levels. Social exclusion arises from macro structural factors and features, and as such can only be effectively addressed by the state, which remains the core actor that can negotiate between competing social interests and facilitate inclusion. The lack of provision of basic resources, coupled with exclusionary policies and institutions at the system level, remains as the most significant hindrance to women's social

[106] Jafar, "Engaging Fundamentalism", 259.

inclusion. As evident through the two cases analyzed here, NGOs largely work to tackle the symptoms rather than the root cause of women's exclusion. Regardless of whether a state is weak, strong, or dysfunctional, the state is still the primary power-broker and negotiator that creates, enforces, mediates, and changes social rules and transforms societies. It is the state that manages the competing interests of multiple social actors and groups, and is tasked with creating a platform of cooperation amongst them. The state certainly functions poorly in Sudan and Pakistan, does not deliver effectively on the basket of social goods, and might even be neglected by NGOs who perceive the role of the state as irrelevant or negligible. But in the end it is still the state that can create and maintain security, ensure law and order, and address overarching issues of instability which impact on the micro and community-level engagement of NGOs.

Much of the theoretical work done on social exclusion has focused on the conditions of highly developed, post-industrial countries (particularly in Europe) and how they have addressed marginalization, unequal access to resources, and other forms of injustice against social sub-groups. The case of SRSP in Pakistan indicates that while NGO efforts may achieve micro-level change of women's status at the household level, altering broader social norms and informal institutions that dictate gender relations is a much more difficult feat. The VSLA development interventions of PI in North Kordofan, Sudan, have provided insight into the challenges faced by the INGO in engaging women in income-generating activities. Women in this study focused on securing their basic needs and assumed the role of "care-takers" at the household and community levels due to the state's failure to provide basic political goods, as well as the women's prioritization of the domestic sphere. Both these cases indicate that while grass-roots empowerment may be achieved at a micro level, social inclusion of women is something that can only be achieved with the active involvement of the state.

10

WHITHER PALESTINE?

WEAK STATE, FAILED STATE, OR NO STATE AT ALL?

Glenn E. Robinson

The purpose of this chapter is twofold. The first purpose is to explore the history and characteristics of Palestinian statehood in the West Bank and Gaza Strip, and ask to what degree can Palestine even be considered a state? The second purpose is to identify the primary dynamics under which proto-state institutions have been built since the signing of the Declaration of Principles (the first Oslo Accord) in 1993. This chapter finds that while Palestine enjoys some of the attributes of statehood, primarily international recognition, it would be wrong to classify Palestine as a state. It further finds that the construction of Palestinian state institutions has been primarily shaped by three dynamics, all of which will create serious dysfunctions if Palestine ever does become independent: institution-building under a suffocating colonial system of rule, a rentier state type of political economy, and a legacy of personalized anti-institutionalism used by Yasir Arafat to consolidate power after Oslo (a dynamic I refer to as "the politics of antithesis").

Early Palestinian State-Building Attempts

In the century prior to the 1967 war, Palestinian state-building efforts were limited. The dominant Palestinian political efforts in this period focused more on nation-building and independence than on constructing an institutional and legal framework for a state. Both the construction of a national identity and actual independence are certainly important for the success of statehood, but they are not necessary prerequisites, as the Zionist experiment showed. On the eve of its formal independence in 1948, Israel had neither an Israeli national identity nor liberation, but had constructed the institutional foundation for a successful state. Indeed, Israel still today has no strong *Israeli* national identity, but its state is rather strong and has survived for more than six decades.

In the late Ottoman period, there were no substantial Palestinian state-building efforts. Indeed, the very notion of an independent state of Palestine emerging from Ottoman control was hardly a topic of conversation, much less the focus of any sustained political movement. Moreover, during this period, there was virtually no Palestinian national identity or nationalist movement per se. As Muhammad Muslih has shown, elite Palestinian national identity in the late Ottoman period consisted of dominant notable leaders who espoused Ottomanism, and estranged members of the same notable class who increasingly adopted the language of Arabism in response to the "Turkification" of the Ottoman state under the Young Turk movement. Palestinian nationalism per se was not in the political mix.[1] Rashid Khalidi largely agrees, dating the formation of Palestinian national identity to the "critical years" of 1917–23.[2] Thus, while Palestine as a geographical concept roughly equivalent to "the holy land" has been in use for over two millennia, neither Palestine as a state nor Palestine as a political identity had much currency under the Ottomans.

The idea of a Palestinian state and concomitant Palestinian nationalism emerged with the British Mandate for Palestine when the specific territory of Palestine—today's Israel, West Bank, and Gaza—was drawn by the British. The Palestinian national movement clearly emerged under Mandatory author-

---

[1] Muhammad Y. Muslih, *The Origins of Palestinian Nationalism* (New York: Columbia University Press, 1988).

[2] Rashid Khalidi, *Palestinian Identity: The Construction of Modern National Consciousness* (New York: Columbia University Press, 1997). See also Y. Porath, *The Emergence of the Palestinian–Arab National Movement, 1918–1929* (London: Frank Cass, 1974).

ity, as did some efforts actually to construct a state. Under the terms of the Mandate and Article 22 of the Covenant of the League of Nations, Palestine was designed to emerge eventually as an independent state. That said, the national movement and the construction of a national identity received far more attention than actual state-building efforts. Palestinian state-building was essentially thwarted by British power. In a formal sense, Palestinian state-building efforts were to be managed by an "Arab Agency" parallel to the Jewish Agency, which did succeed in its state-building efforts under the British. However, the Arab Agency never got off the ground, primarily because the Palestinians were required to accept the Balfour Declaration as integral to the work of the Arab Agency. The demand that Palestinians accept a British promise to make Palestine a "national home for the Jewish people" was an obvious non-starter among the Palestinians and, as Tom Segev has shown in detail, British policy under the Mandate consistently favored Zionist interests and undermined Palestinian interests, at least until 1939.[3]

Palestinian institution-building during the Mandate was likewise thwarted by elite rivalry among the dominant notable families of Palestine. No doubt part of the institutional weakness of Palestinian society was the nature of the society itself: a poor, underdeveloped, largely subsistence agrarian (peasant)-based society with strong extended familial ties is rarely fertile soil for the growth of strong proto-state institutions. That said, notable family rivalry for influence undermined most nascent attempts at institution-building by Palestinians in the Mandate.[4] In addition, Palestinian elites who promoted nationalism—in part as a response to Zionism—were split on which nationalism to privilege: a broader Arab nationalism (*qawmiyya*) that was beginning to gain traction in the 1930s and 1940s as Ba'thist as other forms of Arabism emerged, or a particular Palestinian national identity (*wataniyya*) distinct from the Arab nation.

The *Naqba*, or Disaster, of 1948 left Palestinian society shattered and fragmented under different political rulers, and state-building efforts largely ceased until the 1960s. Those Palestinians left in Israel lived under military rule until 1966, and any notion of independent state-building was strictly prohibited.[5] Jordan similarly frowned upon any institutional or political

---

[3] Tom Segev, *One Palestine, Complete: Jews and Arabs under the British Mandate* (New York: Metropolitan Books, 2000).

[4] See Issa Khalaf, *Politics in Palestine: Arab Factionalism and Social Disintegration 1939–1948* (Albany: SUNY Press, 1991); and Muslih, *Origins*.

[5] See Ian Lustick, *Arabs in the Jewish State: Israel's Control of a National Minority*

expression of national Palestinian aspirations in the West Bank, with the Hashemites assuming the Palestinian national portfolio for themselves. Development investment was largely limited to the East Bank as well, prompting tens of thousands of Palestinians to move across the Jordan River during the 1948–67 period, further undermining any chance of Palestinian state- or nation-building inside the West Bank. One consequence of Jordan's policy for Palestinians to disavow national politics and focus instead on the local was the flourishing of municipal government on the West Bank during this period.[6] The Gaza Strip was administered by Egypt, which did not object to Palestinian national organizing as long as Cairo remained the ultimate master. The All Palestine Government (established in September 1948) helped run Gaza from 1948 to 1959, although it was itself based in Cairo following the 1948 war and was largely ineffectual and symbolic. Egypt under Gamal Abd al-Nasir was largely responsible for the creation of the Palestine Liberation Organization in 1964, but kept it under a tight leash until after the 1967 war, when Cairo lost its dominant role over the PLO.

The 1967 war set in motion dynamics that refocused Palestinian national aspirations toward a two-state solution with Israel instead of in place of Israel.[7] The PLO's 1974 Ten Point Program is widely considered its first formal step toward recognition of a two-state solution, although the plan fell far short of explicit recognition of a two-state solution. This would come in its 1988 Declaration of Independence, which formally recognized Israel and the legitimacy of a two-state solution, and which helped set the stage for the mutual recognition letters exchanged between Israel and the PLO in 1993 as part of the Oslo peace process.

Is Palestine a State Today?

The state of Palestine, bounded by the 1967 borders, was formally declared by Palestinian Authority President and PLO head Mahmud 'Abbas in 2012; it

---

(Austin: University of Texas Press, 1980); and As'ad Ghanem, *The Palestinian–Arab Minority in Israel, 1948–2000* (Albany: SUNY Press, 2001).

[6] See Moshe Ma'oz, *Palestinian Leadership on the West Bank: The Changing Role of the Mayors under Jordan and Israel* (London: Cass, 1984).

[7] The best and most detailed description of this transition can be found in Yezid Sayigh, *Armed Struggle and the Search for State: The Palestinian National Movement, 1949–1993* (New York: Oxford University Press, 1997, in conjunction with the Institute for Palestine Studies).

was then formally recognized by the United Nations General Assembly as a "non-member observer state" on a lopsided 138–9 vote, and by 2013 enjoyed individual recognition from 132 states, or over two-thirds of the member states of the United Nations. Some analysts go back further to suggest that Palestinian statehood began with the Palestine National Council's Declaration of Independence in 1988, with the UN partition resolution (UNGAR 181) of 1947, or even with the 1924 League of Nations Mandate for Palestine.[8] There are problems with all of those arguments, primarily having to do with the lack of a sovereign claim over a specific territory; for example, the 1988 Declaration did not identify the specific territory that was being claimed for independence, but did approve (for the first time) UNGAR 181. Yet the territorial allocation in UNGAR 181 is significantly different from the 1967 borders. In any case, there is no question that, at least beginning in 2012, Palestinians have unequivocally claimed a sovereign state and have specified that the 1967 borders define its boundaries.

Just because the Palestinians have claimed statehood—as a current reality, not a future goal—does that make it so? When is a state really a state? Under the Westphalian system of states that has dominated first Europe and then the world since 1648, two attributes of statehood are fundamental.[9] First, a state must have effective control over its claimed territory; and second, a state must be recognized as the legitimate sovereign by other states. Neither of these characteristics is absolute. As to the former, there are many instances of states that have not had effective control over much of their claimed territory. For example, a principled (and principal) reason why Taiwan lost its recognition by the United Nations in favor of Beijing was the fact that Taiwan did not have effective control over mainland China, a territory over which it claimed to be sovereign. Obviously, geopolitical considerations also played a significant role in this change. More recently, how many states in the Middle East

---

[8] For a rich discussion of the legal arguments concerning Palestinian statehood, see John Quigley, *The Statehood of Palestine: International Law in the Middle East Conflict* (Cambridge: Cambridge University Press, 2011).

[9] For a provocative discussion on the attributes of statehood in the Westphalian system, see Charles Tilly, "War Making and State Making as Organized Crime", in Peter Evans, Dietrich Rueschemeyer, and Theda Skocpol, eds., *Bringing the State Back* (Cambridge: Cambridge University Press, 1985). A most interesting discussion of the Westphalian system applied to the Arab world can be found in Ian S. Lustick, "The Absence of Middle Eastern Great Powers", *International Organization*, Vol. 51, No. 4 (Autumn 1997).

exercise effective control over all their claimed territory? Does Tripoli have effective control over southern or even eastern Libya? Is effective control in these areas at best episodic? Does the Egyptian state exercise effective control over the Sinai Peninsula, outside the Sharm al-Shaykh enclave? Likewise, the Yemeni state based in Sana'a can only in reality claim episodic control over much of its claimed territory.

While effective control of claimed territory is considered central to the Westphalian model, today it is often practiced in the breach. More accurately, effective control only really matters when someone else is claiming to be the rightful sovereign of that same territory. For example, there are large swathes of Syria today (2013) that the Damascus-based Syrian state no longer controls, and there is an alternative claimant to sovereign legitimacy over those lands. This reality will compel other states to reconsider to whom they should give sovereign recognition, particularly if the current contestation lingers and deepens further. In the absence of such contestation, the lack of effective control is not in practice a serious deterrent to recognition of sovereignty in the modern world. Episodic control is often a more accurate gauge.

Does the state of Palestine meet the first criterion of effective control over its claimed territory? The simple answer is no, for two reasons. First, Israel has effective control over all the land borders around and airspace over the West Bank, so all people and goods that enter or exit any part of the West Bank are controlled by Israel. Likewise, Israel controls most of the land borders and all of the sea border and airspace of the Gaza Strip, with the exception of the Rafah border with Egypt. Thus, it is Israel, not Palestine, that exercises effective control over the broad territory of the land claimed by Palestine. Indeed, it is this argument of effective control that leads many experts to conclude that Israel is still legally considered the occupying power in Gaza, even though its colonization efforts ended in 2005 with the withdrawal of IDF forces to the border area and the dismantling of settlements.

Second, by signing the Oslo Accords, the Palestine Liberation Organization (PLO) agreed to give up effective control over the large majority of the West Bank. Oslo broke the West Bank into four categories. "Area A" consisted of those areas in which the Palestinian Authority (PA)[10] had both civil and secu-

[10] PA is actually shorthand for PISGA, the Palestinian Interim Self-Governing Authority, created by the Oslo accords for the interim period prior to the signing of a "final status settlement". Under the terms of Oslo, the PA was to have a five-year lifespan that began with the signing of the Cairo accord in May 1994; therefore, the

rity control. These were the areas wherein most of the Palestinian population was concentrated, but which consisted of only about 20 percent of the West Bank.[11] Most Palestinian urban areas fell under Area A, although Hebron was governed by a separate protocol negotiated in 1997. It is important to note that while the PA had extensive control over Area A, it did not claim actual sovereignty over these lands until 2012, and Israel never stopped military incursions to arrest or kill wanted militants there.

"Area B" was West Bank lands in which Israel maintained security control and the PA exercised civil authority (that is, it provided many government services). Prior to the second Intifada, Israel's security presence on a routine basis consisted of joint patrols with PA security forces, although again Israel would conduct special raids in Area B without consulting with its PA counterparts, further underlining the lack of sovereignty exercised by the PA. Area B lands made up about 20 percent of the West Bank, and contained several hundred Palestinian villages.

Israel maintained full security and civil control over "Area C" lands, which comprised fully 60 percent of the West Bank. Area C lands contained all settlements and military areas, virtually all the Jericho Valley outside the municipal boundaries of the city of Jericho, all Jewish-only "bypass roads",[12] and, importantly, large areas that settlement councils had marked for expansion at a later date.

PA was legally supposed to expire in May 1999. (The Cairo accord is also known as the Gaza–Jericho agreement; Yasir Arafat had to be compelled by his Egyptian hosts to sign the document.) The PA has faced many legal uncertainties about a number of its elements, including the expiration of the 'Abbas presidency and the termination of the PA by treaty in 1999.

[11] I say "about" both because the amount of territory in Area A varied over time, and because Israelis and Palestinians have very different ways of measuring the West Bank. In defining the territory of the West Bank, Israel routinely does not include East Jerusalem, the north-west quadrant of the Dead Sea, and the "no-man's land" near Latrun, all of which are properly part of the West Bank.

[12] Bypass roads in the West Bank were primarily meant to link settlements with each other and with Israel proper, bypassing Palestinian towns and villages. Only cars with yellow (Israeli and Jewish settler vehicles) or white (UN/international vehicles) license plates were allowed to use these roads. Vehicles with green (Palestinian) license plates were not allowed to use such roads. Gaza, until 2005, had a similar discriminatory road system, albeit less complex because Gaza has fewer roads of any sort.

Until 2005, the Gaza Strip had essentially the same kind of land allocations, but used different nomenclature. According to Oslo, settlements and military areas (primarily along the border area) in Gaza were not accessible to Palestinians. Gaza also had Jewish-only roads until de-colonization took place in 2005.

A fourth category of lands under Oslo were those territories that were simply excluded from any kind of Palestinian claims at all, not even reaching Area C levels of inclusion. These lands remained under the full and direct authority of Israel in every way, without even the possibility of being transferred to either partial or full Palestinian control (minor amounts of territory were transferred from Area B to Area A lands in the 1990s). Excluded lands included East Jerusalem (as defined by Israel following the 1967 war and the extension of Israeli law to these new territories) and the north-west quadrant of the Dead Sea, which, under international law, "belongs" to the West Bank—or, more precisely, whichever sovereign power is recognized to exercise sovereign authority over the West Bank. Israel maintained full and unequivocal authority over the western half of the Dead Sea under Oslo, including that quarter which is attached to the West Bank under the norms of international law.

The second criterion of statehood in the Westphalian model is recognition by fellow states: essentially, other states must acknowledge that the new state is now a member of the club. By this criterion, the state of Palestine has greater claim. Indeed, it is one of the very few states in the world that were created by the UN, with large majority support among all the members. Israel is also in that elite group, having been legally created by the UN in November 1947. As of April 2013, 132 of the UN's 193 member states had formally extended diplomatic recognition to the state of Palestine as bounded by the 1967 borders. By contrast, even though Israel has been in existence for over six decades, only 160 member states of the UN formally recognize it. This is an all-time high: for much of its history, and especially in the period following the 1967 Arab–Israeli war, when many African and Asian countries broke diplomatic ties with Israel, Israel had the lowest rate of international *de jure* recognition of any country in the world. Even the formal birth of Israel at the United Nations (UNGAR 181) was only approved by a vote of 33–13, or 72% of the vote. Compared with the 2012 UN vote on Palestine, which garnered a 94 percent positive vote, Israel's diplomatic acceptance by the international community has been weaker than Palestine's in important ways.

One final point on the issue of whether there is, in fact, a state of Palestine today: how do the PLO and the PA now relate to the state? Mahmud 'Abbas proclaimed the state of Palestine in the name of the PLO, which made sense, as the PLO was recognized under Oslo as the official representative of the Palestinians, and has had formal standing with the United Nations as an observer since 1974. In addition, the PLO had formal status in the Arab League as the "sole legitimate representative of the Palestinian people". Thus, for the PLO to bring forth the application for recognition of the state of Palestine was proper, even though there had been no recent action by the PLO and especially the Palestine National Council (the broadest decision-making body of the PLO) to authorize this move specifically. However, what is now the relationship between the PLO and the state of Palestine?

Ironically, the declaration of the state of Palestine may well have removed the PLO as the political center of gravity for the Palestinians. The primary vehicle for Palestinian national aspirations since the 1960s, the PLO is now likely to play second fiddle to the state of Palestine when it comes to representing Palestinian interests internationally. Indeed, the PLO may well fade into political oblivion as a result of its creation of the state of Palestine. Adding to the irony, the PLO will have essentially been replaced by the PA, as the state of Palestine is essentially the PA with a new name. The president is now the president of the state instead of the PA; cabinet ministers now have a letterhead that says their ministries are of a state instead of an "authority"; parliamentarians now legislate for a state instead of the PA, although their circumstances have not changed on the ground.[13] The PLO helped create the PA as part of the Oslo process, and the PA was to last no longer than five years. The PA has now effectively devoured its creator.

In official Palestinian eyes, the PA no longer exists and there is really no longer much of a role for the PLO to play. If and when negotiations restart with Israel, will the Palestinian negotiators present themselves as representing the state of Palestine or as representing the PLO, which had been the case up to the point of statehood? Will official negotiators be appointed by Mahmud 'Abbas, president of Palestine, or Mahmud 'Abbas, head of the PLO? It may be a distinction without a difference at some levels, but it would mark a symbolic end to the PLO. As the state of Palestine pushes aside the PLO, it also continues the major political change started in 1993 to shift the center of Palestinian politics from the diaspora Palestinian community—which is really

---

[13] The PA's parliament, also known as the Palestinian Legislative Council, or PLC, has not met since 2007 because of Israel's arrest of many of its members and because of the rift between Fatah rule in the West Bank and Hamas rule in Gaza.

what the PLO has primarily represented—to historical Palestine. The shift does have important political implications for the place of the diaspora in the future, and its probable further alienation from Palestine. This is likely to be a source of unrest and political turbulence in the future.

By way of conclusion to this section, it is fair to say that the state of Palestine has not yet been much of a state, given that it does not have effective control over the territory it claims in the West Bank, East Jerusalem, and the Gaza Strip (putting aside the issue of current Hamas control there). On the other hand, its level of *de jure* diplomatic recognition, both bilaterally by over 130 states and through the United Nations as of 2012, is quite impressive. In some ways, the state of Palestine can be compared to exiled governments that still enjoyed broad international recognition, even while they exercised little to no control over their territory. An example of this would be the Kuwait government in 1990, forced into exile with Iraq's invasion. No state recognized Iraq's annexation of Kuwait—thus, Kuwait's sovereignty as a state was maintained by international consensus—and the Kuwaiti government maintained its status even in the absence of effective control over its territory. In this case, however, Kuwait had been a functioning state and there was good reason to believe that it would return to that status in short order, as in fact it did. The state of Palestine has never exercised effective control over its purported territory, and there is good reason for pessimism that it ever will. But like those who viewed the emperor without clothes, few states want to say out loud that the state of Palestine may never reach fruition. It is a useful fiction for virtually all states—from Israel to the Arab League, from the US to the EU—to maintain the rhetorical possibility of real Palestinian sovereignty emerging from a never-ending "peace process". To tell the emperor that he has no clothes would entail unfathomable risk, similar to the frightful possibilities of concluding that hoped-for and real Palestinian sovereignty is likely not to occur. Then what?

Dynamics Shaping Palestinian Institution-Building

Palestinian state- or proto-state-building has been deeply shaped by several dynamics, which themselves have created deep structural realities that will continue to inform Palestinian governing institutions for many years to come. Three such dynamics deserve special mention and will be briefly discussed below. First, Palestinian state institutions built under the terms of Oslo have been created in the shadow of Israeli colonialism and military occupation, and often reflect the interests of the colonial power more than those of the occupied population. Second, Palestine is essentially a rentier or distributive state that receives the large majority of its governing funds from outside powers, either Israel or foreign donors. There are some important differences, especially Palestine's inability to control the flow of rents to its government coffers, but some critical rentier similarities have clearly emerged and have deeply shaped both central and municipal institutions. Third, the nature of the consolidation of power by the Arafat regime, and in particular the "inside–outside" dynamic, created a politics of antithesis that both personalized institutions and downplayed the importance of institutionalized governance. While the death of Arafat in 2004 relieved some of these pressures, the way in which power was consolidated has deeply impacted the nature of Palestinian state institutions. I will discuss each of these three issues in turn.

Institution-building under Occupation

Joseph Massad spoke of the "colonial effects" of British rule in Jordan, and specifically the long-lasting and generally negative impacts British colonialism had on Jordanian legal and military institutions.[14] The fact that they were built under the watchful eye of Glubb Pasha and others shaped these Jordanian state institutions in tangible ways decades after British rule ended. For the Palestinians, Israeli occupation authorities have exercised a far more intrusive and shaping role since Oslo than the British ever did in Jordan. No Palestinian institution of governance has gone untouched by this pervasive Israeli dynamic. In short, Palestinian state institutions have been constructed to meet not only the needs of the Palestinian public, but also the interests of Israel.

The most obvious Israeli shaping of Palestinian institutions has occurred in the security sector, where Palestinian security forces have been principally formed to ensure the safety and security of Israelis from militant attacks. The professionalization of Palestinian security forces in the West Bank since 2005 has redoubled those efforts, particularly under the prime ministership of Salam Fayyad. Senior Israeli security officials regularly praise Palestinian security forces for their ability to protect Israeli interests and "keep the peace". But even from the outset of the Oslo process, the construction of the Palestinian police and security forces served dual masters: Arafat's calculations of consolidating power, and Israel's calculation that an authoritarian Palestinian

---

[14] Joseph A. Massad, *Colonial Effects: the Making of National Identity in Jordan* (New York: Columbia University Press, 2001).

Authority was likely to be better at cracking down on Hamas and other opponents of Oslo.

All PA ministries likewise had to respond to and be shaped by Israeli interests. The Palestinian Water Authority, for example, does not control West Bank water supplies, as Israel continues to take well over 80 percent of the West Bank's water, and Palestinian institutions needed to function around this fact.[15] Municipal planners always needed to be wary of Israeli restrictions on Palestinian building, which often resulted in sub-optimal outcomes. Villages would have to locate water tanks and crops away from Area C-designated lands, even when those locations made the most sense; towns could not undertake normal growth and development if that meant encroaching on lands that a settlement wanted for future use; no municipal authority could rely on the free flow of goods and services, or even the ability to reach constituents, given Israeli checkpoints and closures. The Ministry of Health inherited an Israeli system that had been in place for nearly three decades; the Ministry of Industry had strict Israeli restrictions on the kinds of industrial development it could pursue.

Indeed, state institutions dealing with economic growth were among the most constrained and shaped by Israel's interests. Israeli impacts on the Palestinian economy and its institutions have been profound since the 1967 war. During the first decade of occupation, Palestinian household income rose sharply, primarily because Palestinians began working in the Israeli labor market, where wages were significantly higher than could be found on the farms of the West Bank or the camps of Gaza. Palestinian unskilled and semi-skilled labor became critical to Israel's construction and agricultural sectors and, later on, to its service sector as well. About one-third of the Palestinian labor force worked in Israel. Even during the second decade of Israeli rule, many measurements of Palestinian economic activity rose, despite the burgeoning settlement project that took off in the early 1980s, which often made the flow of labor, goods, and services much more difficult. While household income figures were good during this time frame, Palestinian institutional development around economic activity stagnated. Sara Roy referred to such institutional weakness as "de-development" in her political economy study of the Gaza Strip.[16] Perhaps reflecting Roy's argument, the Oslo period led to a clear "de-industri-

---

[15] For a recent critical study of the West Bank water situation, see http://www.alhaq. org/publications/Water-For-One-People-Only.pdf

[16] Sara Roy, *The Gaza Strip: The Political Economy of De-Development* (Washington, DC: Institute for Palestine Studies, 1995).

alization" of the Palestinian economy, as manufacturing dropped from 18 percent of GDP in 1995 to just 11 percent in 2011. During the same period the number of agricultural workers nearly doubled, the opposite trend of what typically happens in modernizing economies.[17]

The first Palestinian Intifada (1987–93) led to a sharp downturn in economic activity for Palestinians, which is typically the case in areas experiencing political turbulence. However, the single biggest factor negatively impacting the Palestinian economy was Israel's decision in early 1992 to begin to close off its labor market to Palestinians. Israel increasingly imported low-skilled foreign workers to replace Palestinian laborers. This closing of Israel's labor market to Palestinians intensified over time, particularly with the building of Israel's "security barrier" around the West Bank and a similar fence around Gaza, such that today, virtually no Palestinian from the West Bank or Gaza is allowed to enter Israel, let alone work there. With few exceptions, the one-third of the Palestinian labor force that had worked in Israel now needed to find local employment, or else, more often than not, remained unemployed.

Palestinian expectations for Oslo included a significant improvement in their economic situation, an expectation that was largely dashed both before and after the second Intifada (2000–2004). There are many studies that detail the economic plight of Palestinians in the West Bank and Gaza over the past two decades, which in any case is not the focus of this current discussion.[18]

The Oslo process strongly and formally linked Palestinian economic institutions to Israel, beginning with the 1994 Paris Protocol that governed economic relations between the two. While the Protocol enacted a number of technical details (e.g. recognizing that the PA had the power to levy taxes), its primary function was to maintain the existing and subservient nature of Palestinian economic dependence on Israel. The principal vehicle for this was the creation of a "customs union" that prevented the establishment of any kind of economic border between Israel and the PA. Generating an economic border would have provided the PA with greater economic autonomy from Israel, but Israel rejected this, threatening to prevent any Palestinians from working in Israel if the PA did not sign the Protocol.[19] The Protocol mandates

---

[17] See World Bank, *Fiscal Challenges and Long Term Economic Costs*, 19 March 2013, 13–15.

[18] The best economic analysis has come from the World Bank. See its many reports and larger studies at www.worldbank.org/we

[19] http://www.btselem.org/freedom_of_movement/paris_protocol. A technical addendum to the Paris Protocol came into effect on 1 January 2013.

that all the PA's foreign trade must pass through Israeli seaports, airports, or border crossings, allowing Israel to exercise final control over Palestine's international trade. The Protocol also stipulates the taxes Israel will collect and turn over to the PA from this trade. It should be noted that this process has often been subject to delays and withholdings, depending on the amount of political pressure Israel wanted to assert on the PA. This is no small matter, as Israeli tax transfers to the PA have accounted for about 75 percent of the PA's annual revenues on average, an issue that will be discussed more fully in the section on rentier states, below. While Palestinian state institutions have somewhat improved their own revenue collection system, they have been stunted by the PA's enormous reliance on Israeli collection institutions.

Extensive Israeli restrictions on Palestinian economic activity have compelled the growth of the PA, now state, public sector to help absorb Palestinian labor. The closure policy begun the year before Oslo was signed rapidly shrank the Palestinian labor force that was working in Israel from about one-third of the total Palestinian labor force to about 7 percent by 1997. Today, only a small handful of Palestinians receive permits to work in Israel, and sneaking in to work in the black labor market is virtually impossible with both Gaza and the West Bank walled in. The PA has had to absorb much of that lost labor, greatly expanding the public sector. From 1998 to 2009, the public sector share of employment grew from 17 to 26 percent; as well, public sector services provided by the PA nearly doubled to 30 percent in the 1994–2011 period, as the public sector needed to pick up the slack caused by Israeli restrictions on the private sector.[20]

Infrastructure is another sector where Palestinian state institutions have been fundamentally shaped by Israeli interests. Typically, a state builds and is responsible for the basic infrastructural needs of its society, including roads, water, electricity, and telecommunications. In all of these areas, PA activity has been thwarted by Israeli restrictions. The PA has been provided limited access for road construction and maintenance in Area C, fully 60 percent of the West Bank, and has even less access to West Bank water supplies, which Israel considers a deep national interest. In a detailed 2013 study, the respected Al-Haq organization in Ramallah described the water situation in the West Bank as "water apartheid" for the benefit of "one people only".[21] The state of Palestine has virtually no control over its own water system. Much of the electrical grid

[20] World Bank, *Fiscal Challenges*, 13 and 20.
[21] http://www.alhaq.org/publications/Water-For-One-People-Only.pdf

in the West Bank is still controlled by Israeli interests (about 95 percent, according to the World Bank), largely because it also services Jewish settlements there. The degradation of infrastructure has been particularly pronounced in Gaza, due to both the massive destruction of infrastructure brought on by Israel's assault in the brief 2008–9 conflict, and to Israel's restrictions on what Gaza can import to rebuild its infrastructure. In short, where Palestinian state institutions are responsible for infrastructure, limited access offered by Israel has often exacerbated degradation; in other cases, Palestinian infrastructure is still directly dependent on Israel for provision of services.

A final example concerns the ability of Palestinian state institutions to promote and deliver exports. Once again, Israel's interests, often pronounced as security concerns, have deeply impacted how Palestinian institutions can function. As noted, under the terms of Oslo, all Palestinian international trade must go through Israel first. Delays and other hindrances have made Palestinian export of goods nearly impossible, meaning that the vast majority of Palestinian exports simply go to Israel. In 2011, this was the case for fully 86 percent of all Palestinian exports, mostly low value-added exports such as stone and agricultural products.[22]

It should be added that the international donor community, primarily driven by US interests, has largely enabled the colonial logic of institution-building in Palestine. There has been precious little donor commitment to building Palestinian state institutions that deviate from Israeli colonial interests in the West Bank. Ironically, Gaza under Hamas rule may well be developing more genuinely independent state institutions. While Gaza remains desperately poor, with one-third of its labor force unemployed, since 2007 its state institutions have developed outside the colonial context, and thus may represent a more authentic expression of Palestinian state-building—for better or worse.[23]

Palestine as a Rentier State

There is a vast literature on rentier states, with a well-established general finding that oil wealth impedes democratic development.[24] What is far less studied

[22] World Bank, *Fiscal Challenges*, 16–18.
[23] For a good discussion on Hamas' version of state-building in Gaza, see Yezid Sayigh, *Hamas Rule in Gaza: Three Years On*, Crown Center for Middle East Studies 41, Brandeis University, March 2010.
[24] The most recent seminal book on the topic is Michael L. Ross, *The Oil Curse: How*

is the impact of other forms of international rents on the political development of states. Laurie Brand's work on Jordanian foreign policy took as its organizing principle the notion of "budget security" and the centrality of capital transfers from foreign patrons (UK, US, Gulf). This was every bit a rentier-type system, with typically about half of Jordanian government revenues coming from these international strategic rents.[25] My own earlier work on Jordan argued that it was a fiscal crisis in the rentier state system there that led to the period of relative liberalization beginning in 1989.[26]

International rents that accrue directly to the government's treasury shape political outcomes, and are not limited to oil or other natural resources. Strategic rents are as common as oil rents, but rarely account for the overwhelming majority of government revenues. Oil states typically have 75 percent or more of budget revenues come from the sale of oil on international markets. Strategic rents, or the renting of a country's foreign policy, rarely account for even half of budget revenues in the recipient countries, and are thus not generally as determinative as oil rents in shaping domestic political outcomes.

Palestine is an odd sort of rentier state. The vast majority of its government budget revenues come from international sources, but not in the usual way. Under the Paris Protocol formula, Israel collects customs tariffs and VAT (Value Added Tax) for the PA and passes these revenues directly to the PA coffers. During the early years of Oslo, these transfers, called "clearance revenues" by the PA Ministry of Finance, accounted for nearly 80 percent of all PA government revenues; more recently, they have dropped to about 70 percent; in fact, they accounted for exactly 70 percent of the $2.1 billion total PA revenues in 2012.[27] The transfers are routinely withheld by Israel when tensions are high, although they are then released later. Israel also regularly deducts delinquent water and electricity bills prior to transferring the monies to the PA.

In addition to the "clearance revenues" provided by Israel, the PA has received annual transfers from other countries, although the amounts have

---

Petroleum Wealth Shapes the Development of Nations (Princeton, NJ: Princeton University Press, 2012). Ross's argument is summarized as follows: "Countries that are rich in petroleum have less democracy, less economic stability, and more frequent civil wars than countries without oil."

[25] Laurie A. Brand, *Jordan's Inter-Arab Relations: the Political Economy of Alliance Making* (New York: Columbia University Press, 1995).

[26] Glenn E. Robinson, "Defensive Democratization in Jordan", *International Journal of Middle East Studies*, 30 (1998).

[27] World Bank, *Fiscal Challenges*, 8.

varied widely, both from year to year, and from what was pledged to what was actually delivered. Some of these monies have gone to direct PA budgetary support, while others fund specific projects in the West Bank and Gaza, freeing up PA revenues to be applied elsewhere. International donor assistance amounts to about $1 billion per year; this figure does not count other revenues that went to rebuild Gaza after the 2009 conflict.

While it is a bit like comparing apples to oranges, Israel's tax transfers to the PA combined with donor assistance from abroad provide roughly 85 percent of Palestine's government revenues, meaning that approximately 85 percent of those revenues come from abroad, in one manner or another. That puts Palestine on the high end of the rentier state spectrum. But Palestine's rents are very different in fundamental ways. Most obviously, the government of Palestine does not control its own rents. It cannot decide to increase or decrease their flow as states with oil can and do, depending on the market. Palestine is utterly dependent on other states to come through with the monies, requiring periodic pressure from the US to prompt Israel to release funds that it owes the PA. Other states have regularly pledged levels of financial assistance and then not delivered as much as was pledged, not delivered in a timely manner, or not delivered at all. There is little that Palestine can do other than protest, putting it in the same camp as countries that rely on strategic rents; however, unlike those other countries, Palestine lacks the autonomy to sell its strategic assets to other bidders, as Israel remains central to Palestine's revenues.

While far from a typical rentier state, Palestine has suffered from some of the same institutional maladies associated with a rentier political economy. The most striking of these has been the creation of a personalized, soft authoritarian system of rule. Despite some hopeful beginnings, Palestine is hardly democratic. Prior to 2006, there were a handful of democratic elections, including a national election in 1996 and a series of municipal elections. However, there have been no democratic elections since 2006, and since then, the PA has essentially ruled by decree. For the most part, Palestine has been best characterized as a soft authoritarian political system, either under Yasir Arafat, when it was accompanied by the construction of a cult of personality, or more recently under Mahmud 'Abbas.

A second rentier feature is general institutional weakness, particularly in state institutions related to extraction. Palestinian state institutions remain quite weak across the board, but it is not entirely clear to what extent this is linked to the rentier nature of the state, the still relative newness of the institutions, Israeli limitations, or other factors. The World Bank has concluded that the financial institutions of the state are actually in relatively good shape for independence.[28] But what the rentier nature of Palestine does suggest is that if independence actually comes, state institutions are not likely to strengthen appreciably without a more direct extractive relationship between state and society. By contrast, distributive state institutions in Palestine, like those in other rentier states, are in relatively good condition.

A third typical rentier characteristic is the concentration of power at the top, without meaningful decentralization and empowered local governments. Once again, Palestine shares this characteristic, in spite of the fact that there has been a relatively robust history of municipal government in both the West Bank and Gaza since 1948. But once again, it is difficult to untangle the impacts of several factors that push toward the concentration of power at the center: the rentier nature of the state, where resources accrue directly to the center, the nature of the consolidation of power by Arafat and the PA (see below), or the international focus since 1993 on building institutions of power at the top, not at the level of local government. The Oslo process has witnessed the relative decline in local authority in Palestine, as power and resources have been concentrated at the political center. If the rentier structure of revenue accrual remains in place, it seems likely that the trend toward power concentration would continue were Palestine to gain its independence.

A related point, also common in rentier states, is the lack of capacity to do meaningful planning, especially at the local level. In oil states, this lack of planning is based on the windfall, boom-or-bust nature of revenues. Meaningful long-range planning can only be reasonably undertaken when there is relative certainty about the level of resources likely to be available over the coming three to five years. When revenues are boom or bust, depending on the oil market, those resources that do become available tend to be used for one-off patronage-based allocations instead of for investment in rational long-range planning. PA revenues do not fluctuate quite as much as those in oil rentier states, but there clearly does exist a windfall element to PA revenues, based on whether or not foreign pledges actually materialize (and when), and whether or not Israel chooses to punish the PA by not delivering on tax transfers. As a result, long-range planning, both by the PA and especially at the local level, has been sporadic at best and rarely actually implemented. Donor-driven infrastructure-improvement projects tend to have the best record in this regard, but that is because of the leverage the donors can bring to bear to get planned projects completed.

[28] World Bank, *Fiscal Challenges*.

Other common rentier characteristics have not been as apparent in Palestine. This is particularly true of the usual "de-politicization" often witnessed in rentier states, where the average citizen has little interest in being politically active and thereby risking access to resource streams from the state. Rather, public politics in rentier states tends to be concentrated in socio-cultural issues, not bread-and-butter economic issues. While Palestine has no shortage of socio-cultural wedge issues, there is no question that broader political discourse in Palestine has been far from constrained.

The Politics of Antithesis

A third major shaper of Palestinian state institutions since Oslo was the nature of the consolidation of power by the Arafat regime, particularly during the 1990s. The legacy of this dynamic continues. When Arafat returned to historic Palestine in 1994, he discovered that the society in the West Bank and Gaza had evolved according to its own circumstances since 1967, including the rise of a new type of political elite. This new type of leadership, most of whom were members of the PLO, was politically tied to the Tunis-based PLO, but had not organically evolved under the authority of Yasir Arafat and the other "outside" PLO leaders. This tension was commonly referred to as the "insider–outsider" dynamic, and I have described it in detail elsewhere as a contest between an "Oslo elite" and an "intifada elite", defined as those people who came to positions of communal leadership in the West Bank and Gaza in the 1980s.[29] The Oslo elite consisted of Arafat and other top returning PLO officials, and was backed up by 100,000 returning Palestinians, many based in the police and security forces.

The logic of Arafat's consolidation of power was to sideline the indigenous intifada elite politically and to empower both the personnel and the political system associated with the returning PLO leaders. I refer to this process as a "politics of antithesis", in that the system of authority constructed by the intifada elite was systematically dismantled by Arafat and replaced with its opposite. The politics of antithesis took a number of forms; I will discuss four of them here.

First, and most obviously, Arafat appointed his own people, mostly outsiders (or "the Tunisians", as they were sometimes called), to virtually all key positions of power throughout the PA bureaucracy, police, and security forces.

[29] I have explored this elite conflict in several venues, including originally in Glenn E. Robinson, *Building a Palestinian State: The Incomplete Revolution* (Bloomington, IN: Indiana University Press, 1997).

Second, and more fundamentally, Arafat consolidated power by de-emphasizing institutions and empowering personalized authority, including a cult of personality surrounding himself. The best predictor of power in the PA in the 1990s was not the official position of any individual, but rather his closeness to Arafat. There are many examples of ministers who would essentially be overruled by their more politically connected underlings. The intifada elite was more "modern" than the Oslo elite in that they built institutions as their basis of authority, which was seen in the extensive mobilization campaign of the 1980s.[30] Since institution-based authority worked to the political benefit of the intifada elite, the Oslo elite de-emphasized institutions as the primary source of authority, and privileged personalized authority instead.

The intifada elite also had a greater predisposition toward democracy, again seen in the politics of the West Bank and Gaza in the 1980s, with its focus on grass-roots democracy. Given demographics, an extensive democratization program in the PA, especially at the local level, would have empowered the intifada elite. Hence, national elections were held just once in the first thirteen years after the signing of Oslo, and local elections were never fully carried out. Instead of democracy, an ideology of neo-patrimonialism was promoted, with its emphasis on personal authority and patronage.

A fourth area where the politics of antithesis could be seen was the campaign of demobilization carried out after Oslo. The Oslo elite viewed empowered grass-roots politics as a significant threat to their consolidation of power, as it would empower their indigenous rivals. In many ways, Israel allowed Arafat to return to historic Palestine as a means to end the intifada and its grass-roots mobilization against Israel. Thus, a campaign of social demobilization was a logical consequence of Oslo, further enhancing the concentration of power in the hands of the small Oslo elite.

The politics of antithesis was largely successful in that the intifada elite was effectively marginalized in various ways. Some were simply pushed out of political life, while others were co-opted into the system that Arafat built. Some top members of the intifada elite, like Marwan Barghouti, still remain in Israeli prisons. This would suggest that the intifada elite never really coalesced into a political class for itself, even if it clearly was an identifiable force in Palestinian politics for a generation. Moreover, the dramatic sharpening of the divide between Hamas and Fatah following the 2006 elections largely

---

[30] See Robinson, *Building a Palestinian State*; and Joost R. Hiltermann, *Behind the Intifada* (Princeton, NJ: Princeton University Press, 1993).

trumped and replaced the inside–outside cleavage that so dominated the first decade of Palestinian self-rule.

State institutions in any new or emerging state are always shaped by various dynamics, and are not simply constructed in a vacuum. Palestine is not unique in creating new institutions in the shadow of colonialism or neo-colonialism, nor is it unique in having its institutional configuration reflect a rentier political economy. Certainly Arafat and the Oslo elite were not history's only returning "victors" to assume power following some form of national liberation and seek to consolidate power in ways that distorted political dynamics in the newly (partially) liberated zones. What is unusual in the Palestinian case is to have had all three of these profound shaping dynamics occur at the same time.

Conclusion: Stateness with Governance?

Palestine has never enjoyed existence as a fully realized nation-state. Whether Ottoman, British, Jordanian, Egyptian, or Israeli, foreign powers have for centuries been the dominant sovereign power in the land of Palestine. Under Ottoman rule, this was not seen as a problem, as neither a separate Palestinian national identity nor attempts to build an independent sovereign Palestinian state existed. In the twentieth century, as new and independent Arab states came into existence, the lack of Palestinian statehood was deemed a much more pressing problem, particularly in the light of growing Zionist claims to the land and, ultimately, the creation of Israel in 1948 on 77 percent of the land of Palestine. The evolution of Palestinian state claims is well recorded elsewhere and briefly noted in this chapter. Statehood claims became more pronounced with the Oslo peace process in 1993, and especially with the actual claim of Palestinian statehood by Mahmud 'Abbas in 2012. International recognition of Palestinian statehood is rather extensive and convincing, certainly more convincing than actual territorial control by the state of the territory it claims for statehood. The pivotal process of building state institutions in Palestine has been distorted by the realities of the continued Israeli occupation, by the rentier nature of government revenues, and by the exigencies of the consolidation of power by an external Palestinian elite.

In spite of its institutional deformities, it would not be fair to conclude that Palestine is a failed state when it has not been given the opportunity to be a real state, independent from Israel. Nor could we conclude that it is a weak state for the same reason. Palestine exists in a surreal place; it has wide legal recognition and an extensive institutional network that looks very much like what a state should look like, but it does not really exist in the full sense of statehood and independence.

Perhaps Palestine today is best understood as a kind of state, but one that really does not enjoy actual governance. It exists on paper and there are ministries, police, and other manifestations of stateness. But Palestine is not allowed to exercise actual governance, at least not to any reasonable extent. A state that does not govern is essentially a fiction, but perhaps a fiction that is convenient to have continue in the eyes of many actors. If Palestine were to become a truly independent state, then social scientists could seek to measure its capacity and strength as a state. But if Israel's occupation is permanent, as many analysts suspect is the case, then Palestine would, of course, be considered a state that never really came to be. Palestine would then probably be known to history as the world's most famous stillborn state.

11

DIASPORAS AND STATE-(RE)BUILDING IN THE MENA REGION

POTENTIALS AND CONSTRAINTS

Laurie A. Brand

The uprisings that broke out across the Middle East/North African region beginning in winter 2010–11 have swept away authoritarian leaders in four countries, led to modest reforms in two others, triggered brutal repression in one, and civil war in another. While many aspects of the unfolding of these revolts and transitions have received significant attention, often overlooked is the role that members of some of these countries' respective diasporas have played. In some, exiles have returned to participate in demonstrations or to take up arms, in others expatriates have gone home to lead political movements, and in several the right to vote has been extended so that members of the diaspora communities may have a greater stake in the processes of political rebuilding going forward.

This chapter examines key elements in the relationship between MENA state diaspora communities and possible nation- and state-(re)building in transitional political systems. To do so, it considers the literatures on weak states and on diaspora–home state relations. After briefly examining the possible lessons from the literature on diaspora involvement in conflict and in peace-building, it moves on to a more detailed consideration of two key factors, one economic and one political—remittances and political institutions—and their implications for the role of expatriates in home state-(re)building.

Weak State, Fragile State

The use of the term "failed state" has become so common in policy and journalistic discussions as to have lost much of its conceptual power. While its academic use is older, it came into vogue in policy circles post-9/11, as concerns grew about the implications for international (read Western, largely US) security of states like Somalia and Afghanistan. Since then, its application has extended well beyond countries in which central government authority has broken down to include a range of countries suffering from a host of deficiencies in capacity and sovereignty.[1] As a result, some analysts and scholars have instead adopted the term "weak state",[2] although this term, too, is problematic, for it implicitly establishes a dichotomy which invites comparison with what constitutes a "strong state". Nor is it particularly helpful to think instead in terms of a continuum from weak state to strong state, since there are many variables at work that may produce or characterize strength or weakness, and they are unlikely all to align in a single country for easy classification along a spectrum. Indeed, those who have taken a more conceptual approach to the issue recognize the degree to which these terms may mask more than they illuminate.

My interest, which derives from a concern for just domestic economic and political development, not the security concerns of external actors, leads me to jettison the terms entirely, and focus instead on some of the key attributes of what have been termed weak or fragile states. To do so, I draw on the work of Call, who suggests we focus on gaps in capacity, security, and

---

[1] Robert I. Rotberg, *When States Fail: Causes and Consequences* (Princeton, NJ: Princeton University Press, 2004); Zaryab Iqbal and Harvey Starr, "Bad Neighbors: Failed States and Their Consequences", *Conflict Management and Peace Science*, Vol. 25, No. 4 (2008), 315–31; Patrick Stewart, "Weak States and Global Threats: Assessing Evidence of Spillovers", working paper, Vol. 23 (Washington, DC: Center for Global Development, 2006); Edward Newman, "Failed States and International Order: Constructing a Post-Westphalian World", *Contemporary Security Policy*, Vol. 30, No. 3 (2009), 421–43.

[2] Charles T. Call, "The Fallacy of the 'Failed State'", *Third World Quarterly*, Vol. 29, No. 8 (2008), 1491–1507; Newman, "Failed States".

legitimacy.[3] Capacity refers to the scope and strength of the state in delivering or seeing to the delivery through approved actors of at least a minimal level of public goods and services: defense, law and order, public health, macroeconomic management, and disaster relief. The security gap refers to a situation in which the state fails to provide minimal levels of security "in the face of organized armed groups",[4] although I would argue that this should be extended to include basic policing services as well. Finally, a legitimacy gap exists when "a significant portion of political elites and society reject the rules regulating the exercise of power and the accumulation and distribution of wealth".[5] As others have pointed out, measuring legitimacy is a difficult proposition, but indications of lack of agreement on the rules governing the distribution of power and resources can be gauged, if imperfectly, by examining degrees and types of societal activism as well as the extent of regime repression. Finally, and certainly related to the degree of state and regime legitimacy, may be a fourth gap, which here we shall call the national identity gap: the relationship between the process of state-building—referring to institutional capacity—and nation-building,[6] a complex process of developing identity and cohesion at the state level.

State Performance Gaps and Diaspora

In considering the relationship between these four gaps and the potential role of diasporas in contributing to state- and nation-(re)building, one must first stipulate that the very existence of some diasporas, or at least their size, is a direct function of the state failures or inefficiencies that rebuilding would or should seek to address. Indeed, a majority of emigrants have left their homes either because the state was incapable of generating sufficient employment to enable them to remain, or because political turmoil or repression directly threatened them. It is also important to note that many diasporas have their origins not just in the failures of the post-independence state, but in the eco-

---

[3] Charles T. Call, "Beyond the 'Failed state': Toward Conceptual Alternatives", *European Journal of International Relations*, Vol. 17, No. 2 (2010), 303–26.

[4] Ibid., 307.

[5] Ibid., 308.

[6] Dominik Heiling, "Anatomy of a 'Political Chameleon': Re-examining Fluid Shapes and Solid Constants of Nationalism and Nation Building", Crisis States Research Centre Discussion Paper No. 17 (Series 2), London School of Economics and Political Science (2009).

nomic and political relations established under colonialism. Indeed, the bases of economic exploitation and underdevelopment of human capital resulting in labor recruitment abroad can in many cases be traced to the period of European control. The ways in which these areas were initially incorporated into the world economy established structural relationships that have been difficult to break or significantly modify. As a result, even in countries where there has been notable investment in education, such as Tunisia or Jordan, the domestic economic structure has been unable to absorb the countries' production of human capital.

On the other hand, post-independence leaderships have not always been eager or successful in restructuring domestic political economy relations in such a way as to transform the country's productive base. In such cases, exporting labor is a much less disruptive development strategy than attempting to reconfigure internal financial and investment structures and educational priorities in order to expand employment significantly. As a result, some countries lose what may be significant educational investment through a brain drain, while they hope to recoup some of the losses through remittances or perhaps through subsequent transfer of knowledge, social capital, and expertise. Indeed, the export of human capital in the form of emigration has become a kind of development strategy, in some cases at a national level (as in .the case of Jordan), but also at the level of the family.

As for diasporas populated largely by those who have fled conflict situations, the proximate cause of instability may have been a capacity or security gap, but the root causes more likely lie in crises related to legitimacy and nation-building. Lack of agreement on the rules of economic and political power distribution, and the resultant failure to incorporate regions, ethnoreligious groups or others into a meaningful, inclusive sense of national identity may trigger instability that can, in extremis, lead to massive out-migration. In the MENA region, this has certainly been the major driver of the additional expansion of the Lebanese diaspora, and (exacerbated by external involvement) it is fueling the development of a new Syrian diaspora at the time of this writing. Of course, conflict-triggered diasporas can also be the result, not of state failure, but of colonialism and armed external intervention, as in the case of the initial creation of the Palestinian diaspora in the 1947–8 Palestine war, and in Iraq after 1990 and especially after 2003.

The Concept of Diaspora

Just as the concept of state fragility or weakness must be examined in all its dimensions, so too must the notion of diaspora. Most fundamentally, a diaspora is not an undifferentiated "entity". It may be used as shorthand to refer to all members of a particular nationality and/or their descendants outside the country or origin or homeland, but it should in no way be construed as implying homogeneity or uniformity among its "members". As the vast literature makes clear, diasporas may replicate the same ethnic/cultural/religious/regional disparities and differences as the homeland population. They may also, for economic or political reasons, disproportionately represent some groups over others.

In considering how a diaspora's various characteristics and components may shape its potential role in the home country, a number of basic elements must be considered. First, what is the reason for the diaspora's existence in the first place? Did it evolve as the result of migration for economic reasons (usually employment), or because of discrimination, political oppression, or conflict? The answer to these questions may well condition the way emigrants view their homeland and the degree or ways in which they are (willing to become) involved. For example, since the vast majority of remittances are sent to family members, the emigrant's view of the government of the state of origin may be relatively unimportant. If the migrant left because of economic marginalization or political persecution, s/he may still be keen on assisting family members left behind as they struggle under difficult conditions. However, if we are interested in the success of the home state government when it seeks to mobilize emigrant resources to address capacity gaps, then one factor may well be the way the emigrant views that government. Is it trustworthy, so that investing back home seems a patriotic (and financially sound) activity, or is the government viewed as corrupt or repressive, thus generally triggering hesitation if not avoidance on the part of the migrant?

Related to the reasons for the diaspora's emergence will be the resources at its disposal: in other words, the emigrant's capabilities to engage in the sending state.[7] Is the diaspora of relatively recent formation, and hence perhaps

---

[7] Hazel Smith, "Diasporas in International Conflict", in Hazel Smith and Paul Stares, eds., *Diasporas in Conflict: Peace-Makers or Peace-Wreckers?* (New York: United Nations University Press, 2007), 3–16, 9; Milton Esman, "The Factors Conducive to Diaspora Investment: Comparing China, Armenia and Ireland", in Jennifer M. Brinkerhoff, ed., *Diaspora and Development: Exploring the Potential* (Boulder, CO: Lynne Rienner, 2008), 99–112.

FRAGILE POLITICS

with limited economic resources, or is it well-established? However, even if it is well-established, diaspora members may be less attached to the sending country, and therefore less likely to send remittances back, although contemporary evidence seems to suggest that length of residence abroad is not a primary indicator of continuing diaspora interest or commitment.[8] Also of relevance to diaspora members' capability and desire to engage with the sending state are conditions in their respective host countries. Do conditions of residence permit easy travel back and forth? Are there restrictions on financial transfers, or on establishing or belonging to associations affiliated with the home state?

Bilateral ties between the sending and host state of any particular diaspora community may also come into play, with state-level relations either facilitating or obstructing connections. For example, Smith notes that "host states can change the opportunity structures available for diaspora contributions in such a way as to channel contributions to peacemaking and dissuade the negative contributions of peace-wreckers".[9] Conversely, of course, host states can play a pernicious role in dealing with a diaspora community if it serves their economic or political interests. Also of potential importance are the differences in political freedoms between sending and receiving states, and even among receiving states, in explaining the opportunities and constraints members of the diaspora may face in becoming involved back home. While significant variation exists, democratic states are likely to be more open to transnational involvements of a variety of sorts, whereas authoritarian states may well place restrictions on such activities.

Finally, looking at the other side of the ledger, how active is the sending state in (re)engaging the diaspora? Gamlen distinguishes three types of diaspora engagement strategy: remittance capture, diaspora networking (cultivating links between the homeland and its diaspora), and diaspora integration (recognizing the diaspora as a constituency that is marginalized from the homeland).[10] Østergaard-Nielsen makes a distinction between direct strategies—those that target the countries of origin—and indirect strategies that

[8] Alejandro Portes, Cristina Escobar, and Alexandria Walton Radford, "Immigrant Transnational Organizations and Development: A Comparative Study", *International Migration Review*, Vol. 41, No. 1 (2007), 242–81.

[9] Smith, "Diasporas", 13.

[10] Alan Gamlen, "Diaspora Engagement Policies: What are They and What Kinds of States Use Them?" (Working paper, Vol. 32, University of Oxford: Centre on Migration, Policy and Society, 2006).

254

work through a third country or other actor to target the country of origin.[11] The former consists of economic or other contributions, while the latter involves lobbying or pressuring institutions or members of the international community. Thus, to understand the nature of the relationship, it is critical to examine existing capacity gaps: what sorts of instruments or institutions exist, how effectively are they used, and which new ones may the home state need or seek to develop? How receptive is the state of origin to civil society activity or initiatives? Indeed, how eager is it for the effective, as opposed to perhaps merely symbolic, participation of the diaspora? What efforts have been made to collect relevant data to help in effectively connecting and usefully mobilizing diaspora human, social, and economic resources? Are the forms of interaction all top-down, or are there serious initiatives to understand and engage the emigrants' concerns? Here again, the gaps noted at the outset, particularly those of capacity, legitimacy, and national identity, will influence the way the sending state engages with diaspora communities and vice versa.

Diasporas: Support for Conflict or for Peace?

To date, most of the interest in expatriate involvement in the homeland—as opposed to work on diaspora community lobbying of the host state—has focused on the question of expatriate involvement in conflict and post-conflict rebuilding.[12] Much of the literature focuses on a handful of cases, with Ireland,[13] Sri Lanka[14] and Somalia[15] prominent among them. Some large stud-

---

[11] Eva Østergaard-Nielsen, "The Politics of Migrants' Transnational Political Practices", *International Migration Review*, Vol. 37, No. 3 (2001), 760–86.

[12] Daniel Byman, Peter Chalk, Bruce Hoffman, William Rosenau, and David Brannan, *Trends in Outside Support for Insurgent Movements* (Santa Monica: RAND Corporation, 2001); Ashok Swain, ed., *Diasporas, Armed Conflict and Peacebuiding in Their Homelands* (Uppsala: Uppsala Universitet, 2007); Hazel Smith and Paul Stares, eds., *Diasporas in Conflict: Peace-Makers or Peace-Wreckers?* (New York: United Nations University Press, 2007).

[13] Feargal Cochrane, "Irish-America, the End of the IRA's Armed Struggle and the Utility of 'Soft Power'", *Journal of Peace Research*, Vol. 44, No. 2 (2007), 215–31.

[14] Camilla Orujela, "Distant Warriors, Distant Peace Workers? Multiple Diaspora Roles in Sri Lanka's Violent Conflict", *Global Networks*, Vol. 8, No. 4 (2008), 436–52.

[15] Cindy Horst, "The Transnational Political Engagements of Refugees: Remittance Sending Practices amongst Somalis in Norway", *Conflict, Security & Development*, Vol. 8, No. 3 (2008), 317–39; Jorgen Carling, Marta Bivand, and Cindy Horst,

ies, such as those of Collier and Hoeffler, suggest a correlation (although not causation) between civil war (or its re-igniting) and the existence of large diasporas, but their cases are all of US-based diaspora communities.[16] Among others, Lyons has noted that "diaspora groups created by conflict and sustained by traumatic memories tend to compromise less and therefore reinforce and exacerbate the protracted nature of conflicts. In some cases this tendency strengthens confrontational leaders and organizations and undermines others seeking compromise" as they "provide key financial support and contribute to the framing of conflicts through their control over media outlets and other institutions where political strategies are debated and leaderships and strategies legitimized".[17] However, there are also important examples of diaspora groups becoming active advocates for peace.[18] Thus, being outside the homeland can open up the space for diaspora members either to transcend divisions in the homeland or to exacerbate them. Diaspora groups may organize and raise money for arms and other equipment to prosecute war, or for relief, reconstruction, and development.

Even when a conflict ends, diaspora contributions may not be politically neutral. For example, Orujela shows in the Sri Lankan case that, depending upon the way that the diaspora engages in homeland politics, it can either reproduce the grievances that led to the initial conflict or mitigate the elements that fueled it. "Belligerent parties can co-opt development initiatives, exacerbate inequalities, frustrations and distrust, discourage cooperation and confirm enemy images."[19] Development can become a "continuation of war by other means".[20]

In some cases, rebel groups themselves may largely function from abroad, as was the case with the ANC in South Africa. In the MENA region, of course, one of the best examples is that of the PLO, which was funded in part by a

---

"How does Conflict in Migrants' Country of Origin Affect Remittance-Sending? Financial Priorities and Transnational Obligations among Somalis and Pakistanis in Norway", *International Migration Review*, Vol. 46, No. 2 (2012), 283–309.

[16] Paul Collier and Anke Hoeffler, "Greed and Grievance in Civil War", *Oxford Economic Papers*, Vol. 56, No. 4 (2004), 563–95.

[17] Terrence Lyons, "Conflict-Generated Diasporas and Transnational Politics in Ethiopia", *Conflict, Security & Development*, Vol. 7, No. 4 (2007), 529–49, 530, 539.

[18] Cochrane, "Irish-America".

[19] Orujela, "Distant Warriors", 439.

[20] Ibid., 448.

Liberation Tax collected by Arab governments from Palestinian workers.[21] There are many anecdotes of diaspora support for various Lebanese factions, perhaps most notably Hezbollah, and also well-documented is the participation of American Jews in supporting the establishment of the state of Israel, from financial contributions to fighting in the 1948 war. Another example is that of Iraqi expatriates in planning and advocating the 2003 invasion of Iraq. This last example underlines the importance of distinguishing between the actions of "a diaspora" and a handful of expatriates with particular political interests and influence that intersect with those of a more powerful external actor.

In general, then, to explore how a diaspora community may be involved back home, whether in development or conflict, one must understand its historical evolution—economically, politically, demographically, and geographically. It is also critical to bear in mind that a diaspora's composition and role change over time. Smith notes the possible shift from peace-wrecker to peace-maker, but one can imagine other types of shifts. And of course members of the same diaspora may play contradictory roles.[22] Indeed, a review of the literature makes clear that broad claims cannot be sustained that diasporas contribute consistently either to peace or conflict, state-building, or to any other specific goal such as political openness or the status quo. One must instead look at individual situations to determine the range of possibilities, as well as the range of likely outcomes.

MENA Diasporas

If we take a minimalist definition of diaspora—a series of communities (of significant size in relation to country population) resident long-term outside the homeland—then in the MENA region, classified by country of origin (rather than a sub or transnational ethnicity),[23] we can talk about Moroccan, Tunisian, Algerian, Egyptian, Sudanese, Palestinian, Palestinian/Jordanian, Israeli, Syrian, Lebanese, Turkish, Iraqi, Yemeni, and Iranian diasporas. Clearly, the home states of these diasporas vary dramatically according to the criteria for classifying states as weak or strong: state legitimacy, extent of state sovereignty, ability to deliver public goods and services effectively, capacity to

[21] Laurie Brand, *Palestinians in the Arab World: Institution Building and the Search for State* (New York: Columbia University Press, 1988).

[22] Smith, "Diasporas", 10.

[23] Were we to take sub or transnational actors, we could speak about a Coptic diaspora, a Maronite diaspora, a Kurdish diaspora, a Kabyle diaspora, and so on.

maintain internal and external security, presence of socio-economic and political fragilities, and degree of national identity consolidation.

A brief discussion of diasporas that have issued from states of the MENA region cannot do justice to the full range of variation within and among them. For our purposes here, in order to understand their possible contributions to nation- or state-building in the country of origin, it is perhaps most useful to think of them first as falling into one of two categories: economic/labor or conflict diasporas, although in some cases over time the same diaspora may be characterized by elements of both.

Lebanon has one of the oldest diasporas, with significant migration to Africa and the Americas beginning in the 1860s. While some of the outmigration after the turn of the century owed to the desire of Christians to avoid the Ottoman draft, the majority of those who left did so because of the collapse of the silk industry and the increasing pressure on land in Mount Lebanon. While perhaps a third of those who left ultimately returned and contributed to significant socio-economic changes as a result of their experiences abroad,[24] those who settled permanently outside Lebanon formed the basis of the oldest and most far-flung of Arab Middle Eastern diasporas.[25]

In several other states, the "tradition" of migration dates to the colonial period, and owes a debt to the nature of the colonial relationship. Algeria, in particular, but Morocco and Tunisia as well, serve as prime examples. The impoverishment of Algerians under French settler colonialism combined with the metropole's need for additional labor power, starting from World War I, to lay the basis for a labor recruitment relationship. After independence, Maghribis from all three countries continued to migrate to France (and from there, increasingly to other parts of western Europe), because of the inability of post-independence governments to address effectively a range of development problems shaped in part by the colonial legacy.

The other major migration wave—this time within the MENA region— resulted from the combination of continuing low standards of living in some countries and the development of the oil industry in others with limited infrastructure and human capital. Emigration from the Levant to the Gulf states began after World War II. It therefore coincided with the Arab defeat in

---

[24] Akram Khater, *Inventing Home: Emigration, Gender, and the Middle Class in Lebanon, 1870–1920* (Berkeley: University of California Press, 2001).

[25] Albert Hourani and Nadim Shehadi, eds., *The Lebanese in the World: A Century of Emigration* (London: I. B. Tauris, 1992).

Palestine in 1948 and the creation of the first major MENA refugee waves of the modern era. Particularly negatively affected were Jordan, Syria, and Lebanon, all three of which had only recently secured independence and none of which had a strong state or robust economy. The migration continued, but did not expand dramatically until the 1970s, when the tremendous increase in the price of oil provided the Gulf states with undreamed of resources to engage in their own projects of state institutional and commercial development. In this climate, the existing migration paths were further expanded as more Palestinians, Jordanians, Syrians, and Lebanese went to the Gulf, as did growing numbers of Egyptians, Yemenis, South Asians, etc. In all these cases, the consequent benefit to the sending state of unemployment alleviation, poverty reduction, and budgetary support rendered outmigration a critical structural, and not just passing, element in state economic development calculations. It enabled these states to avoid (or at least postpone) difficult decisions about economic and political reform.

This is not to say that conflict and war have not played a role in diaspora creation. The most obvious example is that of the Palestinians, more than 700,000 of whom were driven from or fled their homes as a result of the 1948 war and the establishment of the state of Israel. While Jordan enfranchised those who came to reside within its boundaries (which were themselves expanded to include part of historic Palestine), this was not the case with the other Arab states in which Palestinian refugees came to reside in significant numbers—most notably Lebanon, but also Syria, and to a lesser extent Egypt and Iraq. The resulting precariousness of the Palestinians' economic and political situations led many to seek improved employment opportunities elsewhere. Thus a diaspora initially created by brutal settler colonialism expanded further geographically for economic reasons. Lebanon, on the other hand, witnessed a transformation in the other direction. A diaspora that had developed for economic reasons dramatically grew in size and changed in sectarian composition as a result of the outbreak of civil war in 1975. More recently, a significant Iraqi diaspora has emerged, first as a result of the 1991 war and the subsequent draconian sanctions regime; it then expanded following the 2003 invasion and the 2006 descent into civil war. Currently, the region is witnessing the development of a significant Syrian diaspora since, as of this writing, perhaps a million and a half Syrians have fled the fighting in their homeland, taking refuge overwhelmingly in Lebanon, Turkey, and Jordan.

Diasporas and Development: the role of remittances

Outside the literature on diasporan involvement in conflicts, the literature on migrant contributions to the sending state focuses overwhelmingly on remittances, which can be divided into several different categories.[26] One type is social capital, which takes the form of transnational production and supply-chain networks among diasporans, which can benefit home country firms. Another is human capital, such as the expertise mobilized by programs like UNDP's TOKTEN (Transfer of Knowledge Through Expatriate Nationals), which can be directed to governments, firms, or NGOs. The obvious advantages of these "transfers" are those of language and cultural similarity as well as presumed familiarity and sensitivity, although there is also the possibility that length of residence outside the country may render diasporans out of touch or generate distrust and resentment among those who remained "back home" through difficult times.[27] Another form of transfer is through what have been termed nostalgic products and services: everything from foods imported from home, to travel back and forth. Finally, and most often written about, are financial and in-kind remittances: monies and consumer goods going to households, financial donations to communities, and capital investment in the form of real estate, portfolio, and direct investment in businesses.

The impact of the various kinds of financial transfers needs to be understood as having very different meanings or effects, depending upon which level is analyzed. At the state level, financial remittances are critical to the health of many national economies. An important source of foreign exchange, they can compensate for diminishing inflows of hard currency from other sources. They can also have a powerful multiplier effect on GDP, job creation, consumption, and investment.[28] In addition, "remittances have allowed for the delay of unpopular structural adjustment policies—mainly price corrections and exchange rate devaluations—that would otherwise have to be undertaken".[29]

[26] Liesl Riddle, "Introduction to Part 2", in Jennifer M. Brinkerhoff, ed., *Diaspora and Development: Exploring the Potential* (Boulder, CO: Lynne Rienner, 2008), 91–8.
[27] Derick W. Brinkerhoff and Samuel Tadesse, "Recruiting from the Diaspora: The Local Governance Program in Iraq", in Jennifer M. Brinkerhoff, ed., *Diaspora and Development: Exploring the Potential* (Boulder, CO: Lynne Rienner, 2008), 67–87.
[28] Donald F. Terry, "Remittances as a Development Tool", in Donald F. Terry and Steven R. Wilson, eds., *Beyond Small Change: Making Migrant Remittances Count* (Washington, DC: Inter-American Development Bank, 2005), 3–20.
[29] Mohammed El-Sakka, "An Overview of Remittances in the Middle East and North

On the household level, remittances have become critical to the survival of millions of families. They are used for school fees, food, and clothing; and to start small businesses, purchase land, or build or upgrade homes. Much of the literature criticizes the expenditure of remittances on short-term consumption rather than on savings or investment. To the degree that they promote the purchase of imported and luxury goods, they may be responsible for harmful demonstration effects that exacerbate trade imbalances and reduce savings.[30] However, this negative view of remittances overlooks the degree to which they have had a positive impact on the quality of life for families of poor or modest means. Remittances can also make savings accounts, loans, mortgages accessible to lower levels of society; they can be the "point of entry for many remitters and their families to the formal financial system".[31]

In thinking about the relationship between state-building and diasporas, it is important to underline that remittances should be viewed as indicators of state economic failure,[32] and as a reflection of global inequity.[33] The tendency in some of the literature to turn to look to them as a path to development, as implicitly an alternative to external development assistance[34] or to significant domestic economic reform, is a serious misrepresentation. The advantage of remittances over other development solutions derives from the fact that they fit the notions of neo-liberal capitalism and the minimal role of the state. That does not, however, render them a panacea or an alternative to meaningful reform. Rather than celebrating them as the potential solution to capital shortages and insufficient investment, they should instead be viewed as an anti-poverty strategy on a family level in the context of economic stagnation or the failure of state economic development strategies: in other words, as a manifestation of inferior state capacity. Their continuation is an indicator of "the heroic endurance of family values across time and space".[35]

Africa", in Donald F. Terry and Steven R. Wilson, eds., *Beyond Small Change: Making Migrant Remittances Count* (Washington, DC: Inter-American Development Bank, 2005), 319–40, 329.

[30] Ibid., 328.

[31] Terry, "Remittances", 11.

[32] Ibid., 15.

[33] Ezra Rosser, "Immigrant Remittances", *Connecticut Law Review*, Vol. 41, No. 1 (2008), 1–62, 52.

[34] Kathleen Newland, ed., *Diasporas: New Partners in Global Development Policy* (Washington, DC: Migration Policy Institute, 2010).

[35] Rosser, "Immigrant Remittances", 42, 51.

For decades, the countries of North Africa viewed the emigration of their nationals abroad primarily in terms of the labor safety valve it represented. This impersonal and largely instrumental view of the emigrants was clear in the language that was used by the state to refer to them. They were simply Tunisians or Moroccans "working abroad", suggesting that the fact of their being "workers" was what most centrally defined them.[36] However, as economic crises set in during the 1980s, MENA states in general became more aware of the other value of emigrants: the role of their remittances in providing hard currency to help replenish state coffers. Indeed, expatriate remittances have come to constitute one of the top three sources of hard currency in most of the region's labor exporters.

Egypt, Lebanon, and Morocco are among the top ten remittance-receiving countries in the world, thus indicating the importance of the transfers, not only in absolute terms for any given MENA country, but also comparatively. That said, any statistics regarding financial transfers must be viewed with the understanding that they are likely to be underestimates. First of all, while probably declining in proportion to other forms of transfer, cash remittances continue to be a part of the equation, and yet they bypass official accounting. Second, remittances may also be repatriated in-kind, as emigrants returning for visits may bring with them everything from cars and mattresses to clothes and computers. Also important is the actual institutional capacity of the state to measure such flows. While attention to and instruments for doing so have improved over time, they vary from country to country, and are imperfect even in the best of circumstances.

Although the literature on the determinants of remittances is relatively limited, studies suggest that they vary considerably over time and space. Like other sources of export income, remittances are subject to conditions of the market, as well as a host of political considerations. One basic element is the sheer number of migrants working abroad. Here host country policy shifts can be significant. Following the jump in oil prices in 1973, a number of key European countries decided that they could no longer afford to keep open doors to immigration. France, for example, instituted a policy of encouraging repatriation, with the goal of encouraging primarily Maghribi immigrants to

[36] Laurie Brand, "Émigré, Mughtarib, 'Amil f-il-Kharij: La Langue et les Institutions des Relations Etat-Expatries", in Stéphane Dufoix, Carine Guerassimoff, and Anne de Tinguy, eds., *Loin des Yeux, Près du Cœur* (Paris: Presses de Sciences Po, 2010), 129–46.

return home. It concomitantly encouraged family reunification for those who decided to remain, assuming that the arrival of family members would staunch the outflow of hard currency. In practice, however, few Maghribis took the repatriation incentives. Instead, many brought their families to Europe, thus creating the basis of an unintended consequence: multi-generational, family-based diaspora communities.

As for economic factors, a 1992 study found "the main determinants of the inflow of remittances to be the level of income in the host country, the black market exchange rate premium, the domestic inflation rate, and the length of stay abroad".[37] Another suggests that levels of income in both host and home countries have a positive impact on the inflow of remittances to the home country, as do consistent and sound macroeconomic policies at home.[38] Over time, the forces of globalization have come to play an important role as "remittances have surged with the rise of transnational networks based on the 'five Ts': tourism, transportation, telecommunications, nostalgic trade and transfer of remittances".[39] If one focuses not just on individual migrants, but diaspora organizations, they can serve as important intermediaries between traditional development actors and local communities in identifying needs and priorities and communicating them to donor organizations, NGOs, and the like.[40] However, in general "remittances remain financial flows in search of financial products. Too few financial institutions offer transnational families affordable financial products or options. Public authorities have lagged in creating enabling environments to leverage these flows."[41] Here again, inferior state capacity has meant sub-optimal attraction and use of these financial flows.

Concerns have been expressed that length of residence abroad would gradually lead to a decrease in interest in repatriating funds; however, remittances have instead continued to grow. In the MENA region this is true both for communities in countries in which permanent resettlement and citizenship

---

[37] El-Sakka, "An Overview", 333.

[38] Ibid.

[39] Terry, "Remittances", 17.

[40] Jennifer M. Brinkerhoff, "The Potential of Diasporas and Development", in Jennifer M. Brinkerhoff, ed., *Diaspora and Development: Exploring the Potential* (Boulder, CO: Lynne Rienner, 2008), 1–15, 13.

[41] Manuel Orozco and Steven R. Wilson, "Making Migrant Remittances Count", in Donald F. Terry and Steven R. Wilson, eds., *Beyond Small Change: Making Migrant Remittances Count* (Washington, DC: Inter-American Development Bank, 2005), 375–94.

are a possibility, such as the North African communities in Europe, and for those in which not only citizenship, but even ownership of immovable property is excluded, as in the Gulf oil states. A brief examination of World Bank statistics on remittances for the region bears this out, even for those countries that have been affected by the Arab uprisings.[42] Morocco has shown gradual growth, with some ups and downs over the years, but with continuing increases since 2002. With the exception of only a few years, Tunisia shows a secular increase, with the period since the revolution continuing that trend: $2.004 billion for 2011 and $2.202 billion estimated for 2012. Syria shows a drop in the early 1980s, and continuing and even lower levels in the 1990s, but a dramatic increase between 2002 and 2003 ($0.135–$0.889 billion), rising to $2.079 billion in 2011 and an estimated $2.079 billion for 2012. In Egypt we find a drop between 1993 and 1994, but then a continuing increase, with dramatic jumps between 2006 and 2007 (from $5.330 to $7.656 billion) and then between 2009 and 2010 (from $7.150 to $12.453 billion). The years since the revolution also show increases, with $14.453 billion for 2011 and an estimated $17.971 billion for 2012.

What then of the fate of remittances during periods of political crisis or war? There is still a dearth of information on how conflict in the sending country may interact with other variables in affecting remittance levels.[43] In the case of Algeria, which suffered a military coup in 1992 and then a descent into a bloody internal insurgency that lasted for a decade, one finds that remittances continued through the worst of the violence: 1992, $1.390 billion; 1993, $1.140 billion; 1994, $1.395 billion, 1995, $1.120 billion. However, for 1996 there was a drop to only $0.88 billion, then $1.060 billion in 1997, another drop in 1999 and 2000 ($0.790 billion) and then $1.070 billion in 2002, $1.750 billion in 2004 and up to a high of $2.460 billion in 2005. Since then, there has been significant variation in the numbers. Algeria historically has done a poorer job of attracting remittances through official channels than its Maghribi neighbors, and so it is difficult to draw any definitive conclusions from these numbers. However, there is no secular decline, and remittances remained high during the worst years of the internal violence.

[42] World Bank, "Migration and Remittances", http://econ.worldbank.org/WBSITE/ EXTERNAL/EXTDEC/EXTDECPROSPECTS/0,,contentMDK:21121930 ~menuPK:3145470~pagePK:64165401~piPK:64165026~theSit ePK:476883,00.html (accessed 27 May 2013).

[43] Nadje Al-Ali, Richard Black, and Khalid Koser, "Refugees and Transnationalism: The Experience of Bosnians and Eritreans in Europe", *Journal of Ethnic and Migration Studies*, Vol. 27, No. 4 (2001), 615–34.

In Jordan, the statistics indicate a major jump between 1992 and 1993 ($0.844–$1.040 billion), probably because of the return of Jordanian workers to the Gulf after the departures and expulsions of 1990–91. Then we see continuous growth, reaching a highpoint in 2008 ($3.794 billion), with a drop to $3.453 billion in 2011 but an estimated $3.530 billion in 2012, even as domestic economic crisis continued to grow. Yemen also witnessed a significant drop with the 1990 Gulf war, when much of the community in Saudi Arabia was forced to leave ($1.498 billion in 1990 down to $0.998 billion in 1991). However, levels have gradually moved back up so that the 2012 estimates are again at $1.498 billion. Finally, the West Bank and Gaza show regular growth from 1995 until 2003, when remittances dropped to $0.563 billion from $1.036 billion, perhaps as a result of the second intifada. They then began to rise again to reach $1.545 billion, a constant figure since 2010.

As for diaspora involvement in development projects, Gallina argues that "the success of the projects [from expatriate remittances] is based on factors such as sustainability, empowerment of local beneficiaries, reproducibility, visibility in the host and home country, and ownership of the communities in the villages of origin, while the failures have instead been caused by limited access to financial resources, difficulties in travelling back and forth for the promoters of the project, the difficulty in finding reliable institutional interlocutors in the home country".[44] Iskander, who studied the successful experiences of Moroccan expatriates resident in France who invested in electricity generation back home, makes the important point that "policy interventions are most effective in forging a link between emigration and development when they actively connect with the social processes through which local actors determine the value of migration-generated resources".[45] "The resources are not what cause local change; remittances in and of themselves do not flow into a given locale to either spark or hinder economic growth. Rather, the social processes that move those resources and give them meaning are what create change."[46]

In sum, remittances are critical elements in the budgets of a number of MENA countries. Depending upon how they are channeled and used, on a

[44] Andrea Gallina, "Enhancing Workers' Remittances for Development in the Mediterranean Partner Countries", *CARIM Analytic and Synthetic Notes* (European University Institute: Robert Schuman Centre for Advanced Studies, 2008), 22.

[45] Natasha Iskander, "Diaspora Networks for Creating National Infrastructure: Rural Morocco, 1985–2005", in Jennifer M. Brinkerhoff, ed., *Diaspora and Development: Exploring the Potential* (Boulder, CO: Lynne Rienner, 2008), 163–83, 163.

[46] Ibid., 169.

family or community level, they may reduce poverty and open the way to small-scale investment, or they may be used for consumption of luxury goods. On a national level, they can make the difference between dwindling and stable hard currency reserves, thus reinforcing solvency, but perhaps also postponing the implementation of needed economic and political reforms. In either case, however, they must be understood as an indicator of malaise in state economic development capacity. Diaspora contributions can help mitigate some of the most severe impacts of unsuccessful development strategy; they may be key to poverty reduction particularly in times of crisis; and in some cases, they may result in the establishment of successful local-level initiatives or businesses. They should not, however, be looked to as a path to broader economic development or as a solution to rebuilding significant capacity at a national level.

Diasporas and Political Development—diaspora engagements

Just as with diaspora economic contributions, the political involvement of expatriates may take varying forms and be of differential salience. Today there is a tendency among those seeking to overthrow or transform repressive regimes to look to diaspora communities as a source of ideas and activities that may push for democratization "back home".[47] Not surprisingly, however, from the other side of the equation—that of the authoritarian state—there is a long tradition of viewing diaspora communities as potentially subversive. Key examples are those of the Soviet and Chinese Communist approaches to their respective diaspora for decades following the revolutions. However, the record of the same diaspora may be mixed. In the case of Ethiopia, for example, at times "diaspora organizations played key roles in pushing for change, including promotion of human rights, press freedom, competitive elections, and other elements of good governance. At other times, they bolstered chauvinist leaders with little commitment to democracy or militant leaders with records of human rights abuses."[48] As a result, home state leaders may view the diaspora as an asset or as an antagonist.

In the context of today's technologies of globalization, diasporans may engage in various informational or media activities to raise awareness interna-

[47] Orujela, "Distant Warriors", 439.
[48] Terrence Lyons, "Conflict-Generated Diasporas and Transnational Politics in Ethiopia", *Conflict, Security & Development*, Vol. 7, No. 4 (2007), 529–49, 539.

tionally regarding conditions at home. Through YouTube, Facebook, Twitter and other social media, there is unprecedented direct informational output from insiders to expatriates. Members of the diaspora may also engage in lobbying and other activities that can raise the profile of developments in the country of origin, just as they may be in a better position to access international funding, facilities, and expertise. The Armenian, Greek, and Jewish diaspora communities in the US are obvious examples. In short, at least in some cases, "Diaspora members have become critical agents of social, political and cultural change...through voting, engaging in political activities and participating in political debate."[49]

Portes et al. show that beyond the generalization that home loyalties and nostalgia endure among expatriates, individual diaspora communities behave quite differently when it comes to politico-cultural organization.[50] In comparing the Columbian, Dominican, and Mexican communities, they find Columbian organizations to be more middle class, and more professional and religious in orientation. Dominican organizations, on the other hand, tend to be overwhelmingly political, with a strong presence of homeland political parties in major diaspora communities. However, in neither case has the involvement of the home state gone much beyond the symbolic. Both governments seem too weak and poor to implement large-scale programs, and therefore major initiatives have come from the private sector. Mexicans, on the other hand, are notable for their establishment of a large number of hometown associations, which have generated important developmental effects in the sending communities, in part owing to the Mexican government's focus on partnering with them.[51]

In addition to the various civil society organizations that may be established by diaspora communities,[52] central to understanding the relationship between diaspora communities and state-building are the various forms of socio-political engagement created by states of origin to involve the diaspora.[53] For

---

[49] Cindy Horst, "The Transnational Political Engagements of Refugees: Remittance Sending Practices Amongst Somalis in Norway", *Conflict, Security & Development*, Vol. 8, No. 3 (2008), 317–39, 324.

[50] Portes, "Immigrant Transnational Organizations".

[51] Ibid., 276–7.

[52] Ludger Pries and Zeynep Sezgin, *Cross Border Migrant Organizations in Comparative Perspective* (London: Palgrave Macmillan, 2007).

[53] Laurie Brand, *Citizens Abroad: States and Their Expatriates in the Middle East and North Africa* (New York: Columbia University Press, 2006).

example, over the years, states throughout the MENA region have established separate ministries or branches of ministries to address the concerns of expatriates; they have offered language and culture classes through embassies or in conjunction with the host state; and they have provided special facilities, such as imams to tend to the religious needs of the emigrant communities (and to try to promote particular interpretations of Islam). They have also established summer programs for the children of expatriates to enable them to learn about the "mother" country; and in some cases, as in increasing numbers of countries around the world, they have accepted dual citizenship. Perhaps most interesting from the point of view of the evolution of the political system, since the Arab uprisings, a number of countries have implemented or expanded the right to vote accorded to their diasporans.

How significant are such policies for trying to understand the possibilities of diaspora involvement in state- and nation-(re)building? An examination of the evolution of the role of state institutions devoted to emigrants should provide clues as to the changing nature of the regime, but also to the development of the view of state elites toward the role, both actual and potential, of communities abroad. A few examples should suffice to illustrate the point. In the case of Lebanon, as the country was coming to independence in 1946, the overwhelmingly Maronite Kata'ib party of Pierre Jumayyil argued strongly in favor of a range of state efforts—including enfranchising those Lebanese in the diaspora who had lost their citizenship—aimed at strengthening the ties between expatriates and the homeland. These efforts are easily understood in the context of a political system in which confessional affiliation and the balance among different sects was (and is) critical to the internal balance of power. Hence, initiatives aimed at the diaspora, which counted a plurality if not a preponderance of Maronites, sought to reinforce the power of Maronites in particular, and Christians in general.

Another set of very different examples can be seen in the Maghribi cases. Here, first Algeria, then Tunisia, and finally Morocco established what were called *amicales*, or friendship societies, for their emigrants in Europe. In the Algerian case, the post-1962 *amicale* was the heir of an FLN-affiliated organization that had operated during the revolution, the goal of which was to mobilize, but also monitor, Algerians abroad. Its later Tunisian and Moroccan counterparts maintained the primary purpose of monitoring the emigrant communities to discipline dissent and enforce loyalty. A third example may be seen in the case of Jordan, which organized a series of expatriate conferences in the mid-1980s. The goals of this series of meetings were twofold: to interest expatriates in investing in the kingdom as the impact of the regional recession began to hit home, and to compete with the PLO for the political loyalty of Jordanians of Palestinian origin who constituted a majority of Jordanians in the Gulf diaspora communities.

Some of these institutions have changed their missions over time. For example, in the case of Morocco in the 1990s, the *amicale*'s role was downgraded as two other institutions, the Hassan II Foundation for Moroccans Resident Abroad and a separate ministry devoted to the Moroccan community abroad, were established. In the case of Jordan, once King Hussein cut administrative ties with the West Bank in July 1988, the regime abandoned the series of expatriate conferences. In other countries, such as Syria and Yemen, separate ministries devoted to expatriates were established in the early 2000s as the first initiatives in such state "outreach" to the diaspora.

The question of the effectiveness of these institutions is another matter, and it should be judged from both the sending state and the expatriate sides of the ledger. In the case of the *amicales*, they seem to have been successful in monitoring and intimidating the communities in Europe, which was their primary task from the point of view of their respective states. From the point of view of the emigrants, however, unless one was closely linked to the regime, these institutions offered few services that the emigrants really needed. Celebrations at embassies for national or religious holidays were far less important than would have been state efforts aimed at protecting the emigrants' labor and human rights. One survey of Moroccans regarding their view of the Hassan II Foundation found that while many emigrants had heard of it, few had had any dealings with it;[54] and the expatriate conferences held by Jordan produced little in the way of expatriate investment or state extension of services. In general, then, these institutions have reflected the same capacity gaps observed in other state institutions, just as they have been marked by the authoritarian nature of the home state regime. The result has been, in general, a failure to address emigrants' needs, either because that was never their real *raison d'être* or because of insufficient institutional capacity. Thus, even when the state's intention was to involve or serve the diasporans rather more, the implementation has fallen far short of expectations.

How then might we think about what role expatriates might play in the political state-building of their countries of origin in the context of the transitions currently underway in the region? Here, let us focus on one of the most

[54] Ibid., 86, 87.

interesting developments in diaspora–home state relationship since winter 2010–11: the expansion of expatriate voting rights. First granted by Australia in 1902, out-of-country voting (OCV) expanded slowly in the early decades of the twentieth century as only a few countries followed suit, generally offering the vote to members of the military or other government employees stationed abroad.[55] Not until the 1980s did the phenomenon become more widespread, and what followed in the 1990s was a dramatic increase in the number of countries that devised a variety of arrangements, depending upon the types of elections in which the expatriate is permitted to participate, the eligibility requirements, as well as the mechanics and logistics by which the vote is carried out. According to the most comprehensive survey available, that of May 2007, 115 countries and territories had extended some form of this right, of which the MENA region counted Algeria, Bahrain, Iran, Iraq, Oman, Sudan, Syria, Tunisia, and Yemen.[56] Israel and Turkey permit nationals residing abroad to vote, but only if they return to do so.

Algeria was the first state in the region to institute OCV, in 1976. Iran did so following the revolution, in 1980. Morocco followed suit in 1984, even establishing separate parliamentary seats for expatriates, but then rescinding the right for the 1993 parliamentary elections, although it reinstated the right for expatriates to vote in referenda in 1997. In Tunisia, in 1988 President Ben 'Ali accorded Tunisian expatriates the right to vote in presidential elections and referenda.[57] Bahrain legalized the right in 2002 as did Yemen, although it has never been implemented by San'a. Iraq first used OCV for the post-Saddam elections in 2005, while Syria allowed expatriate participation in the presidential referendum of 2007.

In each of these cases, the meaning of the vote for the expatriates varied, although all were in the context of an authoritarian system (or occupation, for Iraq). In Algeria, initially, since participation was considered a manifestation of loyalty, many Algerians seem to have voted as part of an expected performance of loyalty. However, the presidential elections of 1995 in particular, which confirmed Liamine Zeroual as president, attracted a great deal of interest since Algerians hoped they would pave the way to ending the domestic

---

[55] E. Sensenig-Dabbous, *Absentee Voting Survey: Laws + Practice* (white paper, Beirut: LERC, Notre Dame University, 2005), 6.

[56] International Institute for Democracy and Electoral Assistance, *Voting from Abroad: The International IDEA Handbook* (Stockholm: IDEA, 2007).

[57] Laurie Brand, "Authoritarian States and Voting from Abroad: North African Experiences", *Comparative Politics*, Vol. 43, No. 1 (2010), 81–100.

insurgency. Thus, in this instance, their participation was intended to contribute to a rebuilding of domestic stability back home. In the other country cases, however, with the exception of Iraq, participation in the elections was generally viewed as an obligation imposed by the authoritarian state, the results of which were known in advance.

Since the beginnings of the Arab uprisings, however, there have been significant changes. In Tunisia, shortly after the overthrow of Ben 'Ali, the right to vote from abroad was extended to include parliamentary elections, and eighteen seats in the new parliament were created for diaspora community representatives. Both Egypt (fall 2010) and Libya (summer 2012) instituted OCV for the first time, for parliamentary and presidential elections as well as referenda; and Morocco (2012) reinstituted OCV for parliamentary elections, although it adopted a cumbersome method (proxy voting) which was widely criticized.

More important than simply the extension of the vote was the process by which it was "won" in several of these cases. In both Tunisia and Egypt there was extensive expatriate civil society activity that secured the new voting provisions. Among Egyptian diasporans, the development was even more dramatic than among Tunisians, because it took law suits which were ruled on only a few weeks before the first round of parliamentary elections in November 2011 to lead the transitional authorities to approve OCV. In the Libyan case, the extension of OCV also appears to have been the result of pressure from expatriate civil society and diplomatic missions. The significant difference in the Libyan case is that owing to the late nature of the decision and the inferior state capacity (in comparison with Tunisia and Egypt), balloting was made available in only a handful of countries (most notably not Egypt and Tunisia), and the assistance of the International Organization for Migration was secured through UNDP.[58] Also significant has been the registration and turnout. While in general OCV seems to attract about 10 percent of eligible expatriate voters, in the case of Tunisia, some 40 percent participated. In the case of Egypt, the initial rounds of parliamentary elections suffered because of lack of time to register; still, some 355,000 out of an estimated total (not just voting age) expatriate population of about 3.5 mil-

[58] Laurie Brand, "Restructuring State–Expatriate Relations? Out-of-Country Voting and Political Transitions in the MENA Region" (paper presented at the annual meeting for the European University Institute, Mediterranean Conference, Mersin, Turkey, 20–23 March 2013).

lion registered. Particularly notable were the large numbers of registrants among those resident in non-democracies, who constituted the preponderance of the voters, with the largest number (142,700) in Saudi Arabia. In the case of Libya, some 8,000 voted, the numbers affected by the fact that the large concentrations in Egypt and Tunisia were told they lived close enough to return home to vote. In the Moroccan case, the state released total numbers—not separate statistics for the expatriates—so it is more difficult to gauge the involvement.

Several conclusions may be drawn from these examples. The first is that the countries in which the transitions have moved the farthest have also done more to involve their diaspora communities effectively.[59] Tunisia is at one end of the spectrum while Morocco is at the other, although it should be mentioned that OCV was at least proposed in the Jordanian parliament in 2012 as part of discussions surrounding a new electoral law, but it was quickly dismissed. Second, civil society groups in the diaspora as well as some in-country groups concerned with civil and political rights made OCV a high-profile issue and managed to convince or force the new state authorities to include it. In so doing, they took advantage of the political openings created by the revolutions to begin to restructure the relationship between the home state and the diaspora communities. The result, at least initially, has been the expression of a clear desire by diasporans to participate in selecting decision-makers and law-makers who will oversee the next stages of the transitions. Moreover, the numbers of those participating from abroad has had an impact on the domestic outcome. In the case of Tunisia, for example, nine of the eighteen expatriate seats went to candidates from El-Nahdah, thus constituting more than 10 percent of the party's parliamentary representation. In the case of Egypt, the numbers were significant in the presidential elections, which were decided by less than 883,000 votes: more than 225,000 expatriates voted for the Muslim Brotherhood's Muhammad Mursi, while some 75,000 voted for his opponent Ahmad Shafiq. Finally, there appears to be just as great an interest in participating in politics back home in diaspora communities in authoritarian states as in democratic host states; and in communities in countries in which citizenship and long-term settlement are possible (Europe and North America) as in country contexts where they are not (the Gulf states).

[59] I detail this argument in Laurie Brand, "Arab Uprisings and the Changing Frontiers of Transnational Citizenship: Voting From Abroad in Political Transitions", *Political Geography*, forthcoming.

In sum, expatriates' securing the right to vote should be understood as part of the process of rebuilding the political system in each of these countries in more pluralistic, participatory, and effective ways. The extension of the vote may also be seen as part of the process of laying the groundwork for political systems more fully respectful of the rule of law, and based more on the concept of real citizenship, as opposed to "subjectness". These steps toward more inclusive political systems should be viewed as critical preconditions to addressing the four gaps in capacity contributing to state fragility that were discussed at the outset.

Conclusions

There is often the presumption that those living in the diaspora constitute a constituency that can easily be mobilized to push for economic development or political reform in the state of origin. As we have seen, however, reality is far more complicated. Many expatriates are interested in conditions "back home", but in some cases only in matters related to the family or local community. Others may simply be interested in finding ways to improve their access to decision-makers to tap into or further develop rent-seeking relationships. Still others may seek to contribute to causes that stoke or perpetuate conflict or inequalities in the sending state. To evaluate the potential of any diaspora (or part of it) to become involved economically, politically, culturally or otherwise in the state of origin, one must first examine the various communities that compose a diaspora to determine their length of residence abroad, degree of economic success, resources at their disposal, degree of integration into the host state, and any subnational or transnational identity or affiliation. Also critical is an understanding of the full complexity of the nature of the relationships between the host states and the diaspora communities, as well as between the host state and the sending state.

Thus, one central conclusion is that one cannot a priori assume any particular potential role for a diaspora in the state of origin. Only a careful examination of the history and composition of the diaspora will enable us to suggest likely or appropriate forms of involvement in (re)building "back home". Close case comparisons may provide some clues, but it is critical to keep in mind that the forms and opportunities for diaspora intervention and influence change over time, all the more so today with the dramatic developments in technology allowing for swifter and more continuous communication, easier transfer of funds, more frequent travel, and the like. Nor should analysts harbor illusions about diaspora potential. On the economic front, while in some countries remittances will no doubt continue to play a key role in raising families' standards of living, and may contribute to some small business development, just as they help maintain national levels of hard currency reserves, under no circumstances should they be viewed as an engine for development or the answer to economic malaise. At best they may contribute—most likely on the margins—to what needs to be a much broader and deeper strategy for economic transformation. Similarly, on the political front, the involvement of the diaspora may be an important indicator of a political opening during a transitional period, but it is at best a participant in, not a catalyst of, that change. Diaspora communities may support programs and initiatives that seek to rebuild or reinvigorate state capacity; however, they should not be looked to as the primary initiator or trigger of nation- or state-building.

12

STATE CAPACITY AND AID EFFECTIVENESS IN WEAK STATES IN THE GREATER MIDDLE EAST

Mark McGillivray

Arguably one of the greatest challenges in international development concerns weak states. These states tend to have the greatest need for aid, yet by most accounts they tend to have the most limited capacities to absorb aid effectively for development purposes. While the needs of weak states are typically quite clear, based on agreed indicators, the reverse is the case regarding absorptive capacity. This chapter identifies various dimensions of absorptive capacity. It then devises a composite index of absorptive capacity for individual recipient countries. Values of this index are derived for 140 developing countries, including ten that are located in the Greater Middle East. Among the latter group of countries are a number that according to standard definitions can be considered weak states. The index scores of this sub-group of countries are given special consideration from a donor aid allocation perspective. Policy relevance of these scores is also considered.

There are lofty development expectations for aid to weak, failing, or fragile states. Among these expectations are to help establish and sustain peace, prevent a slide into civil collapse, and to achieve and sustain growth and development over time. It is not surprising therefore that countries widely thought to be weak, failing, or fragile receive very large amounts of aid relative to other developing countries. The top three largest recipients in terms of aggregate official development assistance (ODA) volumes during 2007 to 2011 were three countries that are widely held to be weak, failing, or fragile: Iraq, Afghanistan, and the Democratic Republic of Congo. These three countries received 14 percent of the global ODA budget shared among 153 countries and territories over this period.[1]

What precisely a weak, failing, or fragile state might be is a matter of some conjecture. Yet irrespective of precisely what definition we might use, from a development perspective these states have two dominant characteristics. The first is that they tend to be among those with the greatest need for aid. This is typically due to them having very low multidimensional development achievements, including high levels of both income but also poverty. The second is that within them there are very limited capacities to convert foreign development aid into development results, be it in terms of higher economic growth, lower poverty, or higher overall standards of living. These characteristics combine to make the promotion of development in weak, failing, or fragile states one of the greatest, if not the greatest challenge facing aid donors and the international community generally.

In development circles, a country is often thought to have a weak capacity to absorb aid for development purposes if it has policies that are bad for development and poorly performing institutions. It is, indeed, by these criteria that countries in development circles have been considered fragile. A well-known measure of the quality of policies and institutional performance is the World Bank's Country Policy and Institutional Assessment (CPIA).[2] Thus the OECD's Development Assistance Committee has used the CPIA to define fragile states as low-income countries in the bottom two quintiles of that measure.[3] For example, three low-income Greater Middle East countries fall into the bottom two quintiles of the most recent CPIA scores: Afghanistan, Pakistan, and Yemen.[4]

---

[1] Organisation for Economic Co-operation and Development (OECD), *International Development Statistics On-line* (Paris, 2013).

[2] World Bank, *IDA16: Delivering Developing Results*. Report from the Executive Directors of the International Development Association to the Board of Governors (Washington, DC: World Bank, 2010).

[3] OECD, "Principles for good International Engagement in Fragile States" (Paris: OECD, 2005).

[4] World Bank, *Open Data* (Washington, DC: World Bank, 2013). The World Bank does not publish CPIA scores for countries that are ineligible to receive aid from the

This chapter does not take issue with using CPIA scores solely to assign the fragile state classification, although it does note in passing that this approach is problematic. It does, however, take issue with using the CPIA as a sole measure of absorptive capacity. It considers the CPIA to be too narrow a measure of a country's capacity to absorb aid for development purposes: in particular, it looks only at the capacity of the recipient country and not at the capacity of donors to deliver development results in these countries. Accordingly, the first task of this chapter is to develop and apply a new, more comprehensive cross-recipient country measure of the capacity to absorb for development purposes. It builds on the work of Feeny and De Silva in this task.[5] The chapter then highlights the numerical values of this measure—the Absorptive Capacity Index (ACI)—for countries in the Greater Middle East (which is treated as the Middle East traditionally defined, plus the North African countries, Afghanistan, and Pakistan), and compares these values to the amounts of aid these countries have received in recent years. Inferences for the likely development effectiveness of this aid are then drawn. The chapter concludes with policy implications, particularly concerning the amounts of aid allocated to weak states in the Greater Middle East.

The chapter consists of a further four sections. It begins with a discussion of the concept of absorptive capacity and what it means for aid effectiveness. It then outlines a new measure of absorptive capacity (the ACI), followed by numerical values of variants of this measure. These values are also compared with aid amounts received by Greater Middle Eastern countries. Policy implications for aid to Greater Middle Eastern countries, those classified as fragile according the above-mentioned OECD criteria in particular, are discussed in the conclusion.

Absorptive Capacity and Aid Effectiveness

The existence of absorptive capacity constraints (ACCs) and diminishing returns to foreign aid has long been recognized. Chenery and Strout first

---

International Development Association. Among these countries are the Middle Eastern countries of Iraq, Libya, and Syria and the territory of West Bank and Gaza. If the first three of these states were classified as low income and the fourth classified as a country, they would almost certainly satisfy the OECD fragile state definition.

[5] S. Feeny and A. de Silva, "Measuring Absorptive Capacity Constraints to Foreign Aid", *Economic Modelling*, Vol. 29, No. 3 (2012), 735–33.

documented diminishing returns to aid caused by the problem of absorptive capacity over forty years ago.[6] This issue is becoming increasingly pertinent as international donors scale up their aid to record levels, and, arguably, it is a problem that has largely been ignored by policy-makers. In economics, the concept of absorptive capacity is well known and often relates to the ability of a country to utilize physical capital productively. It is often found that there are diminishing returns to capital. In other words, the productivity of physical capital (investment) falls as its level increases. Since international donors often fund capital and investment, this interpretation of absorptive capacity can readily be applied in the context of foreign aid. Yet not all foreign aid is provided to fund profitable investment opportunities, and therefore a broader view of the concept is required. Human capital elements are part of this view. Those administering aid inflows, from both the recipient and donor country sides, will have limits to the amounts of aid they can effectively deal with, no matter how competent they might be. And like the productivity of capital, this will vary among donors and recipients.

The linked notions of ACCs and diminishing returns to aid effectiveness in the context of a single country are depicted in Figure 1. Development is measured in the vertical axis of Figure 1. This can be any of the typical development objectives to which aid is subject, such as growth, inequality, poverty reduction, health, education, and per capita income. Aid is measured on the horizontal axis and can be either ODA in absolute levels or relative to population or GDP. The basic story emanating from Figure 1 is that there can be too much of a good thing owing to absorptive capacity constraints. That is, the incremental impact of aid increases as aid increases up to a certain level of aid, commences to decrease, and eventually becomes negative. In Figure 1, aid increases development up to the level of aid A_m, still increases but at a decreasing rate up to level A_n. Up to A_n aid results in higher development than would otherwise be the case (without aid), but beyond this level actually leads to lower development than would otherwise be the case, be it lower poverty reduction, increases in health and education levels, or growth in per capita income. Aid levels up to A_n can be considered the "do no harm" range for aid allocation, this phrase reflecting a well-known principle among aid practitioners.

The vast majority of aid effectiveness literature has examined the impact of foreign aid on per capita economic growth rates in recipient countries.

---

[6] H. Chenery and A. M. Strout, "Foreign Assistance and Economic Development", *American Economic Review*, Vol. 56, No. 4 (1966), 679–733.

Figure 1: Diminishing Returns to Aid Effectiveness

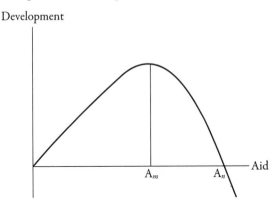

Virtually all studies that test for diminishing returns confirm the existence of a relationship depicted in Figure 1 (with respect to growth), providing strong empirical evidence for the existence of ACCs in recipient countries.[7] Unfortunately, no studies have to date tested for such a relationship between aid and its other intended development outcomes, including poverty reduction. This is a great pity as there is a valid argument that these outcomes are ultimately more important than income growth.

Various estimates of A_m are provided by these empirical studies. This is not surprising given that measures of aid, samples of developing countries, and time periods differ among these studies. Drawing on the parameter estimates from a number of these studies, Feeny and McGillivray estimate that diminishing returns set in when foreign aid accounts for about 20 percent of a recipient's GDP, and that donors should exercise caution in providing a level of aid in

[7] See, for example, H. Hansen and F. Tarp, "Aid Effectiveness Disputed", *Journal of International Development*, Vol. 12 (2000), 375–98; H. Hansen and F. Tarp, "Aid and Growth Regressions", *Journal of Development Economics*, Vol. 64 (2001), 547–70; R. Lensik and H. White, "Are there negative returns to aid?" *Journal of Development Studies*, Vol. 37, No. 6 (200)1, 42–64; J. Hudson and P. Mosley, "Aid, policies and growth: in search of the holy grail", *Journal of International Development*, Vol. 114 (2004), 191–216; D. Roodman, "The Anarchy of numbers: aid, development and cross-country empirics", CGD working paper No. 32 (Washington, DC: Centre for Global Development, 2004); M. Clemens, S. Radelet, and R. Bhavani, "Counting Chickens when they hatch: the short-term effect of aid on growth", CGD working paper No. 44 (2004).

excess of this threshold as this implies lower incremental impact, the caution provided below notwithstanding.[8] The corresponding level of A_n is 40 percent of recipient country GDP. Since these thresholds are estimated from studies using cross-country data, it represents an average threshold for developing countries as a group. Clearly, the actual threshold will vary among countries.

There is an important caution or caveat regarding any implicit aid alloca-tion decision rules that might be transmitted by Figure 1 and the research findings discussed above. This figure and these findings are best interpreted as relating to particular points in time, in the short run. If we accept the 20 percent threshold, donors would provide this amount on average if they want to maximize the short-run impact of aid. Donors might, as they should, also have an eye to the long run, trading off current development for higher levels of development in the long run. This is particularly relevant for weak, fragile, or failing states. Donors might, for example, want to establish the precondi-tions for long-run development (such as rebuilding damage to physical and human capital in an immediate post-conflict country) by providing in excess of A_m, possibly even A_n. But this case becomes very weak if yearly allocations remain above these thresholds for extended periods of time.

That the specific level of aid at which diminishing returns begin will vary across recipient countries provides the motivation for constructing an index of absorptive capacity for individual countries.[9] Aid effectiveness studies point to a number of different capacity constraints which help explain the finding of diminishing returns to foreign aid. The following types of capacity con-straints are identified: capital constraints; policy and institutional constraints; macroeconomic constraints; donor practices; and social and cultural con-straints.[10] Each type of ACC is now discussed.

Capital Constraints

Capital constraints include human and physical capital constraints. Low levels of human capital might prevail in recipient country public sectors, limiting

[8] S. Feeny and M. McGillivray, "Scaling up foreign aid: will the 'big push' work?" *World Economy*, Vol. 34, No. 1 (2011), 54–73.

[9] Ibid. Feeny and McGillivray note that if ODA accounted for 20 percent of GDP in all recipient countries, the global aid budget would need to increase to US$ 1,466 billion. This is a level far in excess of the levels implied by an outright doubling of aid, or where it accounts for 0.7 percent of all donors' GNI.

[10] P. de Renizo, "Increased aid versus absorptive capacity: challenges and opportuni-ties towards 2015", *IDS Bulletin*, Vol. 36, No. 3 (2005), 14–19.

their ability to put additional amounts of aid to good use. For example, at a central (administrative) level, public sectors might face a shortage of skilled or adequately trained civil servants to manage and administer foreign aid flows from overseas. Given the way in which flows are administered, public sector officials are likely to be responsible for a broad range of reporting requirements to different aid donors. They will also be responsible for hosting donor missions and dealing with staff from overseas agencies. All these activities will take valuable time and resources away from core government tasks and functions. Recipient public-sector staff might also lack the necessary skills and technical expertise for aid project identification, preparation, and evaluation.[11] The constraint becomes more binding with poor donor practices in delivering aid, discussed below. Reducing this and the institutional administrative burden of aid is one of the objectives of the Paris Declaration on Aid Effectiveness, to improve its quality.

Human capital constraints also exist at a sector level. In particular, recipient country health and education sectors are increasingly being targeted as donors seek to assist with progress towards the millennium development goals (MDGs). However, a lack of qualified or trained staff in health and education in some countries will impede the effectiveness of additional resources aimed at achieving these goals. Such concerns are substantiated by the McKinsey Group, which finds that human resources are the primary barrier to scaling up immunization programs.[12] Moreover, Killick argues that there is a worsening shortage of human resources in Africa, compounded by the brain drain and high mortality rates.[13]

Physical capital constraints relate largely to infrastructure constraints. Extensive and well-maintained infrastructure will play an important role in ensuring that additional financial resources will lead to tangible progress toward the MDGs. Delivering essential services such as health, education,

[11] R. Reyes, "Absorptive capacity for foreign aid: the case of the Philippines" (Manila: International Center for Economic Growth and Philippine Institute for Development Studies, 1993).

[12] N. Dreesch, C. Dolea, M. DalPoz, A. Goubarevm, O. Adams, M. Aregawi, K. Bergstrom, H. Fogstad, D. Sheratt, J. Linkins, R. Scherpbier, and M. Youssef-Fox, "An approach to estimating human resource requirements to achieve the Millennium Development Goals", *Health Policy and Planning*, Vol. 20 (2005), 267–76.

[13] T. Killick, "Don't throw money at Africa", *IDS Bulletin*, Vol. 36, No. 3 (2005), 14–19.

water, and sanitation will require physical infrastructure (such as schools, hospitals, and clinics) but also transport infrastructure (such as roads, bridges, and ports). Improving telecommunications, energy infrastructure, and irrigation systems will also assist in improving productivity and securing economic growth. In the absence of such infrastructure, the costs in delivering services to intended beneficiaries in rural areas will remain very high.

Policy and Institutional Constraints

A well cited finding in the empirical aid effectiveness literature is that weak macroeconomic policy and institutional environments undermine the positive impact of foreign aid.[14] While the robustness of this finding is often disputed, there is a widely held view that recipient countries should have appropriate economic and social policies in place in order to maximize the effectiveness of additional aid.

Strong institutions offer incorporate effective financial management systems; strong systems of accountability and transparency; high levels of law and order; a strong legal and judicial environment; and a democratic electoral process. Mechanisms also need to be in place to deal with the administration of aid programs, including long-term national development plans and medium-term development strategies to which aid programs can be aligned. An efficient planning department is also required to ensure that aid is aligned with national priorities and is coordinated effectively among different donors. For these reasons, the absence of sound policies and institutions can limit the effectiveness of additional aid.[15]

[14] C. Burnside and D. Dollar, "Aid, policies and growth", *American Economic Review*, Vol. 90, No. 4 (2000), 847–68; C. Burnside and D. Dollar, "Aid, policies and growth: revisiting the evidence", World Bank Policy Research working paper No. 3251 (Washington, DC: World Bank, 2004); P. Collier and D. Dollar, "Aid allocation and poverty reduction", *European Economic Review*, Vol. 46 (2002), 1475–1500.

[15] While aid can be used to improve policies and institutions in recipient countries, at high levels it can also become part of the problem, leading to institutional destruction and weak systems of domestic accountability. A number of studies identify adverse impacts of foreign aid on institutions and the level of governance in recipient countries. S. Knack, "Aid dependence and the quality of governance: a cross-country empirical analysis", World Bank Policy Research working paper No. 2396 (Washington, DC: World Bank, 2000); D. Brautigam and S. Knack, "Foreign aid, institutions and governance in Sub-Saharan Africa", *Journal of Economic*

The response of recipient fiscal policy to aid is another important aspect of this constraint. Specifically, recipient governments might change their spending and revenue raising behavior in response to foreign assistance. If foreign aid is fungible, it might lead to an increase in expenditures viewed as undesirable by donors, or recipients might devise inappropriate expenditure plans. Additional aid flows might also increase the scope for corruption and financial mismanagement. Arguably, the most important concern is whether large amounts of aid reduce the amount of tax collection efforts by recipient governments. Very low tax bases relative to aid flows can also lead to a high level of aid dependency, undermining democracy since recipient governments become more accountable to their aid donors than to their own electorates.[16]

Macroeconomic Constraints

Very high levels of foreign aid can potentially have adverse macroeconomic impacts. Such impacts are widely referred to as "Dutch disease" impacts of aid. High levels of assistance can lead to an appreciation of a recipient's Real Exchange Rate (RER) and therefore to a loss of export competitiveness.[17] This problem arises when the increase in demand for a recipient's currency leads to a nominal exchange rate appreciation and when aid is spent on domestic (non-

---

Development and Cultural Change, Vol. 52, No. 2 (2004), 255–86. These findings are not undisputed, but they do point to a need to be cautious when scaling up, in order to ensure that additional aid does not undermine the objective of strengthening institutions.

[16] The empirical evidence on the relationship between aid and tax is mixed. Results from fiscal response studies are clearly recipient-specific, with aid found to lead to either increases or falls in tax revenues, depending on the sample of countries under consideration. Using other techniques, D. Brautigam and S. Knack, "Foreign aid, institutions and governance in Sub-Saharan Africa" found that higher levels of aid are associated with lower shares of tax to GDP in developing countries; while Bourguignon et al. identified that tax effort increased when aid increased, in a study of eleven African countries: F. Bourguignon, A. Gelb, and B. Versailles, "Policy, aid and performance in Africa: the G11 and other country groups" (Washington, DC: World Bank working paper, 2005).

[17] The term was originated by *The Economist* for a rather different context: reflecting the paradoxical impact of discovering natural gas deposits in the North Sea on the Dutch manufacturing sector, which resulted in the appreciation of the Dutch real exchange rate. P. S. Heller, "Pity the finance minister: issues in managing scaling up of aid flows", IMF working paper No. Wp/05/180 (Washington, DC: International Monetary Fund, 2005).

tradable) goods and services, thereby increasing their price and raising costs, or drawing resources away from the export (tradable) sector. Given the importance of the export sector in many developing countries, these so-called "Dutch disease" impacts could undermine the positive impacts of aid on growth and poverty education.

Findings in the literature relating to macroeconomic constraints are ambiguous. Evidence of the Dutch disease impacts of aid are confirmed by Rajan and Subramanian for a sample of developing countries, by Adenauer and Vagassky for a sample of African countries, by Laplagne et al. for some Pacific countries, and by White and Wignaraja in the case of Sri Lanka.[18] However, little or no evidence of aid-induced Dutch disease has been found by Ouattara and Strobl and Killick and Foster in samples of African countries, by Nyoni in the case of Tanzania, and by Sackey in the case of Ghana.[19] Mixed results have been identified for Pacific countries by Fielding.[20]

Arguably, there are other more important constraints to expanding the export sector in developing countries, and the adverse effects of aid on a recipient's RER may be overstated. Barder argues that it is very unlikely that increases in foreign aid will lead to Dutch disease impacts if aid flows are sustained and predictable.[21] Gupta et al. demonstrate that the likelihood of

---

[18] R. G. Rajan and A. Subramanian, "What undermines aid's impact on growth?" IMF working paper No. 05/126 (Washington, DC: International Monetary Fund, 2005); I. Adenauer and L. Vagassky, "Aid and the real exchange rate: Dutch disease effects in African countries", *Interconomics: Review of International Trade and Development*, Vol. 33, No. 4 (1998), 177–85; P. Laplagne, M. Treadgold, and J. Baldry, "A model of aid impact in some South Pacific microstates", *World Development*, Vol. 29, No. 2 (2001), 365–83; H. White and G. Wignaraja, "Exchange rates, trade liberalization and the aid: the Sri Lankan experience", *World Development*, Vol. 20, No. 10 (1992), 1471–80.

[19] B. Ouattara and E. Strobl, "Do aid flows cause Dutch Disease? A case study of the CFA Franc countries", discussion paper No. 0330 (University of Manchester, School of Economic Studies, 2003); T. Killick and M. Foster, "The macroeconomics of doubling aid to Africa and the centrality of the supply side", *Development Policy Review*, Vol. 25, No. 2, (2007), 167–192; T.S. Noyoni, "Foreign aid and economic performance in Tanzania", *World Development*, Vol. 26, (1998), 1235–1240; H. A. Sackey, "External aid flows and the real exchange rate in Ghana", AERC Paper No. 110. Nairobi: African Economic Research Consortium, (2001).

[20] D. Fielding, "Aid and Dutch disease in the South Pacific", United Nations University—World Institute for Development Economics Research (UNU-WIDER), Research Paper No. 2007/50.

[21] O. Barder, "A policymakers' guide to Dutch disease", Center for Global Development, Working Paper No. 91, (Washington, DC: Center for Global Development, 2006).

Dutch disease impacts from aid depends on how much aid is spent (rather than accumulated as reserves) and how much is "absorbed" (where foreign exchange is used to purchase imports).[22] Whether the recipient economy is supply-constrained is also likely to be an important factor mediating the impact of aid on the recipient's RER and its export competitiveness.

Donor Practices

An additional constraint on the ability of recipients to absorb more aid effectively stems from the way in which aid is delivered by the international community. Developing countries are usually recipients of aid from a large number of donors. As noted above, the delivery of aid imposes an administrative burden on recipient-country public-sector officials. This administrative burden becomes larger when donors work in isolation from one another and use different procedures for monitoring and evaluation. As donors scale up foreign aid, the burden will be further exacerbated by an increasing number of donors and a high degree of donor proliferation and fragmentation. The 2005 Paris Declaration on Aid Effectiveness seeks to minimize this burden.

Donor proliferation relates to donors providing aid to a large number of recipient countries, implying that each individual recipient has to deal with a large number of donors. Fragmentation refers to donors funding a large number of projects and programs across different sectors, which often results in duplication. There is a growing body of literature which documents the constraints caused by poor donor practices. The impacts and degree of donor proliferation and fragmentation have been identified by Morss, Knack and Rahman, Acharya et al., and Roodman.[23] Importantly, donor proliferation and fragmentation are likely to increase in the future with the scaling up of aid.

---

[22] S. Gupta, R. Powell and Y. Yongzheng, "Macroeconomic challenges of scaling up aid to Africa: a checklist for practitioners", (Washington, DC: International Monetary Fund, 2006).

[23] E. R. Morss, "Institutional destruction resulting from donor and project proliferation in Sub-Saharan African countries", *World Development*, Vol. 12, No. 4 (1984), 465–70; S. Knack and A. Rahman, "Donor fragmentation and bureaucratic quality in aid recipients", World Bank Policy Research working paper No. 3186 (Washington, DC: World Bank, 2004); A. Acharya, A. de Lima, and M. Moore, "Proliferation and fragmentation: transaction costs and the value of aid", *Journal of Development Studies*, Vol. 42, No. 1 (2006), 1–21; D. Roodman, "Aid proliferation and absorptive capacity", CGD working paper No. 75 (Washington, DC: Center for Global Development, 2006).

Donors are also responsible for other aspects of aid delivery which could hamper its effectiveness. Volatile and unpredictable aid flows have a disruptive impact on annual budgets and fiscal planning. Studies have identified a high degree of volatility in aid flows, which hampers aid effectiveness and has been shown to increase over time.[24] Aid flows are found to be more volatile than other sources of government revenue, and volatility is also likely to increase with the scaling up of aid. In summary, the constraints engendered by poor donor practices on the ability of countries to absorb more aid are clearly important, and this remains undisputed in the literature.

Social and Cultural Factors

Social and cultural factors also represent a constraint on the effective use of additional aid flows. These constraints relate to a lack of demand for health and education services in some developing countries. Even if schools and clinics are built and are well staffed, people may not necessarily attend them.[25] Relieving such constraints lies beyond the scope of international donors, but should be a consideration when scaling up aid programs in particular countries.

Measuring the Absorptive Capacity of Developing Countries

It is important to motivate the development of the ACI clearly, given recent critiques of composite or "mash-up" indices.[26] The ACIs are developed in order to assist donors in allocating their annual aid budgets across developing countries. This is important given the strong evidence of diminishing returns to aid and that low levels of absorptive capacity limit aid effectiveness. The

---

[24] R. Lensink and O. Morrissey, "Aid instability as a measure of uncertainty and the positive impact of aid on growth", *Journal of Development Studies*, Vol. 36, No. 3 (2000), 31–49; D. Dollar and V. Levin, "The forgotten states: aid volumes and volatility in difficult partnership countries", paper prepared for the Development Assistance Committee (DAC) Learning and Advisory Process on Development Partnerships (Paris: OECD, 2005); A. Bluir and A. J. Hamann, "Volatility of development aid: from the frying pan into the fire?" *World Development*, Vol. 36, No. 10 (2008), 2048–66; D. Fielding and G. Mavrotas, "The Volatility of aid", *Economica*, Vol. 75, No. 299 (2008), 481–94.

[25] P. de Renizo, "Increased aid versus absorptive capacity: challenges and opportunities towards 2015", *IDS Bulletin*, Vol. 36, No. 3 (2005), 14–19; M. Clemens, C. Kenny, and T. Moss, "The trouble with the MDGs: confronting expectations of aid and development success", *World Development*, Vol. 35, No. 5 (2007), 735–51.

[26] M. Ravallion, "Mashup Indices of Development", World Bank Policy Research working paper No. 5432 (Washington, DC: World Bank, 2010).

ACI is designed to capture the most important factors which inhibit the effectiveness of aid at a country level. Importantly, country rankings based on the ACI are shown to be robust to different weightings of the index components. The index can be used to augment existing aid allocation models and replace other ad hoc measures of institutional capacity and policy strength. *Ceteris paribus*, higher levels of aid should be provided to countries with higher levels of absorptive capacity and vice versa.

The index needs to meet a number of criteria to be of use to policy-makers, including a very high level of country coverage and a high degree of simplicity for the sake of transparency and duplication. This chapter therefore devises an index which incorporates data that are available for a large number of countries, and which is easy to calculate and update. The inclusion of the specific components of the index, the proxies used to measure them, and the robustness of the index rankings with respect to alternative weighting systems are discussed below.

Drawing on the review of the aid effectiveness literature presented above, the ACI incorporates three major components of absorptive capacity: (i) capital constraints (including human capital and infrastructure constraints); (ii) governance constraints (including policy and institutional constraints); and (iii) donor practices. This choice of constraints as index components is strongly justified by the findings of the aid effectiveness literature concerning their importance. There is a very broad consensus throughout the literature that each of these constraints can hamper the use of additional aid. Moreover, data that can adequately measure these constraints are widely available for developing countries. While less importance is attached to the other two constraints discussed above (macroeconomic and social/cultural), they might still be relevant to certain countries. Donors can augment the ACI with other country-specific information where appropriate.

These types of constraints, how they are measured, and the source of data are presented in Table 1 below. Descriptive statistics for all of the variables are provided in Table A1 of the Appendix.

The choice of the variables employed to measure the three constraints warrants some discussion. All of the variables provide important information relating to the key constraints that have been identified by the literature as hampering the effectiveness of foreign aid.

The health and education sectors are assuming ever greater importance as donors scale up aid in attempts to achieve the MDGs. However, a shortage of skilled professionals in these sectors will limit the productive use of additional financial resources. Proxies for human capital constraints therefore include the number of doctors, nurses, and primary and secondary school teachers per thousand people. A skilled civil service is also required to handle high levels of foreign aid. Much foreign aid is provided directly to recipient governments, placing large administrative and other demands on government staff. An adult literacy variable is included as a proxy for the capacity of the staff in recipient public sectors. Physical capital constraints are captured by the extent of paved roads. This is justified on the grounds that a lack of road infrastructure will impede the delivery of basic services, even when additional resources are available. To achieve the MDGs, more remote locations of recipient countries need to be targeted and poor road systems will increase the costs and weaken the viability of servicing remote communities.

Proxies for the policy and institutional constraints include the World Bank's governance indicators. These indicators have excellent coverage for developing countries, have been used in numerous empirical studies, and are correlated with other measures of institutional strength. It is assumed that countries with low values for governance have less capacity to utilize additional aid flows effectively, and that returns on aid-funded investments will be lower. The quality of donor practices is measured using the number of donors providing aid to the recipient and the extent of aid fragmentation (both as a ratio to the log of government expenditures). These variables capture the donor-imposed administrative burden associated with aid. The greater the number of donors and the higher the level of fragmentation, the more time recipient public sectors spend on aid administration. Although these constraints could be relieved over the long term (including through the use of aid), they will be binding in the short term, restricting the effectiveness of aid.

The sensitivity of country rankings from a composite index to the weightings attached to the index components must be examined. Three methods for weighting the different components (constraints) of the composite index are adopted. The sensitivity of country rankings and policy implications to these different methods are analyzed and discussed below.

In the first method, an equally weighted index is constructed. Each of the fourteen variables used to measure the four different constraints are standardized to lie between 0 and 1.[27] The variables are averaged at a constraint level to

[27] The governance variables are constructed so that they have an effective range from −3 to 3. The variables are scaled to lie in the range (0,1) by adding 3 to each variable and then dividing it by 6. A score close to 1 (0) indicates that the level of governance enables a high (low) level of absorptive capacity. A similar procedure is applied to the variables that represent capital constraints. Actual values are divided

provide an indication of the importance of the three different constraints at a country level. The values for the three different constraints are then combined with an equal weighting to calculate the ACI. Using this method, the index is calculated for all 140 recipients of ODA, even in cases where data are not available for all of the variables. The index is referred to as ACI1.

Table 1: Components of the absorptive capacity index

Component	Measurement	Source	Year
Capital			
Human capital	(i) Number of doctors per thousand people	World Bank (2009a)	Latest available
	(ii) Number of nurses per thousand people		
	(iii) Number of primary school teachers per thousand people		
	(iv) Number of secondary school teachers per thousand people		
	(v) Adult illiteracy		
Infrastructure	(i) Paved roads (percent of total)	World Bank (2009a)	Latest available
Governance			
Policy and institutional	(i) Voice and accountability	World Bank (2009b)	2008
	(ii) Political instability		
	(iii) Government effectiveness		
	(iv) Regulatory quality		
	(v) Rule of law		
	(vi) Control of corruption		
Donor			
Donor practices	(i) Ratio of the number of DAC donors to the log of government expenditures	OECD (2009a)	2005/6 average
	(ii) Ratio of fragmentation (number of donors accounting for less than 10 percent of Country Programmable Aid (CPA)) to the log of government expenditures		

by the maximum value for each variable. This gives a score from 0 to 1 where 1 (0) indicates a high (low) level of absorptive capacity. For the donor constraint variable, the following formula was applied (maximum value—actual value)/maximum value. This was so that the score was reversed to provide a consistent interpretation with the other constraints.

The ACI1 can be criticized for its equal weighting of its various components. At the same time, assigning different weights to the different dimensions of absorptive capacity must be readily justifiable. Factor analysis provides a useful and widely used method for calculating alternative weights for the index components, particularly when the variables used in the construction of an index are correlated. Factor analysis is a statistical technique that groups variables according to their degree of co-movement. Variables are grouped into (fewer) factors according to their co-movements.

The latent components of the index of absorptive capacity are defined by the number and composition of the groupings. A (factor) score can be calculated at the constraint level and a composite index is devised by combining the factor scores for each country. Each factor indicates which set of variables has the most association with it. Two methods of combining the factor scores are utilized. The first takes a simple average of the factor scores and the resulting index is referred to as ACI2. The second takes a weighted average of the factor scores, with the weights determined by the relative proportion of the total variance explained. This composite index is referred to as ACI3.[28] The "Further" details of the factor analysis are provided in the Appendix.

ACI Scores

This chapter proceeds by examining the sensitivity of country rankings to different ACI (with different constraint weightings). Table 2 below presents the rank correlations between the different aggregate indices of absorptive capacity. It indicates that there is a very high degree of correlation between the three different composite indices. This implies that rankings and policy recommendations based on rankings of absorptive capacity change very little with the index employed.

Table 2: Correlations between alternative methods

	ACI1	*ACI2*
ACI2	0.95	
ACI3	0.87	0.97

Note: correlations are based on the 66 nations that are common to all three applications.

[28] Note that the indices cannot be calculated for countries with missing data for any of the variables.

The ACI is intended to be a more comprehensive measure of the capacity to absorb aid for development purposes than the CPIA. Its empirical correlation with the CPIA is therefore of special interest. The two indices are positively correlated, but the correlation is not high. The simple correlation between the two indices is a relatively low 0.45. A scatter plot between the two indices is shown below in Figure 2.

Figure 2: Scatter plot of ACI and CPIA

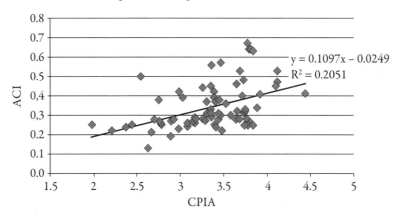

$y = 0.1097x - 0.0249$
$R^2 = 0.2051$

Country ACI scores are reported only for ACI1, owing to the high correlations between the three variants of the index. These scores are shown in Appendix Table A6. ACI scores for the Greater Middle Eastern countries for which requisite data are available are reproduced in Table 3. These countries are grouped threefold. Afghanistan, Pakistan, and Yemen are grouped together on the basis of them falling into the bottom two quintiles of the 2011 CPIA. The next group is Iraq, Libya, and Syria; owing to current political and civil conditions in these countries, they might also be considered weak states. The remaining group is treated as a residual one, containing what might broadly be described as non-weak countries. It should of course be noted that all states are weak to various degrees or in certain dimensions, so the emphasis here is on relativities.

On the basis of the information shown in Table 3 (in comparison with that in Table A6), it can be observed that Afghanistan has the second lowest ACI among the 140 countries for which index values can be calculated. Pakistan and Yemen are in the bottom 20 percent of countries based on ACI scores. Bahrain, Libya, and Saudi Arabia are in the top 10 percent of countries. Some might find this surprising in the case of Libya, given recent political events in that

FRAGILE POLITICS

country, although one should keep in mind that the latest data for which the ACI can be calculated mainly pre-date the recent turmoil in this country.

Table 3: Absorptive Capacity Index scores for Greater Middle Eastern countries[a]

	ACI	
Country	Value	Rank
Afghanistan	0.13	139
Pakistan	0.26	119
Yemen, Rep.	0.26	120
Iraq	0.34	86
Libya	0.59	13
Syrian Arab Republic	0.47	40
Bahrain	0.58	14
Iran, Islamic Rep.	0.39	70
Jordan	0.46	44
Lebanon	0.40	65
Oman	0.50	30
Saudi Arabia	0.61	11

[a] A number of Greater Middle East countries are excluded from this table, purely owing to data needed to calculate Absorptive Capacity Index scores not being available at the time of writing this chapter.

The ACI values are interesting in their own right, but are of greater relevance if used to make judgments about the possible effectiveness of aid to the countries in question. It is possible to use these values to examine whether countries are receiving appropriate levels of aid. This involves estimating the specific threshold at which diminishing returns set in for each individual country. In order to do this, it is assumed that for a country with an average ACI, the threshold is where aid accounts for 20 percent of a recipient's GDP. This is justified on the basis that aid growth studies, as discussed above, point to this threshold existing for the average developing country. The threshold is adjusted for individual countries by scaling it by a factor equal to its ACI score relative to the average ACI. This is the input threshold shown in Table 4. Comparing this threshold with actual aid levels gives some indication, for a short-run per capita income growth perspective, of the effectiveness of ODA to the Greater Middle East.

Table 4 suggests that, with one exception, aid to all Greater Middle Eastern countries can be increased without any loss in its incremental impact on

3292

growth. On the contrary, provided the thresholds shown in Table 4 are not exceeded, increasing aid to these countries will increase its incremental impact on growth. The exception is Afghanistan. ODA in 2011 to Afghanistan was more than six times the input growth efficient level, at which the incremental impact of aid on growth in the short term is maximized. This does not, on the grounds provided above, provide a case for immediately reducing aid to Afghanistan, although it does provide a caution against providing such high levels into the future. What it does suggest, however, is an extremely strong case for building absorptive capacity in Afghanistan. This is hardly a surprising finding, but the weight attached to this policy priority from Table 4 possibly is. At the very least, it adds to the case for building absorptive capacity in Afghanistan. Achieving improvements in the various components of the ACI is no easy task. But the logical starting point is for donors to improve their own allocative practices. Further policy implications of these findings are provided below.

Table 4: Absorptive Capacity and 2011 ODA levels

Country	ACI	Input ODA:GDP threshold (%)	Actual ODA:GDP (%)	Difference
Afghanistan	0.13	6.5	40.9	−34.4
Pakistan	0.26	13.0	1.6	11.4
Yemen, Rep.	0.26	13.0	2.3	10.7
Iraq	0.34	17.0	2.8	14.2
Libya	0.59	29.5	n.a.	n.a.
Syrian Arab Republic	0.47	23.5	0.2	23.3
Bahrain	0.58	29.0	n.a.	n.a.
Iran, Islamic Rep.	0.39	19.5	n.a.	n.a.
Jordan	0.46	23.0	3.6	19.4
Lebanon	0.40	20.0	n.a.	n.a.
Oman	0.50	25.0	n.a.	n.a.
Saudi Arabia	0.61	30.5	n.a.	n.a.

n.a. denotes that the requisite GDP data to calculate the ODA to GDP ratio and the difference shown in the last column of the table were not available at the time of writing this chapter.

Conclusion and Policy Recommendations

An enormous challenge in international development concerns weak states. These states tend to have the greatest need for aid, yet by most accounts they tend to have the most limited capacities to absorb aid effectively for development purposes. So while their need provides a compelling case for high levels of aid relative to other countries, their absorptive capacities suggest a case for low levels of aid relative to other countries. While the needs of weak states are typically quite clear, based on agreed indicators of need, the reverse is the case regarding absorptive capacity.

This chapter identified various dimensions of absorptive capacity. It then devised a composite index of absorptive capacity for individual recipient countries. Values of this index were reported for 140 developing countries, including ten located in the Greater Middle East. Among the latter group of countries are a number that according to standard definitions can be considered weak states. These countries are Afghanistan, Pakistan, and Yemen. The index scores of all Greater Middle East countries were given special consideration from a donor aid allocation perspective. It was found that Afghanistan is currently receiving far more aid from a growth perspective than its absorptive capacity would suggest, and that as a consequence donors need to work very hard and very quickly to address this issue, or else the task of securing peace and outgoing development in this country will be made all the more difficult. This is not at all to imply that aid levels to Afghanistan necessarily need to be reduced from current levels; simply that it is vitally important that its absorptive capacity be increased.

How should donors do this? Firstly, they need to identify and understand the drivers of absorptive capacity identified in this chapter, Secondly, they should identify which of these drivers they can actually drive and how. Thirdly, they need to act and start to drive the identified drivers—as mentioned above, drivers that they can most obviously drive at their own allocative practices. These policy recommendations do not solely apply to Afghanistan. Increasing the absorptive capacity of all Greater Middle Eastern countries will mean that aid effectiveness there will increase, they can be provided with more, and even greater development dividends can be achieved. Of course it needs to be remembered that donors do not provide aid purely for developmental reasons. Foreign policy and other objectives are important. But it is hard to achieve any lasting objectives, developmental or otherwise, if aid does not achieve significant and lasting development results.

APPENDIX

Table A1: Descriptive statistics for absorptive capacity constraint variables

Variable	Minimum	Maximum	Median	Mean	Standard deviation
Primary school teachers per 1,000 people	1.32	11.70	4.91	5.14	1.92
Secondary school teachers per 1,000 people	0.55	15.35	4.79	4.87	3.25
Paved roads (percent of total)	0.80	100.00	27.80	38.39	30.85
Doctors per 1,000 people	0.02	5.91	0.49	0.98	1.16
Nurses per 1,000 people	0.19	12.51	1.50	2.33	2.51
Adult literacy	26.18	99.79	84.28	77.79	20.03
Voice and accountability	−2.24	1.24	−0.29	−0.40	0.80
Political instability	−3.28	1.40	−0.21	−0.36	0.87
Government effectiveness	−2.51	1.48	−0.56	−0.48	0.63
Regulatory quality	−2.77	1.58	−0.46	−0.48	0.70
Rule of law	−2.69	1.28	−0.54	−0.49	0.64
Control of corruption	−1.90	1.32	−0.53	−0.46	0.59
Number of donors	2.00	30.00	20	18.12	6.52
Fragmentation	0.00	25.00	13	12.17	5.63
Donors/log (Govt Exp.)	0.12	1.44	1.01	0.95	0.34
Fragmentation/log (Govt Exp.)	0.04	1.02	0.7	0.66	0.28

Note: See Table 1 for variable descriptions; sample size varies between 115 and 140.

Table A2: Description and source of variables used in the empirical analysis

Variable	Description	Source
GDP per capita growth	Annual average growth in real GDP per capita (PPP)	Penn World Tables
Initial GDP per capita	GDP per capita (PPP) at the beginning of each period (logged)	World Bank (2010)
Ethnic fractionalization	Chance that two people drawn at random from the population will speak the same language	Roodman (2004)
Assassinations	Number of assassinations per capita	Roodman (2004)
Population	Population	World Bank (2010)
Inflation	Average annual rate of growth in the Consumer Price Index (CPI)	World Bank (2010)
Trade	Sachs-Warner trade openness index (values for 1998 used for years after 1998)	Roodman (2004)
Aid to GDP	Ratio of net Official Development Assistance (ODA) to GDP	OECD (2010)
ACI1, ACI2, ACI3	Composite Indices of Absorptive Capacity	Author's calculations

Factor analysis

The calculation of ACI2 includes all fourteen variables listed in Table A3 and is calculated for 90 countries. Presented below is the factor loading matrix with three columns, each representing a latent component of absorptive capacity.

The numbers in Table A3 are typically referred to as factor loadings. These loadings can be thought of as correlations, in particular, how the variables correlate with a particular factor. Loadings above 0.5 in magnitude are highlighted to help identify the different factors. The first factor has been denoted as *Governance* as the variables that define this factor (i.e. that have the highest loading) all relate to governance.

The second factor clearly measures *Capital*, as all the variables that load highly define the stock of physical and human capital. The third factor, *Donors*, primarily measures donor characteristics. This last factor is also determined by the number of primary school teachers per 1,000 people. While it is expected that this variable belongs in the *Capital* factor, it is only marginally above 0.5 in magnitude and can be attributed to an aberration in the data rather than as a variable which defines the factor.

Table A3: Factor loading matrix (N=66)

Variable	Governance (Factor 1)	Capital (Factor 2)	Donors (Factor 3)
Primary school teachers per 1,000 people	0.206	−0.527	
Secondary school teachers per 1,000 people		0.863	−0.206
Paved roads (percent of total)		0.565	−0.138
Doctors per 1,000 people		0.93	
Nurses per 1,000 people	0.823		
Adult literacy		0.282	0.709
Voice and accountability	0.62	−0.113	
Political instability	0.61	0.25	−0.254
Government effectiveness	0.936	0.147	
Regulatory quality	0.859	0.159	0.101
Rule of law	0.92	−0.19	
Control of corruption	0.893	−0.211	
Number of donors		−0.372	0.88
Fragmentation		−0.213	0.946

Note: factor loadings between−0.1 and 0.1 are suppressed.

Unlike the first two factors, *Donors* measures the lack of absorptive capacity. As the level of *Governance* and *Capital* increases, a country's ability to absorb aid increases. However, as the number and fragmentation of donors increase, a nation's capacity to absorb aid would be expected to decrease. This negative relationship is consistent with the negative factor loading of primary school teachers.

In order to increase the sample of countries for which ACI3 is created, two variables are omitted from the analysis: adult literacy and paved roads. The results of this exercise are presented in Table A4 below.

An important feature of this table is that the factors are defined in the same way as in Table A3. This is despite the inclusion of an additional sixteen countries. Therefore, the latent variables *Governance, Donor,* and *Capital* appear to provide robust factors. The only discernible difference between Tables A5 and A6 is that the order in which the factors appear has changed. This indicates that the relative importance of the factors has changed (albeit marginally). Importance is typically measured by the proportion of variance explained. In both cases the three factors collectively explain at least 70 percent of the variation in the dataset; and in both cases the *Governance* factor captures approximately 30 percent of the variation. In the first application the *Donor* factor captures 16 percent of the variation, whereas in the second instance it represents 20 percent of the variation. The results for *Capital* are 24 percent and 19 percent for the first and second applications respectively.

Table A4: Factor loading matrix (N=82)

Variable	Governance (Factor 1)	Donors (Factor 2)	Capital (Factor 3)
Primary school teachers per 1,000 people	0.281	−0.485	
Secondary school teachers per 1,000 people		−0.213	0.854
Doctors per 1,000 people			0.872
Nurses per 1,000 people		−0.148	0.781
Voice and accountability	0.665	−0.132	
Political instability	0.553	−0.372	0.112
Government effectiveness	0.943		0.14
Regulatory quality	0.87		0.166
Rule of law	0.919	−0.211	
Control of corruption	0.897	−0.241	
Number of donors	−0.106	0.913	−0.25
Fragmentation		0.988	−0.108

Note: factor loadings between−0.1 and 0.1 are suppressed.

In Table A5 the correlations between the individual constraints from ACI1, ACI2, and ACI3 are presented. The results in this table indicate that there is a high correlation between all three methods. This implies that the simple ACI1 methodology is providing very similar information as the approaches based on factor analysis denoted by ACI2 and ACI3.

Table A5: Correlations at the factor level

	Governance (ACI1)	Governance (ACI3)
Governance (ACI2)	0.96	0.99
Governance (ACI3)	0.95	

	Capital (ACI1)	Capital (ACI3)
Capital (ACI2)	0.96	0.99
Capital (ACI3)	0.93	

APPENDIX

	Donor (ACI1)	Donor (ACI3)
Donor (ACI2)	0.96	0.99
Donor (ACI3)	0.96	

Note: correlations are based on the 66 countries that are common to the three indices.

Table A6: Absorptive Capacity Index country scores

	ACI	
Country	Value	Rank
Afghanistan	0.13	139
Albania	0.37	77
Algeria	0.46	45
Angola	0.27	114
Antigua and Barbuda	0.72	1
Argentina	0.52	26
Armenia	0.53	24
Azerbaijan	0.53	25
Bahrain	0.58	14
Bangladesh	0.22	135
Barbados	0.69	2
Belarus	0.62	10
Belize	0.49	32
Benin	0.30	98
Bhutan	0.41	59
Bolivia	0.31	94
Bosnia and Herzegovina	0.40	66
Botswana	0.51	27
Brazil	0.41	60
Burkina Faso	0.26	121
Burundi	0.24	130
Cambodia	0.29	100
Cameroon	0.29	101
Cape Verde	0.47	41
Central African Republic	0.38	73
Chad	0.24	131
Chile	0.51	28
China	0.36	80
Colombia	0.36	81
Comoros	0.50	31

Congo, Dem. Rep.	0.21	137
Congo, Rep.	0.19	138
Costa Rica	0.49	33
Cote d'Ivoire	0.28	102
Croatia	0.58	15
Cuba	0.54	21
Djibouti	0.27	115
Dominica	0.64	6
Dominican Republic	0.41	61
Ecuador	0.35	84
Egypt, Arab Rep.	0.38	74
El Salvador	0.36	82
Equatorial Guinea	0.44	51
Eritrea	0.22	136
Ethiopia	0.24	132
Fiji	0.49	34
Gabon	0.48	36
Gambia, The	0.31	95
Georgia	0.41	62
Ghana	0.34	87
Grenada	0.67	4
Guatemala	0.40	67
Guinea	0.26	122
Guinea-Bissau	0.28	103
Guyana	0.39	71
Haiti	0.28	104
Honduras	0.30	99
India	0.32	91
Indonesia	0.35	85
Iran, Islamic Rep.	0.39	70
Iraq	0.34	86
Jamaica	0.47	42
Jordan	0.46	44
Kazakhstan	0.56	19
Kenya	0.27	116
Kiribati	0.39	72
Korea, Dem. Rep.	0.28	105
Kyrgyz Republic	0.46	46
Lao PDR	0.28	106
Lebanon	0.40	65
Lesotho	0.38	75
Liberia	0.28	107
Libya	0.59	13
Macedonia, FYR	0.48	37

APPENDIX

Madagascar	0.33	89
Malawi	0.31	96
Malaysia	0.51	29
Maldives	0.45	49
Mali	0.28	108
Marshall Islands	0.38	76
Mauritania	0.28	109
Mauritius	0.64	7
Mexico	0.49	35
Micronesia, Fed. Sts.	0.34	88
Moldova	0.48	38
Mongolia	0.37	78
Morocco	0.44	52
Mozambique	0.25	123
Myanmar	0.23	133
Oman	0.50	30
Pakistan	0.26	119
Saudi Arabia	0.61	11
Syrian Arab Republic	0.47	40
Yemen, Rep.	0.26	120

INDEX

'Abbas, Mahmoud: 234–5, 247; President of Palestine, 230, 235, 243

Abboud, General Ibrahim: regime of, 175

Abdali (tribe): 31–2; conflict with Fadhli, 38

Abdulmutallab, Umar Farouk ('Underpants Bomber'): Northwest Airlines Flight 253 Attempted Attack (2009), 62

absorptive capacity constraints (ACCs): 277–81; human/infrastructural, 281–2, 287–8; macroeconomics, 283–4; policy and institutional, 282–3, 287

Acharya, A.: 285

Aden Live: 48

Afewerki, Isseyas: external political budget of, 186

Afghanistan: 12, 21, 23, 27, 82, 87–8, 93, 97, 101, 108, 203, 250, 276, 291, 293–4; Bonn Agreement (2001), 91; borders of, 211; Kabul, 88–9; Kabul Province, 91–2; National Solidarity Programme (NSP), 89–90; Operation Enduring Freedom (2001–), 83, 96–7, 107, 205; Parliament (*Wolesi Jirga*), 91; Soviet Invasion of (1979–89), 91

African National Congress (ANC): 256

African Union (AU): 189, 193; High-Level Implementation Panel (AUHIP), 190–1; High Level Panel on Darfur (AUPD), 187

al-Ahmar, Abdalla bin Hussein: 40

bin Ahmayd, Wissam: 114–15

Ahmed, Imam: death of (1962), 35; family of, 35

'Alawite: 140

Algeria: 257, 268, 270; Algiers, 86; use of OCV in, 270–1; War of Independence (1954–62), 268

Ali, Mohammed: 31

All Palestine Government: establishment of (1948), 230

Amal Movement: 129, 136; members of, 125

Amazigh (ethnic group): 99; Berbers, 102, 118

Angola: 186

Ansar al-Shari'a: 42, 45, 75, 79; Benghazi Seminar, 107–8; ideology of, 109; members of, 110

anthropology: 151, 156, 160; political, 152

Arab-Israeli War (1948–9): 252, 257–9

Arab League: members of, 235

303

Arab Spring: 1, 12, 16–18, 21, 27–8, 44, 46, 53, 116, 138–9, 249, 264; Bahraini Uprising (2011), 17, 139; Egyptian Revolution (2011), 17, 62, 139, 193; Libyan Civil War (2011), 17, 100–1, 105, 107, 111–13, 118; Syrian Civil War (2011–), 17–18, 120, 141–3, 259; Tunisian Revolution (2010–11), 17, 62, 138–9, 193, 271; Yemeni Revolution (2011–12), 17, 30, 44–5, 62–4

Arabic (language): 21, 74, 101, 103

Arabism: 228

Arafat, Yasser: 26, 227, 243–4; consolidation of power under, 245–7; death of (2004), 237

Argentina: AMIA Building Bombing (1994), 131; Buenos Aires, 131; Israeli Embassy Bombing (1992), 131

Asian Development Bank (ADB): 87

al-Assad, Bashar: 132; regime of, 120, 135

al-Assad, Hafez: 127–9, 132

atheism: 162

Attas, Abu Baker: supporters of, 47

Australia: 270

Ba'ath Party (Iraq): purging from political and military posts, 93, 95

Ba'athism: 229

al-Badawi, Jamal: house arrest of (2007), 76

Badr, Imam: renouncing of Imamate (1970), 36, 45

Bahrain: 18, 270, 291; Shia population of, 17; Uprising (2011), 17, 139; use of OCV in, 270

Bakil (tribal federation): 38; funding provided to, 60

Baladi, Jallal: 79

Balfour Declaration (1916): 229

Bangladesh: 207; War of Independence (1971), 204

Barak, Ehud: electoral campaign of, 132

Barghouti, Marwan: 246

Barqa Council: demonstrations organised by, 103–4

Barthes, Roland: 162

al-Bashir, Omar: 17, 25, 171, 177, 180, 187, 195–6, 203; Framework Agreement with SPLM-N, 193; ICC warrant issued for (2008), 189, 191, 206; rise to power (1989), 172, 175

al-Beidh, Ali Salem: 48

Beja Congress: 176

Belgium: Brussels, 86

Bemba, Pierre: 186

Ben Ali, Zine El Abidine: awarding of OCV to Tunisia expatriates, 270; regime of, 139; removed from power (2011), 17, 271

Bennett, Tony: definition of marginality, 165

Berri, Nabih: 125, 136

Bilhaj, 'Abd al-Hakim: 106, 109

Bolivia: 7

Bonaparte, Napoleon: 31

Bornstein, Avram: 157

Bosnia-Herzegovina: 101

Botswana: 55

Bozizé, François: regime of, 186

Brand, Laura: 242

Bremer, L. Paul: CPA Administrator, 93

British Empire: 30, 45, 50

Bulgaria: Burgas, 123

Bureau of Investigative Journalism: 61

Bush, George W.: 56; administration of, 135

Buzan, Barry: theory of state strength components, 15

Call, Charles: 148, 250–1; concept of state weakness, 10
Canada: Montreal, 86
capacity: 2, 10, 250, 253, 257–8; concept of, 251; erosion of, 23; financial, 174; international influences on, 11–12; limited, 25; minimal, 11; political, 10; public, 198; state weakness as function of, 11; structural, 58
capital: 156; constraints, 280–1, 287; human, 252, 278, 280; physical, 278, 280; political, 171, 187, 189, 195–6
capitalism: 151; monopoly, 158; neo-liberal, 261
Central African Republic: 186
Chad: 181, 185–6; government of, 187
Chenery, H.: 277–8
China, People's Republic of: 139, 266; Beijing, 231
Chomsky, Noam: 148
Christianity: 134, 154, 156, 163, 165, 167; militias, 119
citizenship: 35–6, 167, 263–4, 272–3; depriving group of, 102; dual, 268; equal, 168
civil society organizations: 26; established by diasporas, 267
Coalition of the Willing: 23, 82
Coalition Provisional Authority of Iraq (CPA): 93–5
Cold War: 22, 35, 45
collective action: efforts to control, 96; transnational, 96
Collier, Paul: 256
colonialism: 154–6, 158, 203, 236, 252; settler, 258–9
communism: 91, 93, 178–9
constitutionalism: 156, 167
Creative Associates: 70–1
Cyprus: Nicosia, 86

Da'wah Party: Lebanese branch of, 125

Déby, Idriss: foreign policy of, 187
democracy: 86, 96; promotion of, 94–5, 97; role in state legitimacy, 14; suppression of, 97
Democratic Republic of Congo: 2, 276
Democratic Republic of Yemen: 41
development assistance: 65; use in stabilization efforts, 66–7
diasporas: 26, 249–50, 252, 256–7, 260, 266–9, 273–4; civil society organizations established by, 267; concept of, 253; conflict, 258; economic, 258; emergence of, 253–4, 259; engagement strategies, 254–5; financial remittances of, 261–6; MENA, 252, 257–9, 262–6, 268; networking, 254; out-of-country voting (OCV), 270–1; role in peace-building efforts, 255–6; role in state-building efforts, 251–2, 261, 267
Druze Progressive Socialist Party: 126
Dussel, Enrique: 158–9

East Timor: 89
Ecuador: 7
Egypt: 18–19, 26, 29, 34, 104, 136, 185, 247, 257; 23 July Revolution (1952), 35; Cairo, 230; French Invasion of (1798–1801), 31; Free Officers Movement, 35; government of, 185; remittance-receiving activity in. 262; Revolution (2011), 17, 62, 139, 193; role in administration of Gaza Strip, 230; Sharm al-Shaykh, 232; use of OCV in, 271–2
Ennahda: 106
Eritrea: 185; Asmara, 186; role in internal Sudanese affairs, 185–6
Ethiopia: 186, 190, 266; airlifting of Jewish population to Israel, 179; government of, 183–4

European Union (EU): 102, 236

Facebook: 267
Fadhli (tribe): conflict with Abdali, 38
Fadlallah, Sayyed Mohammad Husayn: 126
failed state concept: 22, 29, 34, 42, 55–6, 147–9, 173; gradations of, 7; shortcomings in discourse of, 3–6, 49–51, 55–6, 100, 250; state–centric posture of, 42
Fatah: 246
Feeny, S.: 277, 279–80
Feierstein, Gerald: US Ambassador to Yemen, 63–4, 67
First Intifada (1987–93): 245–6; economic impact of, 239
First World War (1914–18): 258
foreign aid: 277–9, 288–9, 294; absorptive capacity (ACI), 275, 277–8, 286–7, 289–93; donor fragmentation, 285; donor proliferation, 285; Dutch disease impacts, 284; example programmes, 281–2; impact of, 282; impact of social and cultural factors on, 286–7; recipient Real Exchange Rate (RER), 283, 285; returns, 277–8, 280
Foreign Policy: Failed State Index (2013), 22, 55, 145–6, 148–50, 173
Foster, M.: 284
France: 139, 258, 265; government of, 72; Paris, 89, 116
Free Syrian Army (FSA): territory held by, 141
Fukuyama, Francis: 81
Future Movement: 137

Gall, Charles: 4
Galloway, George: 82
Gamlen, Alan: thoughts on diaspora engagement strategies, 254

Garang, John: 183
Gates, Robert: US Secretary of Defence, 63, 67
Gause, F. Gregory: 37, 39
Ghana: 55, 284
Ghani, Ashraf: concept of 'syndrome of dysfunctionality', 8
al-Gharyani, Shaykh Sadeq: Grand Mufti of Libya, 109
al-Ghayid, 'Abd al-Wahhab: family of, 107
Giustozzi, Antonio: 89
globalization: 13, 263; technologies of, 266–7
governance: conceptions of, 81–2; collapsed, 83; divide-and-rule, 154, 183; local, 86; 'othering', 157; peripheral, 183; self-, 150; spaces of, 89; statist national, 96
Guatemala: 7
Gulf Cooperation Council (GCC): 56, 59; Yemeni Agreement, 41–2, 46, 49

Hadi, Abd Rabbuh Mansur: 47, 75
Haiti: 7
Hamas: 236, 238, 246; provision of arms to, 186–7
Hamzeh, Nizar: 128
al-Hariri, Rafiq: 124; assassination of (2005), 135–6
Hashid (tribal federation): 38; funding provided to, 60
Hassan II Foundation for Moroccans Resident Abroad: 269
Hehir, Aidan: 5
Hezbollah: 18, 24, 120, 124, 128–9, 131, 134, 137–40, 142; accusation of role in terrorist attacks, 126, 131; cadres of, 125–6; corporatist structure of, 123; electoral performance of (1992), 129; establishment

of (1985), 120, 125; Hezbollah's
Political Document (*Al-Wathiqa
al-Siyasiya li-Hezbollah*) (2009),
137–8; members of, 123, 130; mili-
tary/security capabilities of, 122–3;
'Open Letter to the Downtrodden
in Lebanon and the World', 125;
participation in al-Saniora cabinet, 136–7; role in Qusayr battles
(2013), 141–3; resistance activities
of, 130
Higgins, Lieutenant Colonel William:
kidnapping of (1988), 127
al-Hitar, Hamood: 77
Hoeffler, Anke: 256
Human Development Index: Low
Human Development Category, 208
Huntington, Samuel: 37
Hussein, Saddam: 177; regime of,
92–3; removed from power (2003),
135, 270

identity: relationship with legitimacy,
15
India: 30; British Raj, (1858–1947) 33;
Delhi, 86; Mumbai, 86
Indonesia: 207
informal economies: 56; presence of
women in, 201, 209–10
institutionalism: focus on state col-
lapse, 5, 7
Integrated Management of Childhood
Illness and Community-Led Total
Sanitation: 224
International Committee for the Red
Cross: attacks targeting, 107
International Criminal Court (ICC):
arrest warrants issued by, 189, 191,
206
International Energy Agency (IEA):
116

International Monetary Fund (IMF):
178–80, 188; structural adjustment
programmes of, 45
International Organization for Migration (IOM): 271
Iran: 17, 24, 26, 43, 129, 136, 138, 141,
143, 257, 270; funding provided
by, 59; Islamic Revolution (1979),
270; Revolutionary Guards, 119;
Tehran, 48, 126, 138–9, 141; *wilayat
al-faqih*, 128
Iran-Iraq War (1980–8): 19
Iraq: 12–13, 23, 26, 87, 92, 97, 100–1,
127, 139, 236, 252, 257, 270, 276,
291; Baghdad, 12, 86, 93–5;
Baghdad City Council, 93; Baghdad
Interim City Advisory Council,
93; Basra, 94; economy of, 92–3;
Al-Eyaldia, 95; Fallujah, 94–5; Hilla,
94; Mosul, 94–5; Najaf, 94; Operation Iraqi Freedom (2003–11), 19,
82, 92–3, 96–7, 107, 135, 252, 257,
259; Ramadi, 95; Shia population of,
94–5; state-building efforts in, 94–5;
Sunni population of, 94; Tallafar, 95;
use of OCV in, 270; Zumar, 95
Iskander, Natasha: 265
Islah Party: members of, 47
Islam: 34, 107, 154, 205, 268; five
pillars of, 163; fundamentalist, 205;
Hajj, 163; political, 178, 203; Sharia,
158, 204; Shia, 17, 48, 94–5, 119,
123, 129, 136, 142, 186; Sufi, 103,
105, 109; Sunni, 94, 101, 136, 140,
142, 186; Zaydi, 48
Islamic Amal: 125–7
Islamic Jihad: 136
Islamic Revolutionary Committees:
125
Islamic State: declaration of Caliphate
(2014), 12

Islamic State in Iraq and the Levant
(ISIL): 9, 12
Islamism: 99–101, 105–6, 108,
110–12, 114, 164, 171, 177–8,
180–2, 216–17; political, 104, 204;
radical, 204; Shia, 125
Israel: 35, 123, 137–8, 228, 233, 246,
257, 270; borders of, 135; Hebron,
233; Independence of (1948), 228,
247, 259; Invasion of Lebanon
(1982–2000), 120, 124–5, 132–4;
labour market of, 239; Occupied
Territories, 27, 134, 232–4, 248; role
in Palestinian budget, 242–3
Israel Defence Forces (IDF): 125, 132,
134; Operation Accountability
(1993), 131–2; Operation Cast
Lead (2008–9), 241, 243; Operation Defensive Shield (2002), 134;
Operation Grapes of Wrath (1996),
129, 132; withdrawal from Gaza
(2005), 232

Jabril, Mahmud: leader of National
Forces Alliance, 106
al-Jifry, Abd al-Rahman: Vice-Pres-
ident of Democratic Republic of
Yemen, 41
jihad: 109–10
jihadism: 177; militant, 62, 70–1
Johnson, Chris: 88; criticisms of NSP,
90
Jordan: 115, 136, 229–30, 242, 247,
252, 257, 259, 268; Emirate of Tran-
sjordan (1921–46), 237; government of, 242; remittance-receiving
activity in, 265
Judaism: 179, 233, 257
Jumayyil, Pierre: 268
Justice and Constitution Party (JCP):
electoral performance of (2012),
105–6

Justice and Equality Movement (JEM):
alliances of, 193

Kahalani, Avigdor: Israeli Minister of
Domestic Security, 132
Kaplan, Seth: 13–14
Khalidi, Rashid: 228
Al Khalifa, Hamad bin Isa: regime of,
139
Khatmiyya Sect: 175–6
Khomeini, Ayatollah Ruhollah: Death
of (1989), 129
Kiir, Salva: 190; incorporation of mili-
tias into Sudanese military, 184
Killick, T.: 284
kinship: 86–7; networks, 102
Knack, S.: 285
Komey, Guma Kunda: 182–3
Korea Gas: 72
Kosovo: 101
Kurds: territory inhabited by, 94–5
Kuwait: 21, 188; Iraqi Invasion of
(1990), 19, 127, 177, 236

labour: 156, 258, 262, 269; black
labour, 240; division of, 177; domestic, 223; flow of, 238; gendered participation of 218; market, 209–10,
239; Mexican, 39; recruitment, 252;
skilled, 19
bin Laden, Osama: funds provided to
Sudanese government, 180
League of Nations: Covenant of, 229;
Mandate for Palestine (1924), 231
League of the Sons of Yemen: 47;
members of, 41
Lebanese Armed Forces (LAF): 122,
132, 137; shortcomings of, 143
Lebanese Civil War (1975–90): 17–18,
26, 120, 126–7, 259; Ta'if Accord
(1989), 18, 121, 127–8; War of the
Camps (1985–7), 126

Arab tribes in, 179; Blue Nile, 176, 193–4, 203, 219; budget of, 180; Christian missionary activity in, 154; Comprehensive Peace Agreement (CPA)(2005), 181, 187–9, 193; Darfur, 24, 167, 176, 179, 181, 203; Darfur Rebellion (1991), 182; Darfur War (2003–), 181–2, 187; Doha Document for Peace in Darfur, 187; Eastern Sudan Peace Agreement (2006), 187; economy of, 172–3, 220; Elections Act (2008), 217–19; GDP per capita, 190; government of, 171–2, 187, 190, 204, 206–7, 218–19; Independence of (1956), 24, 156–8, 175, 185; Juba Agreement (2006), 184; Kassala, 167; Khartoum, 167, 176, 181–2, 184–5, 187, 189–90, 193, 206; legal code of, 204; literacy rates in, 217–18; Ministry of Welfare and Social Security, 218; North Kordofan (NK), 205–7, 219–22, 226; Nuba, 176; oil infrastructure of, 180; political life in, 172–8; Second Civil War (1983–2005), 185; Shia population of, 186; socio-economic inclusion/exclusion of women in, 204–5, 216–17, 219–20, 222–3; South Kordofan, 193–4, 198–9, 203, 206, 219; Sunni population of, 186; Transitional Military Council, 179

Sudanese Communist Party: 175
Sudanese People's Liberation Army/Movement (SPLA/SPLM): 176–7, 179, 181, 191–2; activity in government, 181; budget of, 184; Eighth Division of, 190; fragmentation of, 184; origins of, 183–4
Sudanese People's Liberation Movement-North (SPLM-N): 194; alliances of, 193; Framework Agreement with Omar al-Bashir, 193
Support Front of the People of Greater Syria (*Jabhat al-Nusrah li-Ahl al-Sham*): members of, 140
Sweden: 173
Syria: 12–13, 15, 24, 31, 100, 110, 120, 128, 135–6, 257, 259, 269–70, 291; 'Alawite population of, 140; Aleppo, 141; borders of, 140–1; Civil War (2011–), 17–18, 120, 141–3, 259; Damascus, 126, 129, 133, 136, 139–41, 232; Golan Heights, 130, 133; government of, 131; Homs, 141; military of, 126; Qusayr, 141–3; Sunni population of, 140

Tabu (ethnic group): 99, 118; kin networks of, 102; targeted by Qadhafi regime, 102
Taiwan: 231
Taliban: Pakistani, 211; territory held by, 205
Tanzania: 284
terrorism: 9, 87, 126, 131
Tibaijuka, Anna: former Executive Director of UN-HABITAT, 88
Tilly, Charles: theory of role of war in enhancing state power, 18
tribalism: 39
tribes: 7, 22, 46, 80, 99–100, 102, 183; confederations, 39–40; elders, 109; kin networks of, 102; leadership structure, 32, 38; recognition of, 33; social relations of, 29–30, 38; tribal identities, 86
Tripoli Military Council: members of, 106
Tuareg (ethnic group): 99, 102, 118; kin networks of, 102